HTML
A Beginner's Guide

Third Edition

HTML
A Beginner's Guide

Third Edition

Wendy Willard

New York   Chicago   San Francisco
Lisbon   London   Madrid   Mexico City
Milan   New Delhi   San Juan
Seoul   Singapore   Sydney   Toronto

The **McGraw·Hill** Companies

McGraw-Hill books are available at special quantity discounts to use as premiums and sales promotions, or for use in corporate training programs. For more information, please write to the Director of Special Sales, Professional Publishing, McGraw-Hill, Two Penn Plaza, New York, NY 10121-2298. Or contact your local bookstore.

HTML: A Beginner's Guide, Third Edition

234567890 CUS CUS 01987

ISBN-13:   978-0-07-226378-7

ISBN-10:   0-07-226378-4

Sponsoring Editor   Wendy Rinaldi
Editorial Supervisor   Patty Mon
Project Editor/Manager   Claire Splan
Acquisitions Coordinator   Alex McDonald
Technical Editor   Karl Hilsmann
Copy Editor   Mike McGee
Proofreader   Paul Tyler
Production Supervisor   George Anderson
Composition   Lucie Ericksen
Illustration   Lyssa Wald
Cover Designer   Jeff Weeks

To Corinna and Caeli—that you might remember your mom once knew some "cool stuff," even when HTML becomes for you what 8-track tapes are to me. "Heaven and earth will pass away, but my words will never pass away."
—Luke 21:33

About the Author

Wendy Willard is a freelance consultant offering design and art direction services to clients. She also teaches and writes on these topics, and is the author of several other books including *Web Design: A Beginner's Guide* and *Photoshop 7: Tips & Techniques* (both published by McGraw-Hill/Osborne). She holds a degree in Illustration from Art Center College of Design in Pasadena, California, where she first learned HTML in 1995.

Wendy's passions include all aspects of digital design; drawing, painting, and photographing Maine; Chop Point School & Camp; and anything related to the Web. She lives and works in Maryland with her husband, Wyeth, and their two young daughters.

Contents at a Glance

PART II
Beyond HTML

PART III
Appendixes

Contents

PART I
HTML Basics

PART II
Beyond HTML

Acknowledgments

Thanks to Rachel, the first edition's *non-technical* editor, for spending hours reading this material with a critical eye, pointing out things she didn't understand in the text that I needed to clarify. I wouldn't turn a chapter in without you reading it first! Thanks to Karl, this edition's technical editor, for making sure everything is *still* clear, concise and accurate.

Thanks to everyone at McGraw-Hill/Osborne for making it easy to update this book. Thanks to the readers of the previous editions for pointing out errata and suggesting additions, so I could make the third edition even better than the first two.

A special thanks to Chop Point, for providing the real-world project in the book.

And finally, Wyeth, Corinna, and Caeli—you are my inspiration and my reward..

Introduction

When I was first approached about writing this book, I must admit that my thought was, "Another HTML book—how many do we need?" I learned HTML by experience when there was only one version of Netscape, and it had been a long time since I'd even looked at an HTML book. But after I researched the other HTML books on the market, I felt compelled to write a book that gives readers a realistic, easy-to-understand approach to learning HTML, while at the same time offering real-world practice activities and advice on related issues.

HTML: A Beginner's Guide is that book, offering you practical tools and knowledge that can easily be applied to a variety of development situations, without the boring rhetoric or lengthy technical fluff. This book tells you what you need to know, when you need to know it.

In revising this book for its third edition, I again reviewed competing books to determine what readers wanted and needed in a "new" HTML book. Again and again, I saw that you wanted a book that combined HTML and cascading style sheets in a way that was easy to understand and use. Furthermore, readers clamored for a beginning-level HTML book that covered the standards-compliant way to code useable web pages. This is that book.

Who Should Read This Book

Since this book is geared toward anyone with little or no prior HTML knowledge, it's perfect for anyone wishing to learn HTML. If you are a stay-at-home mom who wants to create a web site for your family, you've come to the right place. If you are a business professional seeking to acquire web development skills, this is the book for you. If you are interested in learning HTML, this book is for you.

You don't need to know anything about computer programming or web development in order to learn HTML, and you certainly don't need to know either of those things to get a lot from this book.

What This Book Covers

The book is divided into three parts——HTML Basics, Beyond HTML, and Appendixes.

Part I, "HTML Basics," covers all you need to know in order to start coding effective and efficient web pages with HTML. Part I consists of 12 modules, in which information is broken up into manageable chunks. Each module contains one or more step-by-step, real-world projects to give you practice performing the suggested concepts. In addition to the HTML taught therein, each module provides details on how cascading style sheets can be used to accomplish the same or similar techniques.

Module 1, "Getting Started," helps you understand the Web by answering common questions such as "Who created HTML?" and "Who maintains HTML?" and also by tackling the anatomy of a web site, web browsers, and XHTML. Issues surrounding how to plan your web site, using HTML editors, and learning from the pros are also discussed.

Module 2, "Basic Page Structure," explains beginning terminology such as tags, attributes, and nesting while also describing naming conventions and proper page structure.

Module 3, "Color," gives you details on how to work with and reference color in your web pages. Hexadecimal color and the web-safe color palette are also discussed.

Module 4, "Working with Text," teaches you how to use HTML and Cascading Style Sheets to format text within your web pages, whether that means changing the font style or color, adding line breaks and emphasis.

Module 5, "Working with Links," discusses the core of HTML: hypertext links. This module gives details on how to add and customize links in your web pages, whether you're linking to another web page, a section on a web page, or an e-mail address.

Module 6, "Working with Images," helps you use images in your web pages by describing different image types, how to add them to a page, and how to link to and from them. Additional tips on using images in web pages are also provided.

Module 7, "Working with Multimedia," explains different types of multimedia you can add to your pages and tells how to do so in ways that work in multiple browsers.

Module 8, "Creating Lists," teaches you how to create and format the three different types of lists available in HTML, as well as how to style them with CSS.

Module 9, "Using Tables," tackles the somewhat tricky but very useful topic of HTML tables. In step-by-step fashion, this module takes you through creating a very basic table structure and then formatting it with CSS.

Module 10, "Developing Frames," offers you ways to break your web pages up into separate window frames, each with different pieces of content. Both standard and inline frames are discussed, as well as how to format each.

Module 11, "Employing Forms," discusses a key ingredient for most web sites—forms providing communication methods for customers. Various types of input controls are taught, including textfields, checkboxes, file uploads, select menus, and buttons, as well as information about processing forms with scripts and additional formatting techniques.

Module 12, "Positioning Page Elements," is a completely new module in this edition of the book, tackling how to move content around on the page without ever touching the HTML code and only updating a single style sheet.

Part II, "Beyond HTML," gives you an introduction into several additional areas related to building web pages with HTML. If you're only interested in learning HTML, you might be able to skip these sections, but if you're wondering what comes next after you learn HTML, I recommend checking out the modules in Part II. All of the modules in Part II also include sections called "Learn More," which provide additional resources for those interested in pursuing the topic.

Module 13, "Creating Your Own Web Graphics," contains a review of popular web graphics software, as well as guidelines you can use when creating images for the Web. This module also discusses issues that impact design decisions and web graphics file formats. Even if you don't have a graphics editor, the module lists several places where you can download demos for free to practice the concepts taught.

Module 14, "Web Content," discusses ways to ensure the on-screen readability of your web pages, how to create effective links and printer-friendly pages. In addition, this module provides essential dos and don'ts for working with web content.

Module 15, "Dynamic Content," offers you an introduction to JavaScript, a technology used to add dynamic aspects to otherwise static HTML pages, and Dynamic HTML. Sample scripts allow you to add the current date and time to a web page, make form fields required, and change page elements when users point to them.

Module 16, "Making Pages Available to Others," teaches you to prepare your pages for online distribution before guiding you on important decisions such as where to host your site, what domain name to use, and how to upload the site. Testing, submission to search engines and directories, and general marketing tips are also discussed.

Part III, "Appendixes," provides additional information in quick-reference formats and puts commonly used details at the fingertips of both beginning and advanced HTML coders.

Appendix A, "Answers to Mastery Check," contains the answers to the questions asked at the end of each module.

Appendix B, "HTML/CSS Reference Table," outlines all of the HTML tags and CSS properties taught in the book in an easy-to-read alphabetical reference format.

Appendix C, "Troubleshooting (FAQs)," provides answers to commonly asked questions from beginning and advanced HTML coders.

Appendix D, "Special Characters," lists the character entities used to embed special characters, such as the copyright symbol and an ampersand, into a web page.

Appendix E, "File Types," includes a list of the file types you are most likely to encounter while creating web pages, as well as a brief description and MIME type for each.

How to Read This Book

The content is structured so that you can read a single module as needed or the entire book from cover to cover. While beginners should read through the book, module by module, in order to efficiently grasp the concepts taught, intermediate and advanced users can use certain modules as reference materials.

The projects at the end of each module build upon each other, but you could certainly adapt a specific module to your own needs if you read them out of order.

Special Features

Each module includes Tips, Notes, and Cautions to provide additional reference information wherever needed. Detailed code listings are included, many times with certain tags or features highlighted with further explanation.

Many modules contain Ask the Expert question-and-answer sections to address potentially confusing issues. Each module contains Critical Skills exercises, Progress Check segments, and step-by-step projects to give you a chance to practice the concepts taught thus far. These projects are based on a real-world web development project I worked on for a non-profit called Chop Point in Woolwich, Maine.

Mastery Checks are included at the end of each module to give you another chance to review the concepts taught in the module. The answers to the Mastery Checks are in Appendix A.

You can download the content for the Chop Point projects from Osborne's web site (**www.osborne.com**) or my web site (**www.wendywillard.com**).

Throughout the development of this book, our objective has always been to provide you with a cohesive, easy-to-understand guide for coding HTML to help you get up and running in no time. As you'll hear me say countless times, HTML is not that difficult and is definitely within your reach. I applaud your decision to learn HTML and encourage you to use the Internet to its fullest potential both during the learning process and in your ensuing web development aspirations. As Module 1 discusses, visit the web sites you love and love-to-hate to determine how they accomplished various features. Follow the links identified in the book for additional information, and don't forget to perform your own web searches for related content. Have fun and good luck!

Part I

HTML Basics

Module 1

Getting Started

3

For as long as I've been involved in making web pages, people have asked me to teach them the process. At the start, many are intimidated by the thought of learning HTML. But fear not! After all, one of the reasons I decided to attend art school was to avoid all the math and science classes. So, as I tell my students . . . if I could learn HTML, so can you.

HTML is not rocket science. Quite simply, it is a means of telling a web browser how to display a page. That's why it's called *HTML,* which is the acronym for *Hypertext Markup Language.* Like any new skill, HTML takes practice to comprehend what you are doing.

Before we dive into the actual creation of web pages, you must first understand a few things about the Internet. I could probably fill an entire book with the material in this initial chapter, but the following should provide you with a firm foundation.

CRITICAL SKILL
1.1

Understand the Internet as a Medium for Disseminating Information

When you're asked to write a term paper in school, you don't sit down and just start writing. First, you have to do research and learn how to format the paper. The process for writing and designing a web page is similar.

The Anatomy of a Web Site

Undoubtedly, you've seen a few web sites by now. Perhaps you know someone who's a web guru, and you've watched him navigate through a web site by chopping off pieces of the web address. Have you ever wondered what he's doing? It's not too difficult. He just knows a little about the anatomy of a web site and how the underlying structure is laid out.

URLs

The fancy word for "web address" is *uniform resource locator,* also referenced by its acronym *URL* (pronounced either by the letters U-R-L or as a single word, *url,* which rhymes with "girl"). Even if you've never heard a web address referred to as a URL, you've probably seen one—URLs start with http://, and they usually end with .com, .org, .edu, or .net. (Other possibilities include .tv, .biz, and .info. For more information, see **www.networksolutions.com.**)

Every web site has a URL—for instance, Google's is **www.google.com**. The following illustration shows another example of a URL as it appears in a common web browser (Firefox) on the Mac.

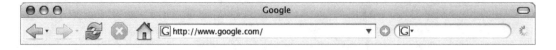

One part of a URL is the *domain name*, which helps identify and locate computers on the Internet. To avoid confusion, each domain name is unique. You can think of the domain name as a label or shortcut. Behind that shortcut is a series of numbers, called an *IP address*, which gives the specific address of where the site you're looking for is located on the Internet. To draw an analogy, if the domain name is the word "Emergency" written next to the first-aid symbol on your speed dial, the IP address is 9-1-1.

NOTE

Although many URLs begin with "www," this is not a necessity. Originally used to denote "World Wide Web" in the URL, using www has caught on as common practice. The characters before the first period in the URL are not part of the registered domain, and can be almost anything. In fact, many businesses use this part of the URL to differentiate between various departments within the company. For example, the GO Network includes ABC, ESPN, and Disney, to name a few. Each of these is a department of go.com: abc.go.com, espn.go.com, and disney.go.com. Type in **www.abc.com** in the address bar of your favorite web browser, and you'll notice the URL changes to abc.go.com. That's because www.abc.com is an alias—or a shortcut—for abc.go.com.

Businesses typically register domain names ending in a .com (which signifies a commercial venture) that are similar to their business or product name. Domain registration is like renting office space on the Internet. Once you register a domain name, you have the right to publish a web site under that name on the Internet for as long as you pay the rental fees.

TIP

Wondering whether *yourname.com* is already being used? You can check to see which domain names are still available for registration by visiting a registration service like **www.godaddy.com** or **www.networksolutions.com**.

Web Servers

Every web site and web page also needs a web server. Quite simply, a *web server* is a computer, running special software, which is always connected to the Internet.

NOTE

Some people talk about the computer as the server, as in "We need to buy a new server." Others call the software the server, saying "We need to install a new web server." Both uses of the word essentially refer to the same thing—web servers make information available to those requesting it.

Ask the Expert

Q: I've heard the phrase "the World Wide Web" used so many times, but I'm a little confused about what it actually means and how it relates to the Internet.

A: The *World Wide Web* (*WWW* or the *Web*) is often confused with the Internet. While the precursor to the Internet was originally created during the Cold War as a way to link sections of the country together during an emergency, the actual term "Internet" wasn't used until the early 1970s. At that time, academic research institutions developed the Internet to create better communication and to share resources. Later, universities and research facilities throughout the world began using the Internet. In the early 1990s, Tim Berners-Lee created a set of technologies that allowed information on the Internet to be connected through the use of *links* in documents. The language component of these technologies is Hypertext Markup Language (HTML). If you want to find out more, a good resource on the history of the Internet is available at **www.isoc.org/ internet-history**.

The Web was mostly text-based until Marc Andreessen created the first graphical web browser in 1993, called Mosaic, which paved the way for the use of video, sound, and photos on the Net. As a large group of interconnected computers all over the world, the Internet comprises not only the Web, but also things like *newsgroups* (online bulletin boards) and e-mail. Many people think of the Web as the graphical or illustrated part of the Internet.

When you type a URL into your web browser or click a link in a web page, you send a request to the server housing that information. It's similar to the process that occurs when you dial a phone number with your telephone. Your request "calls" the computer that contains all the files necessary to show you the web page you requested. The computer then "serves" and displays all the pages to you, usually in your web browser.

Sites

A URL is commonly associated with a web site. You've doubtless seen plenty of examples of such addresses on billboards and in television advertising. For instance, **www.amazon.com** is the URL for Amazon's web site, while **www.cbs.com** is the URL for CBS.

Most commonly, these sites are located in directories or folders on the server, just as you might have your C: drive on your personal computer. Then, within this main site, there may be several folders, which house other sections of the web site.

For example, Chop Point is a summer camp and K–12 school in Maine. It has several main sections of its web site, but the most notable are "camp" and "school." If you look at the URL for Chop Point's camp section, you can see the name of the folder after the site name:

www.choppoint.org/camp

If you accessed the main page for the school, the URL changes to:

www.choppoint.org/school

Pages

When you visit a web site, you look at pages on the site that contain all its text, graphics, sound, and video content. Even though a web page is not the same size or format as a printed page, the word "page" is used to help us differentiate between pages, folders, and sites. The same way that many pages and chapters can be contained within a single book, many pages and folders (or sections) can also be kept within a web site.

Most web servers are set up to look automatically for a page called "index" as the main page in any folder. So if you were to type in the URL used in the previous example, the server would look for the index page in the "camp" folder, which might look like the following.

www.choppoint.org/camp/index.html

If you want to look for a different page in the camp folder, you could type the name of that page after the site and folder names, keeping in mind that HTML pages usually end with .html or .htm, such as in:

www.choppoint.org/camp/dailyactivities.html

Web Browsers

A *web browser* is a piece of software that runs on your personal computer and enables you to view web pages. Web browsers, often simply called "browsers," interpret the HTML code and provide a visual layout displayed on the screen. Browsers typically can also be used to check e-mail and access newsgroups.

The most popular browser is Microsoft Internet Explorer (also called IE). As of this writing, some estimates give IE upwards of 75 percent of the market share. One explanation is that IE comes preinstalled with Windows and few people seek out alternative browsers. Apple's preinstalled browser with the Mac O/S is Safari.

Most of the other popular browsers are part of a breed called "Mozilla-based" browsers. This name comes from the fact that each browser is based on a framework named Mozilla, which has its roots in the old Netscape browser. The most popular Mozilla-based browser is Firefox, which is available for both Windows and Mac operating systems.

Browsers are updated regularly, changing to address new aspects of HTML or emerging technologies. Some people continue to use older versions of their browsers, however. This means, at any given time, there may be two or three active versions of one browser, and several different versions of other browsers being employed by the general public.

What if there were several versions of televisions, which all displayed TV programs differently? If this were true, then your favorite television show might look different every time you watched it on someone else's television. This would not only be frustrating to you as a viewer, it would also be frustrating for the show's creator.

Web developers must deal with this frustration every day. Because of the differences among various browsers and the large number of computer types, the look and feel of a web page can vary greatly. This means web developers must keep up-to-date on the latest features of the new browsers, but we must also know how to create web pages that are backwards-compatible for the older browsers many people may still be using.

TIP

To keep current on statistics about browser use, visit **www.w3schools.com/browsers/browsers_stats.asp**.

Internet Service Providers

You use an *Internet Service Provider* (*ISP*) to gain access to the Internet. This connection can be made through your phone line with a company like Verizon, AT&T, AOL, or Earthlink, or you can connect through a cable line with a company like Comcast or Time Warner.

Many companies offer you a choice of browsers, and may even provide a particular web browser customized with quick links for things like checking your e-mail and reading local news. However, some companies may support only one browser, such as *America Online* (*AOL*). To locate an ISP with local service in your area, visit **http://thelist.internet.com/areacode.html** and click your phone number's area code.

TIP

Most browsers can be easily customized, meaning you can change the text sizes, styles, and colors, as well as the first page that appears when you start your browser. This is usually called your "home" page or your "start" page, and it's the page displayed when you click the "home" button in your browser. For easier access, many people change their home page to a search engine or a news site customized according to their needs. These personalized sites are often called portals and also offer free e-mail to users. A few examples are Yahoo!, Google, and MSN.

Looking to the Future

In its earliest years, HTML quickly went through many iterations, which led to a lack of standardization across the Internet. The *World Wide Web Consortium* (W3C—**www.w3.org**) publishes a list of recommendations, called standards, for HTML and other web languages. The last official standard for HTML was HTML 4.01.

In an attempt to set standards, the W3C rewrote HTML 4.01 using *Extensible Markup Language* (*XML*). The resulting set of standards was called *Extensible Hypertext Markup Language* (*XHTML*), and even provided a way for HTML to handle alternative devices, such as cell phones and handheld computers.

XHTML 1.0 offered many new features to make the lives of web developers easier, but was poorly supported by web browsers at its launch in 2001. Since then, the W3C has updated its recommendation to XHTML 2.0. This edition of *HTML: A Beginner's Guide* was revised to incorporate XHTML throughout the entire book, and to remove any old—and no longer supported—HTML tags.

Progress Check

1. What is a web browser?

2. List some parts of a URL.

CRITICAL SKILL
1.2 Plan for the Audience, Goals, Structure, Content, and Navigation of Your Site

In addition to learning about the medium, you also need to do the following:

- Identify your target audience

- Set goals for your site

- Create your web site's structure

---

1. A web browser is a piece of software that runs on your computer and enables you to view web pages.

2. Domain name, folder, file

- Organize your web site's content

- Develop your web site's navigation

Identify the Target Audience

If you are creating a web site for a business, a group, or an organization, you are most likely targeting people who might buy or use the company's products or services. Even if your site is set up purely for the purpose of disseminating information, you must target a certain audience. Consider whether you have existing research regarding your client or user base. This might include demographics, statistics, or other marketing information, such as age, gender, and web experience.

TIP

If your site represents a new company or one that doesn't already have information about its clients' demographics, you might check out the competition. Chances are good that if your competition has a successful web site, you can learn from them about your target audience.

Knowing your target audience will influence how you design and develop your web site. For example, if you are developing a site for beginners to learn about the Internet, you want to create a site that is extremely easy to use and does not stray from standard computer conventions.

Once you identify your target audience, you need to think about what functions each part of that audience can perform at your site. Try drawing up a chart like Table 1-1 to make your

User Group	Functions Performed	Ages	Gender	Web Experience
Current customers	- bank online - contact customer service - research additional services/products	16+	male/ female	varies
Potential customers	- research services/products - contact sales	16+	male/ female	varies
Potential employees	- search job openings - research company - contact HR	18–60	male/ female	varies
Financial consultants	- research services/products - view company financials - contact sales	30–60	male/ female 60/40	savvy

Table 1-1 Functions Performed by a Target Audience

plans. The example in the table is designed for a bank, but you can use it as a starting point for any site you create.

You can use this information to determine the appropriate direction for the site. I like to break down the audience into two major sectors: the "accidental tourists" and the "navy seals." Most sites have a little of both. Have you ever surfed a certain site, and then wondered how you got there from here? This is the "accidental tourist," a.k.a. the serendipitous visitor. At the other end of the spectrum is the student on a mission—looking for a specific piece of information for a homework assignment. I call these the "navy seals."

TIP

Does your site target mostly "navy seal" visitors? These individuals prefer search engines, especially when trying to locate information quickly. Providing a good search engine or site map on your site can greatly increase your repeat visitors.

Set Goals

Since the Web's inception, millions of new web sites have been created. To compete in such a large market, you need to set clear goals for the site. For instance, the site might

- Sell products/services
- Recruit potential employees
- Entertain
- Educate
- Communicate with customers

Always remember the goals when developing the site to avoid unnecessary content. If a page on your site doesn't meet one of the goals, it may confuse or turn away visitors.

Create the Structure

Once you align your site's goals with the functions performed by the target audience, you will see a structure forming. Consider a site whose primary goal is to sell office supplies to businesses and whose secondary goal is to recruit potential employees. This site would most likely contain two main topic areas: shop for office supplies and browse available jobs.

Many people use tree diagrams, such as the one shown in Figure 1-1, to help define the structure of the site. Others use flow charts or simple outlines.

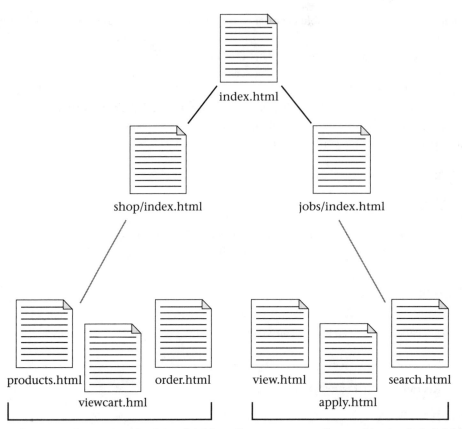

These pages are all stored in the "shop" folder. These pages are all stored in the "jobs" folder.

Figure 1-1 A tree diagram showing a portion of the structure for a sample office supply site

Organize Content

All the content for the site should fit under each of the topic areas in the site structure, and you might have several subcategories in each topic area. So, the "shop for office supplies" section from the previous example might be broken down into several subcategories, according to the different types of products available. Table 1-2 shows how the category names might relate to the folder names.

Category Name	Folder Name
Paper	shop/paper/
Pens	shop/pens/
Software	shop/software/
Furniture	shop/furniture/
Furniture, Desks	shop/furniture/desks/
Furniture, Chairs	shop/furniture/chairs/
Furniture, Bookcases	shop/furniture/bookcases/

Table 1-2 Content Organization

Develop Navigation

After the site structure has been defined and the content has been placed into the structure accordingly, you will want to plan out how a visitor to this site navigates between each of the pages and sections. A good practice is to include a standard navigation bar on all pages for consistency and ease of use. This navigation bar probably should include links to your home page and any major topic areas. It should probably also contain the name of your business or a logo so a simple visual clue lets the user know she has not moved beyond your site by accident.

Highlighting the current section on the navigation bar is important, so visitors can more easily distinguish where they are in your site's structure. This means if your site has two sections— jobs and resumes—the jobs button would look different when you were inside that section and, in some way, should identify it as the current section.

In addition, consider giving your visitors as many visual clues as possible to aid in the navigation of your site (see Figure 1-2). This might be accomplished by repeating the page name in:

- The page's title (the text that appears at the top of the browser window, as well as in search engines)

- The page's filename

- A headline

- Buttons and links to the page (highlighted if you are viewing that page)

This tab is a different color to show the visitor in which section this page is located

The page title lists the name of the site as well as the page and section names

The URL clues the visitor to the name and location of the page being viewed

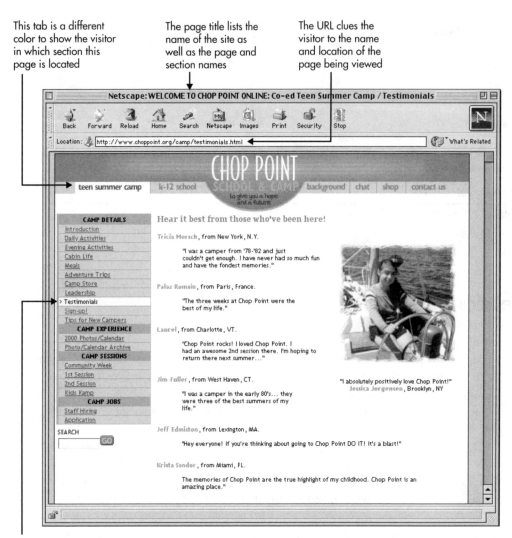

This link is highlighted to remind the visitor which page he/she is visiting

Figure 1-2 The page name is repeated several times.

CRITICAL SKILL
1.3 Identify the Best HTML Editor for You

At some point, you may wonder: "Why go to the trouble of learning HTML if I can use a program that does it for me?" With so many new software packages available to help you develop HTML, that's a valid question. The bulk of the software packages can be broken up into two main categories: text-based HTML editors (also called code-based HTML editors) and *What You See Is What You Get* (*WYSIWYG*—pronounced *wizzywig*) editors. However, most of the current WYSIWYG editors also have sophisticated HTML-editing capabilities.

With so many options available, it can be difficult to determine the best tool for your needs. To help, I've outlined a few of the most popular for you here. This is by no means an exhaustive list of valid HTML editors. It is merely meant to help get you started by pointing out the key benefits of each.

Text- or Code-Based HTML Editors

Text-based editors require you to know some HTML to use them. They can be customized to help speed your coding process, and often have sophisticated checks and balances in place to check for errors in coding. Hundreds, if not thousands, of editors exist. I've listed a few of the most popular text-based HTML editors here, and encourage you to try out a few before settling on one.

- **CoffeeCup HTML Editor**—www.coffecup.com (Windows)
- **CuteHTML**—www.globalscape.com (Windows)
- **HotDog Pro**—www.sausage.com (Windows)
- **NoteTab**—www.notetab.com (Windows)
- **BBEdit**—www.barebones.com (Mac)
- **uEdit**—www.uedit.tk (Mac)

TIP

Most of these tools have free demo versions you can use before buying.

WYSIWYG HTML Editors

WYSIWYG editors don't require HTML knowledge. Instead of looking at the HTML of your pages, you are shown a "preview" of how the page will look in a browser. This way you can simply drag-and-drop pieces of your layout as you see fit. These types of programs can have some drawbacks, but they can also be quite useful for the purposes of learning different aspects of HTML or for quickly publishing a basic web page. The most popular WYSIWYG editors are

- **Macromedia Dreamweaver (www.adobe.com/dreamweaver/)**, which is available for both the Macintosh and the PC. It offers benefits such as customizable features and automated production, and is integrated with graphics tools such as Macromedia Fireworks. Because of its ease of use in both the preview pane and the code view, Dreamweaver has arguably become the industry standard for professional web page developers.

●   **Adobe GoLive (www.adobe.com/golive/)**, which is also available for both the Macintosh and the PC, has garnered a large portion of professional web designers, particularly those who like its integrations with the rest of the Adobe Creative Suite. GoLive's development environment enables designers and coders to work quite well together.

●   **Microsoft FrontPage (www.microsoft.com/frontpage/)**, which is also available for both the Macintosh and the PC (although in different versions). It boasts integrated support for other products in the Microsoft Office suite, and offers advanced features such as sample forms and site management tools. For this reason, FrontPage's largest market share continues to be amateur site developers and small businesses.

Which Is Best?

Many web developers prefer to use the text-based HTML editors, rather than have a WYSIWYG editor do it for them, for the following reasons:

●   **Better control**   WYSIWYG editors may write HTML in a variety of ways—although not all of them will have the same outcome. For example, Microsoft FrontPage sometimes uses proprietary code that is not understood by Netscape's browsers. This means your pages can look different in each browser. Unfortunately, this has caused many of these programs to be labeled "WYSINWYG" or What-You-See-Is-NOT-What-You-Get.

●   **Faster pages**   WYSIWYG editors often overcompensate for the amount of code needed to render a page properly, and so they end up repeating code many more times than necessary. This leads to large file sizes and longer downloads.

●   **Speedier editing**   The large-scale WYSIWYG editors often take a lot of memory and system resources, slowing both the computer and the development process.

●   **More flexibility**   Many WYSIWYG editors are programmed to "fix" code they think is faulty. This may make you unable to insert code or edit the existing code as you wish.

That said, current WYSIWYG editors have come a long way in terms of control and flexibility. They even offer web developers advanced features such as the capability to code DHTML and JavaScript. With the ability to dig right into the code and still see a visual representation of the output, it's no surprise that editors like Dreamweaver have become so popular. In fact, Dreamweaver is the tool I use for most of my web development.

Note that:

- *Dynamic HTML* (or *DHTML*) allows web page content to be easily changed and customized on the fly, without having to send and receive additional information from the server. Style sheets, used especially in DHTML, are discussed throughout the book.

- *JavaScript* is a scripting language designed to give web pages more interactivity than can be achieved through HTML. Even though the name might make you think otherwise, JavaScript is different from Java, which is a full programming language. You will read more about JavaScript in Module 15.

Both text-based HTML editors and WYSIWYG editors have their benefits. My recommendation is to download free trials of the various programs and decide for yourself which one works best for your needs.

To achieve the purposes of this book, you are free to use any editor or software package you like, although to begin, I recommend you use the basic text editor that came with your computer system, such as SimpleText (Macintosh) or Notepad (Windows). Once you have the basics of HTML down, you can move on and experiment with other available programs.

CRITICAL SKILL

1.4 Learn from the Pros Using the View Source Command of Popular Web Browsers

One of the best ways to learn HTML is to surf the Web and look at the HTML for sites you like (as well as those you don't like). Most web browsers enable you to view the HTML source code of web pages, using the following commands:

- In your favorite web browser, choose View | Page Source or View | Source.

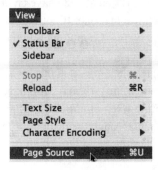

You'll notice there are often additional types of code visible. For example, aside from standard HTML code, you might also find references to other files on the server, or even other types of scripts or code altogether. Furthermore, what you're seeing in the View Source display is only what has been sent by the server for the browser to display. This means there may have been other code used to actually tell the server where to get this code, when to send it, or even how to send it.

If you'd like, you can even print or save these pages to review at a later time or to keep in a reference library. Because the Web is *open source*, meaning your code is free for anyone to see, copying other developers' code is tempting. But remember, you should give credit where credit is due and never copy anything protected by a copyright, such as graphics and text content.

NOTE

A few browsers don't let you use View Source. If you find you cannot view the HTML source of a web page, try saving the page to your local hard drive, and then opening it in a text editor instead.

Project 1-1 Developing a Web Site

The best way to practice HTML is to develop web sites. While developing a personal site might be fun, I think you can sometimes learn more about the whole development process by working on a site for a business or organization. In fact, volunteering your time to develop a web site for a nonprofit organization is a wonderful way to start.

Throughout the course of this book, I'll give you projects that relate to the development of such an organization's web site. If you already have an organization in mind for which you want to develop a site, then use that one. If not, you can use the organization I used while creating examples for this book—Chop Point Summer Camp and School, located in Woolwich, Maine.

All the files needed to complete the projects in this book for Chop Point can be downloaded from **www.osborne.com** or **www.wendywillard.com**. In addition, you can view my version of the web site anytime by visiting **www.choppoint.org**.

This specific project takes you through the planning phase of the web development project. Goals for this project include

- Identifying your target audience

- Setting goals for your site

- Creating your web site's structure

- Organizing your web site's content
- Developing your web site's navigation

Step by Step

1. Spend some time researching your organization. Try to learn as much about its business as possible. If you know people within the company, do some interviews to help you identify your target audience, as well as the site goals. If you can't speak with them, visit other similar sites to determine what type of people the competition is targeting. Some questions to ask and things to consider include

- What business problem(s) will the web site address? What do you want to accomplish? What are your goals for the web site?
- Who are the targeted users/visitors of the site? Do you have any existing research regarding your client or user base, such as demographics, statistics, or other marketing information?
- To determine the appropriate direction for the site, you must match the targeted users and the functions they will perform when visiting the site. For example, will the targeted users be "accidental tourists" directed to the site by an advertisement, or potential investors looking for the financials? How do the audience demographics affect this? (You can use a table like the following to help you plan the targeted users and the functions they might perform at the site. An example is shown for Chop Point.)

User Group	Functions Performed at Site	Ages	Web Experience
1. Potential campers	- check session dates - sign-up - get more information	10–18	moderate - high
2.			
3.			

2. After you decide on the target audience and goals for the site, it's time to evaluate your content. This is best accomplished through conversations with the people you're developing the site for. If this isn't possible, be creative and come up with a list of content you think could be appropriate.

3. Use the answers to the following questions as a springboard for building the structure of your site. Then develop a tree diagram, similar to the one shown in Figure 1-1, to identify all the pieces of your site and where they fit within the overall structure.

- Does an official logo have to be used on the web site?
- Is all the content written and available in digital format?

(continued)

1

Getting Started

Project
1-1

Developing a Web Site

● What are the main sections of the site? Does all the content fit within those sections?

● List all the content for the site. Assign each piece of content to a section (as necessary) and define the filenames.

Project Summary

Before you begin writing the actual HTML for your web pages, you need to know something about the site you are creating. The questions asked in this project should get you off to a good start and help you build a solid foundation for your web site. In the next module, you'll continue working with this site as you write the code for one of the pages.

✓ Module 1 Mastery Check

1. What is a web browser?

2. What does HTML stand for?

3. Identify the various parts of the following URL:
   http://www.osborne.com/books/webdesign/favorites.html
   _____ :// _____ / _____ / _____ / _____

4. What is WYSIWYG?

5. Fill in the blank: Every new version of HTML will be built on the foundation of
   _____.

6. What is the program Macromedia Dreamweaver used for?

7. What is the most popular web browser?

8. Fill in the blank: When you type a URL into your web browser, you send a request to the _____ that houses that information.

9. What does the acronym "URL" stand for?

10. What organization maintains the standards for HTML?

11. How can you give your site's visitors visual clues as to where they are in your site's structure?

12. Fill in the blank: A good practice is to include a standard _____ on all pages for consistency and ease of use.

13. Fill in the blank: Selling products and recruiting potential employees are examples of web site _____.

14. Fill in the blank: Before you can begin developing your web site, you must know a little about the site's target _____.

15. If your site represents a new company or one that doesn't already have information about its client demographics, where might you look for information?

Module 2

Basic Page Structure

N ow that you know a little about the Web and what to think about before creating a web page, let's talk about the basic structure of an HTML page.

2.1 Create an HTML File

At their very core, HTML files are simply text files with two additional features.

1. *HTML files have an .html or .htm file extension.* A *file extension* is an abbreviation that associates the file with the appropriate program or tool needed to access it. In most cases, this abbreviation follows a period, and is three or four letters long. In the following example, notice that the Yahoo! home page ends in an .html file extension.

Location: http://www.yahoo.com/index.html

2. *HTML files have tags.* Tags are commands or code used to tell the computer how to display the page content. After choosing View | Page Source or View | Source, you can see some of the HTML tags in Yahoo!'s home page.

```
view-source: - Source of: http://www.yahoo.com/
<a href=r/sq>Finance</a>
<a href=r/pl>Games</a>
<a href=r/g3>GeoCities</a>
<a href=r/gp>Groups</a>
<a href=r/wm>Health</a>
</div>
<div class=u>
<a href=r/hl>Horoscopes</a>
<a href=r/jb>HotJobs</a>
<a href=r/yg>Kids</a>
<a href=r/0z>Local</a>
<a href=r/m2>Mail</a>
<a href=r/mp>Maps</a>
<a href=r/oa>Mobile</a>
</div>
<div class=u>
<a href=r/mf>Movies</a>
<a href=r/uf>Music</a>
<a href=r/i2>My Yahoo!</a>
<a href=r/dn>News</a>
<a href=r/ps>People Search</a>
<a href=r/pr>Personals</a>
<a href=r/fo>Photos</a>
</div>
<div class=u>
<a href=r/rl>Real Estate</a>
<a href=r/sh>Shopping</a>
<a href=r/ys>Sports</a>
<a href=r/ta>Travel</a>
<a href=r/tg>TV</a>
<a href=r/yp>Yellow Pages</a>
<div class=mr><a href=r/xy>All Y! Services...</a></div>
</div>
</div>
</div>
<div id=wm>
```

NOTE

You might also see more advanced types of pages on the Internet, such as Microsoft's Active Server Pages (.asp) or those written in the Extensible Markup Language (.xml). These are beyond the scope of the traditional HTML page and follow different standards.

Naming Conventions

Remember the following few points when naming your HTML files.

- Although in most cases it doesn't matter whether you use .html or .htm, you should be consistent to avoid confusing yourself, the browser, and your users.

NOTE

Wondering why some people use .html and some use .htm? Older systems such as Windows 3.1 and DOS could not understand four-letter file extensions, so anyone creating web pages on those systems used .htm as the extension. In any case, because the first three letters of .html and .htm are the same, those systems simply ignored the "l" and recognized the file type without any problems.

- Some web servers are case-sensitive, so remember this when naming and referencing filenames and try to be consistent. If you name your file MyPage.html, and then reference it later using mypage.html, you may end up with a broken link. One good technique is to use only uppercase or lowercase to name your files. This way, if you see a file with a letter in it that doesn't match, you know instantly that file is probably the problem. Even the pros run into case-sensitivity problems on an almost daily basis.

- Use simple filenames with only letters and numbers. Don't use spaces, punctuation, or special characters. (Dashes (-) and underscores (_) are allowed.) Good examples might be home.html, my-story.html, and contactme.html.

TIP

While it's perfectly acceptable to use an underscore (_) in a file or folder name, I suggest using a dash instead. Underscores can easily become confused with an underline, especially when displayed as a link on a web page (because links are usually underlined).

These same recommendations hold true for any folder names you use. If you were creating a web site that had your favorite links, family photos, and résumé, you might find it useful to put each of those things in a separate folder.

 TIP

If you decide to use Microsoft Word or WordPad to type your HTML, you need to choose the file type "Text Document" or "Text Only" and give the file an .html extension the first time you save it. This is because both of those programs default to saving "Word for Windows" or "Microsoft Word" documents with a .doc extension.

CRITICAL SKILL
2.2 Preview an HTML File in a Browser

You can view HTML files located on your personal computer within your own web browser. It isn't necessary for your files to be stored on a web server until you are ready to make them visible on the Internet.

When you want to preview a page, open your web browser and choose File | Open (or Open Page or Open File, depending on your browser), and then browse through your hard drive until you locate the HTML file you want to open.

If you're going to make frequent changes to the HTML file in a text editor, and then switch back to a web browser to preview the page, keeping both programs (a text editor and a web browser) open at the same time makes sense. When using a basic text editor, the steps to edit and preview HTML files are

1. Open/return to your HTML file in a text editor.

2. Edit your HTML file in a text editor.

3. Save your HTML file in a text editor.

4. Open/return to your HTML file in a web browser.

5. Click the Refresh button in Internet Explorer or the Reload button in Netscape in your web browser to update the HTML page employing the changes you just made to it.

By keeping your HTML file open in both a text editor and a browser, you can easily make and preview changes.

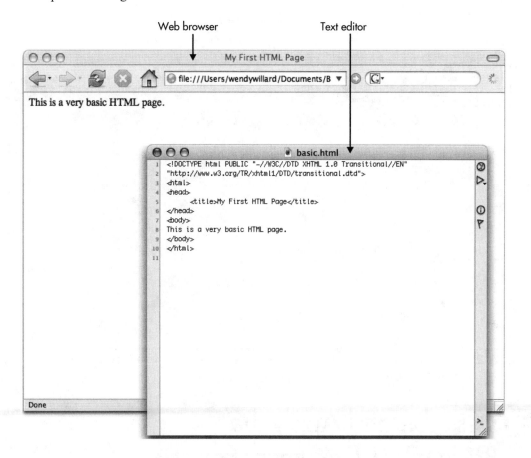

If you're using a graphical or WYSIWYG editor, the steps are slightly different because these types of programs include a browser preview option. For example, Macromedia Dreamweaver offers three ways to work with an HTML file. One option is to view only the code, as you would in a basic text editor. Another option is to work in the preview mode, moving page elements around on the page by clicking and dragging. Finally, you can use a combination, where the code is visible on part of the screen and the browser preview is visible on the rest (as shown in Figure 2-1).

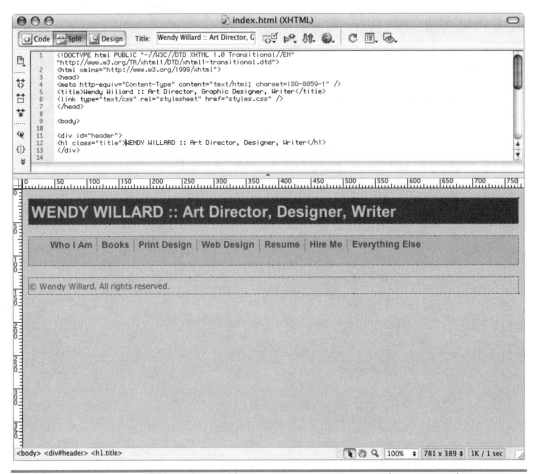

Figure 2-1 Accessing both the code and browser preview at once with Macromedia Dreamweaver

CRITICAL SKILL
2.3 Describe and Apply the Basic HTML Document Format

An *HTML entity* or *tag* is a command used to tell the computer how to display content on a page. This command is similar to what happens behind the scenes when you highlight some text in a word processor and click the Italic button to make the text italicized.

With HTML, instead of clicking a button to make text italicized, you can type a tag before and after the text you want to emphasize, as in the following:

```
<em>Reminder:</em> There will be no band practice today.
```

You can easily recognize tags because they are placed within *brackets* (< >), or less-than and greater-than symbols.

Did you notice that the tag to emphasize text and make it italic is em? Given that piece of information, can you guess the tags to add a paragraph or create items in a list?

Purpose	Tag
Create paragraphs	<p>
Create list items	<li>
Add a line break	

Now do you believe me when I say HTML is not rocket science? Don't worry—most of the tags are pretty intuitive and easy to remember.

Types of Tags

In HTML, there are usually both *opening* and *closing* tags. For example, if you use <p> as an opening tag to signify where to start a new paragraph, you have to use a closing tag to signify where that paragraph ends (unless you want your entire page to be contained within one paragraph). To do so, use the same tag with a forward slash placed before it: </p>. Table 2-1 shows a list of basic HTML page tags.

Opening Tag	Closing Tag	Description
!DOCTYPE	n/a	- Tells the browser which set of standards your page adheres to - Lists the standard (see the section "The Three Flavors" later in this chapter) - Identifies the location of the standard by linking to the URL
<html>	</html>	- Frames the entire HTML page
<head>	</head>	- Frames the identification information for the page, such as the title, that is transferred to the browser and search engines
<body>	</body>	- Frames the content of the page to be displayed in the browser window
<title>	</title>	- Gives the name of the page that will appear at the top of the browser window and be listed in search engines - Is contained within <head> and </head>

Table 2-1 Basic HTML Page Tags

NOTE

Even though older versions of HTML didn't need every tag to be closed, current versions do require it.

Attributes

Many tags have additional aspects that you can customize. These options are called *attributes* and are placed after the tag but before the final bracket. Specific attributes for each tag are discussed as we move through the book. But to give you an idea of how attributes work, let's look at an example using the img tag.

```
<img src="mypicture.jpg" width="100" height="100" alt="A photo of me" />
```

In this example, the base tag is img, which tells the browser I want to insert an image at this spot. The attributes are width, height, and alt. Each attribute has a *value*, which comes after an equal sign (=) and is placed within quotation marks.

There's no need to repeat the img tag, because multiple attributes can be included in a single tag. When you add attributes to a tag, you only put them in the opening tag. Then, you only need to close the tag (not the attributes). Note that this tag is one that doesn't have an official closing tag. In fact, old versions of HTML didn't require the img tag be closed at all. When you encounter tags like this, simply place the closing / before the final bracket, as shown in the code example.

Required Tags

All HTML pages need to have the html, head, and body tags, along with the DOCTYPE identifier. This means, at the very least, your pages should include the following:

```
<!DOCTYPE html PUBLIC "-//W3C//DTD XHTML 1.0 Transitional//EN"
"http://www.w3.org/TR/xhtml1/DTD/transitional.dtd">
<html>
<head>
     <title>My First HTML Page</title>
</head>
<body>
This is a very basic HTML page.
</body>
</html>
```

Here is the result of this page when displayed in a browser.

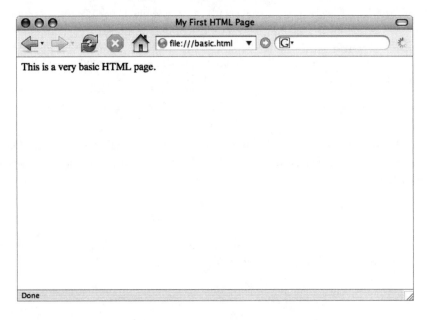

To test this basic HTML page for yourself, try the following:

1. Open a basic text editor, such as SimpleText (Mac) or Notepad (PC).

2. Copy the previous code into a new text document.

3. Save it as a text-only file (ASCII text) and name it **test.html**.

4. Launch your browser and choose File | Open File (Firefox or Safari) or File | Open (Internet Explorer).

5. Browse your hard drive to locate the test.html file, and you're off and running!

The Three Flavors

The W3C has specified the current version of HTML be available in three flavors, or versions, to accommodate the transition time during which developers and browsers migrate from HTML 4.0 to XHTML. You need to identify your page with one of these three flavors to help the browser validate it. Because most of your pages will probably fall into one of the three categories, you can simply copy-and-paste the doctype from one page onto all the others.

1. **XHTML Transitional**   This is the category under which the majority of existing pages probably fall, because it allows those HTML 4.01 tags that are deprecated, as long as the rest of the page adheres to XHTML rules, such as closing all tags (even ones like `br`, that aren't required to be closed in regular HTML). Pages that are transitional are prepared for XHTML, but are also compatible with older browsers that don't understand XHTML. To validate your pages against this flavor of XHTML, use

```
<!DOCTYPE html PUBLIC "-//W3C//DTD XHTML 1.0 Transitional//EN"
"http://www.w3.org/TR/xhtml1/DTD/transitional.dtd">.
```

2. **XHTML Strict**   Pages that fall into this category don't contain any deprecated tags. Instead, they are structurally very clean. To validate your pages against this flavor of XHTML, use

```
<!DOCTYPE html PUBLIC "-//W3C//DTD XHTML 1.0 Strict//EN"
"http://www.w3.org/TR/xhtml1/DTD/xhtml1-strict.dtd">.
```

3. **XHTML Frameset**   Sites using HTML frames to divide the pages must identify with the frameset flavor of XHTML. To validate your pages against this flavor of XHTML, use

```
<!DOCTYPE html PUBLIC "-//W3C//DTD XHTML 1.0 Frameset//EN"
"http://www.w3.org/TR/xhtml1/DTD/frameset.dtd"">.
```

Validating Against These Doctypes

Wondering why you even need to *validate* your HTML against a particular doctype? The purpose of validation is to help identify potential problems a browser might encounter when displaying your page. Because browsers render pages based on the official HTML specifications (as dictated by the W3C), it makes sense to double-check your pages against those specs as part of your testing.

The official W3C validation service can be found at **http://validator.w3.org**. Once you get there, you'll notice you can use several different methods to test or validate your pages.

- **Validate by URL**   If your page is already live on the Internet, you can simply enter the page's URL (address), and the tool will seek to validate your page.

- **Validate by file upload**   If you're working on pages currently stored on your hard drive (but not live on the Internet), you can upload those pages to the online validator.

- **Validate by direct input**   Alternatively, you can simply copy-and-paste the code into an online form at the validation service.

Regardless of which method you choose, the results will be the same. The validator will give you a passing or failing grade. If your page fails to validate against the standard you've listed in your code, the tool will also tell you why the page fails. For example, it might tell you if you've used a particular attribute in the wrong tag, or if you've used a tag that's not in the spec.

Ask the Expert

Q: **I typed the previous HTML into a text file, but when I tried to preview the page in my browser, nothing happened. Why?**

A: There are several possible reasons why your page might appear blank. First, review the code in the previous example and compare it line by line with the code you typed. Forgetting a closing tag or maybe just a forward slash (/) is easy. Sometimes it's helpful to take a quick break before returning to scrutinize your page. If you do make a change, be sure to save the file in your text editor, before clicking Refresh or Reload in your web browser.

   If you're certain the code in your page matches the example, try resaving your file under a new name. Close your browser, then relaunch your web browser and open the page in the browser again.

   Additional troubleshooting techniques are located in Appendix C.

Progress Check

1. What is an attribute?

2. How can you preview your web page in a browser?

Capitalization

Original versions of HTML were case-insensitive and, in fact, very forgiving. This means all of the following examples would be considered the same by the browser:

- `<html>`
- `<HTML>`
- `<HTml>`

---

1. An attribute is an optional feature of a tag that can be customized.

2. Choose File | Open File (Safari or Firefox) or File | Open (Internet Explorer) and browse your hard drive until you locate the file you want to preview. Alternatively, your graphical HTML editor may have built-in ways of previewing the page.

That said, current versions of HTML (XHTML) are case-sensitive and require all tags to be lowercase. Of the three previous examples, the browser would properly interpret only the first. For this reason, I recommend using all lowercase tags.

Quotations

Current versions of HTML/XHTML require all values to be placed within straight quotation marks, as in the following example:

— The value of the attribute

```
<p style="font-family: verdana;">
```

Nesting

The term *nesting* appears many times throughout the course of this book and refers to the process of containing one HTML tag inside another.

— The em tag is nested within the strong tag.

```
<strong>This text is bold and <em>italic</em></strong>
```

There is a proper and improper way to nest tags. All tags should begin and end starting in the middle and moving out. Another way of thinking about it involves the "circle rule." You should always be able to draw semicircles that connect the opening and closing versions of each tag. If any of your semicircles intersect, your tags are not nested properly.

Using the following example, the first one is proper because the `strong` tags are both on the outside and the em tags are both on the inside.

```
<strong><em>These tags are nested properly.</em></strong>
<strong><em>These tags are not nested properly.</strong></em>
```

Even though both may work in some browsers, you need to nest tags the proper way to ensure that your pages display the same across all browsers.

Spacing and Breaks

Let's look closely at some example HTML to identify where proper spacing should occur. (Note, the `a` tag and `href` attribute are used to link something, in this case text.)

No space is between the brackets and the tag.

No spaces should be between a tag and the text it affects.

```
<body>
<a href="http://www.google.com" title="Search Google">Search Google</a>
```

A single space should be between tags and attributes.

A single space should be between attributes.

Two places exist within an HTML file where you might like to add breaks:

- In between tags, to help you differentiate between sections of the page
- In between lines of text within the body of the page

Spacing and Breaks Between Tags

The first place you might like to add breaks is in between tags, as in the following example.

```
<html>
<head>
    <title>My First Web Page</title>
</head>
```

Although this is not required, most people use the ENTER or RETURN key to separate tags with line breaks. Others also indent tags that are contained within another tag, as in the previous example: the `title` tag is indented to show it is contained or nested within the `head` tag. This may help you to identify the tags more quickly when viewing the page in a text editor.

Spacing Between Lines of Text

The second place you add breaks is between the lines of text in the body of the page. If you use the RETURN or ENTER key on your keyboard to add a line break in between two lines of text on your page, that line break will not appear when the browser displays the page.

```
<!DOCTYPE html PUBLIC "-//W3C//DTD XHTML 1.0 Transitional//EN"
"http://www.w3.org/TR/xhtml1/DTD/transitional.dtd">
<html>
<head>
    <title>My first Web page</title>
</head>
<body>
Welcome.

Thank you for visiting my first Web page. I have several other pages
that you might be interested in.
</body>
</html>
```

In the previous code, I pressed the RETURN key twice after the word "Welcome." In this example, you can see that the browser ignored my returns and ran both lines of text together.

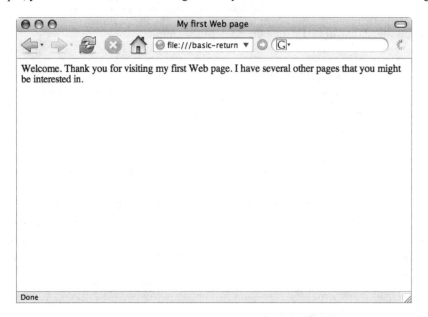

To make those line breaks appear, I'd have to use a tag to tell the browser to insert a line break. Two tags are used for breaks in content.

```
<br />
<p></p>
```

The br tag inserts a simple line break. It tells the browser to drop down to the next line before continuing. If you insert multiple br tags, the browser will drop down several lines before continuing.

The p tag signifies a paragraph break. The difference between the two is that paragraph breaks cause the browser to skip a line, while line breaks do not. Also, the p tag is considered a *container* tag because its opening and closing tags should be used to contain paragraphs of content. The br and p tags are discussed in more detail in Module 4.

NOTE

Because the br tag doesn't contain any text, as the p tag does, it doesn't have an opening and closing version. Instead, you place a slash before the closing bracket to "terminate" the tag, as in: <br />.

If I enclose each of these paragraphs in p tags, like the following:

```
<p>Welcome.</p>
<p>Thank you for visiting my first Web page. I have several other
pages that you might be interested in.</p>
```

the browser will know to separate them with a blank line. The following screen shows how the browser displays the text now that I have contained each of the paragraphs in p tags.

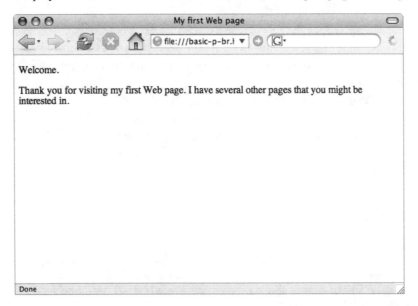

In addition, HTML neither recognizes more than a single space at a time nor does it interpret a tab space as a way to indent. This means that in order to indent a paragraph or leave more than one space between words, you must use style sheets (see Module 4 or Appendix D) or special characters.

Progress Check

What's wrong with these tags?

1. `<strong><em>This text is bold and italic.</strong></em>`

2. `< strong >This text is bold.< / strong >`

---

1. These tags aren't nested properly. The correct order should be `<strong><em>This text is bold and italic.</em></strong>`

2. No spaces should appear within the tags.

Use Character Entities to Display Special Characters

As crazy as this sounds, you shouldn't include any characters in your HTML files that you can't type with only one finger. This means, if you have to hold down the SHIFT key to type an exclamation mark or a dollar sign, you will need to use a *character entity* to include that special character in your HTML file.

Even though you might be able to type a certain character on your computer system without any problems, some characters may not translate properly when visitors to your web site view your page. So, I recommend you use character entities to maintain consistency across computer systems.

Character entities can be typed as either a numbered entity or a named entity. All character entities begin with an ampersand (&) and end with a semicolon (;). Although every character entity has a numbered version, not every one has a named version. While a full list of special characters is included in Appendix D, a few are listed in the following table to give you an idea of what they look like.

NOTE

A few characters are reserved and given special meaning in HTML. For example, the brackets (< and >) are used to signify HTML tags, while the ampersand (&) is used to begin these entities. If you need to use a bracket within the content of your HTML page, such as when a greater-than symbol is needed, in the case of 3 > 2, you should use the character entity (>) to do so.

Character	Numbered Entity	Named Entity
"	&#34;	&quot;
&	&#38;	&amp;
(nonbreaking space)		
©	&#169;	&copy;
®	&#174;	&reg;
É	&#233;	&eacute;
<	&#60;	&lt;
>	&#62;	&gt;

Having now made the case for using character entities, let me just say here that it's been my experience that certain characters *can* actually be used in a web page without causing any problems. These include straight—not curly—quotation marks ("), exclamation marks (!), question marks (?), colons (;), and parentheses (). While I haven't noticed any of these to cause problems in the majority of browsers, you should still test your pages thoroughly when using any special characters.

2.4 Add Comments to an HTML File

Sometimes you might not want your web site visitors to see personal comments or notes you've added to your web pages. These notes might be directions to another person or reminders to yourself.

Signifies the beginning of a comment

```
<!-- Remember to update this page after the new product becomes available -->
```

A space should appear after the opening comment and before the closing comment.

Space denotes the end of the comment.

Comments are not restricted in size and can cover many lines at a time. The end comment code (-->) doesn't need to be on the same line as the beginning comment code. If you forget to close your comment tag, the rest of the page will not appear in your browser. If this happens, don't be alarmed. Simply go back to the code and close that comment. The rest of the page will become visible when you save the file and reload it in the browser.

2.5 Set Up Style Sheets in an HTML File

I've already mentioned the phrase "style sheets" a few times, but haven't really given them a full explanation yet. Part of the reason is that style sheets weren't really a part of HTML until it was rewritten as XHTML. The purpose of *cascading style sheets* (abbreviated CSS) is to separate the *style* of a web page from its *content*.

The current HTML "rules" dictate that we only use HTML to identify the content of the page, and then use a style sheet to specify the presentation of that content. This not only makes web pages more accessible and useable to all users (regardless of their browsers, platforms, operating systems, physical limitations, and so forth), but also to search engines and other types of software.

TIP

If you've ever used the style drop-down menu in Microsoft Word, you've already used a style sheet of sorts. The most basic style sheet might include a style called "Body Text," that specifies how the body text of the web page should look—which font and color to use, how much space to leave around it, and so on.

Define the Style

To define a basic formatting style, you first must identify which tag you want to affect. This tag is then called a *selector* in CSS. So, if you wanted to specify the style of all the level 2 headlines (<h2>) on a page, you would use h2 as your selector.

```
h2
```

In fact, the selector is essentially the tag without the brackets. With that in mind, can you guess what the selector for <p> would be?

```
p
```

Once you have a selector, you can define its properties. Similar to how attributes work in HTML, CSS *properties* alter specific attributes of a selector. Returning to the previous example, if you want to change the style of the level 2 headlines on your page to a 14-point Verdana font, italic, and blue, you can use the following properties:

```
font-family
font-style
font-size
color
```

When you specify values for properties, you are creating a *declaration* for that selector. The declaration and selector together is then referred to as a set of *rules*, or a *ruleset*. In the typical ruleset, the declaration is enclosed in curly brackets after the selector.

So here are the first few pieces of our ruleset:

```
h2 ◄————————————— Selector
font-family ◄—————————— Property
verdana ◄——————————————— Value
{font-family: verdana;} ◄————————— Declaration
```

And here is how they all fit together to tell the browser to display all level 2 headlines in the Verdana font.

```
h2 {font-family: verdana;}
```

To specify the font size, color and style (italic), we simply add on a few more of those properties.

```
h2 {font-family: verdana;
    font-size: 14pt;
    color: blue;
    font-style: italic;}
```

At this point, you can probably start to see the pattern—a CSS property is followed by a colon, and then its value, which in turn is followed by a semicolon.

Define the Values

As with attributes in HTML, properties have values. Most values can be specified in terms of color, keyword, length, percentage, or URL, as listed in Table 2-2. Length and percentage units can also be made positive or negative by adding a plus (+) or minus (–) sign in front of the value.

Type of Value	Description
Color	When specifying color in a value, you can do so in one of three ways (see Module 3 for more information on color): - hexadecimal code, such as #000000 - RGB values, such as rgb(0,0,0) or rgb(0%,0%,0%) - one of the 17 predefined keywords
Keyword	A keyword is a word defined in CSS that's translated into a numerical value by the browser. For this reason, keywords are often considered relative because, ultimately, it's up to the browser to decide how to render the content. An example of a keyword is small.
Length	In HTML, most units are defined in pixels. In CSS, however, you have the option of using many other types of units. For example, when specifying text sizes with the font-size property, you can use any of the following. (Abbreviations are shown in parentheses.) - points (pt)—72 points in an inch - picas (pc)—12 points in a pica - pixels (px)—a dot on the screen - ems (em)—refers to the height of the font in general - exs (ex)—refers to the height of an x in a particular font - inches (in) - millimeters (mm) - centimeters (cm)
Percentage	Relative percentages can be useful in CSS when used to position elements on a page. This is because percentages allow elements to move around, depending on how large the screen and window sizes are. When used in CSS, a percentage sign (%) following a numerical value, such as 100%, indicates a relationship between the surrounding elements.
URL	When you reference an absolute URL in CSS, use the following form: url(http://www.osborne.com) Similarly, relative URLs (typically those found within the current web site) are referenced in the following manner: url(home.html)

Table 2-2 Types of CSS Values

Create the Structure

After you know a little about the individual parts of CSS, you can put them together to create a few styles. The organization of these pieces depends a bit on which type of style sheet you are creating. CSS offers three types of style sheets:

- **Inline**   Styles are embedded right within the HTML code they affect.

- **Internal**   Styles are placed within the header information of the web page, and then affect all corresponding tags *on the page.*

- **External**   Styles are coded in a separate document, which is then referenced from within the header of the actual web page. This means a single external style sheet can be used to affect the presentation on a whole group of web pages.

You can use any or all of these types of style sheets in a single document. However, if you do include more than one type, the rules of *cascading order* take over: these rules state that inline rules take precedence over internal styles, which take precedence over external styles.

In a nutshell, CSS styles apply from general to specific. This means a ruleset in the head tag of a document overrides a linked style sheet, while a ruleset in the body of a document overrides one in the head tag. HTML styles (such as the now-defunct font tags) inside an inline ruleset override that. In addition, more local (or *inline*) styles only override the parent attributes where overlap occurs.

Inline

Inline styles are created right within the HTML of the page, hence the name. In the previous examples, a declaration was surrounded by curly quotes, but inline declarations are enclosed in straight quotes using the style attribute.

```
<h2 style="font-family: verdana;">
```

You can separate multiple rules by semicolons, but the entire declaration should be included within quotes.

```
<h2 style="font-family: verdana; color: #003366;">
```

Inline styles are best for making quick changes to a page, but they aren't suited for changes to an entire document or web site. The reason for this is that when styles are added to a tag, they occur only for that individual tag and not for all similar tags on the page.

TIP

Inline styles overrule internal and external styles when multiple types of style sheets are found on the same page.

Internal

When you want to change the style of all the h2 tags on a single page, you can use an *internal*, or *embedded*, style sheet. Instead of adding the `style` attribute to a tag, use the `style` tag to contain all the instructions for the page. The `style` tag is placed in the header of the page, in between the opening and closing `head` tags. Here's an example of what an internal style sheet might look like.

```
<head>
<title>CSS Example</title>
<style type="text/css">
h2 {font-family: verdana; color: blue;}
h3 {font-family: verdana; color: red;}
</style>
</head>
```

As the previous example shows, the selector is placed before the declaration, which is enclosed in curly brackets. This entire ruleset can be contained on a single line or broken up into multiple lines, as in the following example.

```
h2
{font-family: verdana;
color: blue;}
```

You can write styles in several ways. The following example is just as valid as the previous one and is preferred by some people because it is easier to read.

```
h2 {font-family: verdana;
    color: blue;}
```

In addition, you can use certain shorthand properties to reduce the amount of coding necessary. For example, instead of specifying both font family (Verdana) and font size (12 point), you could type the following because both properties begin with font.

```
h2 {font: verdana 12pt;}
```

TIP

Module 4 discusses how to style text in much more detail.

External

An *external* style sheet holds essentially the same information as an internal one, except an external style sheet is contained in its own text file, and then referenced from within the web page. Thus, an external style sheet might look like this:

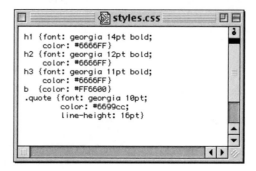

```
styles.css

h1 {font: georgia 14pt bold;
    color: #6666FF}
h2 {font: georgia 12pt bold;
    color: #6666FF}
h3 {font: georgia 11pt bold;
    color: #6666FF}
b  {color: #FF6600}
.quote {font: georgia 10pt;
        color: #6699cc;
        line-height: 16pt}
```

Notice that external style sheets don't use the style tag or attribute, but simply include a list of rulesets as instructions for the browser. Once you create your external style sheet, save it as a text file, with the .css file extension.

Then, return to your HTML file and add the `link` tag to the page header to reference the external style sheet, as in the following example.

This is where the name of
your style sheet is placed.

```
<head>
<title>Using an External Style Sheet</title>
<link rel="stylesheet" type="text/css" href="styles.css">
</head>
```

In this case, I only needed to write styles.css because the style sheet is in the same folder as my HTML page. However, if your style sheet is in a different folder than your HTML page, be sure to reference that path appropriately.

NOTE

External style sheets can be overruled by internal and inline style sheets.

Project 2-1 Creating the First Page of Your Site

To continue with the site you began planning for in the first module, we now begin the first page in your site. Goals for this project include

- Use all the necessary tags to create a basic web page.

- Use a character entity to add a copyright symbol to the page.

- Add space for an internal style sheet in the header of the page.

- Save the page as an HTML file that can be read by a web browser.

- Preview the page in a web browser.

NOTE

All the files needed to complete the projects in this book for the Chop Point site can be downloaded from **www.osborne.com** or **www.wendywillard.com**. In addition, you can view my version of the web site anytime by visiting **www.choppoint.org**.

Step by Step

1. Open a text editor on your computer (such as SimpleText on the Mac or Notepad in Windows). Copy the following code to begin your web page. Feel free to make edits wherever necessary to personalize your site for your organization.

```
<!DOCTYPE html PUBLIC "-//W3C//DTD XHTML 1.0 Transitional//EN"
"http://www.w3.org/TR/xhtml1/DTD/transitional.dtd">
<html>
<head>
<title>Chop Point Camp and School, located in Woolwich, Maine</title>
<style type="text/css">

</style>
</head>
<body>
<p>Chop Point </p>
<p>Chop Point is a non-profit organization operating a summer camp and
PK-12 school in Woolwich, Maine.</p>
</body>
</html>
```

(continued)

2. After the end of the second paragraph, add two breaks and a copyright symbol (©), followed by the year and the name of the organization. (Example: © 2006 Chop Point Inc.)

3. Create a new folder on your hard drive, called **choppoint** (or the name of your organization or web site). Save this file as **index.html** in the folder you just created.

4. Open your web browser and choose File | Open (or Open File, depending on the browser you're using). Locate the file index.html you just saved.

5. Preview the page and compare it to Figure 2-2. If you need to make changes, return to your text editor (SimpleText or Notepad) to do so. Once you have made those changes, save the file and switch back to your web browser. Click the Reload or Refresh button in your browser to update your page according to the changes you just made. The complete code for your page might look like this:

```
<!DOCTYPE html PUBLIC "-//W3C//DTD XHTML 1.0 Transitional//EN"
"http://www.w3.org/TR/xhtml1/DTD/transitional.dtd">
<html>
<head>
<title> Chop Point Camp and School, located in Woolwich, Maine </title>
<style type="text/css">

</style>
</head>
<body>
<p>Chop Point </p>
<p>Chop Point is a non-profit organization operating a summer camp and
PK-12 school in Woolwich, Maine.</p>
<br />
<br />
&copy; 2006 Chop Point Inc.
</body>
</html>
```

TIP

Does your browser window appear blank when you try to preview your page? If so, return to your text editor and make sure you have included all the necessary closing tags (such as </body> and </html>). In addition, if you are using any editor other than SimpleText or Notepad, don't forget to save the file as "text only" within an .html file extension. For more tips, see Appendix C: Troubleshooting.

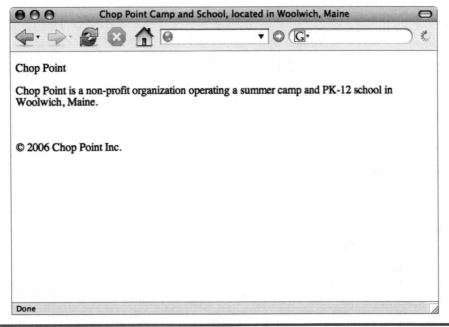

Figure 2-2 Your page should look similar to this one when displayed in a browser, depending on your organization and content.

Project Summary

Every web page needs a few tags to display properly in the browser. This project helps you practice typing those tags and placing them in the correct order on the page.

Getting used to the process of editing, saving, and previewing pages is good because this is used throughout the rest of this book and during the course of your continued web development.

✓ Module 2 Mastery Check

1. What file extensions do HTML files use?

2. The following line of HTML code contains errors. What is the correct way to write this line?

```
<p   This is a paragraph of text    p>
```

3. At the very least, which tags should be included in a basic HTML page?

4. Identify the tag name, attribute, and value in the following line of HTML code:

   ```
   <a href="page.html">
   ```

5. Fill in the blank: XHTML requires all tags to be _____ case.

6. Which option is *not* acceptable for an HTML filename?

   A. myfile.html

   B. my-file.html

   C. my file.html

   D. my1file.html

7. What is the named character entity used to add a copyright symbol to a web page?

8. You just created a web page, and you're previewing it in a web browser when you notice an error. After fixing the error and saving the web page, which button should you click in the browser to view the changes made?

9. Which is the proper way to close the br tag to make it XHTML-compliant?

   A.

   B. </br>

   C.

   D.

   E. </ br>

10. The tags in the following line of code aren't nested properly. Rewrite the code so the tags are nested properly.

    ```
    <p><strong><em>Hello World!</p></em></strong>
    ```

11. How can you rewrite the following text so it doesn't display when the page is viewed in a browser?

    ```
    Hide Me!
    ```

12. Which two options will the browser ignore when they are coded in a web page?

    A. <p>

    B. A tab

    C.

D.

E. Single space with the SPACEBAR

F. Double space with the SPACEBAR

13. Fill in the blank: The p tag is an example of a _____ tag because it contains sections of text.

14. The following line of HTML code contains errors. What is the correct way to write the code?

```
< img src = "photo.jpg" >
```

15. What symbols must surround all HTML tags?

Module 3

Color

51

Each browser has a set of standard colors for web pages that can be customized by the user (see Figure 3-1). If you don't specify otherwise, your pages will display according to the browser's settings.

To change colors on your web page, you need to know the color you want to change it to, as well as the corresponding color value (described in the following section).

CRITICAL SKILL
3.1 Identify the Ways in Which Color Is Referenced in Web Development

At the beginning of time—Web time—the only way to reference color in an HTML page was to use its hexadecimal color value. When CSS became the preferred method of referencing color in web pages, we were permitted to use a variety of other units to measure color, including RGB values, RGB percentages, hexadecimal shorthand, and color names.

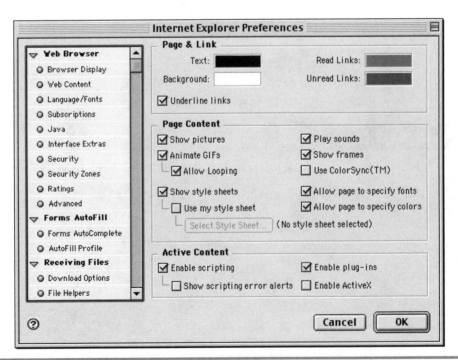

Figure 3-1 Customizing color settings in a version of Internet Explorer

Hexadecimal Color

The "normal" number system in the U.S. is *decimal*—based on the number 10. This means we have 10 units (0–9) to use before we have to repeat a unit (as with the number 10, which uses the 0 and 1).

The *hexadecimal* system (hex) uses the same concepts as the decimal system, except it's based on 16 units (see Table 3-1). Because standard HTML cannot handle decimal color values, the hexadecimal system is used to specify color values on web pages. Instead of making up new characters to represent the remaining units after 9, the hexadecimal system uses the first six letters of the English alphabet (*A–F*).

Computer monitors display color in *RGB* mode, where R = Red, G = Green, and B = Blue. Each letter (R, G, and B) is represented by a value between 0 and 255, with 0 being the darkest and 255 representing the lightest in the spectrum. In RGB, white and black have the following values:

	Red Value	Green Value	Blue Value
White	255	255	255
Black	0	0	0

This is how one graphics program—Adobe Photoshop—displays the RGB values for blue (R:00 G:00 B:255). Most other graphics programs have similar ways of helping you determine the RGB values of your colors.

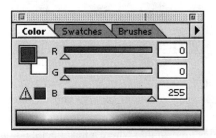

Decimal	0	1	2	3	4	5	6	7	8	9	10	11	12	13	14	15
Hex	0	1	2	3	4	5	6	7	8	9	A	B	C	D	E	F

Table 3-1 Decimal and Hexadecimal Units

In Photoshop, one way to find out what the hexadecimal values are for that shade of blue is to click the triangle in the upper-right corner of that color window and choose Web Color Sliders from the menu.

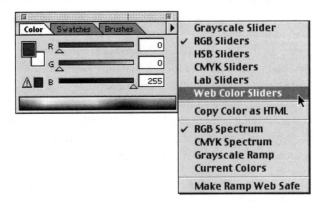

The resulting window shows the corresponding hex values for that same blue are R:00 G:00 B:FF.

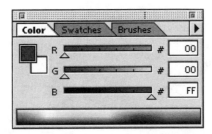

When using hexadecimal color values in an HTML page, you translate the color from decimal (RGB) to hex. Each red, green, or blue value translates into a two-digit hex value. You then combine all three of those two-digit hex values into a single string, preceded by a hash mark. The following is an example where a hexadecimal color is used to change the text in one paragraph to blue.

```
<p style="color: #0000FF;">
```

NOTE

While you previously needed a scientific calculator to convert between decimal and hexadecimal values, many charts, software programs, converters, and even web pages are now available to do this for you.

Hexadecimal Shorthand

When referencing a color that has value pairs, you can use a bit of shorthand to reduce the amount of typing necessary. For example, a color with a hexadecimal code of 003366 can be shortened to 036. This is because each of the two red values is the same, as are that of the blue and green values. A hexadecimal code of 003466 wouldn't work, because the green values—34—aren't the same.

The following shows how the same blue used in the previous code example could be referenced, using hex shorthand.

```
<p style="color: #00F;">
```

NOTE

Hexadecimal shorthand is only allowed when using style sheets—the preferred method of presenting color in your pages. If you previously learned how to use code like this to change page colors, `<font color="#0000ff">`, you can't start using shorthand in those hex values. Only complete hexadecimal codes are permitted in those older, now defunct, HTML tags.

RGB Values and Percentages

Now that style sheets are the preferred method of presenting color in all web pages, we no longer have to struggle with hexadecimal codes. If a color's RGB values are handy, use those in your style sheet in place of the hexadecimal code, like in the following:

```
<p style="color: rgb(0,0,255);">
```

If you don't have the RGB values handy, as when working in some page layout or design programs other than Photoshop, you can also use the RGB percentages, like that shown in the following example.

```
<p style="color: rgb(0%,0%,100%);">
```

Notice that a comma separates each RGB value and the entire set of values is placed inside parentheses. A lowercase `rgb` precedes those parentheses. In the case of the previous code example, R = 0, G = 0, and B = 255. As was the case with hexadecimal shorthand, RGB values and percentages are only used to describe color in style sheets, not the older HTML color tags.

Color Names

HTML 3.2 and 4.0 defined a standard set of 16 colors, which could be referenced by names in addition to hex values. The first version of CSS continued with these 16 colors, and orange was added in CSS 2.1. Although CSS 3.0 finally gives us a larger set of acceptable colors, I don't encourage their use until the browsers have a chance to catch up with the standards. In the meantime, Table 3-2 lists the 17 color names that are almost uniformly supported by browsers.

```
<p style="color: blue;">
```

Color Name	Hex Value	RGB Value
black	#000000	0,0,0
white	#ffffff	255,255,255
silver	#c0c0c0	192,192,192
gray	#808080	128,128,128
lime	#00ff00	0,255,0
olive	#808000	128,128,0
green	#008000	0.128.0
yellow	#ffff00	255,255,0
maroon	#800000	128,0,0
navy	#000080	0,0,128
red	#ff0000	255,0,0
blue	#0000ff	0,0,255
purple	#800080	128,0,128
teal	#008080	0,128,128
fuchsia	#ff00ff	255,0,255
aqua	#00ffff	0,255,255
orange	#ffa500	255,165,0

Table 3-2 Standard Color Names as of CSS 2.1

So Which Should I Use?

The wonderful thing about using style sheets to define color in web pages is that we are free to use any of the previously mentioned methods. This means you can tailor your color presentation method to your particular needs and use whichever makes the most sense to you.

Web-Safe Colors

Have you ever looked at your favorite web site on someone else's monitor and noticed the colors seemed a bit different? This may have been because of different monitor settings. For example, most newer computer systems and monitors are capable of displaying millions of colors. But that wasn't the case only a few years ago, when most DOS-based PCs were set up to display 256 colors or fewer. This reduced color palette means you can't always be assured the color you choose for your web page will be available on the viewer's system.

To compound the problem, Macintosh systems display a different set of 256 colors than their DOS-based PC counterparts. Only 216 colors between the two computer systems (Mac and PC) are the same! Those 216 colors have come to be known as the *web-safe color palette* (see the inside panel of the front cover for a full-color reproduction of the web-safe palette). For a long time, designers were greatly encouraged to use a color from this palette to ensure that the majority of viewers would see approximately the same color selected.

However, ten years after the birth of the web-safe palette, the majority of viewers are now using much better monitors and computers. This means there is significantly less of a push to use web-safe colors, but I still mention them so you are familiar with the palette should you need to absolutely ensure the appearance of a particular color on a web page.

You can easily recognize web-safe colors by their hexadecimal values. Each of the web-safe colors has RGB values that are multiples of 51. So, every color in the 216-color web-safe palette has a hex value made up of the values shown next.

RGB	Hex
0	00
51	33
102	66
153	99
204	CC
255	FF

The color selected in this illustration is not web-safe. This is evident because the green value is #55, which is not a web-safe hex value. To make this color web-safe, you would have to change the green value to #66.

This symbol warns that the color currently selected is not web-safe. Clicking the square box next to the cube causes Photoshop to change the color to the closest web-safe color. →

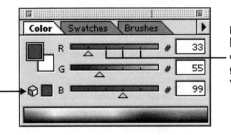

Photoshop's color window has little black lines along each of the three color bars (red, green, and blue) to show where the web-safe values are

Specify Document Colors

The preferred method of changing document colors, such as the background and the text, is with style sheets.

As with any style declaration, you can specify the background, text, and link colors in either an inline, internal, or external style sheet. The actual properties used to do so are the same, however, regardless of which type of style sheet you use. Unlike with the older HTML tags previously used to change document colors, with CSS you aren't restricted to specifying this information within the body tag. In fact, you actually use the a tag (which is used to add links to a web page) to change link colors in CSS. To understand, look at the following example of an internal style sheet:

```
<style type="text/css">
body {background-color: white;
      color: gray;}
a:link {color: blue;}
a:visited {color: purple;}
a:active {color: orange;}
</style>
```

NOTE

Remember, internal style sheets are those placed in between the opening and closing head tags in the HTML code of your web page.

With CSS, you have to consider which tag actually creates the content whose color you want to change, and use that as your CSS selector. So, in the previous inline style sheet example, I first tell the browser to change the background color of the entire page to white (the body tag determines the underlying features of a page, such as background color and default text color). Adding the color property to the body selector also specifies that all text on the page should be, in this case, gray.

Next, I'm telling the browser to select all content affected by a tags (a:link) and to make them blue. When those links have been visited, I want the browser to render them as purple, as indicated by the line a:visited {color: purple;}. And, finally, the color of active links—that is, the color visible when the user is clicking a link—is orange, as defined by the line beginning with a:active.

TIP

Although we used the same property—color—to change the default text color and the various link colors, remember that it is the *selector* (in this case body and a) that tells the browser exactly which color to alter.

Project 3-1 Change the Colors of Your Page

Let's take the index.html page from the previous module, and change the background and text colors of that page. Goals for this project include

- Choosing colors from the web-safe palette.
- Specifying the background and text colors of the web page.
- Referencing the colors with the appropriate color codes.

NOTE

All the files needed to complete the projects in this book for the Chop Point site can be downloaded from **www.osborne.com** or **www.wendywillard.com**. In addition, you can view my version of the web site anytime by visiting **www.choppoint.org**.

Step by Step

1. Open your text editor and load the index.html page saved from Module 2.

2. Add the background-color and color properties to your internal style sheet as the following shows. (Feel free to replace these color values with any you deem appropriate.) Save the file.

```
<style type="text/css">
body {background-color: #ffe188;
     color: 602b00;}
</style>
```

You can find a color in several different ways:

- Pick one from the color palette on the inside front cover of this book.
- Use a color from Table 3-2.

- Choose one from the color-picker in your favorite graphics program (such as Adobe Photoshop).
- Download the HTML Beginner's Guide .zip file, which has your very own web-safe color palette in the Module 3 folder.

3. Open your web browser and choose File | Open Page (or Open File or Open, depending on the browser you're using). Locate the file `index.html` you just saved.

4. Preview the page to determine if you approve of your color choices. If you don't, return to your text editor to make changes. After making any changes, save the file and switch back to the browser. Choose Refresh or Reload to preview the changes you just made.

Project Summary

Using a style sheet to change the colors of your web page is not difficult, but it does require some planning to find a set of colors that work well together. Viewing your pages on several different computer systems can help ensure they all appear as you would like.

Module 3 Mastery Check

1. What is the difference between decimal numbers and hexadecimal numbers?

2. The second two numbers in a six-digit hexadecimal code refer to which color?

3. How many colors are there in the web-safe palette?

4. #036 is hexadecimal shorthand for which complete hexadecimal color code?

5. Fill in the blank: Instead of making up new characters to represent the remaining units after 9, the hexadecimal system uses the first six letters of the _____.

6. Can you use RGB color values to specify color in traditional HTML code?

7. In what additional way is CSS capable of specifying colors?

8. Fill in the blank: Each of the web-safe colors has decimal RGB values that are multiples of _____.

9. Which tag is used as a CSS selector when you want to change the color of a page's links?

10. Which tag is used as a CSS selector when you want to change the background color of a page?

Module 4

Working with Text

Now that you've learned the basics of planning for, opening, editing, and saving a web page, you're ready to learn about editing the content. The original versions of HTML allowed you many ways to format text on a web page. However, most of these methods were *deprecated* by the W3C when they set up the XHTML standards. This means the W3C discourages the use of those tags, in favor of style sheets. Why? Because separating the styling details from the rest of the content makes for a much cleaner, more efficient web page—one more easily understood by browsers, search engines, and even your web site visitors.

The previous edition of this book explained those deprecated HTML tags—such as `<font>` and `<b>`, in case you've heard of them—as well as alternative ways to format text with style sheets. The only reason we continued to use those old tags was because many new browsers weren't yet supporting style sheets. But times have changed, and there is no longer any valid reason for most web developers to use the `font` tag (or any other deprecated tags).

With that said, the rest of this chapter will focus on how to use style sheets to format the text of your web pages.

CRITICAL SKILL
4.1 # Organize Sections of Text

One important aspect of developing a web page is planning—especially when it comes to organizing sections of content on that page. A great strength of style sheets is the ability to easily apply groups of formatting characteristics to whole sections of text. For example, suppose you have three paragraphs and a list making up the main body copy of a page, and you want to see how the text in that section looks with a different font face and size. With the old `font` tag you would need to make multiple code changes just to try a different font. But as long as you've organized your content appropriately and used style sheets, the code changes will be minimal.

The key to all this is the `div` tag. Amazingly, adding a simple `<div>` to the code on your page will cause no outward change in appearance when viewed in the browser. In fact, the `div` tag does *nothing* by itself—it doesn't even cause a line break. It is simply used as a container, allowing you to manipulate its contents later with style sheets.

Identifying Natural Divisions

It's normal for a web page to have natural divisions according to the type of content found in each area of the page. A few common divisions or sections of a page might include the navigation, the body copy, the header, and the footer. The code used to separate each section might look similar to the following:

```
<body>
<div id="header">
Header content goes here.
```

```
</div>
<div id="bodyCopy">
Body copy goes here.
</div>
<div id="footer">
Footer content goes here.
</div>
</body>
```

NOTE

Notice I didn't use any spaces when assigning names to my divs. Instead, I added a capital letter to help readability when multiple words were used in a single div name.

Once you've set up basic divisions like this—and leave the formatting to CSS instead of the HTML tables—the possibilities are endless. Need to move the navigation from the top of your page to the bottom … on ten different pages? If you put all of it into its own div … piece of cake! Not only is it easy to move that entire navigation bar, you only have to edit the style sheet—and not the individual HTML pages—to do so.

DIV + ID

When using the `div` tag to separate content areas, you also need to add the `id` attribute. In the same way that a unique Social Security number is assigned as identification—ID—for each person living in the U.S., so should a unique name be given to each div on a web page. These content areas can then easily be formatted in the site's style sheet, which might look something like the following:

```
#header {border: 1px;}
#bodyCopy {font-family: Verdana; font-size: 12pt;}
#footer {font-size: 10pt;}
```

In the style sheet, the # before each content area name is necessary because this isn't a normal style sheet selector. Instead of using a tag as my selector, like p, I've essentially made up my own selectors and given them names like header and footer. And because I used the `id` attribute to do so, I prefaced my selector name with a pound sign.

SPAN + CLASS

Similar to the `div` tag, the `span` tag also doesn't have any distinct HTML characteristics of its own. The difference with the `span` tag is that it is best used to style *inline*—as opposed to container-level—bits of content.

So while you might use the div tag to add a colored background behind whole sections of your page, you would use the span tag to highlight a single word or phrase within a paragraph. The following shows some code that illustrates this:

```
<head>
<style type="text/css">
#introCopy {background-color: #cccccc;}
.highlight {background-color: #ffcc66;}
</style>
</head>
<body>
<div id="introCopy">
<p>Paragraph 1</p>
<p>Paragraph 2</p>
</div>
<p>Paragraph <span class="highlight">3</span></p>
<p>Paragraph 4</p>
</body>
```

You'll notice I added a pound sign before "introCopy", and a period before "highlight". The difference is simple: "introCopy" was created with an id attribute, whereas "highlight" was created with the class attribute. Even though both were named by me, they need to be prefaced by specific characters to let the browser know where to find them in the rest of the code (in other words, they should follow id or class attributes).

TIP

While there are many people in a *class*, your personal identification (*ID*) is unique to you. This holds true in CSS—id selectors can only be used once on a page, whereas classes can be repeated as many times, and in as many tags, as necessary.

For Some Inspiration

One of my favorite sources of inspiration on this topic is the CSS Zen Garden (**www.csszengarden.com**). This web site shows how one web page can be drastically altered simply by changing the style sheet attached to the page. Each content area of this page is clearly defined in the HTML code. There is the outside container, which includes a "page header", a "quick summary", and a "preamble". Other content areas are the "supporting text", the "requirements", the "benefits", "participation", the "footer", and the "link list".

After dividing his page into these sections, the author then attached a style sheet with directions for how to display each of those content areas. Style sheets are so powerful that a few simple changes to the style sheet can cause the page to appear completely different, as you can see in Figures 4-1 and 4-2.

Figure 4-1 Creator Dave Shea's original design for the CSS Zen Garden

Figure 4-2 One of Shea's additional designs, achieved simply by altering the style sheet (and not the HTML code)

Paragraph Breaks

After you've organized your page into the key content areas, you can further organize the text in those content areas. As discussed briefly in Module 2, HTML is different from traditional word processors because you cannot simply press the RETURN or ENTER key to end a paragraph, and then the TAB key to indent a new one. Instead, you have to use tags to tell the browser where to start and end paragraphs, as well as any other types of breaks.

In earlier versions of HTML, the p tag was used as a one-sided tag (with no closing tag) to signify the end of a paragraph. When the browser saw the <p> in the page, it knew to stop where it was, skip a line, and begin again on a new line to differentiate between paragraphs. The following is an example of how the p tag might have been used originally.

```
Jack and Jill went up a hill<p>
To fetch a pail of water<p>
Jack fell down and broke his crown<p>
And Jill came tumbling after<p>
```

While it used to be perfectly legitimate to use the p tag without a closing tag, as previously shown, the W3C changed the specifications and now recommends otherwise. The p tag now functions specifically as a container for paragraphs. This means you need to use an opening p tag at the beginning of your paragraph, and a closing p tag at the end. If each line in this nursery rhyme were a paragraph, it might look like this:

```
<p>Jack and Jill went up a hill</p>
<p>To fetch a pail of water</p>
<p>Jack fell down and broke his crown</p>
<p>And Jill came tumbling after</p>
```

NOTE

Additional reasons to use both the opening and closing versions of the p tag are that it's required in XHTML and that it's especially important when using style sheets.

Figure 4-3 shows how the browser would render this code. Notice how the p tag forces a blank line between each of the paragraphs or sections.

Even though the p tag is most often used to contain paragraphs of text, it doesn't automatically indent them. There's no regular HTML tag to indent and, as discussed in Module 2, the browser ignores any tabs and multiple spaces you enter using the keyboard.

Instead, you could use the nonbreaking space character entity ( ) several times to indent your paragraphs. In the following example, I used   four times at the beginning of each paragraph to achieve a short indent.

This is the named character entity for nonbreaking space; you have to use this special character to force spaces.

```
<p>    Jack and Jill went up a hill to fetch a pail of water.
Jack fell down and broke his crown and Jill came tumbling after.</p>
<p>    Mary had a little lamb, its fleece was white as snow.
Everywhere that Mary went, the lamb was sure to go.</p>
<p>    Twinkle, twinkle, little star, how I wonder what you
are. Up above the world so high, like a diamond in the sky... Twinkle, twinkle,
little star, how I wonder what you are.</p>
```

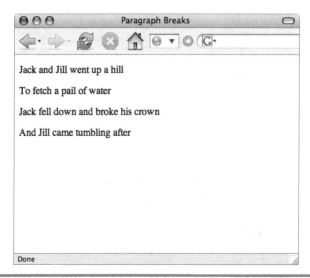

Figure 4-3 Notice that the **p** tags force a blank line between paragraphs.

Indenting with CSS

A more efficient way to indent the first line is to use the text-indent property in your style sheet. In the following example, I specify that the first line should be indented 25 pixels from the left edge of the paragraph:

```
<p style="text-indent: 25px">This is the first sentence in my paragraph...
```

While the preceding example uses an *inline* style to affect this paragraph only, you could add the same declaration to an internal or external style sheet to achieve this effect on all the paragraphs in a page or a whole site. For example, if I wanted all of the paragraphs in the bodyCopy section of my page to be indented 25 pixels, I might add the following declaration to my style sheet:

```
#bodyCopy p {text-indent: 25px;}
```

By placing the p tag selector after my bodyCopy selector, I'm telling the browser to only indent those paragraphs that fall within the bodyCopy div on my page.

NOTE

On the printed page, such as in books and newspapers, paragraphs are indented to ease readability. But on the Web, the p tag automatically adds blank lines between paragraphs to ease readability, thus removing the need for additional indentations.

Line Breaks

You can also use the `br` tag to add a line break in your HTML page. Typing the `br` tag in HTML is the same as clicking the RETURN or ENTER key on your keyboard in a word processor. It causes the browser to stop printing text on that line and drop down to the next line on the page. The following code uses the same nursery rhyme with line breaks instead of paragraph breaks between each line. Figure 4-4 shows how the browser would display this code.

NOTE

Earlier, I mentioned some HTML tags that previously weren't required to be closed. The tag used to add line breaks, `<br>`, is one such tag. To make the `br` tag XHTML-compliant, however, you must add a space and a forward slash before the final bracket.

This tells the browser to stop ──┐
and add a line break.

```
<p>
Jack and Jill went up a hill <br />
To catch a pail of water <br />
Jack fell down and broke his crown <br />
And Jill came tumbling after <br />
</p>
```

Because no closing tag exists for the `br` tag, XHTML requires you to add a space and a / just before the final >.

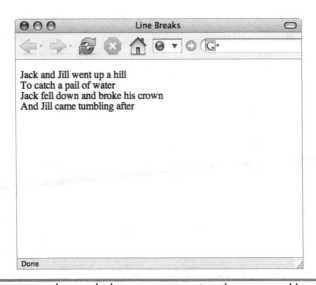

Figure 4-4 The browser understands the **br** tag as a signal to stop and begin again on the next line.

In most cases, it doesn't matter if you click the RETURN or ENTER key after typing <br /> to begin again on the next line (as shown in the preceding code). In fact, that code would have the same output if you let all the text run together, as in the following example:

```
<p>
Jack and Jill went up a hill<br />To catch a pail of water<br />Jack fell down and
broke his crown<br />And Jill came tumbling after<br />
</p>
```

Unlike the p tag, which cannot be repeated to add multiple paragraph breaks in a row, you can use the br tag to add several line breaks. To do so, simply repeat the tag in your HTML file. Figure 4-5 shows how the browser renders this code.

```
<p>
Jack and Jill went up a hill <br /><br /><br /><br />
To fetch a pail of water
</p>
```

Preformat

The only time pressing the RETURN or ENTER key in your page creates line breaks in the browser view is when the pre tag is used. Short for preformat, the pre tag renders text in

Figure 4-5 You can use multiple **br** tags to add as many breaks as you want to your page.

the browser exactly as you type it. Why, then, wouldn't I just use the `pre` tag for everything since it sounds so much easier? Two reasons:

- The `pre` tag usually displays text in a monospaced font, such as Courier, that looks similar to what a typewriter prints. While this may be appropriate for examples of programming code, it probably isn't the look you want for your entire web site.

- The output isn't guaranteed to remain as you envisioned it. Even though you're able to use the TAB key to format text in the `pre` tag, browsers may interpret a tab as a greater or lesser number of spaces than your text editor did. This could cause any tables you lay out to render incorrectly.

The `pre` tag is quite useful for displaying code examples or even creative illustrations.

```
<pre>
This text will display exactly as I type it. Watch this:
      x  |  o  |  o
      ---------------
      x  |  x  |
      ---------------
      o  |     |  x
</pre>
```

Here's how one browser displays the previous code:

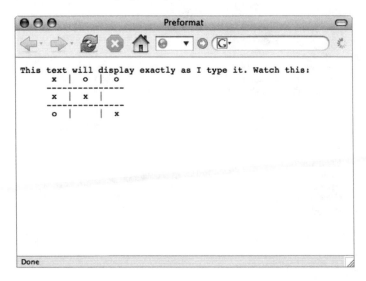

Quotation Blocks and Text Boxes

The `blockquote` tag gives you the option of setting off a long quotation or note that might otherwise get lost within a paragraph of text. This tag indents the entire selection on both the right and the left, and also adds a blank line above and below. The browser determines the exact amount of the indentation, so it may vary from browser to browser. The result of the following code is shown in Figure 4-6.

```
<p>Campers sleep in cabins that hold 10-12 people, including 2 college-age
counselors. The girls' cabins all have showers and toilets, whereas the boys share
a latrine.</p>

<blockquote>Would you like to see a video clip of a cabin? The cabin shown is
called "Manana" and usually houses the oldest girls.</blockquote>

<p>Each summer, campers, ages 12-18, come from all over the world to spend 3 or 6
weeks at Chop Point. In recent years, we have had campers from foreign countries
such as Italy, Switzerland, France, Canada, Mexico, Puerto Rico, Japan, Germany,
Ireland and Brazil (just to name a few).</p>
```

This tells the browser to begin indenting this section of text.

The browser continues to indent the text until it sees the closing `blockquote` tag.

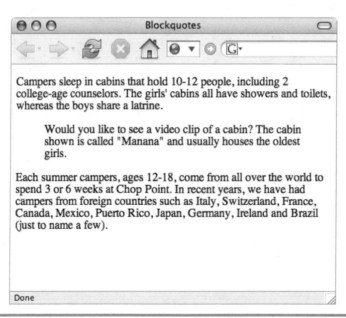

Figure 4-6 Notice how the **blockquote** tag causes the text to be indented on both sides.

TIP

You can include `br` or `p` tags within the content of your `blockquote` to create a group of text lines that are all indented. In addition, you can nest `blockquote` tags to indent text further.

To achieve a specific amount of indentation, as well as control the blank space above and below, you can use CSS's margin and padding properties in your style sheet. Every element on a web page is contained within a box of sorts, or at least it's considered a box in coding standards. I use the following illustration to explain how style sheets handle box properties, specifically in relation to text boxes.

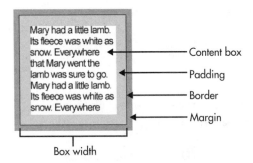

In the previous illustration, notice how the padding is actually contained within the borders of the text box. This means you can use the padding property in a style sheet to give the content a buffer zone of white space on one, two, three, or all four sides, as I did for the `blockquote` tag in the following example.

```
blockquote {padding-bottom: 25 px;
    padding-top: 25px;
    padding-right: 25px;
    padding-left: 25px;}
```

If you do specify a certain amount of padding, such as padding-right: 25px, those 25 pixels are subtracted from the total width of the content box. So if your box is 200 pixels wide by 200 pixels tall, and you code a 25-pixel padding on all four sides, you are left with 150 pixels across and 150 pixels down for the actual content.

The margin property affects the buffer space outside the box boundaries, so it won't subtract space from the overall size of the content box. As with the padding property, you can define the margins for one, two, three, or all four sides of the box, such as in the following:

```
p {margin-bottom: 25 px;
    margin-top: 25px;
    margin-right: 15px;
    margin-left: 15px;}
```

TIP

You might think of margins and padding in terms of a framed painting. The padding affects how far the paint is from the edge of the canvas, while the margin corresponds to how wide the matte and/or frame is.

Horizontal Rules

One way you can separate sections of your web page is to use the hr tag. By default, this tag produces a thin, gray horizontal line called a *horizontal rule*.

```
<p>12/5/02</p>
<p>Tonight's homework is to read chapter 13. Be prepared to answer several
questions about the chapter in class tomorrow.</p>
<hr />
<p>W. Willard, Instructor<br />
Fall, 2006.</p>
```

Although many browsers display horizontal rules a bit differently, a basic one usually looks like that shown next.

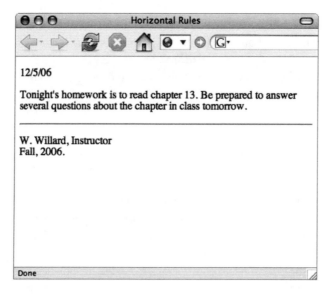

NOTE

Because there is no closing tag for the hr tag (that is, you don't use <hr></hr>), the W3C recommends using <hr /> to officially start and end this tag.

A better way to create horizontal rules involves the border properties shown in Table 4-1 in your style sheets. The use of style sheets to create rules on a web page is much more versatile than HTML. For example, not only can you create horizontal rules, but vertical rules as well. In addition, you can easily alter the size and style of rules on a page, and can place borders around all sorts of page aspects—from images to paragraphs of text.

Alignment

The normal text alignment depends on how text is read across the page in the browser's default language. If text is read from left to right, the normal alignment is left. If text is read from right to left, however, the normal alignment is right. In either case, when text is aligned to one side or the other, the opposite side is *ragged*, in that it doesn't continue all the way to the margin. When text does continue to both margins, it is called *justified*.

The text-align style sheet property allows you to realign text on your page in any of the following ways:

- left
- right
- center
- justify

One benefit of using style sheets in this area is that they also enable you to align text vertically with the vertical-align attribute, as listed in Table 4-2. (In standard HTML, the vertical alignment of text is only possible inside table cells.)

Sample Property and Value	Description	Possible Values
border-bottom-width: thick border-left-width: 4px border-right-width: 6px border-top-width: thin border-width: medium	Controls sizes of an element's borders, individually or as a whole	Can use length units or keywords (thin, medium, or thick)
border-color: #ffffff, #cccccc, #999999, #666666	Specifies the border's color	Can use between one and four color values
border-style: double	Specifies the border's style	Can use none, dotted, dashed, solid, double, groove, ridge, inset, or outset

Table 4-1 Style Sheet Properties Used to Control Borders and Rules

Sample Property and Value	Description	Possible Values
text-align: left	Changes the alignment of the text	Can be left, right, center, or justify
vertical-align: text-bottom	Allows text to be aligned vertically, without the use of tables	Can be specified by relative keywords (baseline, middle, sub, super, text-top, text-bottom, top, bottom) or percentages (Note: negative percentages result in text below the baseline.)

Table 4-2 Style Sheet Text Alignment Properties

The following bit of code provides an example of how embedded style sheets can change the text alignment of three different paragraphs. Figure 4-7 shows how the browser interprets this code.

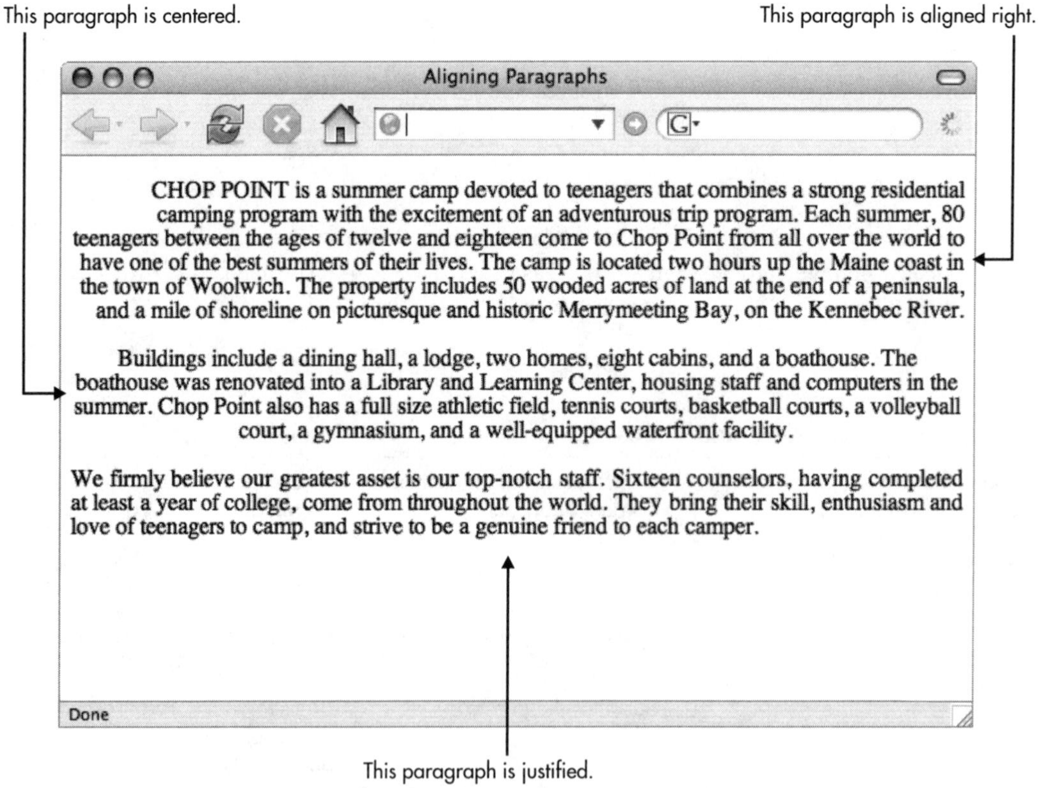

This paragraph is centered.

This paragraph is aligned right.

This paragraph is justified.

Figure 4-7 The following example code is illustrated here, showing different alignment possibilities for the text-align property.

```
<p style="text-align: right;">CHOP POINT is a summer camp devoted to teenagers
that combines a strong residential camping program with the excitement of an
adventurous trip program. Each summer, 80 teenagers between the ages of twelve
and eighteen come to Chop Point from all over the world to have one of the best
summers of their lives. The camp is located two hours up the Maine coast in the
town of Woolwich. The property includes 50 wooded acres of land at the end of a
peninsula, and a mile of shoreline on picturesque and historic Merrymeeting Bay,
on the Kennebec River.</p>
<p style="text-align: center;">Buildings include a dining hall, a lodge, two
homes, eight cabins, and a boathouse. The boathouse was renovated into a Library
and Learning Center, housing staff and computers in the summer. Chop Point also
has a full size athletic field, tennis courts, basketball courts, a volleyball
court, a gymnasium, and a well-equipped waterfront facility.</p>
<p style="text-align: justify;">We firmly believe our greatest asset is our top-
notch staff. Sixteen counselors, having completed at least a year of college,
come from throughout the world. They bring their skill, enthusiasm and love of
teenagers to camp, and strive to be a genuine friend to each camper.</p>
```

But what if you wanted to justify all three of those paragraphs—would you have to add the same style sheet information to each p tag? Definitely not! For one thing, if you planned your page appropriately and separated the content areas with div tags, you could take advantage of that planning by adding the text-align property to the appropriate div selector in your style sheet, instead of any individual tags within each content area. For example, the following code shows how I named one division with the three paragraphs.

```
<div id="CampDescription">
<p>Paragraph 1</p>
<p>Paragraph 2</p>
<p>Paragraph 3</p>
</div>
```

Then, in my site's main style sheet, I use that name—CampDescription—when assigning the formatting of that section. Remember, the # before CampDescription is necessary because this isn't a normal style sheet selector. Instead of using a *tag* as my selector, like <p>, I've made up my own selector and given it the name of CampDescription. And because I used the id attribute to do so (instead of the span attribute), I prefaced my selector name with a pound sign.

```
#CampDescription text-align: justify;}
```

NOTE

Beyond this most basic style of alignment, cascading style sheets also offer advanced alignment and positioning options. Refer to Module 12 for more details.

Project 4-1 Format Paragraphs and Page Elements

This initial project in Module 4 gives you practice in formatting paragraphs and other page elements using the p, blockquote, and div tags. Goals for this project include

- Using the div tag to format a section of the page

- Adding p tags to format the paragraphs

- Using the blockquote tag to format a long quotation

- Adding a horizontal rule to separate sections

NOTE

All the files needed to complete the projects in this book for Chop Point can be downloaded from **www.osborne.com** or **www.wendywillard.com**. In addition, you can view my version of the web site anytime by visiting **www.choppoint.org**.

Step by Step

1. Open your text/HTML editor and load the index.html page saved from Project 3.1. Make the following changes and save the file.

2. Add two to five more paragraphs of text in between the existing paragraph(s) and the copyright information. Use a div tag and id attribute to contain these paragraphs in a section called "campOverview" (or something appropriate to your particular page content). *Those using Chop Point can use the text included in the .zip file available from the Osborne web site, also shown after this numbered list.*

3. Add p tags around each of the paragraphs on the page.

4. Add a quotation (also shown after this numbered list) in between two of the paragraphs. Format using the blockquote tag.

5. Remove the two br tags and add a horizontal rule in between the last paragraph and the copyright information.

6. Use a div tag and id attribute to contain the copyright information in a section called "footer".

7. Open your web browser and choose File | Open Page (or Open File or Open, depending on the browser you are using). Locate the file index.html you just saved.

8. Preview the page to check your work. If you need to make changes, return to your text editor to do so. After making any changes, save the file and switch back to the browser. Choose Refresh or Reload to preview the changes you just made.

Added Paragraphs

The following paragraphs are the added text (mentioned previously in step 2) and can be added to your web page. The text is also included in the .zip file which is available on the Osborne web site.

Chop Point received accreditation from the American Camping Association and opened as a camp in Maine in 1967. Before the founding of Chop Point, the property had been operated as Merrymeeting camp for over fifty years.

Chop Point Summer camp combines a strong residential camping program designed specifically for teenagers, with the excitement of an adventurous trip program. Each summer, 80 teenagers between the ages of twelve and eighteen come to Chop Point from all over the world to have one of the best summers of their lives. The camp is located two hours up the Maine coast in the town of Woolwich. The property includes 50 wooded acres of land at the end of a peninsula, and a mile of shoreline on picturesque and historic Merrymeeting Bay, on the Kennebec River.

Buildings include a dining hall, a lodge, two homes, eight cabins, a new state-of-the-art gymnasium, and a boathouse. The boathouse was renovated into a Library and Learning Center, housing staff and computers in the summer. Chop Point also has a full size athletic field, tennis courts, basketball courts, a volleyball court and a well-equipped waterfront facility.

Chop Point is a recognized non-profit organization and strives to keep campers' and students' fees as affordable as possible. To do this, and still maintain the level of programs that we offer, we rely somewhat on outside donations. We have been provided with generous support from former campers, students, staff and friends. Many of the major improvements to the grounds, facilities and equipment are a direct result of their commitment to Chop Point.

Quotation

The following quote is the added text (as mentioned previously in step 4) and can be added to your web page. It is also included in the .zip file available from the Osborne web site.

What's the greatest asset of Chop Point? Founder Peter Willard said it best: "We firmly believe our greatest asset is our top-notch staff. Sixteen counselors, having completed at least a year of college, come from throughout the world. They bring their skill, enthusiasm and love of teenagers to camp, and strive to be a genuine friend to each camper."

Check Your Work   If you are using Chop Point, you can compare your files to the following code and Figure 4-8.

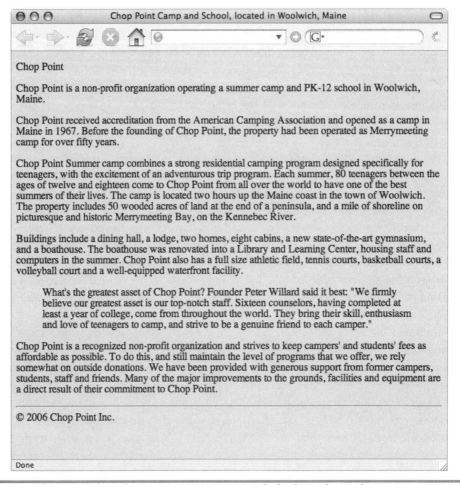

Figure 4-8 If you're using Chop Point, your page might look similar to this.

```
<!DOCTYPE html PUBLIC "-//W3C//DTD XHTML 1.0 Transitional//EN"
"http://www.w3.org/TR/xhtml1/DTD/transitional.dtd">
<html>
<head>
<title> Chop Point Camp and School, located in Woolwich, Maine </title>
<style type="text/css">
body {background-color: #ffe188;
      color: 602b00;}
</style>
</head>
<body>
<p>Chop Point </p>
```

```
<p>Chop Point is a non-profit organization operating a summer camp and PK-12
school in Woolwich, Maine.</p>
<div id="campOverview">
<p>Chop Point received accreditation from the American Camping Association and
opened as a camp in Maine in 1967. Before the founding of Chop Point, the property
had been operated as Merrymeeting camp for over fifty years. </p>
<p>Chop Point Summer camp combines a strong residential camping program designed
specifically for teenagers, with the excitement of an adventurous trip program.
Each summer, 80 teenagers between the ages of twelve and eighteen come to Chop
Point from all over the world to have one of the best summers of their lives. The
camp is located two hours up the Maine coast in the town of Woolwich. The property
includes 50 wooded acres of land at the end of a peninsula, and a mile of
shoreline on picturesque and historic Merrymeeting Bay, on the Kennebec River.</p>
<p>Buildings include a dining hall, a lodge, two homes, eight cabins, a new
state-of-the-art gymnasium, and a boathouse. The boathouse was renovated into a
Library and Learning Center, housing staff and computers in the summer. Chop Point
also has a full size athletic field, tennis courts, basketball courts, a
volleyball court and a well-equipped waterfront facility.</p>
<blockquote>What's the greatest asset of Chop Point? Founder Peter Willard said it
best: "We firmly believe our greatest asset is our top-notch staff. Sixteen
counselors, having completed at least a year of college, come from throughout the
world. They bring their skill, enthusiasm and love of teenagers to camp, and
strive to be a genuine friend to each camper."</blockquote>
<p>Chop Point is a recognized non-profit organization and strives to keep campers'
and students' fees as affordable as possible. To do this, and still maintain the
level of programs that we offer, we rely somewhat on outside donations. We have
been provided with generous support from former campers, students, staff and
friends. Many of the major improvements to the grounds, facilities and equipment
are a direct result of their commitment to Chop Point.</p>
</div>
<hr>
<div id="footer">
&copy; 2006 Chop Point Inc.
</div>
</body>
</html>
```

Project Summary

Page elements can be aligned and formatted using the p tag or the div tag. Because text and element formatting are used on almost every web page, practicing and understanding the capabilities for doing so within HTML is important.

Extra Credit

Try reformatting the page you just completed using an internal style sheet. Some formatting possibilities could be to:

● Justify the paragraphs contained within the campOverview section.

- Specify that the paragraph contained within the `blockquote` tag should be indented 20 pixels on the left only (with no indentation on the right).

- Remove the `hr` tag and instead add the border above the footer using the border property in your style sheet.

CRITICAL SKILL
4.2 Add Headings

One of the earliest means of formatting text was the heading tag. It is available in six levels of importance from `<h1>` down to `<h6>`, as shown in the following code and in Figure 4-9. You might think of these headers as headlines for chunks of text.

This is the opening tag that tells the browser to begin treating this text as a level 1 header.

```
<!DOCTYPE html PUBLIC "-//W3C//DTD XHTML 1.0 Transitional//EN"
"http://www.w3.org/TR/xhtml1/DTD/transitional.dtd">
<html>
<head>
    <title>Header Example</title>
</head>
<body>
<h1>This is an example of a level 1 header.</h1>
<p>This is the text that follows the level 1 header. This is the text that follows
the level 1 header. This is the text that follows the level 1 header.</p>
<h2>This is an example of a level 2 header.</h2>
<p>This is the text that follows the level 2 header. This is the text that follows
the level 2 header. This is the text that follows the level 2 header.</p>
<h3>This is an example of a level 3 header.</h3>
<p>This is the text that follows the level 3 header. This is the text that follows
the level 3 header. This is the text that follows the level 3 header.</p>
<h4>This is an example of a level 4 header.</h4>
<p>This is the text that follows the level 4 header. This is the text that follows
the level 4 header. This is the text that follows the level 4 header.</p>
<h5>This is an example of a level 5 header.</h5>
<p>This is the text that follows the level 5 header. This is the text that follows
the level 5 header. This is the text that follows the level 5 header.</p>
<h6>This is an example of a level 6 header.</h6>
<p>This is the text that follows the level 6 header. This is the text that follows
the level 6 header. This is the text that follows the level 6 header.</p>
</body>
</html>
```

This closing tag tells the browser to stop treating the text as a level 1 header and to return to the default text formatting.

Heading tags are similar to the headings you might use in a word processor like Microsoft Word. They are also like headings in outlines because they should only be used in the proper order, from h1 down to h6.

For example, you wouldn't create an outline that began with a small letter *a* and was followed by the Roman numeral *I*. Instead, you would begin with the Roman numeral *I*, follow

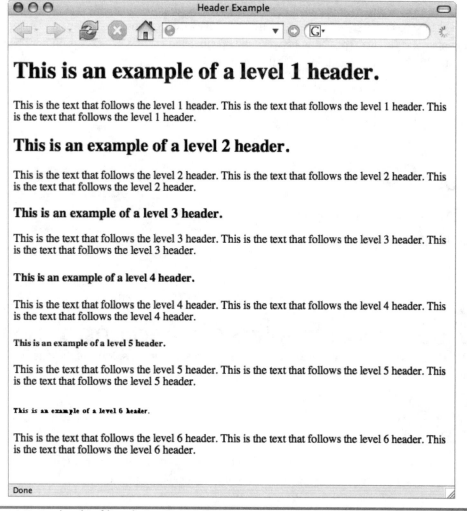

Figure 4-9 Six levels of heading tags exist, with h1 producing large text that is approximately 24 points in size by default, and h6 creating small text sized at 8 or 9 points by default.

that with a capital *A*, and, most likely, follow it with a number *1*. In like manner, an <h1> should be followed by an <h2>, as opposed to an <h3>.

NOTE

Using a heading tag automatically adds breaks before and after the headline because these tags are block-level container tags.

You could quickly adjust the alignment of your headings with an inline style by using `<h3 style="text-align: right;">`. Likewise, you could use h3 as a selector in an internal style sheet (placed in between the opening and closing head tags on your page) to specify the formatting options of all level 3 headings on the page.

```
<style type="text/css">
h3 {text-align: right;}
</style>
```

Progress Check

1. Which h tag creates the largest and most important heading?

2. How could you center a heading?

Add Logical Emphasis to Sections of Text

HTML allows for different types of formatting tags to add emphasis. Most of the tags available can be classified under one of two styles:

- Logical
- Physical

You might consider logical styles to be similar to a person's personality traits, whereas physical styles more closely resemble a person's physical appearance.

Logical Styles

Logical styles define how the affected text is to be used on the page, not how it will be displayed. This means the browser ultimately decides how to display the text (see Table 4-3). For example, if you were writing the HTML for the first sentence in this paragraph, you could use the dfn tag to tell the browser the phrase "logical styles" should be highlighted as a defined term.

```
<dfn>Logical styles</dfn> define how the affected text will be used on the page.
```

---

1. `<h1>`
2. You can use the text-align property in a style sheet to center the heading.

Tag	Description	Typical Graphical Browser Display
<abbr>	Indicates an abbreviation	Not displayed in graphical browsers (each letter is spoken in audio browsers)
<acronym>	Indicates an acronym	Not displayed in graphical browsers (each letter is spoken in audio browsers)
<cite>	Marks a reference to another source or a short quotation	Italic
<code>	Displays a code example	Monospace font (such as Courier)
<dfn>	Highlights a definition or defined term	Italic
<em>	Provides general emphasis	Italic
<kbd>	Identifies text a user will enter (kbd is short for keyboard)	Monospace font (such as Courier)
<samp>	Describes sample text or code, typically output from a program	Monospace font (such as Courier)
<strong>	Provides a stronger general emphasis than with <em>	Bold
<var>	Suggests a word or phrase that is variable and should be replaced with a specific value	Italic

Table 4-3 Logical Styles in HTML

NOTE

The h (heading) tag is also a type of logical style.

In the previous example, the dfn tag would tell the browser to differentiate between the phrase "logical styles" and the rest of the sentence. Exactly how it does so depends on the different browsers, but browsers display it as italicized text.

All logical styles must be opened and closed when they are used in an HTML document. Figure 4-10 shows how these tags are typically displayed.

Physical Styles

Contrary to logical styles, *physical* styles define how to display the affected text. For the most part, these styles display the same, regardless of the browser type. Because they are more reliable with regard to browser display, physical styles are more frequently used than logical styles.

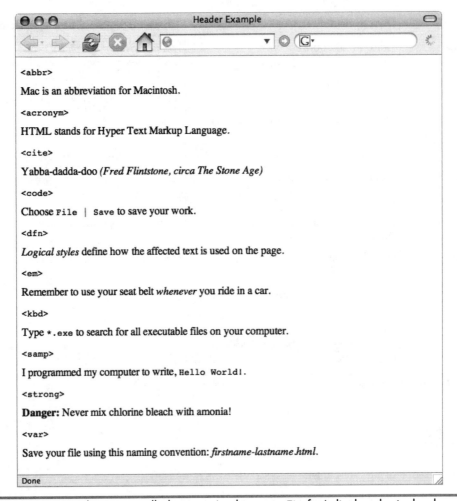

Figure 4-10 Here's how a Mozilla browser (in this case, Firefox) displays logical styles.

As shown in Table 4-4, all physical styles need to be opened and closed when used in HTML documents. A visual representation of these styles is available in Figure 4-11.

Tag	Description
<b>	**Bold**
<big>	Increases the font size by 1 each time it is used (maximum size is 7, default size is 3)
<i>	*Italic*

Table 4-4 Physical Styles in HTML

4

Tag	Description
<tt>	typewriter font
<small>	Decreases the font size by 1 each time it is used (minimum size is 1, default size is 3)
<strike>	~~Strikethrough~~
<sub>	~~sub~~script
<sup>	~~super~~script
<u>	<u>Underline</u>

Table 4-4 Physical Styles in HTML *(continued)*

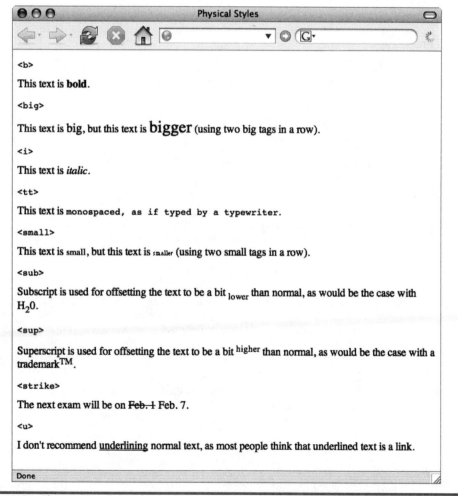

Figure 4-11 This screen shows how physical styles are typically rendered.

The <strike> and <u> tags have been deprecated. The W3C recommends using style sheets instead of these tags. While the other tags listed in Table 4-4 have not been deprecated, you can achieve much richer effects in a more efficient manner through style sheets.

Emphasis with Style Sheets

There are style sheet properties available for each of the HTML physical and logical styles. CSS also enables you to add emphasis in many ways not possible with HTML. For example, while HTML only permits you to add underlines to text, CSS includes properties capable of creating overlines. That and other commonly used properties are listed in Table 4-5.

Sample Property and Value	Description	Possible Values	Notes
font-style: italic	Changes the style of the text, causing it to appear vertical or slightly slanted. Similar to using <i> in HTML.	Can be normal, italic, or oblique.	Italic and oblique appear the same in most cases.
font-variant: small	Lets you specify text as small capitals.	Can use normal or small-caps.	n/a
font-weight: bold	Changes how heavy or thick the font appears. Similar to using <b> in HTML.	Can use keywords (normal, bold, bolder, lighter) or numbers (100, 200, 300…900). Normal is 400, bold is 700; bolder and lighter cause the weight to be one step lighter or darker than the rest of the text.	Some browsers only understand normal and bold.
letter-spacing: 10em	Changes the spacing between the letters. Similar to kerning in other programs and print methods.	Can be specified by a length value (such as 5em) or the keyword normal.	Negative values provide for a tighter, more condensed display, where letters run together.
line-height: 2	Changes the spacing between lines. Similar to leading in other programs and print methods.	Can be specified as a percentage of the font size (such as 200% to achieve a "double-spaced" look), multiples of the font size (1.5 or 2), lengths (72px), or with the keyword normal.	n/a

Table 4-5 CSS Properties Used to Add Emphasis

Sample Property and Value	Description	Possible Values	Notes
text-decoration: overline	Lets you alter the appearance of the text in a variety of ways.	Can use none, underline, overline, line-through, or blink.	Non linked text defaults to none, while linked text defaults to underline.
text-transform: uppercase	Changes the case of the text.	Can use none, capitalize (capitalizes all words), uppercase (makes all letters uppercase), or lowercase (makes all letters lowercase).	n/a
word-spacing: 20em	Changes the spacing between words. Similar to tracking in other programs or print methods.	Can be specified by a length value (such as 20em) or the keyword normal.	Negative values provide for a tighter, more condensed display where words run together.
font-stretch: wider	Lets you expand and condense characters in fonts.	Can be absolute keywords (ultra-condensed, extra-condensed, condensed, semi-condensed, normal, semi-expanded, expanded, extra-expanded, ultra-expanded) or relative keywords (wider and narrower).	Browser support varies.
text-shadow: 10px, 20px, 5px, blue	Allows for text to have a shadow effect.	Can specify a length value for both the top and left side of the shadow, as well as a color and optional color blur radius. (Commas separate these values.)	Browser support varies.

Table 4-5 CSS Properties Used to Add Emphasis *(continued)*

4.4 Style Sections of Text by Changing Font Characteristics

Before you begin changing the font characteristics of a web page, noting that visitors to your web site have the ultimate control over these font characteristics is important. The following screen shows how the user can customize one browser. Users can even choose to use their fonts, overriding page-specified fonts, so you should consider these tags as recommendations for the browser, but never rely on them for your page display.

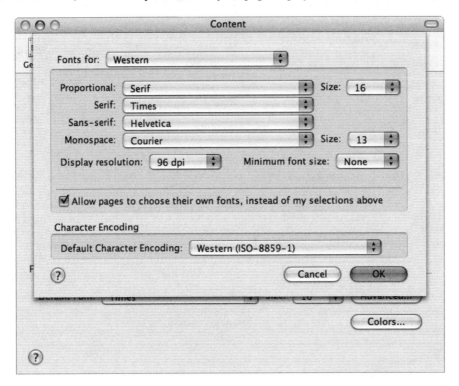

Font Faces

When used in conjunction with the term *font*, the term *face* refers to the name of the font you'd like to use on your page. In style sheets, we specify the font face with the font-family property.

You can use the font-family property to specify virtually any font name you can think of, but the person viewing your web page will be unable to see your page in that font face unless he already has it loaded on his computer. So, if you specify your page to be displayed in Gill Sans font, but the person viewing your page doesn't have Gill Sans, he will see your page in the browser's default font face (usually Times New Roman).

```
<p style="font-family:'gill sans';">This text will be displayed in Gill
Sans.</p>
```

When a style sheet value includes a space, as this one does, use single quotes to contain the value.

To compensate for the possibility that not all visitors will have the font you specify, you can specify backup fonts in the value of the font-family property. If the browser cannot find the first font face listed on the viewer's computer, it then looks for the second font face, and the third, and so forth until it comes up with a match. Once again, if the browser doesn't find a font face listed in your HTML file that is actually installed on the viewer's system, it displays the page in the default font (usually Times New Roman).

NOTE

This process of providing a backup font name is also referred to as cascading.

In this example, the browser would first look for Gill Sans.

```
<p style="font-family:'gill sans', verdana, arial, helvetica;">Here I have given
the browser 4 choices, in hopes that it will find one of them on the viewer's
system.</p>
```

In the previous code, the browser first looks for Gill Sans. If it doesn't find that font face, it looks for Verdana, followed by Arial and Helvetica. If none of those font faces is available, it would display the text in the browser's default font.

Several font faces have become quite popular on the Web. This is because these faces offer the best chance of being installed on a majority of viewers' systems. In addition, most of these fonts have been found to be more readable on the Web than others. (See **http://psychology.wichita.edu/optimalweb/text.htm** for a great comparison on the most readable fonts.) Table 4-6 shows many readable font faces for your pages.

The more products a font ships with, the more likely it is that viewers of your web site will have the font installed. The information on the availability of fonts was drawn from Microsoft's discussion on web typography. To learn more, visit **www.microsoft.com/typography/**.

TIP

Remember, font names may be a bit different across computer systems. Therefore, I recommend using lowercase names and sometimes even including two possible names for the same font. For example, the font Comic Sans can sometimes be installed as Comic Sans or Comic Sans MS. You can code your page to allow for both instances by using: `'comic sans, comic sans ms'`.

Font Name	Example Text	Availability
Arial	ABCdefg 123456 !?@	Comes with Microsoft Office, IE 3+, and most versions of Windows. Also available in Microsoft's web fonts (www.microsoft.com/typography/fontpack/default.htm).
Comic Sans MS	ABCdefg 123456 !?@	Comes with Microsoft Plus! for Windows 95 and most versions of IE.
Courier New	ABCdefg 123456 !?@	Comes with Microsoft Office, most versions of IE, and Windows. Also available in Microsoft's web fonts (www.microsoft.com/typography/fontpack/default.htm). * Courier is a common font supplied by Xfree on UNIX. ** Courier comes with Macintosh System 7+ and some versions of Adobe Type Manager.
Georgia	ABCdefg 123456 !?@	Comes with the supplemental pack of add-ons for IE 4 and later versions of IE. Also available in Microsoft's web fonts (www.microsoft.com/typography/fontpack/default.htm).
Helvetica	ABCdefg 123456 !?@	A common font supplied by Xfree on UNIX. Comes with Adobe Type Manager and Macintosh System 7+.
Impact	ABCdefg 123456 !?@	Comes with Microsoft Office, IE 3+, and most versions of Windows. Also available in Microsoft's web fonts (www.microsoft.com/typography/fontpack/default.htm).
Times New Roman	ABCdefg 123456 !?@	Comes with Windows 3.1, 95, and NT. * Times is a common font supplied by Xfree on UNIX. ** Times comes with Macintosh System 7+ and Adobe Type Manager (versions 3.8, 3.9).
Trebuchet MS	ABCdefg 123456 !?@	Comes with the supplemental pack of add-ons for IE 4 and later versions of IE. Also available in Microsoft's web fonts (www.microsoft.com/typography/fontpack/default.htm).
Verdana	ABCdefg 123456 !?@	Comes with most versions of IE. Also available in Microsoft's web fonts (www.microsoft.com/typography/fontpack/default.htm).
Webdings	[symbols]	Comes with IE 4+. Also available in Microsoft's web fonts (www.microsoft.com/typography/fontpack/default.htm).

Table 4-6 Popular Web Fonts

Progress Check

1. Which style sheet property could you use to change the font face of text on your page?

2. What is the benefit of listing more than one font name when specifying font characteristics in your style sheets?

Font Sizes

You can also use style sheets to change the size of the text. This is accomplished with the font-size property and any of the following possible values, as in: `font-size: 12pt`.

- **Keyword**   xx-small, x-small, small, medium, large, x-large, or xx-large

- **Relative size**   Smaller or larger

- **Absolute size**   Number followed by the unit, as in 12pt (for 12 point) or 8px (for 8 pixels)

Table 4-7 attempts to explain how the font-size keywords correlate to other text sizing measurements. I use the word "attempts" because text sizes can vary greatly given the operating system and browser used to display it.

Default HTML Font Sizes	HTML Headings	CSS Absolute-Size Values	Approximate Point Size
1	h6	xx-small	8
		x-small	9
2	h5	small	10
3	h4	medium	12
4	h3	large	14
5	h2	x-large	16
6	h1	xx-large	18
7			24

Table 4-7   Font Sizes

1. font-family

2. If a visitor to your site doesn't have the first font listed in the face attribute, the browser then looks for the next font name. Using more than one font name increases the chances that one of the fonts is installed on the visitor's computer system.

Although these sizes loosely correspond to the point sizes you use in a word processor, most text in a web page looks a bit smaller on a Mac than it does on a PC (because the two systems render type differently). Figures 4-12 and 4-13 show how the same text sizes might appear differently on a Mac and a PC.

NOTE

Recent versions of browsers that run on the Mac allow users to specify whether they want pages to be displayed in the standard Mac font size, or that of typical Windows-based PCs.

Font Colors

As discussed in Module 3, the CSS color property is used to change the color of any item in the foreground of a web page, including text. Alternatively, the background-color property is

Figure 4-12   This screen shows how the page displays on a Mac.

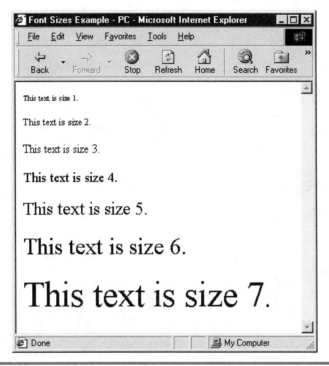

Figure 4-13   This screen shows the same text sizes displayed on a Windows-based PC.

used to change the color of anything in the background of a web page. This means you can attach two color characteristics to a single paragraph, for instance. The following code shows how this might be done to add a yellow highlight behind some purple text.

```
<p style="color: purple; background-color: yellow;">Remember to bring your
notebooks back to class tomorrow, because we will be starting a new unit in
English Literature.</p>
```

Quick Reference
In summary, Table 4-8 lists the most common style-sheet properties used to alter font characteristics.

Sample Property and Value	Description	Possible Values	Notes
font-family: verdana	Changes the font face.	Can use font names. Multiple values are separated by commas.	n/a
font-size: 14pt	Changes the size of the text.	Can use absolute or relative sizes. Absolute sizes can be specified with a numeric value and a unit (such as 12pt) or a keyword (xx-small, x-small, small, medium, large, x-large, xx-large). Relative keywords are larger and smaller.	The default is usually medium, but the size ultimately depends on the user's browser and platform.
color: black	Changes the text color.	Can use hexadecimal code: #000000, RGB values: rgb (0,0,0), or color names: black.	n/a
background-color: #336699	Changes the background color of a page or element.	Can use hexadecimal code: #000000, RGB values: rgb (0, 0, 0), or color names: black.	Can be used with many types of elements (not just text).
font-size-adjust: 1.5	Adjusts the font size, according to which font is actually used to display the page, in cases where several fonts of different sizes are specified in the font-family property.	Can be none or a decimal value. None specifies no size adjusting should take place. When size adjusting is needed, specify the amount of change necessary using a decimal value (such as .75).	CSS2 (browser support varies).
font-weight: bold	Selects the weight of the font.	Can use keywords or a numeric value (100, 200, 300, 400, 500, 600, 700, 800, 900), where 700 is "bold" and 400 is "normal." Can also use relative keywords: bolder and lighter.	n/a
font-style: italic	Selects between normal (Roman) and italic faces within a font family.	Can use keywords normal, italic, or oblique.	n/a

Table 4-8 Style Sheet Properties Used to Alter Font Characteristics

Progress Check

1. The b tag is classified as which type of style?

2. Which style sheet property is used to alter the size of text on a web page?

Project 4-2   Add Styles to Your Web Page

Returning to the index.html page, let's vary the font characteristics of the text on that page and add some physical and logical styles. Goals for this project include

● Adding emphasis to the page where necessary

● Changing the face, size, and color of the text on a page

Step by Step

1. Open your text/HTML editor and load the index.html page saved from Project 4-1.

2. Make "Chop Point" a Level 1 heading.

3. Add "Summer Camp" as a Level 2 headline in between the first and second paragraphs, contained within the campOverview section. Align this headline to the center of the page.

4. Add emphasis to the phrase "Chop Point" in the first paragraph.

5. Change the font face of the first paragraph to one listed in Table 4-6.

6. Change the size of the first paragraph to be approximately 14pt.

7. Change the font face of the campOverview section to a different one than was used earlier.

8. Change the font size of the campOverview section to be approximately 12pt.

9. Change the color of the footer text to a lighter color than the rest of the text on the page.

10. Change the font size of the footer section to be approximately 10pt.

11. Open your web browser and choose File | Open Page (or Open File or Open, depending on the browser you are using). Locate the file index.html you just saved.

(continued)

1. Physical
2. font-size

12. Preview the page to check your work. If you need to make changes, return to your text editor to make changes. After making any changes, save the file and switch back to the browser. Choose Refresh or Reload to preview the changes you just made. If you are using Chop Point to complete this exercise, you can compare your files to the following code and Figure 4-14.

HTML Code

```
<!DOCTYPE html PUBLIC "-//W3C//DTD XHTML 1.0 Transitional//EN"
"http://www.w3.org/TR/xhtml1/DTD/transitional.dtd">
<html>
<head>
<title> Chop Point Camp and School, located in Woolwich, Maine </title>
<style type="text/css">
body {background-color: #ffe188;
     color: #602b00;}
#footer {font-size: 10px;
     color: gray;}
#campOverview {font-size: 12pt;
     font-family: verdana;}
</style>
</head>
<body>
<h1>Chop Point</h1>
<p style="font-family: georgia; font-size: 14pt;"><em>Chop Point</em> is a non-
profit organization operating a summer camp and PK-12 school in Woolwich,
Maine.</p>
<div id="campOverview">
<h2 style="text-align: center;">Summer Camp</h2>
<p>Chop Point received accreditation from the American Camping Association and
opened as a camp in Maine in 1967. Before the founding of Chop Point, the property
had been operated as Merrymeeting camp for over fifty years. </p>
<p>Chop Point Summer camp combines a strong residential camping program designed
specifically for teenagers, with the excitement of an adventurous trip program.
Each summer, 80 teenagers between the ages of twelve and eighteen come to Chop
Point from all over the world to have one of the best summers of their lives. The
camp is located two hours up the Maine coast in the town of Woolwich. The property
includes 50 wooded acres of land at the end of a peninsula, and a mile of
shoreline on picturesque and historic Merrymeeting Bay, on the Kennebec River.</p>
<p>Buildings include a dining hall, a lodge, two homes, eight cabins, a new
state-of-the-art gymnasium, and a boathouse. The boathouse was renovated into a
Library and Learning Center, housing staff and computers in the summer. Chop Point
also has a full size athletic field, tennis courts, basketball courts, a
volleyball court and a well-equipped waterfront facility.</p>
<blockquote>What's the greatest asset of Chop Point? Founder Peter Willard said it
best: "We firmly believe our greatest asset is our top-notch staff. Sixteen
counselors, having completed at least a year of college, come from throughout the
world. They bring their skill, enthusiasm and love of teenagers to camp, and
strive to be a genuine friend to each camper."</blockquote>
<p>Chop Point is a recognized non-profit organization and strives to keep campers'
```

```
and students' fees as affordable as possible. To do this, and still maintain the
level of programs that we offer, we rely somewhat on outside donations. We have
been provided with generous support from former campers, students, staff and
friends. Many of the major improvements to the grounds, facilities and equipment
are a direct result of their commitment to Chop Point.</p>
</div>
<hr>
<div id="footer">
&copy; 2006 Chop Point Inc.
</div>
</body>
</html>
```

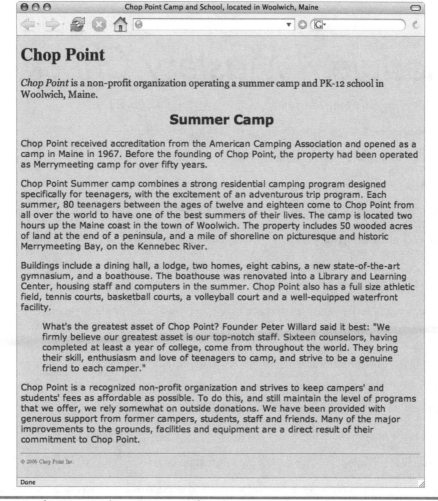

Figure 4-14 If you're working on a page for Chop Point, the results might be similar to this.

Project Summary

HTML and CSS both enable you to add emphasis to your pages, although CSS offers more options than HTML. The key issue when emphasizing certain sections of text onscreen is to make sure your pages are readable and useable to the widest possible audience.

TIP

Do any of your changes continue past where you want them to stop? Make sure to use the appropriate closing tag to tell the browser where to stop. For more tips, see Appendix C.

✓ Module 4 Mastery Check

1. What is the difference between physical and logical styles in HTML?

2. How do you close the br tag to make it XHTML-compliant?

3. What happens when you code three p tags in a row?

4. List two style sheet properties used for text alignment.

5. Name four possible values of the font-size CSS property.

6. What is a characteristic of text rendered in the style of the tt tag?

7. Fill in the blank: You use the _____ attribute of the font tag to specify the font name in which the text should be rendered.

8. Which tag is used to mark a reference to another source or a short quotation?

9. Name the four possible values of the align attribute or the text-align CSS property.

10. Fill in the blank: The process of providing a backup font name in the font-face property is also referred to as _____.

11. How is the div tag different from the p tag?

12. Fill in the blank: The h tag is an example of a _____ style.

13. True/False: The blockquote tag indents text on both the left and right sides.

14. Which style sheet property is a better way to add horizontal lines to a page than the hr tag?

15. What does it mean when tags are deprecated by the W3C?

Module 5

Working with Links

The crux of HTML is its capability to reference countless other pieces of information easily on the Internet. This is evident because the first two letters in the acronym HTML stand for hypertext, or text that is linked to other information.

HTML enables us to link to other web pages, as well as graphics, multimedia, e-mail addresses, newsgroups, and downloadable files. Anything you can access through your browser can be linked to from within an HTML document. In fact, one of the easiest ways to identify the URL of a page you want to link to is to copy it from the location or address toolbar in your web browser. You can then paste it directly into your HTML file.

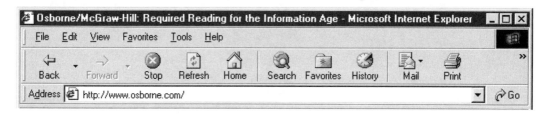

CRITICAL SKILL
5.1 Add Links to Other Web Pages

You can add links to other web pages, whether they are part of your web site or someone else's. To do so requires using the a tag:

```
<a href="http://www.google.com">Use this link to search Google.</a>
```

TIP

While adding a link to your favorite web site on your page is usually considered acceptable, it is never acceptable to copy someone else's content without their permission. If you have any doubts, check with the site's administrator whenever you're linking to a site that isn't your own.

The a tag itself doesn't serve much purpose without its attributes. The most common attribute is href, which is short for *hypertext reference*: it tells the browser where to find the information to which you are linking. Other attributes are name, title, accesskey, tabindex, and target, all of which are discussed in this module.

The text included in between the opening and closing a tag is what the person viewing your web page can click. In most cases, this text is highlighted as a different color from the surrounding text and is underlined, as shown in Figure 5-1.

This is the text in between the opening and closing a tag in the example code

When a visitor to your web site moves the mouse over a link, it usually changes to a hand to show the text can be clicked

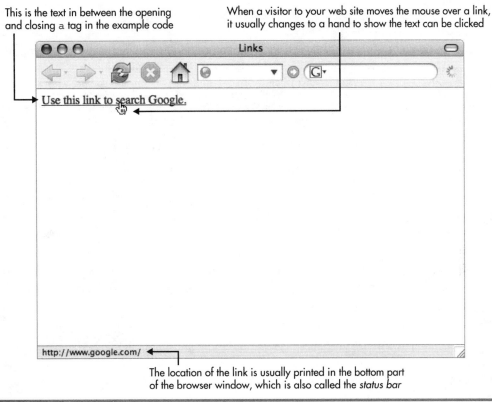

The location of the link is usually printed in the bottom part of the browser window, which is also called the *status bar*

Figure 5-1 This screen shows the browser view of the previous example code.

In deciding what to use as the value of your `href` attribute, consider what type of link you want to use. The following are the two basic types of links.

- Absolute

- Relative

TIP

When you're creating links, carefully consider the wording you want to use to highlight them. I would recommend not using the phrase "Click Here" as your link, because it doesn't tell visitors what they will find when they "Click Here." Most people scan web pages and look for links of interest. If all the links on your pages say "Click Here," visitors will be forced to read the content in detail to determine where to click. Unfortunately, given the short amount of time most people spend on the typical web site, you probably will lose more visitors than you gain with this practice. Compare Figures 5-2 and 5-3 to see how more descriptive links are easier to use.

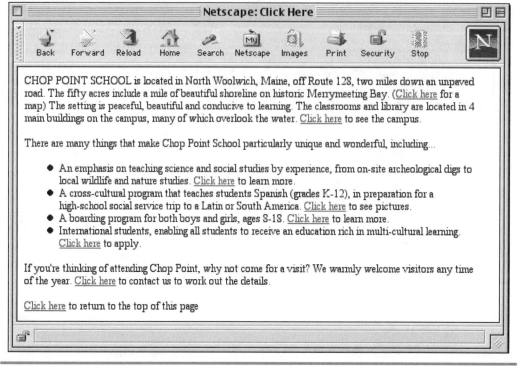

Figure 5-2 This screen shows a page with **"Click here"** used for each link.

Absolute Links

Absolute links are those that include the entire pathname. In most cases, you use absolute links when linking to pages or sites that are not part of your own web site. For example, if you are linking from your web site to Yahoo!, you type **http://www.yahoo.com** as your link.

```
<a href="http://www.yahoo.com">Visit Yahoo!</a>
```

Relative Links

Relative links are so called because you don't include the entire pathname of the page to which you are linking. Instead, the pathname you use is relative to the current page. This is similar to saying, "I live in Summershade Court, about three miles from here," which is relative to wherever "here" is. A more *absolute* way to say this might be "I live at 410 Summershade Court in Anytown, USA 55104."

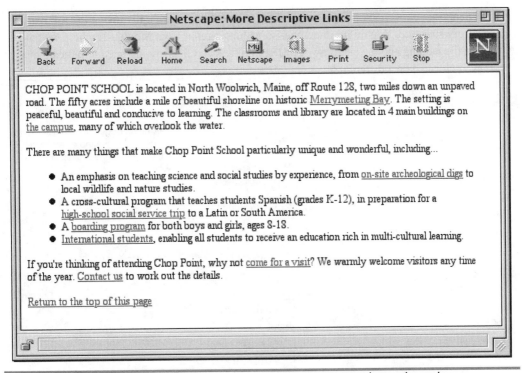

Figure 5-3 This screen shows the same page as that in Figure 5-2 but with much more descriptive link names, making it easier to scan the content of the page.

Relative links are most commonly used when you want to link from one page in your site to another. The following is an example of what a relative link might look like:

```
<a href="contactme.html">Contact Me</a>
```

This link looks for the contactme.html file in the same folder that contains this page. If you were linking to a file in another folder below the current one, the value of your href might look like the following:

```
<a href="wendy/contactme.html">Contact Me</a>
```

If you need to link to a file in a folder above the folder your page is in, you can add "../" for each directory up the tree. So, if the file you are linking to is two folders higher than the one you are in, you might use

```
<a href="../../contactme.html">Contact Me</a>
```

Suppose you were building a web site for yourself and your family, using the following directory structure. You might remember something similar from Module 1, where we talked about file naming and the anatomy of a URL. Folders and files are indented to indicate that they are located on a different level.

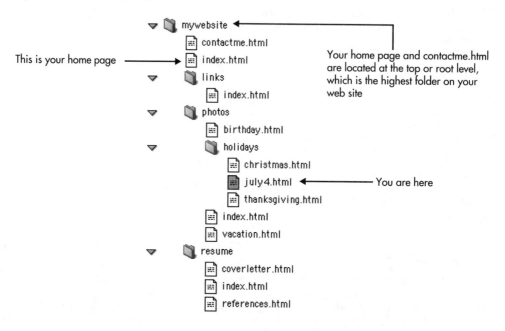

You are working on the highlighted file: july4.html. This file is located two folders down from the home page (index.html) in a folder called *holidays*. If you want to link back to that home page from the july4.html page, you would include a relative link similar to this one:

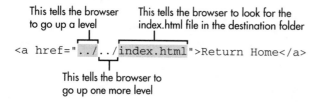

Now, suppose you are working on the birthday.html file and you want to link to the july4.html page. Can you imagine how you would do that?

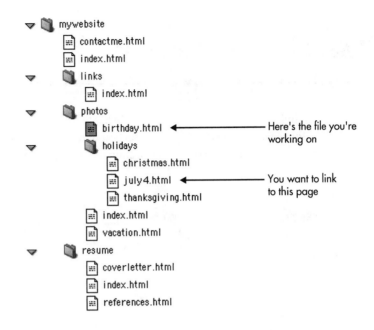

To link from birthday.html to july4.html, use the following code:

```
<a href="holidays/july4.html">Check out these photos from July 4.</a>
```

Because the july4.html file is one folder below the birthday.html file you are currently working on, you simply list the folder name followed by a forward slash and the filename (as shown in the preceding example).

Progress Check

1. Using the preceding illustration as a guide, identify the pathname you would use to link from references.html to contactme.html.

2. Identify the pathname you would use to link back from contactme.html to references.html.

1. ../contactme.html
2. resume/references.html

CRITICAL SKILL
5.2 # Add Links to Sections Within the Same Web Page

When you link to a page, the browser knows what to look for because each page has a name. But sometimes you may want to link to a section of text *within* a page on your web site (see Figure 5-4 for an example). To link to a section of a web page, you must first give that section a name.

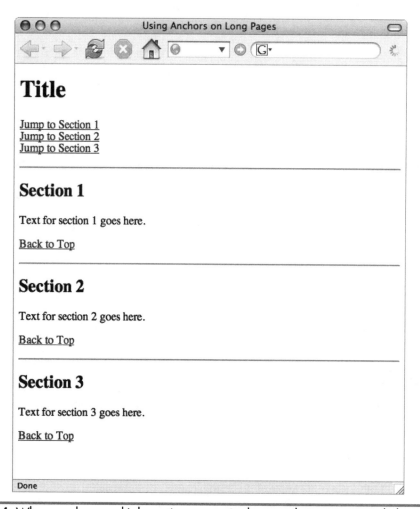

Figure 5-4 When you have multiple sections on a single page that you want to link to, you can use an anchor to name them.

Ask the Expert

Q: **How do I know when to use relative or absolute pathnames?**

A: Whenever you are linking to a page *that is not contained within your web site*, you will probably want to use an absolute pathname. For example, if you are working on the Woolwich Historical Society's web site and you want to link to a historical society for another town, you need to use the full (absolute) pathname to do so.

However, if you are linking to *a page on your own web site* that contains information about that other historical society, then you could use a relative pathname.

Remember, if you do decide to use absolute pathnames to link to a page located in the same folder on your web site, this may cause problems for maintenance in the long run. If, at a later date, you decide to change the name of the folder these files are located in, you need to go back and change all the absolute links. If you used a relative link, though, you wouldn't have to change anything.

Create an Anchor

An *anchor* is a place within a page that is given a special name, enabling you to link to it later. Without first naming a section, you cannot link to it. The following is an example of an anchor:

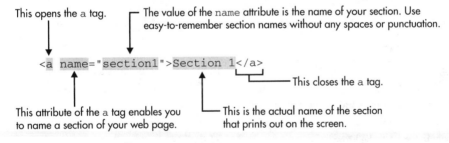

This opens the a tag.

The value of the name attribute is the name of your section. Use easy-to-remember section names without any spaces or punctuation.

`<a name="section1">Section 1</a>`

This closes the a tag.

This attribute of the a tag enables you to name a section of your web page.

This is the actual name of the section that prints out on the screen.

In this example, the phrase in between the opening and closing a tags is displayed in the web page and labels the anchor as "Section 1."

If you prefer not to include a label for your anchor, you can leave that space blank, as in the following example:

`<a name="top"></a>`

Here, you could use this invisible anchor at the top of your page, and then link to it from the bottom of your page. This would enable visitors to return to the top of a long page easily, with only one click and no scrolling (see Figure 5-5 for an example).

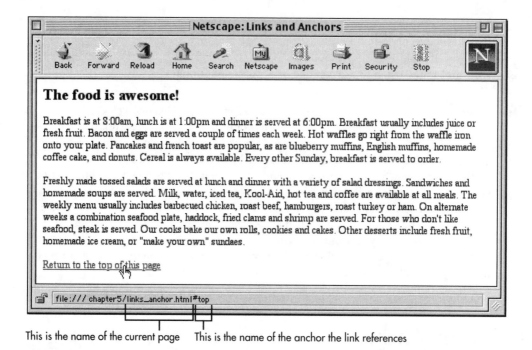

This is the name of the current page   This is the name of the anchor the link references

Figure 5-5 This browser view (of links_anchor.html) shows how an invisible anchor can be used to give visitors an easy link back to the top of the page.

Link to an Anchor

To create the link to an anchor, you also use the a tag and the href attribute, as you would when creating any other type of link. To finish the link, you need to include a hash symbol (#) and the anchor name as the value of the href attribute.

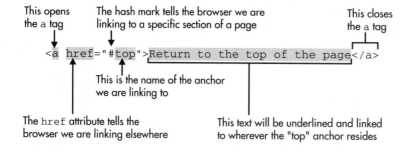

The following shows how it all might look when you code it in an HTML document:

```
<!DOCTYPE html PUBLIC "-//W3C//DTD XHTML 1.0 Transitional//EN"
"http://www.w3.org/TR/xhtml1/DTD/transitional.dtd">
<html>
<head>
     <title>Links and Anchors</title>
</head>
<body bgcolor="#ffffff" text="#000000">
<a name="top"></a>
<a name="food"><h2>The food is awesome!</h2></a>
<p>Breakfast is at 8:00am, lunch is at 1:00pm and dinner is served at 6:00pm.
Breakfast usually includes juice or fresh fruit. Bacon and eggs are served a
couple of times each week. Hot waffles go right from the waffle iron onto your
plate. Pancakes and french toast are popular, as are blueberry muffins, English
muffins, homemade coffee cake, and donuts. Cereal is always available. Every other
Sunday, breakfast is served to order.</p>
<p>Freshly made tossed salads are served at lunch and dinner with a variety of
salad dressings. Sandwiches and homemade soups are served. Milk, water, iced tea,
Kool-Aid, hot tea, and coffee are available at all meals. The weekly menu usually
includes barbecued chicken, roast beef, hamburgers, roast turkey, or ham. On
alternate weeks a combination seafood plate of haddock, fried clams, and shrimp is
served. For those who don't like seafood, steak is served. Our cooks bake our own
rolls, cookies, and cakes. Other desserts include fresh fruit, homemade ice cream,
and "make your own" sundaes.</p>
<a href="#top">Return to the top of this page</a>
</body>
</html>
```

This tag links to the predefined anchor "top"

Another good case for using anchors involves a long page with many small sections, such as the example shown in Figure 5-4. Whenever you do have long pages with several sections, it's nice to offer your visitors a "Back to Top" link to bring them back to the index easily. The following shows the HTML code used to create this page.

```
<!DOCTYPE html PUBLIC "-//W3C//DTD XHTML 1.0 Transitional//EN"
"http://www.w3.org/TR/xhtml1/DTD/transitional.dtd">
<html>
<head>
     <title>Using Anchors on Long Pages</title>
</head>
<body>
<h1><a name="top">Title</a></h1>
<p><a href="#section1">Jump to Section 1</a><br />
<a href="#section2">Jump to Section 2</a><br />
<a href="#section3">Jump to Section 3</a></p>
<hr />
```

This links to the anchor lower on the page named "section1"

This links to the anchor lower on the page named "section 2"

This links to the anchor lower on the page named "section 3"

```
<a name="section1"><h2>Section 1</h2></a>        ←——— The anchor names this "section1"
<p>Text for section 1 goes here.</p>
<p><a href="#top">Back to top</a></p>
<hr />
<a name="section2"><h2>Section 2</h2></a>        ←——— The anchor names this "section2"
<p>Text for section 2 goes here.</p>
<p><a href="#top">Back to top</a></p>
<hr />
<a name="section3"><h2>Section 3</h2></a>        ←——— The anchor names this "section3"
<p>Text for section 3 goes here.</p>
<p><a href="#top">Back to top</a></p>
</body>
</html>
```

NOTE

If the anchor you are linking to is already visible on the screen (such as how the A section is already visible in Figure 5-4), then the browser may not jump to that anchor. Similarly, if the anchor being linked to is at the very bottom of the screen (as the C section is in Figure 5-4), then the browser also may not jump to that anchor, according to your screen size. The reason for this is, if the browser is already at the bottom of the page, it cannot go any further and, therefore, can only try to get as close to the anchor as possible.

If you need to create a link to a specific section with another page (not the one you are currently working on), then you use that page's filename and the anchor name separated by a hash mark (#), as in the following example.

```
<a href="genealogy.html#intro">View names beginning with an "A" on
our genealogy page.</a>
```

In this case, the browser will first look for genealogy.html and then locate an anchor named "intro" on that page.

CRITICAL SKILL
5.3 Add Links to E-mail Addresses and Downloadable Files

Although links to and within web pages are the most common types of links you'll create, you can also link to other types of content on the Internet.

E-mail Addresses

When you want to give someone easy access to your e-mail address, you can include it on your page as a *mailto* link. This means instead of using `http://` in front of your link, you use `mailto:` to preface your e-mail address.

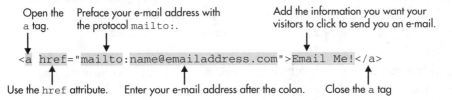

Open the a tag. | Preface your e-mail address with the protocol `mailto:`. | Add the information you want your visitors to click to send you an e-mail.

`<a href="mailto:name@emailaddress.com">Email Me!</a>`

Use the `href` attribute. | Enter your e-mail address after the colon. | Close the a tag

Clicking this link in a browser causes the visitor's e-mail program to launch. Then it opens a new e-mail message and places your e-mail address in the To: box of that message.

NOTE

For a mailto link to work, visitors to your web site must have an e-mail program set up on their computers.

Customize the E-mail Message

Some browsers will even let you add content to the subject and cc fields in the e-mail by entering additional text into the `href` value. To do so, you add a question mark after the end of your e-mail address, and type the word **Subject** followed by an equal sign (=), along with the word or phrase you'd like to use as your subject. This can be particularly useful in helping you distinguish mail sent through your web site from your other e-mail.

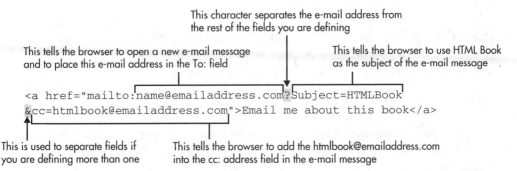

This character separates the e-mail address from the rest of the fields you are defining

This tells the browser to open a new e-mail message and to place this e-mail address in the To: field

This tells the browser to use HTML Book as the subject of the e-mail message

`<a href="mailto:name@emailaddress.com?Subject=HTMLBook`
`&cc=htmlbook@emailaddress.com">Email me about this book</a>`

This is used to separate fields if you are defining more than one

This tells the browser to add the htmlbook@emailaddress.com into the cc: address field in the e-mail message

Remember, no spaces should be in the value of the `href` attribute, unless they are part of the subject line.

Spam-proofing Your E-mail Links

Most people who send spam use programs called mail harvesters to search the Web looking for e-mail addresses. This means any time your e-mail address is listed, displayed, or otherwise included on a web page, you open yourself to potential spam.

What tips these harvesting programs off is the at symbol (@) in your e-mail address, because we all know an e-mail address can't exist without one of those symbols. So the key to spam-proofing your e-mail address is not to display it with an @ symbol.

Using [at] Instead of the @ Symbol

A quick, pure-text way to avoid *displaying* your complete e-mail address on a web page is to replace the @ symbol with something like [at] so savvy visitors can still get your e-mail address, but the harvesting programs miss it. This might make your e-mail address look something like this:

me[at]mail.com

This only works if you merely *display* the e-mail address, and don't *link* to it. For more on that, keep reading.

Using an Image to Replace the @ Symbol

The second easiest way to spam-proof *displayed* e-mail addresses is to replace the text @ symbol with a graphic @ symbol. This causes your site's visitors to see the e-mail address in its entirety, but fools e-mail harvesters because they don't read images.

However, this and the previous technique only work to hide e-mail addresses that are merely *displayed* in the browser. If you're *linking* your e-mail address so people can click it to send an e-mail, you must also hide the version of the e-mail address embedded in the a tag. To do so, try one of the following two tricks.

Using Code to Replace the @ Symbol

The only problem with the first two ways to spam-proof your e-mail address is that they only work if the e-mail address is *displayed* and not *linked*. For example, consider the following:

```
<a href="mailto:me@mail.com">Email Me</a>
```

While the e-mail address is not displayed in the browser view, it's still embedded in the code. When you include your actual e-mail address in the code of a mailto link, harvesting programs reading the actual HTML will still find it!

One way to hide the e-mail address in the mailto link is to replace the @ symbol and period with their decimal equivalents. This means me@home.com might look like:

```
me&#64;home&#46;com
```

`&#64;` is the decimal equivalent of the @ symbol and `&#46;` is the equivalent of a period. The complete a tag using this technique looks like this:

```
<a href="mailto:me&#64;home&#46;com">
```

Most (but regrettably, not all) e-mail programs recognize these decimal characters and will replace them with the appropriate equivalents when preparing the actual e-mail.

Using JavaScript to Hide the E-mail Address   Arguably the most effective way to avoid spammers and still include a mailto link is to hide the e-mail address with some sort of scripting language or other type outside of HTML, such as JavaScript. The following sample script would be placed within your HTML code exactly where your `<a href="mailto:me@home.com">` should have been.

```
<script language="JavaScript">
<!-
var name = "me"
var domain = "mail"
var ext = "com"
document.write("<a href=" + "mail" + "to:" + name + "@" + domain + "." + ext + ">E-mail
Me</a>")
//->
</script>
```

When displayed in a browser, this script prints "E-mail Me" and links it to me@mail.com, all the while never displaying the complete e-mail address in a way spammers can interpret.

TIP

One of the best ways to avoid posting your e-mail address for all to see (and harvest) is to create a web form for visitors to send you e-mail. Refer to Module 11 for more information.

Ask the Expert

Q: What about linking to an RSS feed?

A: RSS—Really Simple Syndication—has grown so quickly in recent years that even though you might not have known what it meant, you've likely seen it referenced at one web site or another. Many news sites and web blogs include little orange or blue rectangular buttons near a story that is available for syndication by the general public. For example, visit **www.foxnews.com/rss** to see a list of the FoxNews content available for syndication.

To "read" such syndicated content, you need to open the RSS feed in a news reader (also called an aggregator). Check out **http://blogspace.com/rss/readers** for a list of some popular news readers.

Anyone can create his or her own RSS feeds. Refer to **www.mnot.net/rss/tutorial** for a great tutorial on doing just that. Once you've created your own syndicated content, you'll need to put a link on your page to advertise that content (similar to those little orange buttons you've probably seen at other sites). Links to RSS feeds look very similar to other HTML links, with a few minor variations: `<a type="application/`**`rss`**`+xml" href="feed.`**`rss`**`">RSS feed for this page</a>`.

FTP and Downloadable Files

The Internet provides many companies with an easy way to transmit files to customers. For example, suppose you purchased a piece of software to protect your computer against viruses. Eventually, your software must be updated so it can recognize new viruses. The quickest and easiest way to obtain such an update is to download it from the company's web site.

When you download files from the Internet that cannot be displayed in your web browser (such as software applications and add-ons), you usually do so by accessing the company's FTP site.

FTP, which stands for *file transfer protocol*, is a way in which you send and receive files over the Internet. Many companies have both HTTP servers, which house their web site, and FTP servers, which house their downloadable files.

To reference a file on an FTP site, you use the `a` tag and the `href` attribute, as in the following example:

```
<a href="ftp://sunsite.unc.edu/pub/">Visit the SunSite FTP</a>
```

Although many FTP files are anonymous and don't require a password for access, some are private. You won't be able to access a private FTP site without a qualified username and password. If you are linking to a private FTP site, you should also consider providing a way for visitors to register or sign up to receive a username and password.

Of course, in some cases, you could have downloadable files located right on your web server with your web page. These might be movies, sounds, programs, or other documents you want to make available to your visitors. You can link to these just as you would any other web page, keeping the proper file extension in mind.

```
<a href="http://www.willardesigns.com/baby.mov">View the baby movie!</a>
```

Project 5-1 Add Links

Returning to the index.html page, let's add links to the web site. A reminder: all the files needed to complete the projects in this book for the Chop Point Summer Camp can be downloaded from **www.osborne.com** or **www.wendywillard.com**. In addition, you can view my version of the web site anytime by visiting **www.choppoint.org**.

Those of you who aren't using Chop Point can tailor the project to your particular needs. Goals for this project include

1. Adding links to web pages

2. Adding links to sections within a web page

3. Adding links to e-mail addresses

Step by Step

1. Open your text/HTML editor and load the index.html page saved from Module 4.

2. Add a link to trips.html that says, "Learn more about our summer camp's adventure trips."

3. Save the file.

4. Create a new file named **trips.html**. Include the text contained in trips.txt in the HTML Beginner's Guide .zip file.

5. Format the phrase "e-mail us" at the end of the fourth paragraph as an e-mail link. Mail should be sent to "camp@choppoint.org." The subject should be "Trips."

(continued)

6. Save this file.

7. Open your web browser and choose File | Open Page (or Open File or Open, depending on the browser you're using). Locate the file index.html you just saved.

8. Click the link you added to ensure it works. The link should bring up the trips.html page.

9. If you need to make changes, return to your text editor to make changes. After making any changes, save the file and switch back to the browser. Choose Refresh or Reload to preview the changes you just made.

TIP

Does your link work? If not, make sure the pathname is correct. Both the index.html and trips.html pages should be located in the same folder. If they aren't, you need to change the pathname to reflect the proper folder name. In addition, be sure to check your capitalization (or lack thereof). Remember, links like this are case-sensitive, so if you named a section "Intro" with a capital I, but linked to "intro" with a lowercase i, then your link won't work. For more tips, see Appendix C.

10. Return to the trips.html file in your text editor.

11. Add anchors to each of the section headings, using the section name (without any spaces) as the anchor name.

12. Add links to each of the anchors you just created so the category names near the top of the page become links to the actual category content below.

13. Add an anchor to the top of the page named **top**.

14. Add **Back to Top** links at the end of each section to enable a visitor to have easy access back to the category listing at the top of the page.

15. Save the file.

16. Return to your web browser and choose Refresh or Reload to confirm your changes. If you're using the Woolwich Historical Society, you can compare your files to the following code and Figure 5-6.

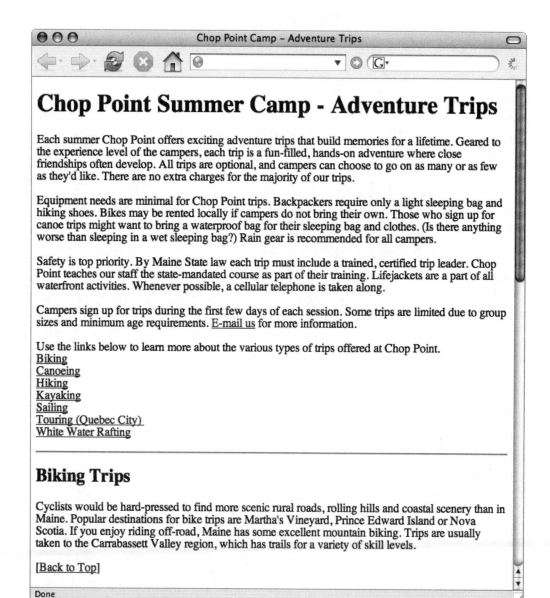

Chop Point Summer Camp - Adventure Trips

Each summer Chop Point offers exciting adventure trips that build memories for a lifetime. Geared to the experience level of the campers, each trip is a fun-filled, hands-on adventure where close friendships often develop. All trips are optional, and campers can choose to go on as many or as few as they'd like. There are no extra charges for the majority of our trips.

Equipment needs are minimal for Chop Point trips. Backpackers require only a light sleeping bag and hiking shoes. Bikes may be rented locally if campers do not bring their own. Those who sign up for canoe trips might want to bring a waterproof bag for their sleeping bag and clothes. (Is there anything worse than sleeping in a wet sleeping bag?) Rain gear is recommended for all campers.

Safety is top priority. By Maine State law each trip must include a trained, certified trip leader. Chop Point teaches our staff the state-mandated course as part of their training. Lifejackets are a part of all waterfront activities. Whenever possible, a cellular telephone is taken along.

Campers sign up for trips during the first few days of each session. Some trips are limited due to group sizes and minimum age requirements. E-mail us for more information.

Use the links below to learn more about the various types of trips offered at Chop Point.
Biking
Canoeing
Hiking
Kayaking
Sailing
Touring (Quebec City)
White Water Rafting

Biking Trips

Cyclists would be hard-pressed to find more scenic rural roads, rolling hills and coastal scenery than in Maine. Popular destinations for bike trips are Martha's Vineyard, Prince Edward Island or Nova Scotia. If you enjoy riding off-road, Maine has some excellent mountain biking. Trips are usually taken to the Carrabassett Valley region, which has trails for a variety of skill levels.

[Back to Top]

Done

Figure 5-6 The Adventure Trips page for Chop Point

(continued)

```
<!DOCTYPE html PUBLIC "-//W3C//DTD XHTML 1.0 Transitional//EN"
"http://www.w3.org/TR/xhtml1/DTD/transitional.dtd">
<html>
<head>
<title> Chop Point Camp - Adventure Trips </title>
</head>
<body>
<h1>Chop Point Summer Camp - Adventure Trips</h1>
<p>Each summer Chop Point offers exciting adventure trips that build memories for
a lifetime. Geared to the experience level of the campers, each trip is a fun-
filled, hands-on adventure where close friendships often develop. All trips are
optional, and campers can choose to go on as many or as few as they'd like. There
are no extra charges for the majority of our trips.</p>
<p>Equipment needs are minimal for Chop Point trips. Backpackers require only a
light sleeping bag and hiking shoes. Bikes may be rented locally if campers do not
bring their own. Those who sign up for canoe trips might want to bring a
waterproof bag for their sleeping bag and clothes. (Is there anything worse than
sleeping in a wet sleeping bag?) Rain gear is recommended for all campers.</p>
<p>Safety is top priority. By Maine State law each trip must include a trained,
certified trip leader. Chop Point teaches our staff the state-mandated course as
part of their training. Lifejackets are a part of all waterfront activities.
Whenever possible, a cellular telephone is taken along.</p>
<p>Campers sign up for trips during the first few days of each session. Some trips
are limited due to group sizes and minimum age requirements. <a
href="mailto:camp@choppoint.org?Subject=Trips;">E-mail us</a> for more
information.</p>
<p>Use the links below to learn more about the various types of trips offered at
Chop Point.<br />
<a href="#biking">Biking</a><br />
<a href="#canoeing">Canoeing</a><br />
<a href="#hiking">Hiking</a><br />
<a href="#kayaking">Kayaking</a><br />
<a href="#sailing">Sailing</a><br />
<a href="#touring">Touring (Quebec City) </a><br />
<a href="#rafting">White Water Rafting</a></p>
<hr />
<a name="biking"><h2>Biking Trips</h2></a>
<p>Cyclists would be hard-pressed to find more scenic rural roads, rolling hills,
and coastal scenery than in Maine. Popular destinations for bike trips are
Martha's Vineyard, Prince Edward Island, or Nova Scotia. If you enjoy riding
off-road, Maine has some excellent mountain biking. Trips are usually taken to the
Carrabassett Valley region, which has trails for a variety of skill levels.</p>
<p>[<a href="#top">Back to Top</a>]</p>
<a name="canoeing"><h2>Canoeing Trips</h2></a>
<p>Canoes are ideal for exploring the rivers and bays of Maine. Before the first
trip, a camper must pass a swimming test and receive instruction in canoeing
safety. One of the most popular trips we take each summer is 70 miles in the
wilderness of Maine along the beautiful and remote Allagash River.</p>
<p>[<a href="#top">Back to Top</a>]</p>
<a name="hiking"><h2>Hiking Trips</h2></a>
<p>For hikers, there are literally hundreds of miles of trails to choose from in
```

```
the White Mountains, Acadia National Park, and Baxter State Park. The scenery is
so breathtaking in the White Mountains that circus founder P.T. Barnum, upon
reaching the top of mile-high Mt. Washington, observed, "This is the second
greatest show on earth." Trips vary between overnight backpacking and day hikes
out of a base camp.</p>
<p>[<a href="#top">Back to Top</a>]</p>
<a name="kayaking"><h2>Kayaking Trips</h2></a>
<p>Kayaking trips are taken in the shelter and safety of the coastal rivers and
bays. Sea kayaks are a fast and efficient way to travel on the water in Maine;
they offer a different experience than your traditional canoe.</p>
<p>[<a href="#top">Back to Top</a>]</p>
<a name="sailing"><h2>Sailing Trips</h2></a>
<p>Many feel that the only way to experience Maine is from the water by boat. Each
summer we take one overnight trip per session aboard a historic schooner such as
the Stephen Taber. There are many islands and harbors to visit during these trips.
The Stephen Taber is the oldest documented sailing vessel in continuous service in
the United States, a National Historic Landmark.</p>
<p>[<a href="#top">Back to Top</a>]</p>
<a name="touring"><h2>Quebec City Trips</h2></a>
<p>300-miles away, Quebec is one of Canada's most interesting areas. Always a
popular trip, Quebec City is perfect for shopping and sightseeing. Highlights
include visits to the Parliament building, the Plains of Abram, and the Cathedral
at Saine Anne de Beaupre. Lodging has typically been in dorms at Laval University
followed by a hearty breakfast. There is an additional charge for this trip.</p>
<p>[<a href="#top">Back to Top</a>]</p>
<a name="rafting"><h2>White Water Rafting Trips</h2></a>
<p>A three-hour drive to the head of the Kennebec River in the Forks begins a
spectacular challenge of the Class IV rapids of the Gorge. Registered Maine guides
using self-bailing rafts make this thrilling experience one to remember. An extra
fee of $75 and a parental release form are required.</p>
<p>[<a href="#top">Back to Top</a>]</p>
</body>
</html>
```

Project Summary

The a tag enables you to add links to many types of information on the Internet. This project gives you practice using that tag to link to another web page, an e-mail address, and sections within the same web page.

TIP

Do each of your target links work? If not, make sure the anchor name is correct. Remember, in most cases links are case-sensitive, so if you capitalized the anchor name, you need to capitalize it again when you link to it. In addition, check to see you have included a hash mark (#) before each anchor name when you link to it (that is, href="#a"). For more tips, see Appendix C.

Extra Credit

1. To prepare for the next project, switch from using an internal style sheet to an external style sheet. (Use the internal style sheet from index.html as the basis for your external style sheet.)

2. Name it **styles.css** and save it in the same folder as the other two files.

3. Add a link to your external style sheet from both index.html and trips.html.

Progress Check

1. Can you fix the following tag?

   ```
   < ahref="http://www.yahoo.com" >
   ```

2. Can you fix the following tag?

   ```
   <a name="top>
   ```

3. Can you fix the following tag?

   ```
   <mailto:name@company.com>
   ```

Style Links

In Module 3, we discussed changing the text and background colors for pages. As with other attributes that change color in HTML pages, you need to specify the color either by hexadecimal code, RGB values, or a predefined color name. A chart of web-safe colors is on the inside of the front cover, and a list of predefined color names is in Module 3.

You specify these colors with style sheets. As with any style declaration, you can specify the background, text, and link colors in either an inline, internal, or external style sheet. The actual properties used to do so are the same, however, regardless which type of style sheet you use.

---

1. Spacing was incorrect. <a href="http://www.yahoo.com">
2. The final quotation mark was missing. <a name="top">
3. The a tag and `href` attribute were missing. <a href=mailto:name@company.com>

You actually use the a tag to change link colors with style sheets, as in the following example:

```
<style type="text/css">
body {background-color: white;}
a:link {color: blue;}
a:visited {color: purple;}
a:hover {color: orange;}
a:active {color: red;}
 </style>
```

This allows you to specify the color of the links before they're clicked.

This allows you to specify the color of the links after they've been clicked and visited.

This allows you to specify the color of the links while the cursor is positioned over them (same as a "rollover").

This allows you to specify the color of the links while they are being clicked.

While this specific style declaration changes the links on the entire page, you could also use classes to adjust only certain link colors. This is particularly handy if, for example, most of the links on your page are the default blue, but the background of your navigation bar is also a deep blue. One way to take care of this is to create a *class* with a different color link, as I did in the following:

```
a.navlinks:link {color: white;}
a.navlinks:visited {color: gray;}
a.navlinks:hover {color: yellow;}
a.navlinks:active {color: orange;}
```

The period tells the browser that a class name follows, which means this declaration only applies to a tags with that class name

After you create the class in the style sheet, you just need to apply it to the links you want affected. This is achieved by adding the class attribute to the appropriate a tags, as in: `<a href="link.html" class="navlinks">`.

Default Link Colors

In most cases, the default link color for browsers is blue. The default visited link color is purple, and the active link color is red. Remember, as with many other features of web browsers, the user ultimately controls these default colors.

TIP

Although not required, and certainly not always possible, staying with a blue/ purple/red color scheme for your link/visited link/active link colors is nice. Visitors to your site may adjust to the navigation more quickly if the color scheme is similar to that of other web sites.

I recommend using the same link colors on all the pages in your web site to give a consistent look and feel across the pages. In addition, it's wise to pick visited link colors that don't stand out as much as your unvisited links. Both of these recommendations enable visitors to scan your page easily and identify which pages they've been to and which ones they haven't visited.

Lastly, remember to test your colors on a number of different computer systems to ensure they appear as you intend. I also recommend changing your monitor settings to black and white for a minute, just to make sure your links are visible in a grayscale environment.

Beyond Colors

If you ever changed link colors with older HTML tags, you know that there wasn't much else you could do to links beyond changing their colors. With CSS, you can style your links to really stand out from the rest of the text on your page. In fact, you can format links in much the same way you learned to style regular text content in the previous module. This means you can substitute link font colors, make links bold or italic, or even change the perpetual underline that comes with text links by default. Table 5-1 contains code to give you a few ideas.

The possibilities are endless, so I encourage you to experiment with ways to creatively style your links. Having said that, I do have a few words of caution:

- Avoid using different size fonts in each link state, unless the size change in no way affects the surrounding content. (It can be very annoying to move your mouse across a web page and then not be able to read the page content because the links become large enough to block the text around them.)

- Avoid making any changes that cause text to move or jump around on the page when a link is activated.

- Make sure to pick colors that complement the rest of the page. While you want your links to be visible, you don't want them to distract the reader.

Link State	Description	Code Used
Normal	Blue Bold	`a:link {color: blue;` `        font-weight: bold;}`
Visited	Purple	`a:visited {color: purple;}`

Rollover	Orange
	Bold
	No underline
	Yellow highlight
		`a:hover {color: orange;`
		`        font-weight: bold;`
		`        text-decoration: none;`
		`        background-color:`
		`yellow;}`

Active	Red Bold	`a:active {color: red;` `        font-weight: bold;}`

Table 5-1 Explanation of Sample Code Used to Style Links

CRITICAL SKILL
5.5 # Customize Links by Setting the Tab Order, Keyboard Shortcut, and Target Window

You can further customize the links on your page by setting the title, tab order, keyboard shortcuts, and target windows. Although the first three options were not supported by older browsers (such as versions prior to 4.0 in Netscape and Internet Explorer), I recommend you become familiar with them because they provide added benefit to users, particularly those with disabilities (such as the hearing- or vision-impaired).

Title

The `title` attribute is actually pretty easy to use and understand, and goes a long way toward helping users navigate a web site. When you add it to a link (or any other page element), you're giving the browser and user a little bit more detail regarding the content—in this case, of the linked file. What the browser does with the contents of your `title` attribute varies, but in most situations the text appears as a "tool tip" when the cursor is placed over the link.

For example, in the following code snippet and illustration, the `title` attribute serves to alert users to the fact that clicking the link will take them to another web site.

```
<a href="http://www.yahoo.com" title="Click this link to leave our
site and visit Yahoo!">Visit Yahoo!</a>
```

TIP

The W3C encourages you to add the `title` attribute to as many page elements as you can—everything from images and links to paragraphs and sections of text—because the `title` attribute can also aid in style sheet development and general page usability.

Tab Order

Frequent users of screen-based forms understand that pressing the TAB key advances your mouse pointer to the next available form field. Usually, the tab order of those fields is specified by the programmer who created the form.

In like manner, you can customize the tab order of links and form field elements on your web page by using the `tabindex` attribute.

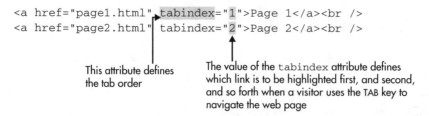

```
<a href="page1.html" tabindex="1">Page 1</a><br />
<a href="page2.html" tabindex="2">Page 2</a><br />
```

This attribute defines the tab order

The value of the `tabindex` attribute defines which link is to be highlighted first, and second, and so forth when a visitor uses the TAB key to navigate the web page

When a visitor uses the TAB key to navigate your web page, each link or clickable element on the page is, in turn, highlighted. If no order has been specified by the `tabindex` attribute (or if the browser doesn't recognize the `tabindex` attribute), the browser will make its best effort to use a reasonable tab order, usually from top to bottom on the page.

After successfully using the TAB key to highlight the link the person wants to visit, he or she can press the RETURN or ENTER key to visit that link.

NOTE

You can use any number between 0 and 32,767 for the value of the `tabindex` attribute, or use a negative number to exclude an element entirely from the tab order.

Keyboard Shortcuts

Many computer users are familiar with some common keyboard shortcuts, such as copy (CTRL-C/Windows or COMMAND-C/Mac) and paste (CTRL-V/Windows or COMMAND-V/Mac). Similarly, you can assign keyboard shortcuts to links in your web page. To do so requires adding the `accesskey` attribute to the a tag.

This attribute defines the keyboard shortcut

```
Click the link or type the appropriate keyboard shortcut and press RETURN to visit
the page of your choice:
<a href="page1.html" tabindex="1" accesskey="1">Page 1</a> (Alt-1)<br />
<a href="page2.html" tabindex="2" accesskey="2">Page 2</a> (Alt-2)<br />
```

The value of the `accesskey` attribute specifies which key the user must enter

A good idea is to include the keyboard shortcut next to your link; otherwise, visitors to your web page wouldn't know it exists. Note that in some versions of IE on Windows, users must press ENTER after typing the `accesskey` to actually visit the web page.

TIP

Try to remember any universal keyboard shortcuts when you come up with your own. You wouldn't want to disable someone's ability to print, for example, in favor of a link in your web page.

Target Windows

Have you ever visited a web site and noticed that a second instance of the web browser opened when you clicked a link? This happens when web developers use the `target` attribute to load links in a browser window other than the one you're currently using.

For example, you might want to offer visitors to your site a link to search Yahoo!, but you don't want to encourage them to leave your site. If you use `_blank` as the value of the `target` attribute in your link to Yahoo!, the browser will launch a new browser window to load **http://www.yahoo.com**.

This attribute is most commonly used to target browser windows other than the one you are currently using

↓

`<a href="http://www.yahoo.com" target="_blank">Search Yahoo!</a>`

↑

This is one possible value for the `target` attribute

Aside from targeting new windows, you can also target specific windows you have named. For instance, instead of using `_blank` to launch a new window, you might use "cars" to launch a window that is named "cars." Then, any time you have a link related to cars, you can add `target="cars"` to your link and all those links will load into the "cars" window. Table 5-2 lists three of the possible options for the `target` attribute. Additional options are discussed in Module 10.

Value of `target` Attribute	Description
_blank	Opens the link in a new unnamed browser window
_self	Opens the link in the same window currently being used
name (where *name* is any name you have given to a window)	Opens the link in the window of that name (if no window is currently open by that name, the browser launches a new window and gives it that name)

Table 5-2 Values for the `target` Attribute

Project 5-2 Customize Links

This final project in Module 5 gives you practice customizing links by changing the default colors, tab order, keyboard shortcuts, and target windows. Goals for this project include

- Changing the link colors for a page

- Targeting a link to open in a new browser window

- Adding titles for all links on a page

Note that all the files needed to complete the projects in this book for Chop Point can be downloaded from **www.osborne.com** or **www.wendywillard.com**. In addition, you can view my version of the web site anytime by visiting **www.choppoint.org**.

Step by Step

1. Open your text editor (SimpleText on the Mac, or Notepad on the PC) and open both the index.html page and the trips.html page saved from Project 5-1.

2. Change the link colors on both pages to the color scheme of your choice. Save all files. (If you created styles.css in the Extra Credit for the previous project, you only need to change the link colors in that one file to alter them on both pages! Refer back to the end of Project 5-1 if you missed it.)

3. Close index.html.

4. Switch to trips.html and add a link to The American Camp Association (**http://www .acacamps.org**) somewhere on the page. Target a new browser window with this link.

5. Add titles to each link with the `title` attribute.

6. Save the file.

7. Open your web browser and choose File | Open Page (Open File or Open, depending on the browser you're using). Locate the file trips.html you just saved.

Preview the page to check your work. If you need to make changes, return to your text editor to make changes. After making any changes, save the file and switch back to the browser. Choose Refresh or Reload to preview the changes you just made. If you're using Chop Point, you can compare your camp.html page to Figure 5-7. The added link might be coded like this:

```
Chop Point is a member of the <a href="http://www.acacamps.org" title="Visit
the ACA Web Site" target="_blank">American Camping Association</a>.
```

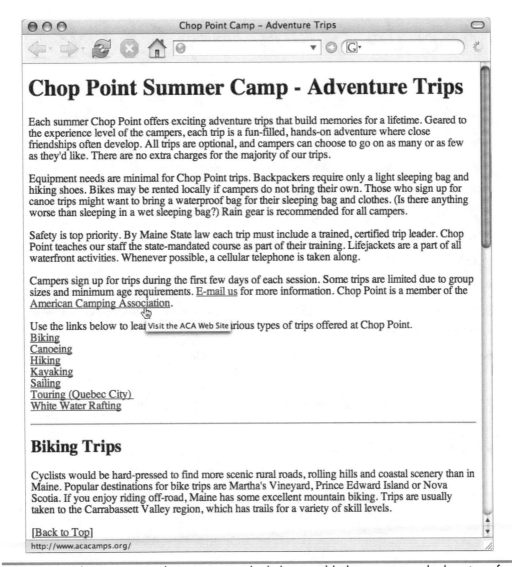

Figure 5-7 When you move the mouse over the link you added, you can see the location of the link in the status bar at the bottom of the screen.

Project Summary

Although users and browsers ultimately control the link colors on your pages, you can make recommendations in your style sheets. This project gives you practice changing those colors, as well as customizing the target windows for your links.

Module 5 Mastery Check

1. What does the `href` attribute do?

2. Which of these can be classified as a relative link?

   a. `<a href="../email.html">`

   b. `<a href="http://www.yahoo.com/email.html">`

   c. `<a href="/email.html">`

   d. `<a href="http://email.yahoo.com">`

3. What must be installed and activated on a user's machine to take advantage of an e-mail link in a web site?

4. How do you tell the browser to launch a link in a new window?

5. Which style sheet selector enables you to change the color of the links on your page after someone has clicked them?

6. In Windows, what must users type to highlight the following link?

   `<a href="contact.html" tabindex="2" accesskey="t">Contact Me</a>`

7. Fill in the blank: After successfully using the TAB key to highlight a link, you must press the _____ key to actually visit that link.

8. Fix the following code.

   `< ahref="contact.html" >Contact Me</a>`

9. Add the appropriate code so that this link enables users to e-mail you at your personal e-mail address.

   `<                    > Email Me </   >`

10. Which tag links to a section within the current page?

    a. `<a href="page1">Page 1</a>`

    b. `<a href="#page1">Page 1</a>`

    c. `<a href="*page1 ">Page 1</a>`

    d. `<a href="page1.html" >Page 1</a>`

11. Which common phrase should always be avoided when naming links?

12. Fill in the blank: By default, all linked text is _____.

13. True/False: A dot-dot-slash tells the browser to go up a level in the directory structure before looking for a file.

14. Which links to a section named *Intro* within the web page named genealogy.html?

    a. `<a href="genealogy.html">Intro</a>`

    b. `<a href="genealogy.html#intro">Intro</a>`

    c. `<a href="genealogy.html#Intro">Intro</a>`

    d. `<a href="genealogy.html=Intro">Intro</a>`

    e. `<a href="genealogy.html=intro">Intro</a>`

15. What does `_blank` do when used as the value of the `name` attribute?

Module 6

Working with Images

133

A t its beginning, information pages on the Internet were text only and didn't contain any images. We've come a long way since then, with some web sites now consisting *solely* of images. While, in most cases, I wouldn't advocate using only images, I do advocate employing images to spice up your web pages wherever they make sense. The saying "a picture is worth a thousand words" definitely holds true for the Internet.

6.1 Use Images as Elements in the Foreground of a Web Page

You can easily add images anywhere on your web page by using the img tag, where img is short for *image*. Add the src attribute (short for source), supply the appropriate value, and you're off and running.

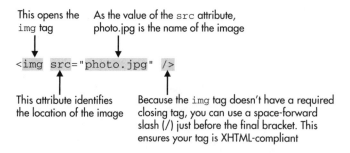

When you use the img tag, you're telling the browser to display the image right within the web page, as shown in Figure 6-1. In doing so, remember the following few things:

- Your image should be in a web-friendly file format, such as GIF, JPEG, or PNG. (See the next section titled "Image File Types.")

- The value of your src attribute should include the correct pathname and location of your file. So, if the image you want to use is not located in the same folder as the HTML page you're working on, you need to tell the browser in which folder that image is located. For example, if you want to include an image located one directory higher than the current directory, you would use src="../photo.jpg", where the ../ tells the browser to go up one directory before looking for the image file. If you want to reference an image from another web site, you could use src="http://www.websitename.com/images/photo.jpg", where the URL is the full name of the image location on the other site.

- In general, each image should serve a unique purpose and add something to your web page. Because visitors have to wait while images download to their computers, it's wise not to bog down your page with gratuitous graphics that serve little or no purpose.

Figure 6-1 By default, the browser displays the image within the web page wherever you type the **img** tag. In this case, the image was the only content on the page, so it was placed at the top of the page.

Image File Types

The most common and widely supported image file types are

● GIF (usually pronounced with a soft *g,* just like the peanut butter—think "choosy designers choose GIF" to help you remember—but many people do pronounce it with a hard *g*)—the acronym for *Graphic Interchange Format*

● JPEG (pronounced *jay-peg*)—the acronym for *Joint Photographic Experts Group*

Because of its compression format, the GIF file type is best suited for flat-color graphics such as comics, illustrations, typography, and line art. In contrast, JPEG was created specifically for photographic imagery and shouldn't be used for flat-color graphics.

A third file type, PNG, has also become widely supported and used in recent years. *PNG,* which stands for *Portable Network Graphics*, has many of the best characteristics from both JPEG and GIF. It's taken some time for it to become popular only because, in times past, it wasn't supported by all the browsers.

For more information on web image file types, see Module 13.

Using Existing Graphics

Whenever you create a web site, you will undoubtedly want to include images. It isn't always necessary to create your own images. In fact, thousands of stock images are available either in computer stores or on the Internet. Some require minimal fees, while others are free. Let's run through a few different types to help you decide what to use.

Stock Photography

The use of photography can often add a sense of professionalism to a business web site, but many businesses don't have the budget to hire photographers to do private photo shoots for them. If you're in this predicament, have no fear. Plenty of stock photography houses offer royalty-free photography to be used for almost any purpose, except for resale.

You can purchase entire CDs of photographs with a particular theme at your local computer or office supply store. These CDs range in cost from $40 to $500, depending on the quality of the work and the type of license you're given.

You can also search online and purchase the right to use an individual photograph. The costs vary according to how you plan to use it. For example, if you want to purchase the right to use a photo only on your web site, you can expect to pay a minimal fee of $25–$50. If, however, you want to use the same image in all your printed publications, as well as in any digital presentations, the fees typically start around $100 and go up from there.

You might also check the software licenses that came with your favorite graphics or presentation program. For instance, registered owners of Microsoft Office have access to Microsoft's free image gallery at **http://office.microsoft.com/clipart**.

When using any stock photography, be sure to read the terms of use and license carefully. While you may find free stock photography, it's often restricted only to noncommercial use. For more links, visit my web site: **www.wendywillard.com**.

Clipart

Whenever you need a stock button, cartoon, line drawing, illustration, or other graphic, you might try searching through some clipart libraries. You can find CDs filled with various types of clipart at your local computer or office supply store for $10–$150. (The cost typically depends on the quantity of graphics you receive.)

Probably thousands of online clip-art galleries exist where you can search for the type of graphic you want. Many artists publish their clipart on the Internet and offer it free for personal use. License fees for commercial use of this clipart are usually affordable but vary greatly according to the artist.

As with stock photography, you may receive some clipart free with the purchase of another software program. For instance, registered owners of Microsoft Office have access to Microsoft's free clipart gallery: **http://office.microsoft.com/clipart**.

For lists of online sources for stock photography and clipart, visit my web site: **www.wendywillard.com**.

Creating Your Own Graphics

If you do not use existing graphics on your pages, you may need to create some of your own or hire a web designer to do so. The best web designers typically have a background in graphic design and know how to make fast-loading, good-looking graphics for the Web. You can locate web designers either by word of mouth or by searching an online directory such as The Firm List: **www.firmlist.com**.

For more information about creating your own graphics, see Module 13.

Project 6-1 Add an Image to Your Web Page

Returning to the trips.html page for Chop Point (or your own organization), let's add an image to the page. Open your text/HTML editor and load the trips.html page that you saved from the second project in Module 5.

NOTE

All the files needed to complete the projects in this book for Chop Point can be downloaded from **www.osborne.com** or **www.wendywillard.com**. In addition, you can view my version of the web site anytime by visiting **www.choppoint.org.** Those of you who aren't using Chop Point can tailor your project to your particular needs.

Step by Step

1. Locate the hiking.jpg image in your Module 6 folder of the .zip archive.

2. Copy and paste the image into the same folder that houses your trips.html file.

3. Add the appropriate code to insert the image into the trips.html page, just below the section title, "Hiking Trips."

4. Save the file.

5. Open your web browser and choose File | Open Page (or Open File or Open, depending on the browser you're using). Locate the file trips.html that you just saved.

6. View the page to ensure the image appears on it. If you need to make changes, return to your text editor to do so. After making any changes, save the file and switch back to the browser. Choose Refresh or Reload to preview the changes you just made. If you're using Chop Point, you can compare your files to the following code and Figure 6-2.

(continued)

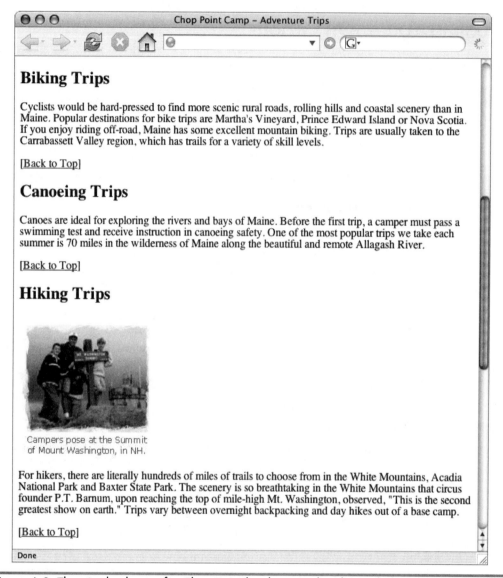

Figure 6-2 The trips.html page for Chop Point has been updated to include an image.

```
...the code before this section remains the same...
<a name="hiking"><h2>Hiking Trips</h2></a>
<img src="hiking.jpg" />
```

```
<p>For hikers, there are literally hundreds of miles of trails to
choose from in the White Mountains, Acadia National Park, and Baxter
State Park. The scenery is so breathtaking in the White Mountains
that circus founder P.T. Barnum, upon reaching the top of mile-high
Mt. Washington, observed, "This is the second greatest show on
earth." Trips vary between overnight backpacking and day hikes out
of a base camp.</p>
...the code after this section remains the same...
```

TIP

Does your image appear? If not, make sure the pathname is correct. Both the HTML page (trips.html) and image (hiking.jpg) should be located in the same folder. If they aren't, you need to change the pathname to reflect the proper folder name. For more tips, see Appendix C.

Project Summary

The img tag enables you to add images to your web pages. This project gives you practice using that tag in its most basic form before we move on to additional formatting techniques.

Progress Check

1. How do you close the img tag so that it is XHTML-compliant?

2. Which attribute is used with the img tag to define the location of your image file?

CRITICAL SKILL

6.2 Specify the Height and Width of Images

After you start adding several images to your web pages, you may notice they sometimes cause the browser to wait a little while before displaying the page. Because they don't know the size of the image, some browsers actually wait until the images are all loaded before displaying the web page.

---

1. Place a space and a forward slash before the closing bracket in the img tag.

2. src

Therefore, you can help speed the display of your web pages by telling the browser the sizes of your images right within the img tag. You do so with the height and width attributes.

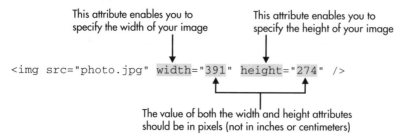

This attribute enables you to specify the width of your image

This attribute enables you to specify the height of your image

```
<img src="photo.jpg" width="391" height="274" />
```

The value of both the width and height attributes should be in pixels (not in inches or centimeters)

If you don't know the size of your image, you can open it in a graphics editor, such as Adobe Photoshop/ImageReady or Macromedia Fireworks, to find out. Or you can use the browser to determine the size of your images.

● **In Firefox/Mozilla for the Mac and PC, as well as in Safari for the Mac**   First, load the image by itself into the browser window (choose File | Open or File | Open Page and locate the image file on your computer). Then, look at the top of the browser window where the title is usually displayed. When you view an image file, these browsers print the width and height of the image (in that order) in the title.

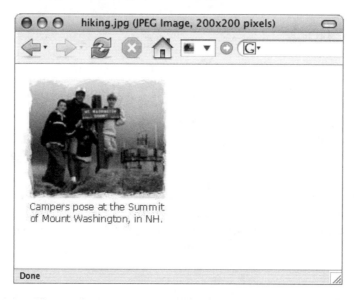

● **In Internet Explorer for the PC**   Load the image into the browser window (choose File | Open and locate the image file on your computer, or drag it from the desktop into an open browser window). Then, right-click the image and choose properties. The size is displayed as *dimensions* (width × height).

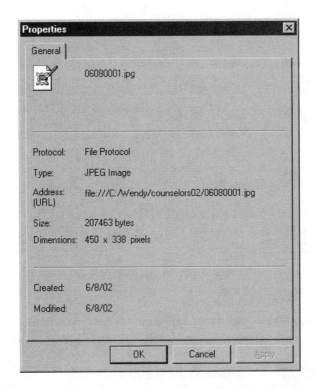

TIP

You can also use the height and width attributes to change the size of an image. For example, if you were given an image that was 50 pixels high by 60 pixels wide, you could change that size by specifying a different size in the HTML (such as 50 pixels wide by 50 pixels high). This causes the browser to attempt to redraw the image at the newly specified size. I don't recommend doing this, though, because it may not only slow down the display of your pages, it may also cause the image to lose proper proportions. Creating the image at whatever size you need it to be within your page is best. For more tips on creating images, see Module 13.

CRITICAL SKILL
6.3 Provide Alternative Text and Titles for Images

Some people visiting your site won't be able to see the images on your pages. A variety of reasons exist as to why this might be the case, but the following describes a few of the most common ones:

- *They have turned images off in their browsers.* Most browsers have a setting in the preferences that enables you to disable images on pages. By turning off images, visitors are able to view web pages more quickly, and then choose which (if any) images they want to see.

- *They are using text-only browsers.* Although a small minority of people using desktop computers have text-only browsers, many of those with handheld devices do use text-only browsers on a daily basis. These handheld devices might include Internet-ready telephones, pagers, and palm-size computers. Additionally, those who are vision-impaired often use text-only browsers with additional pieces of software that read the pages to them. In these cases, your alternate text may be the only way vision-impaired people can understand the purpose of your images.

- *The image doesn't appear.* Sometimes, even though you coded the page properly, the visitor to your site doesn't see every single image on the page. This could happen if too much traffic occurs, or when visitors click the Stop button in their browser before the page has fully loaded.

The good news is you can do something to help visitors to your site understand the content of your images, even if they can't see them. You can use the `alt` attribute of the `img` tag to provide alternative text for an image.

```
<img src="photo.jpg" width="391" height="274" alt="This photo of my
daughter, Corinna, was taken when she was 11 months old." />
```

The text value of the `alt` attribute displays in the box where the image should be located, if the browser cannot find the image or if it isn't set to display images (see Figure 6-3).

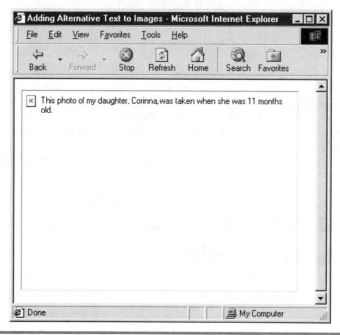

Figure 6-3 This screen shows how the browser displays the alternative text if it cannot find the image. Without that alternative text, viewers wouldn't have any idea what they were supposed to see.

Another great benefit of the `alt` attribute is that even visitors who can see the image can also read the alternative text. For example, when you move your mouse over the image, the alternative text appears in a box near your pointer arrow. This process of showing informative text when the mouse moves over an image is also called a *tool tip* in other software programs.

In addition to the `alt` attribute, it's a good idea to add the `title` attribute to your img tag. While the `alt` attribute specifies alternative text for images in case the images don't load, the `title` attribute can be added to images as well as links and other page elements. It serves as a quick tip for users to briefly explain the contents of the page element or, in this case, the image.

```
<img src="photo.jpg" width="391" height="274" alt="This photo of my
daughter, Corinna, was taken when she was 11 months old."
title="Picture of Corinna at 11 months" />
```

The greatest benefit in using the `title` attribute is that its contents are displayed as "tool tips" in all current browsers, regardless of whether the user has a Windows or Mac operating system.

Link Images to Other Content on a Web Site

In the previous chapter, you learned how to create links to other pieces of information on the Internet. Text phrases were used to mark links and give visitors something to click. You could also use an image to label a link, with or without an additional text marker. Figure 6-4 shows an example of an image used as a link without an additional text label, while Figure 6-5's linked image does have a text label.

Link the Entire Image

To link an entire image, as in Figures 6-4 and 6-5, you need only to add the a tag and the href attribute around the image.

```
<a href="http://www.choppoint.org"><img src="choppoint_468x60.gif" width="468"
height="60" alt="LINK: Chop Point Summer Camp in Woolwich, Maine" /></a>
```

As with any other linked elements in a web page, the visitor's pointer turns to a hand when she moves her mouse over the linked image (refer to Figures 6-4 and 6-5 for examples).

Figure 6-4 Here, an image—in this case an animated banner ad—is used as a link to another web page.

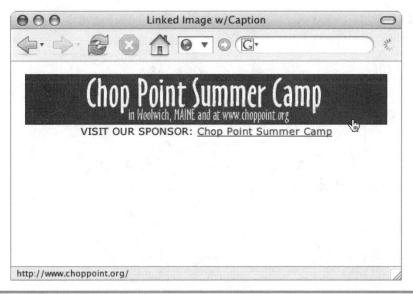

Figure 6-5 As an alternative, a text label has been added in this example to help users understand where the link will take them.

TIP

When I link an image, I like to add "LINK:" to the beginning of my alternative text. This immediately lets users who can't see the image know it is also a link.

Link Sections of an Image

You can also link sections of an image, creating what are called *image maps*. When only sections of an image are linked (as opposed to the entire image), the visitor's pointer only changes to the hand when he moves his mouse over one of the predefined hot spots on the image. Each *hot spot* within an image map can link to its own web page, if wanted.

So, looking back at the photo of Corinna at 11 months, an image map could be used to link her eyes to one web page and her mouth to a different one. Another example of an image map is a picture of the United States, where each state could be designated as a hot spot, with its own link.

In this example, when you move your mouse over the state of Texas, the pointer changes to a hand telling you Texas is a link. You can see in the status bar at the bottom that the Texas hot spot links to a page called texas.html. If you moved your mouse over another state, such as New Mexico, you would see it's linked to newmexico.html.

The technical term for the type of image map discussed here is "client-side image map." *Client-side image maps* are so called because all the work is done on the client's (or visitor's) computer. The "work" I refer to is the computation of where the hot spot is located and to which link it corresponds. All the information about which hot spot is where and what it links to is included within the original HTML file. This makes for easy access by your visitor's web browser because it doesn't have to look for the information elsewhere. The following shows an example of what that code looks like:

First, we have to tell the browser this image will be used as an image map. Use the usemap attribute to do that and tell the browser where to look for the map file

```
<img src="map.gif" width="400" height="244" alt="Click the state you live in."
usemap="#usa" /><br />Click the state you live in.
```

```
<map name="usa">
```
◄————————Then, we name the map . . .

. . . and define each hot spot

```
<area shape="rect" coords="108,132,146,179" href="newmexico.html" alt="New
Mexico" />
<area shape="poly"
coords="181,121,181,147,138,151,143,173,157,173,166,215,202,222,237,186"
href="texas.html" alt="Texas" />
```

```
</map>
```
◄———————— After defining all the hot spots in the image,
don't forget to close the map tag

You use the usemap attribute of the img tag to specify the image as a client-side image map. This attribute works similarly to something you learned in the preceding chapter: links within a page. The reason for this is that the map tag contains a name attribute that enables you to link to it.

When you use the usemap attribute, you reference whatever name you gave to your map in the map tag. So, in the previous example, the image references an image map called "usa" (usemap="#usa"), which is defined further down the page by <map name="usa">.

NOTE

Remember, whenever you reference a client-side image map, you need to use the hash mark (#) before the name of the map to tell the browser you're referencing something contained within a named section of the page.

Let's look at the code a little more closely.

```
<img src="map.gif" width="400" height="244" alt="Click the state you live in."
usemap="#usa" />
```

Here's your basic img tag, with the addition of the usemap attribute. The value of the usemap attribute (in this case, usa) should be enclosed in quotes and preceded by a hash mark (#).

```
<map name="#usa">
```

The map tag surrounds all the other information defining hot spots in your image. The opening and closing tags are both required. The map tag and its enclosed information can actually be located anywhere within your HTML page and needn't be immediately below the corresponding img tag. The name attribute is used with the map tag to enable you to reference it from anywhere else on the page (or any other page, for that matter).

```
<area shape="rect" coords="108,132,146,179" href="newmexico.html" alt="New
Mexico" />
<area shape="poly" coords="181,121,181,147,138,151,143,173,157,173,166,215,
202,222,237,186" href="texas.html" alt="Texas" />
```

In between the opening and closing map tags are area tags for each hot spot. The area tag has four basic attributes (see Table 6-1).

NOTE

Because the area tag doesn't have a closing tag, you need to include the forward slash as a closing character at the end of the tag if you want to make your pages XHTML-compliant. If not, you don't need to include this slash, as the following shows:

```
</map>
```

Finally, you end this section by closing the map tag.

Finding Hot-Spot Coordinates

If you need to, you can use graphics programs to find the coordinates of your hot spots. In fact, a program like ImageReady, which ships with all versions of Photoshop since version 5.5, can help you find the hot spots and even code the image map for you. In ImageReady, you use one of the Image Map Tools to draw shapes around the hot spots, and then you assign the values of the href and alt attributes within the Image Map palette, as shown next:

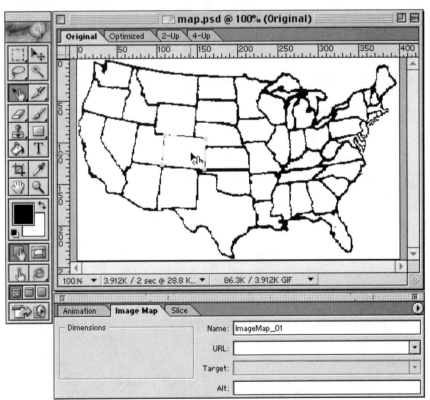

Attribute	Value	Description
shape	rect, poly, or circle	Defines the shape of your hot spot: rect for rectangles, poly for polygons, and circle for circles.
coords	rect: x1, y1, x2, y2 poly: x1, y1, x2, y2, x3, y3 circle: x, y, r	Defines the boundaries of your hot spot, where x and y are the horizontal and vertical coordinates, respectively, and r is the radius (for circles only). - Rectangles are defined by the upper-left and lower-right points. - Polygons are defined by each of their points, in x,y couples. - Circles are defined by the x,y coordinates of the center point and the radius.
href	filename.html	Defines the page to which you want this hot spot to link.
alt	text string	Defines the alternative text that appears for that hot spot.

Table 6-1 Attributes for the **area** Tag

Then when you choose File | Export Optimized As…, you can have the program save the image map code to an HTML file.

However, if you're going to write the code yourself, you can use the standard Paint program that comes with Windows to find coordinates. In this program, when you use the selection tool and move your mouse to the points in question, the coordinates appear in the bottom menu bar.

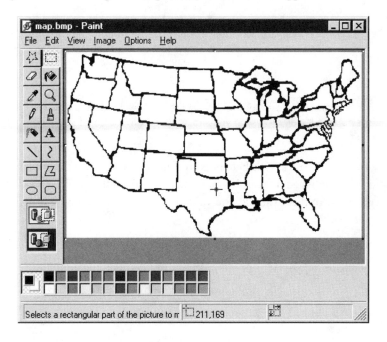

Finally, follow along the outside perimeter of your hot spot, writing down each set of coordinates. With this information, you can create the necessary code for the image map.

NOTE Many other image editing tools, as well as HTML editors, have features that can help you create image maps. In addition, you can even download free or shareware programs that help you write image maps. One example is Mapedit, which is available for PC, Mac, UNIX, and Linux. You can download it from **www.boutell.com/mapedit**.

CRITICAL SKILL
6.5 Style Foreground Images

While the basic img tag provides an easy way to add images to your web pages, you likely want to do a whole lot more than just plop those images down on the page. Style sheets enable you to customize the borders, align images with text, and a whole lot more.

Borders

You might have noticed that many linked images have borders around them. This happens because all linked images automatically have borders, just as all linked text automatically has underlines. The earlier HTML specifications allowed for a border attribute, which was used to specify the size of an image's border, as in the following example:

```
<img src="map.gif" width="400" height="244" alt="Click the state you live in."
usemap="#usa" border="0" /><br />Click the state you live in.
```

NOTE Some versions of Internet Explorer turn off borders for images by default. However, because this is not true for all browsers, you should turn it off yourself if you indeed want it to be off.

The value of the border attribute is expressed in pixels, where the default is 1 for linked images and 0 for nonlinked images. If you wanted to make it thicker, you would use a larger number, such as 4. In this example, the value is 0. This turns the border off completely, making it invisible.

NOTE

You could also use the `border` attribute to add a border to an image that is not linked, by specifying the value as any number greater than 0.

With that said, the W3C retired the `border` attribute and now prefers that you adjust the display of borders with style sheets. One reason for this is that style sheets offer significantly more control over your borders. For example, if you have multiple images on your page and wish to turn the borders off for all of them, instead of adding "`border=0`" to each of the `img` tags on the page, you can add the following code to the page's style sheet:

```
img {border-width: 0;}
```

Actually, you could use `border-style: none;` instead of `border-width: 0;` and it would also make the border invisible. Additional style sheet properties related to borders are listed next.

● **border-width**   Controls the size of the borders, individually (border-left-width, border-right-width, and so on) or as a whole (border-width). Values can be specified in length units (0 or 1, for example) or keywords (thin, thick, or medium).

- **border-color** Controls the border's color by specifying between one and four values. When you specify one value, that color is set for all four border edges. When two values are specified, the top and bottom edges take on the color in the first value and the left and right edges take on the second. When three values are specified, the top is set to the first, the right and left are set to the second, and the bottom is set to the third. When four values are set, the top, right, bottom, and left edges are set, respectively, as in the following example: `img {border-color: #ccc #666 #333 #999;}`. To specify a value for only one side, add the side's name (top, bottom, right, or left) to the property, as in "border-top-color."

- **border-style** Changes the style of the border. Options include

  - none
  - dotted
  - dashed
  - double
  - solid
  - groove
  - ridge
  - inset
  - outset

As you can see, another powerful aspect of the border properties is that they can be altered either as a whole (so the entire four edges look the same) or individually. To alter the characteristics individually, you simply add the side specification (top, bottom, right, or left) to the border property, after "`border`" and before any final characteristic. To give you an idea how this is done, consider the following example and Figure 6-6. Here, I've created a class called "`headshot`", and then set the border properties in my style sheet.

```
.headshot {border-style: double;
          border-left-style: none;
          border-right-style: none;
          border-width: 10px;
          border-left-width: 0px;
          border-right-width: 0px;
          border-color: #C00;}
```

After adding that style declaration to my style sheet, I can add the class reference to my `img` tag to complete the task.

```
<img src="jsmith.gif" alt="John Smith, CEO" class="headshot" />
```

Figure 6-6 The **headshot** class tells the browser to add double, 10-pixel borders to the top and bottom edges of the photo, but leave the left and right edges blank.

TIP

As discussed in Module 4, with style sheets these types of borders can be added not just to images but to any other element on the page! This means you can quickly add border styles to things like table cells or pull-out quotes, or virtually any other piece of content.

Floats

Whenever images appear within a section of text, you may want to alter the alignment so the image floats within the text flow instead of above or below it. (By default, the text starts wherever the image ends and flows below it, as shown previously in Figure 6-6.)

While the text-align property discussed in Module 4 works for basic alignment of text, it does not align images. Module 12 will guide you through the process of more complex alignment and positioning, but before you jump there I want to mention a very quick and easy way to "float" an image on the page—the CSS float property and a value of either left or right.

Floating an Image Within Text

The float property essentially tells the browser to place the floated element nearest whichever browser edge is specified, and then flow the rest of the page's content around it. To say it another way, content automatically flows along the right side of a left-floated image, and to the left side of a right-floated image. For example, if you had a lengthy paragraph of text and wanted to place an image in the upper-right corner of that paragraph, like this:

you could use the float property on that image, and set the value to "right" to tell the browser to keep the image on the right side of the text.

```
<img src="jsmith.gif" alt="John Smith, CEO" width="100" height="116"
style="float: right;" />
```

NOTE

Possible values for the float property are left, right, or none.

Clearing Floats   From time to time you'll encounter an instance in which you actually need to stop or clear a float. One example might involve the same situation I just used—an image floated to the right of a few paragraphs of text. Suppose you wanted to break the long paragraph up into two paragraphs, and then you only wanted the first paragraph to wrap around the image. The remaining paragraph would then take up the entire width of the page. To accomplish this, you have to "clear the float" by adding the `clear` property to the section in question, such as:

```
<p style="clear: right;">Remaining paragraph of text…</p>
```

This causes the paragraph to be "pushed down" until it is below the bottom edge of the floated image, like this:

NOTE

Possible values for the `clear` property are left, right, both, or none.

Floating Groups of Images

Suppose you had a page with lots of images, maybe one with thumbnails of each employee in a company. If all of the images were the same size, it would be very easy to use the float property and let the browser automatically place them in lines across the page. The following code shows one way to accomplish this task, by placing each of the images (and their accompanying captions) into separate divs.

```
<div class="thumbnail">
<img src="jsmith.gif" alt="Jeff Smith, CEO" /><br />
<p>Jeff Smith, CEO</p>
</div>
<div class="thumbnail">
<img src="mclark.gif" alt="Mary Clark, CFO" /><br />
<p>Mary Clark, CEO</p>
</div>
<div class="thumbnail">
<img src="ldaniels.gif" alt="Laura Daniels, CTO" /><br />
<p>Laura Daniels, CTO</p>
</div>
```

Then you would add the declaration for that thumbnail class to your style sheet:

```
.thumbnail {float: left;
     padding: 15px;}
```
◄——————— Adding this property ensures my images have a little breathing room (15 pixels) in between each other.

The `float: left` code tells the browser to put the first image next to the left margin of the page. Then, each subsequent image with the `float: left` style follows suit and sits in a row next to the first image, until it reaches the right edge of the browser. If the browser is open wide enough for all the floated images to fit in a single row, they will do so. If the user has the browser window open only enough for two images to fit in a row, then the remaining images will begin a new row beneath the first row (starting again near the left margin).

This is the true meaning of a "liquid layout" in web design, because the page is able to grow or shrink according to the browser window size. Compare Figures 6-7 and 6-8 to see an example of this floating principle in action.

Figure 6-7 A very simple style sheet allows these three photos to float next to each other on the page.

Figure 6-8 That same style sheet lets the browser move the images according to the width of the browser window.

Padding and Margins

The section "Quotation Blocks and Text Boxes" in Module 4 discusses how to use the padding and margin properties to add blank space within and around an element's borders. Those same properties—margin and padding—can also be applied to images to specify the space around an image on one, two, three, or all four sides.

For example, suppose you wanted to add a small block of space on the left side of an image, but you don't want to add any space on the right side because that side fits perfectly with another image. If you added the margin-left property to your style sheet or within your img tag, you could add space only on the left side.

```
<img src="photo.jpg" width="200" height="200" style="margin-left: 25px;"/>
```

Centering

By this point there's probably a big question still remaining about images and alignment… how to center?! While there isn't a "center" property for images, there is a trick you can use to center an image on the page or within a section. The key lies in changing the way we refer to "centering" an element—in reality what we're doing is making its left and right margins exactly equal.

First, we must tell the browser to display the image as a *block element*. In CSS, block elements will automatically fill the entire available space. So if an image becomes a block element, its margins will grow until they reach the edges of the browser window.

Next, if you tell the browser to make both the left and right margins the same, you will, in effect, center the image. The following is an example of the code you might use to center an image. First, the style sheet:

```
img.centered {display: block;
    margin-left: auto;
    margin-right: auto;}
```

This tells the browser to only apply the style to the centered class when it is used within an img tag

Then, add the name of the class (in this case it's "centered") to the img tag. Figure 6-9 shows the final result in the browser. No matter how wide (or narrow) the browser window is opened, the image remains centered horizontally.

```
<img src="vacation.jpg" alt="On vacation at Disney World"
class="centered" />
```

Figure 6-9   Although there isn't a "center" property in CSS, there are other ways to center
images with style sheets.

Project 6-2 Change Image Characteristics

Returning to the index.html page, let's vary the characteristics of the image you added in the
previous project. In addition, we'll add another image at the top of the page. Goals for this
project include

- Specifying the height and width for an image

- Providing alternative text and a title for an image

- Linking an image to another web page

- Turning off the border for a linked image

- Aligning an image with the text around it

- Adding some buffer space around an image

(continued)

Step by Step

1. Open your text or HTML editor and load the trips.html page saved from Project 6-1.

2. Add the `height` and `width` attributes to the hiking image.

3. Add alternative text and a title to the image.

4. Add 10 pixels of buffer space around the image.

5. Link the image to "hiking.html" and turn off the image's border.

6. Add another photo (rafting.jpg) to the Rafting Trips section, making sure to specify the height, width, and alternative text.

7. Align the hiking.jpg image to the right of the text in that section.

8. Align the rafting.jpg image to the left of the text in that section.

9. Save the file.

10. Open your web browser and choose File | Open Page (or Open File or Open, depending on the browser you're using). Locate the file trips.html that you just saved.

11. Verify that all your changes were made as you expected. If you need to make additional changes, return to your text editor to make changes. When you finish, save the file and switch back to the browser. Choose Refresh or Reload to preview the changes you just made. If you're using Chop Point, you can compare your files to the following code and Figure 6-10.

```
Code before this section stays the same...

<a name="hiking"><h2>Hiking Trips</h2></a>
<a href="hiking.html" title="Click to learn more about our hiking trips"><img
src="hiking.jpg" width="200" height="200" alt="LINK: Campers pose at the summit of
Mount Washington in New Hampshire" style="border:none;float:right;padding:10px;"
/></a>
<p>For hikers, there are literally hundreds of miles of trails to choose from in
the White Mountains, Acadia National Park, and Baxter State Park. The scenery is
so breathtaking in the White Mountains that circus founder P.T. Barnum, upon
reaching the top of mile-high Mt. Washington, observed, "This is the second
greatest show on earth." Trips vary between overnight backpacking and day hikes
out of a base camp.</p>

...code between these sections stays the same...

<a name="rafting"><h2>White Water Rafting Trips</h2></a>
<img src="rafting.jpg" width="250" height="200" alt="LINK: Campers enjoy
```

```
whitewater rafting on a day-trip in Maine" style="float:left;" />
<p>A three-hour drive to the head of the Kennebec River in the Forks begins a
spectacular challenge of the Class IV rapids of the Gorge. Registered Maine guides
using self-bailing rafts make this thrilling experience one to remember. An extra
fee of $75 and a parental release form are required.</p>
<p>[<a href="#top">Back to Top</a>]</p>
</body>
</html>
```

Figure 6-10 This example shows how the Chop Point trips page might appear after making the changes listed in this project.

Project Summary

You can customize the look and style of the images displayed in the foreground of your web pages in many ways. This project gives you practice with many image properties, including links, alignment, borders, and alternative text.

Progress Check

1. How does an image's appearance change when you link it?

2. Why is it important to add alternative text to images?

CRITICAL SKILL
6.6 Use Images as Elements in the Background of a Web Page

Images have another role in a web page, which is in the background. Just as in a theatrical play, where actors may be moving in the foreground while scenery moves in the background, two levels of design also exist in a web page.

The old HTML specifications enabled you to add a single image to be used as the "scenery" in the background of your web page. This was accomplished using the `background` attribute of the `body` tag, as in `<body background="picture.jpg">`. However, the W3C retired the `background` attribute, in favor of using style sheets to specify backgrounds. The latter is done by adding the `background-image` property to a style declaration for the `body` tag:

```
body {background-image: url("picture.jpg");}
```

One great advantage of the `background` property in style sheets is that it can be added to all sorts of page elements, from paragraphs to lists and table cells, using the same format shown for the `body` tag:

```
p {background-image: url("pattern.jpg");}
```

---

1. Linked images have a border around them by default.

2. Adding alternative text to images is important because situations may occur where an image doesn't display. In cases like this, alternative text is shown where the image doesn't display, in order to assist and inform a visitor.

Several benefits arise from using an image in the background as opposed to the foreground.

- You can achieve a layered look in your designs this way, because an image in the foreground can actually be placed on top of the image in the background.

- Background images begin at the top of the page and run all the way to each of the four sides. By contrast, elements in the foreground are subject to borders on the top and left, similar to those that occur when you print something.

- Adding backgrounds to page elements (like navigation bars or footers) can be a great way to set that content apart from the rest of the page.

When you insert a background image with HTML, you need to remember a few other things:

- *All background images tile by default. Tiling* means background images repeat in the browser window as many times as needed to cover the whole screen.

- *You can only include one image in the background.* So, if you want to use two different patterns in your background, they need to be included in a single image file.

- *Text in the foreground must be readable on top of the background.* If you're using dark colors in your background, make sure the text on your page is much lighter. Likewise, try to avoid high-contrast backgrounds because they make it extremely difficult to read any text placed on top of them.

- *Background images should be small in file size.* This avoids a long download time. Take advantage of the fact that the browser repeats a background image and cut your image down as much as possible.

To help clarify these points, look at Figure 6-11. If I told you the darker bar at the top, as well as the word "Corinna" and the stars, are all in the background, could you imagine what the background image itself looks like when it isn't tiled? Figure 6-12 gives the answer.

Because the original image was only 400 pixels tall, the browser was forced to repeat it when the window was opened larger in Figure 6-13.

To compensate for this, I could add additional space to my image, making it long enough to avoid tiling vertically. Testing your pages on different screen sizes is important to ensure your background images are repeating as you expect. See Figure 6-14 for another example.

Figure 6-11 Here, a background image enables me to achieve a layered look because the photo in the foreground lies over the top of the image in the background.

Another way to force the background image to remain stationary is to add the `background-attachment` property to the page's style sheet. This property allows the background to stay in place (when set to "`fixed`") or to move when the page is scrolled (when set to "`scroll`"). Similarly, you can even tell the browser whether or not to repeat your background image at all, using the `background-repeat` property.

```
body {background-image: url("picture.gif");
     background-attachment: fixed;
     background-repeat: no-repeat;}
```

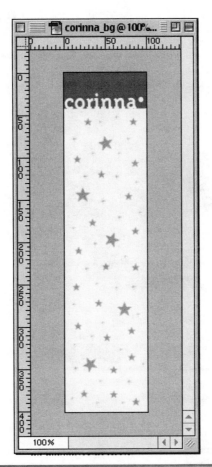

Figure 6-12 Before the image was tiled by the browser in Figure 6-11, it looked like this.

Possible values of the `background-repeat` property are

● **repeat** Specifies the file should repeat both horizontally and vertically (which is the default)

● **repeat-x** Specifies the file should repeat horizontally only

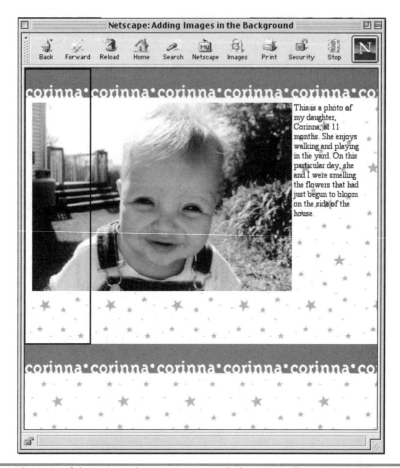

This is a photo of my daughter, Corinna, at 11 months. She enjoys walking and playing in the yard. On this particular day, she and I were smelling the flowers that had just begun to bloom on the side of the house.

Figure 6-13 The size of the original image (100 wide by 400 tall) is outlined here. Because the image is shorter than the browser window, it repeats first to the right and then down.

- **repeat-y** Specifies the file should repeat vertically only
- **no-repeat** Specifies the file should not repeat

Can you imagine what my original image would look like if I wanted the darker-colored bar to run down the left side of the screen instead of across the top? Look at Figures 6-15 and 6-16 for an idea.

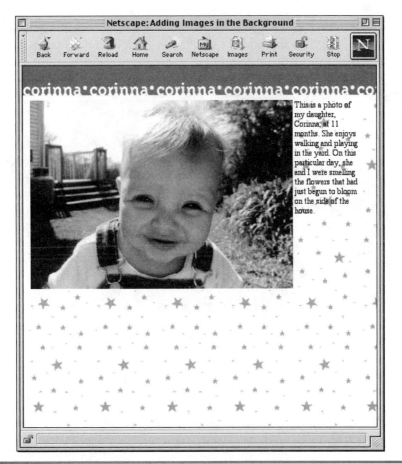

Figure 6-14 Here, I added 600 pixels to the height of the image, making it 1,000 pixels high. This helps to ensure that visitors won't see the darker bar and "Corinna" again on this page.

TIP

You can find many images suitable for background tiles in the same clipart catalogs mentioned earlier in the chapter. For more information about creating your own web graphics like those displayed here, refer to Module 13.

Figure 6-15 When the original image was turned 90 degrees counterclockwise in a graphics program, it created a colored bar down the left side.

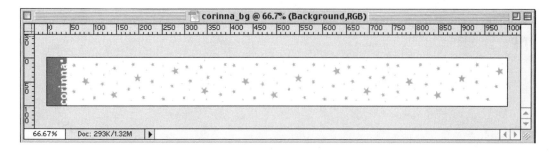

Figure 6-16 The original image used to create the background in Figure 6-15 is shown here. It is 1,000 pixels wide by 100 pixels tall.

Project 6-3 Add a Background Image

This final project in Module 6 gives you a chance to add a background image to your page.

Step by Step

1. Open your text or HTML editor and load the trips.html page saved from Project 5-2.

2. Add one of the patterned images found in the Module06.zip file into the background of the page.

3. Make any changes necessary to the colors of the text on your page in order to ensure it remains readable against the new background.

4. Save the file.

5. Open your web browser and choose File | Open Page (or Open File or Open, depending on the browser you are using). Locate the file trips.html you just saved.

6. Preview the page to check your work. If you need to make changes, return to your text editor to do so. After making any changes, save the file and switch back to the browser. Choose Refresh or Reload to preview the changes you just made. If you're using Chop Point, you can compare your files to the following code and Figure 6-17.

```
<!DOCTYPE html PUBLIC "-//W3C//DTD XHTML 1.0 Transitional//EN"
"http://www.w3.org/TR/xhtml1/DTD/transitional.dtd">
<html>
<head>
<title> Chop Point Camp - Adventure Trips </title>
<style type="text/css">
body {background-image: url("backgrounds/blue-gradient.gif");
      font-family: verdana;}
h1 {color: white;}
</style>
</head>
<body>
...the rest of the code remains the same
```

Project Summary

Adding an image in the background can add depth and appeal to your web pages when used wisely. This activity gives you practice using the background-image property with the body tag to add a background image.

(continued)

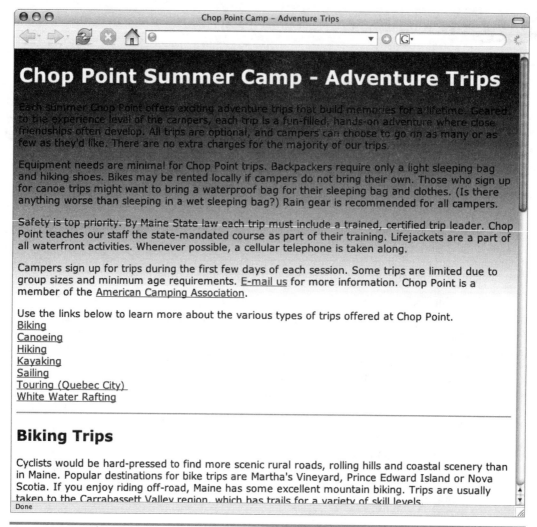

Figure 6-17 When added to the page, this image created the look of a seamless background gradation.

TIP

Having trouble getting your background to display? If so, make sure the image file is located in the same directory as your HTML file. If it isn't, you need to specify the correct file location in the `background-image` property. For more tips, see Appendix C.

Extra Credit

Try reformatting the page you just completed using an internal style sheet. Some formatting possibilities might be to

● Specify that the background image should only repeat along the horizontal axis. You could also try repeating it only along the vertical axis.

● Specify that the background image should remain fixed at the top of the page and should not scroll with the page. Alternatively, you could specify that the background image should always be displayed at the top of the screen, even if the user has scrolled.

✓

Module 6 Mastery Check

1. What does the `src` attribute do?

2. Why is it important to specify the height and width of images in web pages?

3. Which style sheet properties enable you to add blank space around images?

4. Which attribute must be added to the `img` tag to designate the image as a client-side image map?

5. Which two tags are used when defining a client-side image map's name and hot spots?

6. You are creating the code for a client-side image map, and one of the rectangular hot spots has the following coordinates: 0,0 (upper left); 50,0 (upper right); 50,50 (lower right); and 0,50 (lower left). Which are used in the following `coords` attribute?

   ```
   <area shape="rect" coords="_____" href="maryland.html">
   ```

7. Fill in the blank: The value of the height and width attributes is measured in _____.

8. Fix the following code.

   ```
   <img href="contact.jpg" />
   ```

9. Add the appropriate style declaration to use wallpaper.gif as a background for the web page code shown next. Note that the graphic is in the same folder as the HTML file.

   ```
   body {                                    }
   ```

10. What are the four possible values of the `clear` property (used to clear floats)?

11. Fill in the blank: The default value of the `border` property is _____ pixels for linked images and _____ pixels for nonlinked images.

12. True/False: You can achieve a layered look in your designs when an image in the foreground is placed on top of an image in the background.

13. What value must be used with the display property before you can center an image using the method discussed in this module?

```
img.centered {display:                    ;
    margin-left: auto;
    margin-right: auto;}
```

14. Which attribute is used to add alternative text to an image?

15. Which statement is not true about background images?

    a. All background images tile by default.

    b. You can only include one image in the background.

    c. Background images are added to web pages with the `background` tag.

    d. Background images begin at the top of the page and run all the way to each of the four sides.

Module 7

Working with Multimedia

On the Internet, the term *multimedia* is used to refer to presentations of various types of media, such as audio, video, text, graphics, or animation, which are integrated into a single file format. You may have seen multimedia presentations on news or weather sites, where they are used to display audio, video, and text to viewers. Other sites use multimedia to entertain viewers, often in the form of a cartoon or an animated story.

Many forms of multimedia enable visitors to interact with the presentations. For example, a visitor might be watching an animated story, and then click the individual characters to learn more about them before continuing.

The Web itself is often considered multimedia because any web page can contain several different types of media files in it. By default, however, most web browsers are only capable of understanding HTML files, graphics files such as GIF and JPEG, and plain text documents (.txt). Any other file types must be handled through a plug-in, ActiveX control, or helper application. Sometimes these types of controls come preinstalled in the browser, but other times they must be downloaded by the user.

CRITICAL SKILL
7.1 Understand How Plug-ins and ActiveX Controls Are Used with Web Browsers

A *helper application* is an additional piece of software that attempts to do something the browser cannot. If you thought of yourself as the browser, then a helper might be someone who mows your lawn for you, while a plug-in is a ride-on mower that helps you do it yourself. A *plug-in* or an *ActiveX control* helps the browser do something itself, as opposed to the helper application performing the operation for the browser.

NOTE

ActiveX is a brand name used by Microsoft to reference its various technologies that offer added functionality to web browsers.

For example, if your web browser doesn't know how to display a certain type of video file, it first looks for a plug-in capable of doing so. If your web browser doesn't find a plug-in, it might prompt you to download one or look for a helper application loaded on the computer that could display the video. If the browser cannot find a suitable plug-in or helper application, and one isn't downloaded, then it won't be able to display the file. For this reason, I do not recommend including essential information in files requiring plug-ins or helper applications, unless you also provide an alternative text-only version.

Helpers are standalone programs, separate from your browser, which you can purchase for your computer. By contrast, plug-ins and ActiveX controls are usually free and can be easily downloaded from the Internet. In some cases, web browsers even come with certain plug-ins and ActiveX controls. When you download a plug-in, you should receive instructions on how to install it, if necessary.

Many times, the plug-in installs itself and you only need to close and reopen your web browser. Other times, you're asked to place the plug-in in the appropriate folder on your computer and then restart your browser. Once you agree to download an ActiveX control, the browser downloads and installs the control, usually without relaunching the browser.

Identify the Installed Components

You can find out which plug-ins are installed under your browser in a few different ways. For example, the most rudimentary way to check for installed components is to look in the "plug-ins" directory in your browser's application folder. Although Firefox doesn't come with a default plug-in manager, you can download a free one from **www.gozer.org/ mozilla/extensions**.

If you're using Internet Explorer, choose Internet Options from the Tools menu in your browser. Next, click the Programs tab, and then click the Manage Add-ons button to view a list of all add-ons (including ActiveX controls and plug-ins) used by Internet Explorer.

Recognize File Types, Extensions, and Appropriate Plug-ins

You may want to link or embed many different file types in your web pages, but Resource E lists some of the more popular ones. Most file types can be "played" with at least one plug-in or helper application and, quite often, with more than one. If you want to be helpful to your visitors, list the plug-in or helper application they might use to open your files. You could also provide a link to download the appropriate plug-in.

For example, Macromedia Flash, a file type requiring a plug-in, has become so popular that it ships with most current browsers. Even so, you might have visited a web site and noticed a window pop-up saying something about "downloading the Flash player." In any case, Flash files are popular because they're small (which translates as "quick-to-download!") and can include sound, video, interactivity, and animation. Flash files are particularly good for animations and cartoons. Another reason Flash is so popular is that the plug-in used to display Flash files is available for both Windows and Mac systems, as well as Internet Explorer and Mozilla-based browsers.

Some plug-ins and helper applications aren't available for multiple computer systems and browsers, though. This list of plug-ins is changing daily, however. An ever-growing list is maintained at **www.webdevelopersnotes.com/design/list_of_browser_plugins.php3**, complete with the developer web site address and the systems (Windows, UNIX, and Mac) supported.

NOTE

Refer to Appendix E at the back of the book for a list of file types, extensions, and descriptions.

When you're ready to include multimedia files in your HTML pages, consider how you want to include them. Do you want to *link* to them so your visitors can choose whether to download them or view them now? Or do you want to *embed* them within your page, so they appear right within the web browser window? The rest of this module focuses on linking to and embedding several different types of multimedia.

CRITICAL SKILL

7.2

Link to Different Types of Media from a Web Page

A link to a multimedia file is essentially the same as any other link. While embedding a file can sometimes be problematic (as discussed in the next section), a link to a file can be especially useful because links are understood by all web browsers. Figure 7-1 shows how the following code is displayed in a browser, while Figure 7-3 shows the result of clicking the video link.

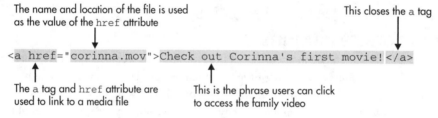

The name and location of the file is used as the value of the `href` attribute

This closes the a tag

```
<a href="corinna.mov">Check out Corinna's first movie!</a>
```

The a tag and `href` attribute are used to link to a media file

This is the phrase users can click to access the family video

NOTE

Including the proper file extension for your media file is important so the browser and operating system can understand and display it. If you're unsure as to which file extension to use, check Appendix E in this book.

Clicking the link shown in Figure 7-1 would cause one of three things to happen, depending on how the system was set up.

- It may prompt the user to download the file and save it for later (see Figure 7-2).

- It may prompt the user to download the file and view it now (see Figure 7-2).

- If the browser recognizes the file as one it is set up to display automatically, it may take over and do just that (see Figure 7-3).

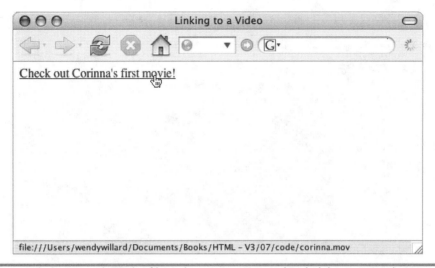

Figure 7-1 A link to a multimedia file is the same as any other link because it also uses the **a** tag and the **href** attribute.

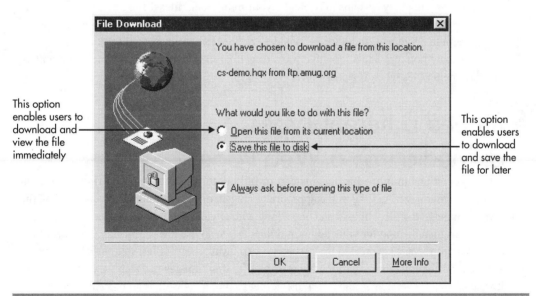

This option enables users to download and view the file immediately

This option enables users to download and save the file for later

Figure 7-2 When the browser doesn't recognize a file type as one it should "play" within the browser, it may prompt the user to download the file.

Figure 7-3 When the link is clicked, the browser may be able to play the video itself if the appropriate plug-in or ActiveX control is installed.

Knowing that many systems may handle your multimedia files differently, try to offer your visitors as much guidance and instruction as possible. For example, list the size of the file you're asking them to download, so they can consider whether they want to wait for it to load to their system. In addition, provide alternative ways of getting the information, and include it within the multimedia files wherever possible.

CRITICAL SKILL

7.3 Embed Different Types of Media into a Web Page

When you embed multimedia files instead of linking to them, they appear right within the context of your page. As long as the appropriate plug-in or ActiveX control is installed on the user's computer, the file will load and play along with anything else that might be on that page.

The original method for embedding multimedia was to use the embed tag. However, that tag was a proprietary tag created by Netscape. As a result, the W3C created the object tag as a method for embedding various types of media, from images to Flash movies and more. It is supported by version 3 (and later) of Internet Explorer, as well as all current versions of Mozilla-based browsers (such as Safari and Firefox).

NOTE

Multipurpose Internet Mail Extension (MIME) is an accepted system of extensions used on computer systems. This standardization makes it easy to specify a file type and feel confident other computers will understand it. Common MIME types for multimedia are image/png, image/gif, image/jpeg, video/mpeg, audio/x-wav, and so forth. Additional MIME types are listed in Appendix E.

Using the Object Tag

When you use the `object` tag, you must tell the browser what type of file you are embedding and where to locate that file. The `type` and `data` attributes are used for this process.

```
<object type="application/x-shockwave-flash" data="movie.swf"
height="60" height="200">
```

Then, after the opening `object` tag, you add any additional properties you want to specify using the `param` tag (short for *parameters*). (Note that the `object` tag enables you to specify the `height` and `width` attributes either in the `object` tag, or in `param` tags, depending on the plug-in employed.) Use the forward slash to make the `param` tag XHTML-compliant because it doesn't have a closing tag.

```
<param name="movie" value="movie.swf" />
<param name="BGCOLOR" value="#ffffff" />
```

Finally, you close the `object` tag.

```
</object>
```

Table 7-1 lists some optional attributes for the `object` tag. Tables 7-2, 7-3, 7-4, and 7-5 list some other parameters you might use when embedding Real Media files, other types of sound files, QuickTime movies, or Flash files. The plug-ins and parameters listed here aren't exhaustive, but are meant to give you an idea of some of the possibilities you have when using them. For more information about any of these, visit the web site of the corresponding plug-in's manufacturer.

TIP

Whenever you embed sound within a web page, it's always considered good practice to display at least some portion of the controls. This lets visitors turn off the sound or adjust the volume as they see fit.

Attribute	Possible Values	Description
`width="#"`	Number of pixels	Specifies the width of the window (video/animation) or controller (sound).
`height="#"`	Number of pixels	Specifies the height of the window (video/animation) or controller (sound).
`border="#"`	Number of pixels	Defines the width, in pixels, of the border.
`name="name"`	*Name*	Gives a (case-sensitive) name to the file so it can be referenced by a script or other method.
`type="value"`	MIME type (see earlier Note)	Specifies the type of file being embedded, which then defines the plug-in needed.
`standby="Text goes here"`	*Text to be displayed*	Specifies text to be displayed while the object is loading.
`tabindex="1"`	Numeric value	Specifies where the element appears in the tab order of the page.

Table 7-1 Attributes for the `object` Tag

Parameter Name	Possible Values	Description
`autostart`	true false	Defines whether the file immediately starts playing when the page is loaded.
`backgroundcolor`	hexadecimal code or color name	Changes the background color of the embedded file. The actual effect varies according to the plug-in used.
`center`	true false	Centers the embedded file in the window.
`console`	name	Identifies this and other embedded controls by naming them.
`controls`	all controlpanel controlpanel, statusbar controlpanel, infovolumepanel playbutton stopbutton	Specifies the style of the controller displayed in the web page.

Table 7-2 Optional Parameters for Real Media Files

Parameter Name	Possible Values	Description
loop	true false	Defines whether a file repeats.
nojava	true false	Stops the Java Virtual Machine from running, causing your embedded file to run only with the plug-in (and not Java).
nolabels	true false	Stops the presentation of label information (such as the author, copyright, and title) on the controller.
nologo	true false	Prevents the RealLogo from displaying.
numloop	number	Specifies the number of times a file will repeat.
shuffle	true false	Plays multiple sounds in random order.

Table 7-2 Optional Parameters for Real Media Files *(continued)*

Parameter Name	Possible Values	Description
bgcolor	hexadecimal code	Changes the background color of the embedded file. The actual effect varies according to the plug-in used.
controls	console playbutton pausebutton smallconsole stopbutton volumelever	Specifies the style of the controller displayed in the web page.
loop	true false # (number of times)	Defines how a file repeats.
volume	number between 0 and 100	Specifies the volume of the sound file.

Table 7-3 Optional Parameters for Most Sound Players

Parameter Name	Possible Values	Description
base	URL	Specifies the base directory for all included links.
play	true false	Defines whether the file begins playing when the page is loaded.
quality	best high autohigh autolow low	Defines the quality level of the embedded file.
scale	showall noborder exact fit	Defines how the embedded file fits within the rest of the web page.

Table 7-4 Optional Parameters for Flash

Parameter Name	Possible Values	Description
autoplay	true false	Defines whether the file immediately starts playing when the page is loaded.
bgcolor	hexadecimal code	Changes the background color of the embedded file. The actual effect varies according to the plug-in used.
controller	true false	Turns on the movie controller. (When true, you need to add 16 pixels to the height of the movie.)
kioskmode	true false	When true, disables the pop-up menu for the movie so users cannot copy or save it.
loop	true false	Defines whether a file repeats.
qtnextn	URL	Identifies a URL for the movie to load when it finishes playing the current one.
qtsrc	URL	Forces the browser to use the QuickTime plug-in to load the file instead of any other video plug-in.

Table 7-5 Optional Parameters for QuickTime Movies

Parameter Name	Possible Values	Description
scale	tofit aspect #	Defines how the embedded file fits within the rest of the web page.
volume	whole number between 0 and 100	Defines the beginning volume for the movie.

Table 7-5 Optional Parameters for QuickTime Movies *(continued)*

TIP

You can learn much more about embedding Flash files by visiting an online tutorial, such as **www.w3schools.com/flash**.

The `object` tag can contain other HTML tags and attributes, including other `object` tags. If the browser is capable of interpreting an `object` tag, it does so and ignores the HTML contained within the opening and closing `object` tags. If it doesn't understand the `object` tag, it uses the HTML included in it instead. The benefit of this is that you can offer a plug-in-free alternative to visitors who may not have or want to use the plug-in. This might be accomplished with code similar to the following:

```
<object type="application/x-shockwave-flash" data="movie.swf">
<param name="height" value="60" />
<param name="width" value="200" />
<param name="movie" value="movie.swf" />
<param name="bgcolor" value="#ffffff" />
<param name="loop" value="false" />
<a href="http://www.adobe.com/products/flashplayer" title="You must
install Flash to access this movie."><img src="movie-pic.jpg"
width="200" height="60" alt="Screen shot of movie - need Flash to
view" /></a>
</object>
```

In this example, I included a link to Adobe's site, with a tool tip (using the `title` attribute) explaining that the user needs to download Flash prior to viewing this file. Then, I added a screen capture of the movie to give users an idea what they might see after downloading the appropriate plug-in. Notice the link and image were added after the `param` tags but before the closing `object` tag.

Ask the Expert

Q: Wow! These tables are a little intimidating. Do I really need to know all this?

A: I completely understand. All this information is intimidating at first. But, rest assured, I only included it so that when you do want to embed a specific type of file later, you can come back to this section and find the particular information that pertains to your plug-in. This information isn't here because you need to memorize every attribute. Given that so many plug-ins (and ActiveX controls) are out there, it would be an impossible task!

The important thing is to understand that you have these tags at your disposal and can customize them according to your needs when the time comes.

Progress Check

1. What are two ways you can reference a multimedia file?

2. Which tag is used to embed a multimedia file within a web page?

Java Applets

You can also use the `object` tag to embed Java applets in your web page. *Java applets* are miniapplications (which is where we get the term *applet*) written in the Java programming language that can run within your browser window. Web developers use these miniapplications to do things that aren't easily accomplished through HTML or other means.

Java applets can be used to add functionality to your web pages, whether through a real-time clock, a mortgage calculator, a stock ticker, or an interactive game.

TIP

Visit **dir.yahoo.com/Computers_and_Internet/Programming_and_Development/ Languages/Java/Applets/** for links to all things related to Java applets.

---

1. Link to the file or embed it
2. `object`

The following is an example of how to embed these applets using the `object` tag.

```
<object classid="applet.class">
Here is my stock ticker.
</object>
```

This attribute of the `object` tag tells the browser which applet to embed and where it is located

This is the alternative text that is displayed when the browser cannot show the applet

You might be able to use many different types of attributes to customize the look of your applet but, for the most part, the attributes will depend on the type of applet you're using. Don't worry—if you search for free or shareware applets online, the developer will usually give you detailed instructions on how to embed the file. If you're writing your own applets, you can tailor the look of your applet within the Java code.

Project 7-1 Add Multimedia to a Web Page

Now you're going to create a link to a video file. If you're using the Chop Point site for your project, you'll link to a short movie showing the inside of one of the camp's cabins.

Note that all the files needed to complete the projects in this book for Chop Point can be downloaded from **www.osborne.com** or **www.wendywillard.com/**. In addition, you can view my version of the web site anytime by visiting **www.choppoint.org**. Those of you not using Chop Point can tailor the project to your particular needs.

Step by Step

1. Open your text or HTML editor and then open the index.html page saved from Project 4-2 in Module 4.

2. Locate the third paragraph below the Summer Camp heading, and add the cabinclip.gif image before the opening p tag of that paragraph.

3. Float the image to the left of the text.

4. Add ten pixels of buffer space to the right of the image.

5. Turn off the image's border.

6. Link the image to cabin.mov.

7. Save the file.

(continued)

8. Open your web browser and choose File | Open Page (or Open File or Open, depending on the browser you're using). Locate the file you just saved. Make sure the link works and the movie plays.

9. If you need to make changes, return to your text editor to make changes. After making any changes, save the file and switch back to the browser. Choose Refresh or Reload to preview the changes you just made. If you're using the Chop Point project, you can compare your files to Figure 7-4 and the following code.

```
... the code before this section remains the same...

<a href="cabin.mov" title="Click to view a short movie showing the inside
of one of our cabins"><img src="cabinclip.gif" alt="LINK: Click to view
the inside of one of the cabins" width="200" height="165"
style="float:left;padding-right:10px;border:none;" /></a>
<p>Buildings include a dining hall, a lodge, two homes, eight cabins, a
new state-of-the-art gymnasium, and a boathouse. The boathouse was
renovated into a Library and Learning Center, housing staff and computers
in the summer. Chop Point also has a full size athletic field, tennis
courts, basketball courts, a volleyball court and a well-equipped
waterfront facility.</p>

... the rest of the code remains the same...
```

Project Summary

The `object` and `embed` tags can be used together to enable you to reach the widest audience. This project gave you a chance to practice using those two tags together to embed a sound file in a web page.

TIP

Does your movie file play? If not, first make sure the pathname is correct. Both the index.html and cabin.mov files should be located in the same folder. If they aren't, you need to change the path name to reflect the proper folder name. Next, make sure you have a plug-in capable of displaying .mov files (such as QuickTime). For more tips, see Appendix C.

Extra Credit

For extra practice, try embedding the movie file instead of linking to it.

Figure 7-4   Those using the Chop Point site can compare their file to this example.

The content shown in the browser window:

Summer Camp

Chop Point received accreditation from the American Camping Association and opened as a camp in Maine in 1967. Before the founding of Chop Point, the property had been operated as Merrymeeting camp for over fifty years.

Chop Point Summer camp combines a strong residential camping program designed specifically for teenagers, with the excitement of an adventurous trip program. Each summer, 80 teenagers between the ages of twelve and eighteen come to Chop Point from all over the world to have one of the best summers of their lives. The camp is located two hours up the Maine coast in the town of Woolwich. The property includes 50 wooded acres of land at the end of a peninsula, and a mile of shoreline on picturesque and historic Merrymeeting Bay, on the Kennebec River.

Click this image to view a video clip of the inside of a girls' cabin. (2MB)

Buildings include a dining hall, a lodge, two homes, eight cabins, a new state-of-the-art gymnasium, and a boathouse. The boathouse was renovated into a Library and Learning Center, housing staff and computers in the summer. Chop Point also has a full size athletic field, tennis courts, basketball courts, a volleyball court and a well-equipped waterfront facility.

What's the greatest asset of Chop Point? Founder Peter Willard said it best: "We firmly believe our greatest asset is our top-notch staff. Sixteen counselors, having completed at least a year of college, come from throughout the world. They bring their skill, enthusiasm and love of teenagers to camp, and strive to be a genuine friend to each camper."

✔ *Module 7 Mastery Check*

1. What's the difference between a plug-in and a helper application?

2. Which tag does the W3C recommend for embedding multimedia in a web page?

3. How can users determine which plug-ins are installed on their computers, and how they can download new plug-ins?

4. What are two ways to include multimedia files in a web site?

5. True/False: Clicking a link to a sound file automatically downloads the file and saves it for later listening.

6. What are two ways to specify the height and width of multimedia files embedded with the `object` tag?

7. Fill in the blank: MIME stands for _____.

8. Fix the following code.

```
<embed href="sillyme.mov" height="100" width="50" />
```

9. Add the appropriate code here to link to wendy.mov. Note that the movie is in the same folder as the HTML file.

```
<html>
<head>
    <title>Home Movie</title>
</head>
<body>
<                            >View my home movie!<        >
</body>
</html>
```

10. Which attribute can restrict a file from replaying after it has played through once?

11. How might you provide an alternative way to view a file that requires a plug-in?

12. True/False: A link to a multimedia file is the same as any other link because it also uses the `a` tag.

13. What is the purpose of the `param` tag?

14. Which attribute of the `object` tag tells where the media file is located?

15. What are Java applets?

Module 8

Creating Lists

ists are everywhere—on your refrigerator, in schoolbooks, next to the telephone, on bills, and in all sorts of other documents. That's why there's a special set of tags just for creating lists. This module focuses on the three different types of lists possible in HTML:

- Ordered lists
- Unordered lists
- Definition lists

Lists are especially useful in web pages to draw attention to short pieces of information. Keep that in mind when you create your lists and try to include short phrases, instead of long sentences, in each list item.

CRITICAL SKILL
8.1 # Use Ordered Lists in a Web Page

An *ordered list* is one in which each item is preceded by a number or letter. For example:
My favorite fruits are

1. raspberries

2. strawberries

3. apples

If you want to create the previous list on a web page, you should use an ordered list. Here's what the HTML code would look like:

This opening tag tells the browser this will be in an ordered list.

```
My favorite fruits are
<ol>
    <li>raspberries</li>
    <li>strawberries</li>
    <li>apples</li>
</ol>
```

This stands for "list item" and distinguishes each item in the list.

The end tag for li is optional in HTML, but required in XHTML.

The end tag for ol is required in both HTML and XHTML. If you forget it, the rest of your text will be indented under the final list item.

NOTE

While it's not required, I indent the list items to make seeing the structure of the list easier.

Notice I didn't include any numbers in my list. This is because I used the `ol` tag to tell the browser this is an ordered list. When browsers see ordered lists, they know to place a number in front of each list item.

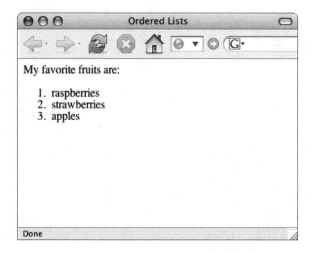

The default type of ordered list uses Arabic numbers, but you can use the `type` attribute to change that. Table 8-1 identifies the different types of ordered lists you can create with the `type` attribute.

To change the type of ordered list, add the `type` attribute and its value to the opening `ol` tag.

```
<ol type="I">
    <li>Introduction</li>
    <li>Understanding the Medium</li>
    <li>Basic Page Structure</li>
</ol>
```

Type Attribute Value	Numbering Style	Example
1	Arabic numbers	1,2,3,...
a	Lowercase alphabet	a,b,c,...
a	Uppercase alphabet	A,B,C,...
i	Lowercase Roman numerals	i,ii,iii,...
I	Uppercase Roman numerals	I, II, III,...

Table 8-1 Ordered List Types

NOTE

The `type` and `start` attributes are deprecated by the W3C, which prefers that you use style sheets to customize the look of your lists, but they are still widely supported by the browsers. Using style sheets to style lists is discussed later in this module.

Here, I changed the type to "I", which tells the browser to place uppercase Roman numerals in front of each list item. So the previous code would create a list like the following:

I. Introduction

II. Understanding the Medium

III. Basic Page Structure

You can also specify the starting number or letter for an ordered list with the `start` attribute. The default for the starting number is 1. To change this, add the `start` attribute to your `ol` tag.

```
<ol type="a" start="3">
    <li>Color</li>
    <li>Working with Text</li>
    <li>Working with Links</li>
</ol>
```

Even though the value of the `type` attribute may be something other than Arabic numerals, the value of the `start` attribute is always an integer. So, in the previous example, `start="3"` actually tells the browser to start the list with the third letter because `type="a"`.

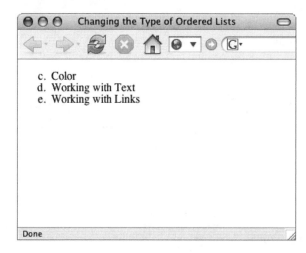

If you want to change an individual value—for example, if you want to make the third item in the list use the letter *g*—you can add the `value` attribute to the specific `li` tag.

```
<ol type="a" start="3">
    <li>Color</li>
    <li>Working with Text</li>
    <li value="7">Working with Links</li>
</ol>
```

As with the `start` attribute, the `value` attribute is always an integer. The browser looks at the value of the third list item and changes it to *g* because the type is *a*.

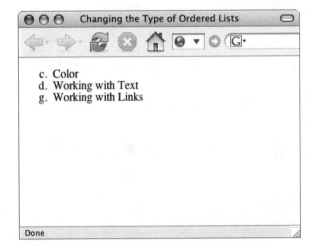

Use Unordered Lists in a Web Page

CRITICAL SKILL
8.2

The second type of list is similar to the first, except *unordered lists* don't use numbers or letters. As the name suggests, unordered lists don't rely on order for importance. These lists use bullets to precede each list item. The following is an example of an unordered list:

- Red

- Green

- Blue

You still use the `li` tag to identify each item in the list but, instead of beginning with the `ol` tag, unordered lists begin with the `ul` tag.

```
<ul>
    <li>red</li>
    <li>green</li>
    <li>blue</li>
</ul>
```

Aside from that, the code used to create the first two types of lists is almost identical. In fact, you can even use the `type` attribute here to change the style of the bullets. Three possible options exist for bullet style:

- **disc**   Usually displayed as a small, filled-in circle

- **circle**   Usually displayed as an open circle

- **square**   Usually displayed as an open (Mac) or filled-in (Windows) square

Initially, all unordered lists default to the disc style, which is usually represented as a small, filled-in circle. However, if you nest unordered lists—that is, if you include an unordered list in another unordered list—the default value changes.

CRITICAL SKILL
8.3 Use Definition Lists in a Web Page

The third type of list you can create in HTML is called a *definition list*. As its name suggests, you might use a definition list to show terms and their definitions. For example, in the following list, the term is listed on the first line, and then the definition is on the line below the term.

W3C

The World Wide Web Consortium was created in 1994 to develop standards and protocols for the World Wide Web.

HTML

Hypertext Markup Language is the authoring language used to create documents for the World Wide Web.

A definition list works just like this one, where you use HTML tags to identify the terms and definitions for each of the list items.

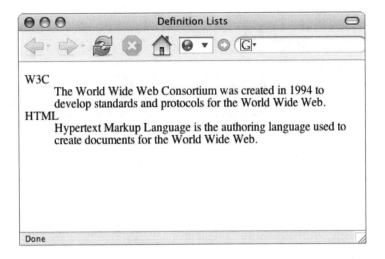

The code to create the page shown in the previous illustration looks like this:

```
<dl>
  <dt>W3C</dt>
    <dd>The World Wide Web Consortium was created in 1994 to develop
standards and protocols for the World Wide Web.</dd>
  <dt>HTML</dt>
    <dd>Hypertext Markup Language is the authoring language used to
create documents for the World Wide Web.</dd>
</dl>
```

You can use more than one dd for each dt if you need to; the browser will just simply indent each line below the dt.

 NOTE

Although it can be quite useful to use the dd tag outside a definition list as a way to indent text, this isn't valid HTML, and it can produce unpredictable results in some browsers. Because indenting text with the dd tag does the same thing as the blockquote tag, you might as well use that tag to indent a block of text.

Combine and Nest Two or More Types of Lists in a Web Page

You can also use another list inside itself or even one type of list inside another type of list. Each time you use a list inside another list, you are *nesting* lists. Perhaps the best example for nested lists is an outline like those created for a term paper.

I. Introduction

II. Part 1

    A. Description

    B. Examples

        1. Reference One

        2. Reference Two

III. Part 2

IV. Summary

Can you imagine what the HTML code would look like for the previous outline? The best solution would be to use a series of nested ordered lists as shown in the following illustration and code.

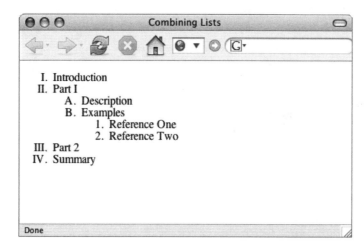

```
<ol type="I">
<li>Introduction</li>
<li>Part I
    <ol type="A">
        <li>Description</li>
        <li>Examples
        <ol type="1">
                <li>Reference One</li>
                <li>Reference Two</li>
        </ol>
        </li>
    </ol>
    </li>
<li>Part 2</li>
<li>Summary</li>
</ol>
```

As I mentioned before, you can also nest one type of list inside another type. For example, you could include a bulleted list inside a definition list to give further clarification to a definition description. Look at the following illustration and code to see what I mean.

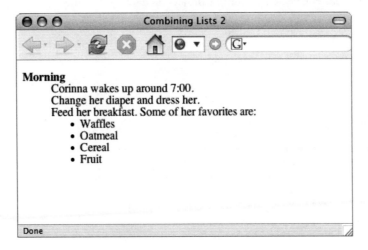

```
<dl>
<dt><b>Morning</b></dt>
    <dd>Corinna wakes up around 7:00.</dd>
    <dd>Change her diaper and dress her.</dd>
    <dd>Feed her breakfast. Some of her favorites are:
    <ul>
        <li>Waffles</li>
        <li>Oatmeal</li>
```

```
        <li>Cereal</li>
        <li>Fruit</li>
    </ul>
    </dd>
</dl>
```

TIP

The most important thing to remember when nesting lists is always to confirm that you have closed each list. If you notice a section of your nested list is indented more than it should be or continues within the list above it, try drawing semicircles from each of the list's opening and closing tags. If any of the circles cross or don't have an ending spot, you may need to recheck your work for errors.

Project 8-1 Use Lists on Your Web Page

Chop Point Summer Camp offers four different sessions each summer, each with its own different requirements for campers. In this project, you create a web page listing camp sessions and requirements. Goals for this project include

- Using an ordered list in a web page
- Using an unordered list in a web page

NOTE

All the files needed to complete the projects in this book for Chop Point can be downloaded from **www.osborne.com** or **www.wendywillard.com**. In addition, you can view my version of the web site anytime by visiting **www.choppoint.org**. Those who aren't using the Chop Point site can tailor the project to their particular needs.

Step by Step

1. Open your text/HTML editor and create a new file entitled **sessions.html**.

2. Type all the HTML tags needed for a basic web page.

3. Specify a white background color and that the entire page should use the Verdana font.

4. Type the content listed in the section (following these steps) titled *Text to Add* (or copy it from the files in the Module 8 folder of the .zip file) and format it appropriately. Therefore, what is bold in the text will become bold in the web page, and so forth.

5. Format the top headline as a Level 1 header.

6. Format the list of sessions as an ordered list using Roman numerals.

7. Format the session requirements lists as unordered lists.

8. Link the phrase "trip program" in the first and second session details to "trips.html".

9. Link the words "email" in the last paragraph to the e-mail address: camp@choppoint.org.

10. Save the file.

11. Open your web browser and choose File | Open Page (or Open File or Open, depending on the browser you're using). Locate the file sessions.html that you just saved. Make sure the file appears as you intended.

12. If you need to make changes, return to your text editor to do so. After making any changes, save the file and switch back to the browser. Choose Refresh or Reload to preview the changes you just made. If you're using the Chop Point site, you can compare your files to the following code and Figure 8-1.

```
<!DOCTYPE html PUBLIC "-//W3C//DTD XHTML 1.0 Transitional//EN"
"http://www.w3.org/TR/xhtml1/DTD/transitional.dtd">
<html>
<head>
<title> Chop Point Summer Camp Sessions </title>
<style type="text/css">
body {background-color: white;
      font-family: verdana;}
.contact {font-weight: bold;}
</style>
</head>
<body>
<h1>Chop Point Summer Camp Sessions</h1>
<p>Each summer, Chop Point holds a total of four camp sessions from June to
August. We have spaces for 40 boys and 40 girls during each session. Additional
```

(continued)

8

Creating Lists

Project
8-1

Use Lists on Your Web Page

```
details such as session length and camper ages are listed below:</p>
<ol type="I"><li>KIDS KAMP</li>
    <ul><li>Traditional overnight residential camping program</li>
    <li>Five days, four nights</li>
    <li>Just for kids ages 8-12* who reside in the state of Maine</li>
    <li>Usually held during the third week of June</li>
    </ul>
<li>COMMUNITY PROGRAM</li>
    <ul><li>Traditional overnight residential camping program</li>
    <li>Five days, four nights</li>
    <li>Just for teens ages 12*-18 who reside in the state of Maine</li>
    <li>Usually held during the last full week of June</li>
    </ul>
<li>FIRST SESSION</li>
    <ul><li>Traditional overnight residential camping program plus an
adventurous <a href="trips.html">trip program</a></li>
    <li>Three weeks</li>
    <li>For teens ages 12-18 from all over the world</li>
    <li>Usually held the first three weeks in July</li>
    </ul>
<li>SECOND SESSION</li>
    <ul><li>Traditional overnight residential camping program plus an
adventurous <a href="trips.html">trip program</a></li>
    <li>Three weeks</li>
    <li>For teens ages 12-18 from all over the world</li>
    <li>Usually held the last week of July and the first two weeks in
August</li>
    </ul>
</ol>
<p>Campers can stay for a minimum of three weeks, or, by attending both
three-week sessions, a maximum of six weeks. In order to ensure that English
is the primary language spoken, we limit the number of French-speaking campers
to 12 per session. The same is true for other nationalities (no more than 12
Spanish speaking, etc.). Spaces for foreign campers fill quickly, so we
recommend signing up as early as possible.</p>
<p>*<em>Local campers who are 12 must choose one program to attend (Kids Kamp
or Community Program) but may not attend both local programs</em>.</p>
<p class="contact">If you are interested in attending a session, please <a
href="mailto:camp@choppoint.org">e-mail</a> us or call 207-443-5860.</p>
</body>
</html>
```

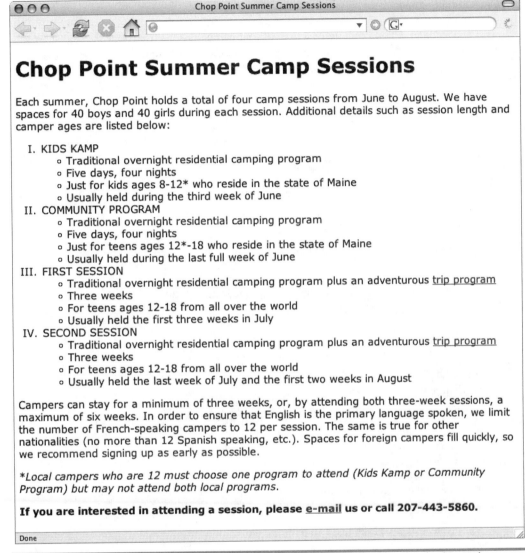

Figure 8-1 If you're using the Chop Point site, you should have a page that looks similar to this.

Text to Add

The following paragraphs (mentioned previously in step 4) should be added to your web page. The text is also included in the .zip file available from the Osborne web site.

(continued)

Chop Point Summer Camp Sessions

Each summer, Chop Point holds a total of four camp sessions from June to August. We have spaces for 40 boys and 40 girls during each session. Additional details such as session length and camper ages are listed below:

I. KIDS KAMP

- Traditional overnight residential camping program
- Five days, four nights
- Just for kids ages 8-12* who reside in the state of Maine
- Usually held during the third week of June

II. COMMUNITY PROGRAM

- Traditional overnight residential camping program
- Five days, four nights
- Just for teens ages 12*-18 who reside in the state of Maine
- Usually held during the last full week of June

III. FIRST SESSION

- Traditional overnight residential camping program plus an adventurous trip program
- Three weeks
- For teens ages 12-18 from all over the world
- Usually held the first three weeks in July

IV. SECOND SESSION

- Traditional overnight residential camping program plus an adventurous trip program
- Three weeks
- For teens ages 12-18 from all over the world
- Usually held the last week of July and the first two weeks in August

Campers can stay for a minimum of three weeks, or, by attending both three-week sessions, a maximum of six weeks. In order to ensure that English is the primary language spoken, we limit the number of French-speaking campers to 12 per session. The same is true for other nationalities (no more than 12 Spanish speaking, etc.). Spaces for foreign campers fill quickly, so we recommend signing up as early as possible.

Local campers who are 12 must choose one program to attend (Kids Kamp or Community Program) but may not attend both local programs.

If you are interested in attending a session, please <u>e-mail</u> us or call 207-443-5860.

Project Summary

Ordered and unordered lists can be great ways to draw attention to important information on your page. This project gave you practice using each type of list, in preparation for using them on your own web pages.

TIP

Is the text after your list indented? If so, check to make sure you closed your lists with the proper ending tag (`</ol>` or `</ul>`). For more tips, see Appendix C.

CRITICAL SKILL

8.5 Style Lists

While there is no style sheet property for actually *creating* lists—that's still done with HTML, as you just learned—there are three properties that can be particularly useful in formatting lists. Table 8-2 provides details. Note that all three properties can only be used to format lists, and no other HTML elements. Finally, each property is recognized only by the most recent versions of the popular browsers.

Sample Property and Value	Description	Possible Values
`list-style-image: url(bullet.gif)`	Changes the appearance of the bullet by replacing it with an image.	Specify the location of the image (URL).
`list-style-position: inside`	Identifies the indentation of additional lines in list items.	Can be `inside` (lines after the first one are not indented) or `outside` (all lines in the item are indented).
`list-style-type: decimal`	Changes the appearance of the bullet or characters at the beginnings of each list item.	Can be none (no bullets), `disc`, `circle`, `square`, `decimal` (numbers), `lower-roman` (lowercase Roman numerals), `upper-roman` (uppercase Roman numerals), `lower-alpha` (lowercase letters), `upper-alpha` (uppercase letters).

Table 8-2 Style Sheet Properties for Formatting Lists

8

Creating Lists

Project
8-1

Use Lists on Your Web Page

Customize the Bullets

For example, suppose you wanted to create a list on a web page in which each item was preceded by an image of a star. You could add an image tag to the beginning of each item in a definition list to achieve this sort of thing, such as with the following code:

```
<dd><img src="star.gif" width="12" height="12" alt="star">The World Wide Web
Consortium was created in 1994</dd>
```

But what if you had 20 items in your list? Adding that long `img` tag to every list item would be tedious. A more efficient alternative is to switch to an unordered list (one with bullets, by default) and use a style sheet in the header of your page to change the regular bullet to the image of your choice. The following illustration and code show how this might work:

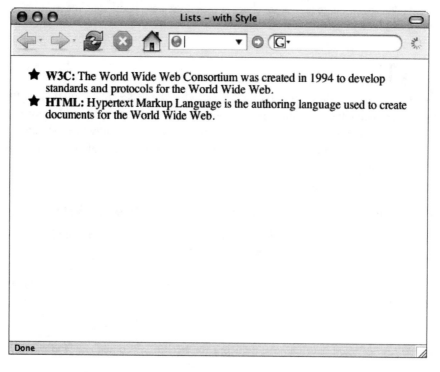

```
<style type="text/css">
li {list-style-image: url(star.gif);}
</style>
```

Customize the Layout

What if you wanted to completely change the layout of your list so it no longer looked like the typical list with bullets and indentations? In the past, web page authors have used tables (such as those created in word processing programs or spreadsheets) to hold each "item" in an irregular list. But style sheets provide an often-overlooked method of easily changing the layout of a list, whether that means simply removing the bullets and indents or going so far as to switch the whole thing from vertical to horizontal.

Vertical Navigation

Probably the most common reason for playing with the layout of a list is to use it as a navigation bar. Consider the navigation bar shown in Figure 8-2. It certainly doesn't look like a list; in fact, it looks more like a bunch of graphical buttons. There are borders separating the links, and the colors even change when you move your mouse over the links.

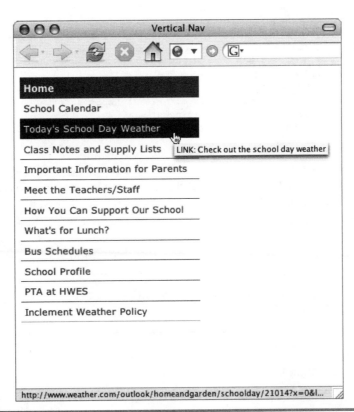

Figure 8-2 CSS made it easy to turn a boring list into a stylish navigation bar.

The actual HTML code used to create that list is shown next:

The entire list is styled according to the "navlist" class in the style sheet.

This first list item is styled as the "active" class because it's the page currently being viewed.

```html
<ul id="navlist">
<li class="active">Home</li>
<li><a title="LINK: School calendar" href="/cgi-bin/calendar/calendar.pl">School
Calendar</a></li>
<li><a title="LINK: Check out the school day weather"
href="http://www.weather.com/outlook/homeandgarden/schoolday/21014?x=0&lswe=2101
4&lswa=SchooldayIndex&y=0">Today's School Day Weather</a></li>
<li><a title="LINK: Class notes for each grade level"
href="classes/index.html">Class Notes and Supply Lists </a></li>
<li><a title="LINK: News for parents" href="info/index.html">Important
Information for Parents</a></li>
<li><a title="LINK: Meet the staff" href="staff.html">Meet the
Teachers/Staff</a></li>
<li><a title="LINK: Support the school" href="support/index.html">How You Can
Support Our School </a></li>
<li><a title="LINK: Lunch menu"
href="http://www.hcps.org/Schools/Menus/default.asp">What's for Lunch?</a></li>
<li><a title="LINK: Bus routes"
href="http://www.hcps.org/schools/bus_routes/BusRoute.asp?School=35">Bus
Schedules</a></li>
<li><a title="LINK: School profile" href="profile.html">School Profile</a></li>
<li><a title="LINK: PTA" href="pta.html">PTA at HWES</a></li>
<li><a title="LINK: Inclement weather news"
href="http://www.hcps.org/Schools/content/InclementWeatherPolicy.asp">Inclement
Weather Policy</a></li>
</ul>
```

Notice how the HTML for the list looks the same as the lists previously created in the beginning of this module. In fact, every bit of the formatting is achieved through the style sheet, which looks like this:

This style declaration specifies that all the text on the page should display in the Verdana font at 10 points.

```css
<style type="text/css">
body {
    font-family:Verdana, Arial, Helvetica, sans-serif;
    font-size: 10pt;
    }

#navlist {
    width: 250px;
    padding-left: 0;
    margin-left: 0;
    border-bottom: 1px solid #cccccc;
    }
```

This defines the characteristics of the navlist section of the page, specifying the width of the buttons (250 pixels), and the bottom edge.

```
#navlist li {
      list-style: none;
      border-top: 1px solid #666666;
      line-height: 200%;
}
```

This defines how each list item within the navlist section should appear, by removing the bullets and indentation, then adding a border of separation between each item. The line-height property allows for some breathing room around each item.

```
#navlist li a {
      color: #990000;
      display: block;
      padding-left: 5px;
      text-decoration: none;
}
```

This defines how each link within those list items should be formatted. The `display: block` line is important to ensure the background-color runs the entire width of the button.

```
#navlist li a:hover {
      color: #ffffff;
      background-color: #333333;
}
```

This defines the rollovers for each link in the list, changing the text color and the background color.

```
.active {
      background-color: #990000;
      color: #ffffff;
      font-weight: bold;
      padding-left: 5px;
}
```

This defines how the button should display when it lists the currently displayed page.

```
</style>
```

Horizontal Navigation

What if you wanted to display the navigation bar horizontally across the page instead of vertically down the page? The reason lists run down the page by default is that they are block-level elements in HTML. As mentioned previously, block-level elements automatically fill the available space.

With that in mind, we can easily make a list display horizontally by specifying it should be displayed as an *inline* element instead of a block-level element with `display: inline`. Figure 8-3 shows a very basic unordered list, with a style sheet applied to turn it into a horizontal navigation bar. The list code looks like the following:

```
<ul id="navlist">
<li class="active">Home</li>
<li><a title="LINK: About Us" href="aboutus.html">About Us</a></li>
<li><a title="LINK: Services" href="services.html">Services</a></li>
<li><a title="LINK: Clients" href="clients.html">Clients</a></li>
<li><a title="LINK: Contact Us" href="contactus.html">Contact
Us</a></li>
</ul>
```

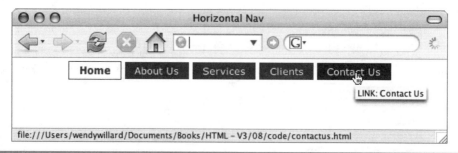

Figure 8-3 Changing the list from block-level to inline allows the items to run horizontally across the page.

And the style sheet looks like that shown next:

```
<style type="text/css">
body {
    font-family:Verdana, Arial, Helvetica, sans-serif;
    font-size: 10pt;
    }

#navlist {
    margin: 0;
    padding: 0;
    text-align: center;
    }

#navlist li {
    list-style: none;
    display: inline;
    }

#navlist li a {
    color: #fff;
    background-color: #900;
    padding: .2em 1em;
    text-decoration: none;
    }

#navlist li a:hover {
    color: #ffffff;
    background-color: #333333;
    }
```

Here, I turn off the bullets and tell the browser to display the list inline (one after another, horizontally across the page).

This specifies how the links in each list item should look.

This specifies how the colors should change when the user rolls over each link in the list item.

```
.active {
    border: 1px solid #900;
    color: #900;
    font-weight: bold;
    padding: .2em 1em;
    }
</style>
```

The final declaration styles the "active" button, by giving it a red border and bold, red text.

Project 8-2 Style Lists Within Your Web Page

In this project, we'll use style sheets to customize the lists created in Project 8-1. Goals for this project include

- Stylizing the bullet in an unordered list
- Creating an inline list for navigational purposes

Step by Step

1. Open your text or HTML editor and return to the sessions.html file saved from the previous project.

2. Replace the Roman numerals in the ordered list with one of the graphical bullets included in the .zip file for this module, such as `star.gif`. (HINT: Try using `ol>li` as your selector, to tell the browser only to use the star for list items *within the ordered list* on your page, not *all the list items* on the page.)

3. Add a new division at the bottom of the page, and call it **navigation**.

4. Create an unordered list in that division, with the following list items:

   - Home
   - Camp Sessions
   - Adventure Trips

5. Link "Home" to the index.html page you've created.

6. Link "Adventure Trips" to the trips.html page you've created.

7. Specify that "Camp Sessions" should use the "active" class in your style sheet.

8. Add the appropriate style declarations to your style sheet to make the list in the navigation division display as a horizontal navigation bar.

9. Turn off the underlines for the links in the navigation bar.

(continued)

10. Continue adding style sheet properties to format the list items with a 1-pixel, solid, black border.

11. Create a class called "active" and give that class a gray background color.

12. Save the file.

13. Open your web browser and choose File | Open Page (or Open File or Open, depending on the browser you're using). Locate the file you just saved. Make sure the file appears as you intended.

14. If you need to make changes, return to your text editor to do so. After making any changes, save the file and switch back to the browser. Choose Refresh or Reload to preview the changes you just made. If you're using the Chop Point site, you can compare your files to the following code and Figure 8-4.

```
<!DOCTYPE html PUBLIC "-//W3C//DTD XHTML 1.0 Transitional//EN"
"http://www.w3.org/TR/xhtml1/DTD/transitional.dtd">
<html>
<head>
<title> Chop Point Summer Camp Sessions </title>
<style type="text/css">
body {
    background-color: white;
    font-family: verdana;}
.contact {
    font-weight: bold;}
ol>li {
    list-style-image: url(star.gif);}
#navigation ul {
    margin: 0;
    padding: 0;}
#navigation li {
    display: inline;
    list-style: none;
    border: 1px solid black;
    padding: 0em .6em 0em .6em;}
#navigation li a {
    text-decoration: none;}
.active {
    background-color: #ccc;}
</style>
</head>
<body>
... the code between these sections stays the same ...
<div id="navigation">
<ul><li><a href="index.html" title="LINK: Return home">Home</a></li>
<li class="active">Camp Sessions</li>
<li><a href="trips.html" title="LINK: Camp adventure trips">Adventure
```

```
        Trips</a></li>
        </ul>
        </div>
        </body>
        </html>
```

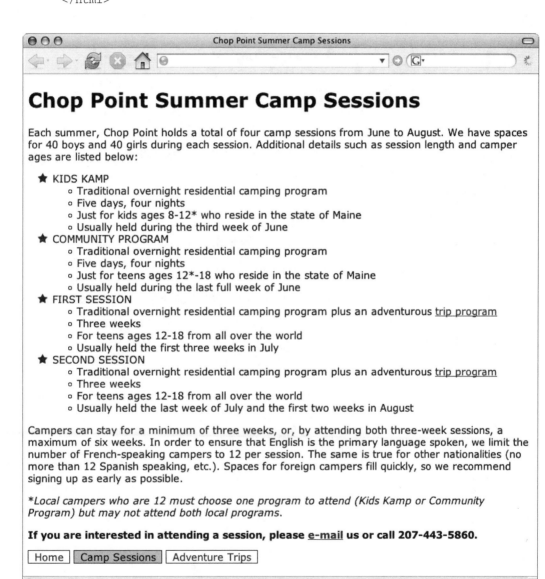

Figure 8-4 If you're using the Chop Point site, your camp sessions page should look similar to this page.

(continued)

Project Summary

Style sheets make it very easy to turn simple lists into elegant navigation bars. This project gave you practice working the various style sheet properties used to do just that.

Module 8 Mastery Check

1. What's the difference between an unordered list and an ordered list?

2. Which tag is used to enclose list items in both ordered and unordered lists?

3. You created an unordered list with four list items. All the content following the fourth list item that should be normal text is indented under the list. What is the most likely cause of this problem?

4. Which HTML attribute changes the numbering style of a list?

5. True/False: You can use more than one dd tag for each dt tag.

6. Which HTML attribute changes the starting letter or number for a list?

7. Fill in the blank: When displayed in a browser, each item in an unordered list is preceded by a _____, by default.

8. Fix the following code.

```
<dl>
    <dd>HTML</dd>
    <dt>Hypertext Markup Language is the authoring language used to
create documents for the World Wide Web.</dt>
</dl>
```

9. Add the appropriate code to turn the following text into an ordered list.

```
<html>
<head>
    <title>My favorite fruits</title>
</head>
<body>

        My favorite fruits, in order of preference, are:

        Raspberries
```

```
        Strawberries

        Apples

</body>
</html>
```

10. Add the appropriate code to cause each item in the following list to be preceded by square bullets.

```
<html>
<head>
    <title>My favorite colors</title>
</head>
<body>

        My favorite colors, in no particular order, are:

        Red

        Blue

        Green

</body>
</html>
```

11. Fill in the blank: The dl tag stands for _____.

12. True/False: When you nest unordered lists, the bullet style remains unchanged.

13. What value is used with the display property to change a list from vertical to horizontal?

14. How can you change a list from using Arabic numbers to lowercase letters?

15. Which CSS property is used to replace the standard bullet in a list with an image?

Module 9

Using Tables

At this point in the book, you've made it through the majority of the basic tags used to create web pages. The next few modules deal with content that can seem a bit more complicated than what you just learned. Don't worry, though, because even the pros struggle with these concepts when they first start (myself included).

CRITICAL SKILL
9.1 # Understand the Concept and Uses of Tables in Web Pages

Even though you might not recognize the terminology, you have undoubtedly seen tables in other printed or electronic documents. In fact, throughout the course of this book, I've used tables to give order to certain sections that might otherwise be confusing. Quite simply, a *table* is a section of information, broken up into columns and/or rows of blocks, called *cells*.

Those of you who use Microsoft Word may be familiar with a menu item in that program called Table that enables you to create tables just like those used in web pages. Microsoft's word processor isn't the only one with tables. Most word processors are capable of letting you format content in tables.

TIP

When considering whether or not to use a table in a web page, first think of how you'd present that same information in a standard word processing program. If you'd use a table in the word processor, you likely should use one in your web page as well. If not, consider another method of presenting that information in your web page.

Another form of a table, either printed or electronic, is the spreadsheet. Along these lines, you might think about a table as a large piece of grid paper, where you get to decide the size of the cells that will hold the information.

To make decisions about how large or small your cells and table should be, you need to do a little planning. Even though HTML tables are created in digital documents, the best way to plan out tables is to use a pencil and paper when you're first learning. As you become more familiar with the structure of a table, you may be able to plan it in your head without first drawing it.

Let's first consider what a table would look like for a simple tic-tac-toe game.

1. Draw a large box on your piece of paper.

2. Divide that box into three columns and three rows.

3. Place an *X* or an *O* in each of the boxes, leaving no boxes empty.

Following these steps will probably get you a piece of paper with a drawing similar to mine.

O	X	O
X	O	X
X	O	X

Now, imagine you want to translate this tic-tac-toe game into a web page. How would you do that? You've already learned that in HTML, you cannot simply tab over to the next column and type an *X* as you might in a spreadsheet application. You can, however, use a table to lay out the tic-tac-toe game's structure.

CRITICAL SKILL
9.2 Create a Basic Table Structure

First, decide how large you want your table, or in this case, how large you want your tic-tac-toe game. Remember, pixels are the units of measure on the screen; inches or centimeters won't get you far in HTML. In the beginning, it'll probably be useful for you to write out your measurements on your drawings. Don't worry, though. Nothing you're doing now is set in stone. You'll be able to make changes later as needed.

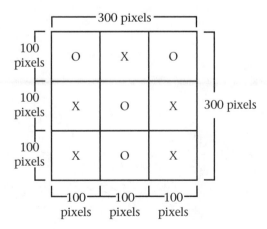

After planning out the dimensions of the table, it's time to get started working on the table structure in HTML.

Table Structure

You need to know about four basic table tags, as described next:

`<table>` `</table>`	The `table` tag is a container for every other tag used to create a table in HTML. The opening and closing `table` tags should be placed at the beginning and end of your table.
`<tr>` `</tr>`	The `tr` tag stands for table row. The opening and closing `tr` tags surround the cells for that row.
`<th>` `</th>`	The `th` tag stands for table header. An optional tag used instead of the `td` tag, this tag defines a cell containing header information. By default, the content in header cells is bolded and centered.
`<td>` `</td>`	The `td` tag stands for table data and holds the actual content for the cell. There's an opening and closing `td` tag for each cell in each row.

With these tags in mind, you can create both basic and complex table structures according to your needs. Say you want to create a basic table structure, such as the following:

Popular Girls' Names	Popular Boys' Names
Emily	Jacob
Sarah	Michael

Your code might look like that shown next:

```
<table>
<tr>
    <th>Popular Girls' Names</th>
    <th>Popular Boys' Names</th>
</tr>
<tr>
    <td>Emily</td>
    <td>Jacob</td>
</tr>
<tr>
    <td>Sarah</td>
    <td>Michael</td>
</tr>
</table>
```

NOTE

While you're not required to indent your `td` or `th` tags, I did so here to help you differentiate between table rows and cells.

Opening and closing `table` tags surround the entire section of code. This tells the browser that everything inside these tags belongs in the table. And there are opening and closing `tr` tags for each row in the table. These surround `td` or `th` tags, which, in turn, contain the actual content to be displayed by the browser.

NOTE

Some browsers show a border around each cell, by default. I discuss more about borders in the section titled "Borders."

Cell Content

You can include nearly any type of content in a table cell that you might include elsewhere on a web page. This content should be typed in between the opening and closing `td` tags for the appropriate cell. All tags used to format that content should also be included in between the `td` tags.

TIP

Want to include a blank cell with no content? Type the code for a nonbreaking space (` `) between the opening and closing `td` tags, and your cell will appear blank. If you have a lot of blank cells, you could add `empty-cells: show;` to the style declaration for your `table` tag.

If we return to our tic-tac-toe game, the following is the code for that table.

```
<table>
<tr>
    <td>O</td>
    <td>X</td>
    <td>O</td>
</tr>
<tr>
    <td>X</td>
    <td>O</td>
    <td>X</td>
</tr>
<tr>
    <td>X</td>
    <td>O</td>
    <td>X</td>
</tr>
</tr>
</table>
```

If you were to create a basic HTML page with this code, save it, and preview it in your browser, you'd see something like the following:

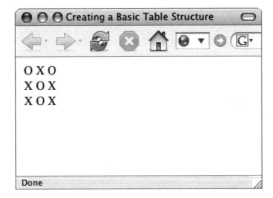

By default, the size of each cell is only as large or as small as the content of the cell. If you typed three *X*s or *O*s in each cell and added a sentence in the center cell, the table would change to look like that shown next:

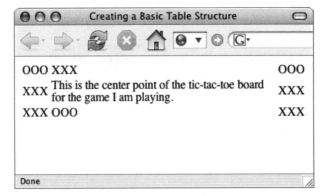

After a certain number of characters, the browser may *wrap* the content. This means it stops printing on that line and continues on the next line. This usually doesn't occur until the table runs up against another element within the page or hits the edge of the window. The default point at which the content wraps varies according to the browser.

Text

You can customize the text within each cell using the tags you learned in previous modules. For example, you can add the b tag to make the text within a cell bold.

```
<table>
<tr>
    <td>OOO</td>
    <td>XXX</td>
    <td>OOO</td>
</tr>
<tr>
    <td>XXX</td>
    <td>This is the center point of the <b>tic-tac-toe board</b> for the game I
am playing.</td>
    <td>XXX</td>
</tr>
<tr>
    <td>XXX</td>
    <td>OOO</td>
    <td>XXX</td>
</tr>
</table>
```

This text is made bold by using the b tag in the cell.

Enclosing the words "tic-tac-toe board" in the center cell with the opening and closing versions of the b tag tells the browser to make that text bold.

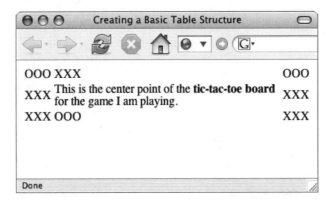

If you want to make all the text in every cell take on the same characteristics, the best solution is to use a style sheet where the td tag was the selector. For example, the style sheet in the following example can be placed in between the opening and closing head tags to change the face and size of text within all the cells created by td tags throughout the entire page.

```
<style type="text/css">
td {font-family: verdana;
    font-size: 10pt;}
</style>
```

Images

You can also add images to any of the cells in your HTML tables. To do so, add the image reference (using the img tag) inside the cell in which you want it to appear. In the following example, I used a graphic of an *O* instead of text wherever the *O* appeared in the game board.

```
<table>
<tr>
    <td><img src="images/o.gif" alt="O" width="19" height="19" /></td>
    <td>XXX</td>
    <td><img src="images/o.gif" alt="O" width="19" height="19" /></td>
</tr>
<tr>
    <td>XXX</td>
    <td><img src="images/o.gif" alt="O" width="19" height="19" /></td>
    <td>XXX</td>
</tr>
<tr>
    <td>XXX</td>
    <td><img src="images/o.gif" alt="O" width="19" height="19" /></td>
    <td>XXX</td>
</tr>
</table>
```

When viewed in the browser, the image *O*s appear where the text *O*s used to appear, as shown next:

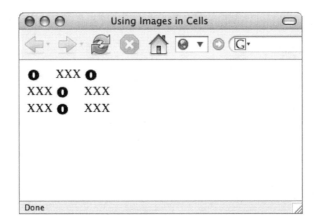

You can also combine text, images, and other types of media (such as animation, sound, and video) within table cells by drawing on many of the tags discussed in previous modules. The key is determining which elements go in which cells.

CRITICAL SKILL
9.3 Format Tables Within Web Pages

You may have noticed by now that all the text in a table appears aligned to the left side of each cell. This, and many other features of a table, can be easily customized with a few table attributes or a style sheet.

Borders

Tables, by nature of their design, have internal and external borders. By default, most browsers set the border size to zero, making them invisible. However, borders can be quite useful for tables of statistical information, for example, where it's necessary to see the columns to understand the data better. The key is understanding the three attributes related to the use of these borders.

TIP

When a table with borders is viewed in a text-based browser, the borders are represented as dashes for the horizontal borders, and as pipes (|) for the vertical borders.

NOTE

You can also use the border properties in a style sheet to format the borders of your tables, specifically the border-width, border-style, and border-color properties. See the section titled "Horizontal Rules" in Module 4 for details.

The border Attribute

Even if you ultimately want your table borders to be invisible, a great way to see how your table is shaping up while you're building it is to turn on all the table borders temporarily. You can do so by adding the `border` attribute to the `table` tag and specifying a whole number greater than zero.

```
<table border="3">
```

Changing the border size to "3" for my tic-tac-toe table lets you see more clearly where each cell begins and ends because it turns on all the internal and external borders. The larger the number you specify, the thicker the borders become.

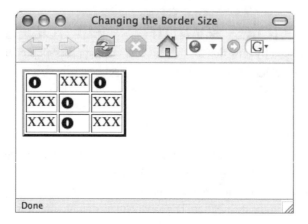

NOTE

If you don't want your borders to appear, it's best to specify border="0" in the `table` tag. That way, you're sure your borders will be invisible, even if the browser defaults to something else.

The frame Attribute

The `frame` attribute specifies which of the external borders surrounding the table will be displayed. Several possible values exist for this attribute, as described in the following table.

NOTE

This attribute was not supported by versions of Netscape prior to version 6 and versions of Internet Explorer prior to version 5.

Value	Description
void	Turns off all four sides (same as `border="0"`)
above	Turns on the top border only
below	Turns on the bottom border only
hsides	Turns on the horizontal borders (left and right) only
vsides	Turns on the vertical borders (top and bottom) only

Value	Description
lhs	Turns on the left-hand side border only
rhs	Turns on the right-hand side border only
box	Turns on all four sides (same as `border="n"`)
border	Turns on all four sides (same as `border="n"`)

You can use this attribute multiple times in a single table, so you could, for example, turn on only the top and left-hand side borders. The code to do this might look like the following.

```
<table border="2" frame="lhs" frame="above">
```

Remember, to use the `frame` attribute, the `border` attribute must be set to a whole number greater than zero.

The rules Attribute

The `rules` attribute can be used to specify those internal borders of a table that should be displayed. As with the `frame` attribute, this attribute only works if you have specified a border size greater than zero. When the `rules` attribute and the `border` attribute are both specified, the `rules` attribute takes precedence in browsers that support it.

 NOTE

This attribute was not supported by versions of Netscape prior to version 6 and versions of Internet Explorer prior to version 3.

```
<table border="1" rules="cols">
```

A value of `cols` tells the browser to display only the vertical internal borders that lie between the columns.

Several possible values exist for the `rules` attributes, as listed in the following table.

Value	Description
none	Turns off all internal borders
groups	Turns on the vertical internal borders between groups of columns and/or rows*
rows	Turns on the internal borders between rows only (horizontal)
cols	Turns on the internal borders between columns only (vertical)
all	Turns on all internal borders

*You'll learn how to designate groups of columns later in this module, in the "Group and Align Columns" section.

The following illustration shows how the browser displays the tic-tac-toe table when the rules are set to "none" and the frame is set to "box" (with a border size of 3).

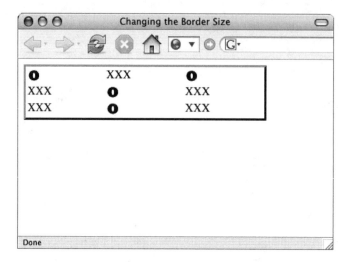

Cell Padding and Spacing

When the borders are visible for a table, it's easier to see how much space is around the content and in between the cells. Two attributes can be added to the `table` tag, so you can control those types of spaces.

- **cellpadding**   Space between the content within the cell and the edges of that cell
- **cellspacing**   Space in between each of the individual cells

First, `cellpadding` affects the amount of space between the content and the edge of the cell. When the borders are visible, increasing the cell padding can give extra *buffer space* around the text, so it doesn't run into the borders.

Second, `cellspacing` affects the amount of space between each of the cells in the table. While not located inside the actual cells, this space can be increased to allow for a gutter between multiple cells, similar to the blank space between columns in a newspaper.

The values for both of these attributes should be expressed in pixels, as a whole number greater than 0. A value of 0, in effect, turns off the cell padding or cell spacing, causing the cells to butt up against one another.

The following illustration shows two examples of different `cellpadding` and `cellspacing` values.

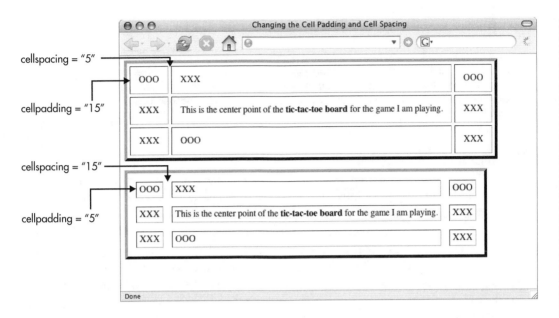

In the first table, the `border` is 5 pixels wide, the `cellpadding` is 15 pixels wide, and the `cellspacing` is 5 pixels wide. This creates a rather large buffer zone around the cell content, but a sm30
all amount of space in between each of the cells.

```
<table border="5" cellpadding="15" cellspacing="5">
```

When those values are reversed in the second table, so the `cellpadding` is 5 pixels wide and the `cellspacing` is 15 pixels wide, the space between the cells is increased while the space around the text in each cell is reduced.

```
<table border="5" cellpadding="5" cellspacing="15">
```

The latest version of the CSS specification also provides a style sheet property to alter table spacing in web pages. Specifically, the border-collapse property is useful when you need to turn off all the cell padding and cell spacing so there is no space between the cells at all. This property might be used in either of the following two ways:

- **border-collapse: collapse** Turns off all the space between the cell borders.
- **border-collapse: separate** Maintains the space between the cell borders. (Use the border-spacing property to specify exactly how much space there should be.)

TIP

For a bit more control, you can also use the padding and margin properties with style sheets to format the cell padding and spacing of tables. Note that entire tables can be styled with both the padding and margin properties, while individual cells can include padding, but no margins. Refer to the section "Quotation Blocks and Text Boxes" in Module 4 for details.

Width and Height

When I first introduced tables, I mentioned planning out the size of your tables ahead of time. This is particularly important if the table you are creating needs to fit within a predetermined amount of space on your page. In "the old days," we used `height` and `width` attributes in the `table` tag to specify the desired dimensions for tables. While that practice is frowned upon by the W3C now, you can still achieve the same results by adding the height and width properties to your style sheet. If you don't specify them in your code, the browser chooses the size based on the amount of content within each cell and the amount of available space in the window.

Let's say I want to include that tic-tac-toe game in my web page, but I only had an available space on my page that measured 200 pixels wide by 200 pixels high. Because tables have a tendency to "grow" according to the amount of content in them, I might want to restrict the height and width of my table, to avoid it growing out of that 200×200–pixel area I designated for it. I could do so by specifying the dimensions in my style sheet. Provided there was only one `table` tag on my page, I could even use `table` as my selector.

```
table {width: 200px; height: 200px; border: 3px solid black;}
```

NOTE

If there were multiple tables on my page, I could style each one independently by adding the `class` attribute to each `table` tag, and then styling the classes uniquely in my style sheet.

In this case, I would specify an *absolute size* for my table, one that shouldn't change if the browser window were larger or smaller.

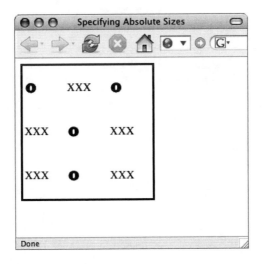

On the other hand, if I didn't care about the exact measurements of my table, but I only wanted it to take up 50 percent of the window and no more, I could use a percentage in the value of those attributes.

```
table {width: 50%; height: 50%; border: 3px solid black;}
```

This is called *relative sizing* because I'm not specifying absolute pixel dimensions but, instead, sizes that are relative to the browser window opening. Compare the next two illustrations to see how, with relative sizing, the table size varies according to the window size.

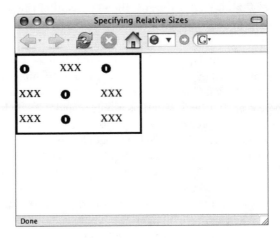

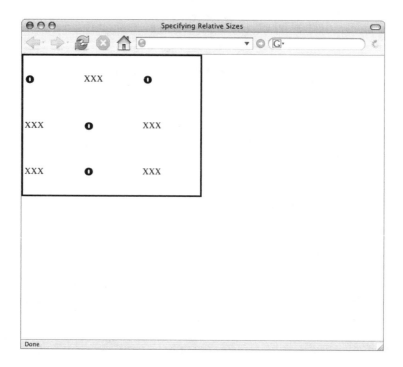

Ask the Expert

Q: **Wait! When I try that, my table doesn't fill 50 percent of the screen vertically, only horizontally!**

A: If you're following along by typing these code examples into your own HTML editor and then viewing the pages in your own browser, you likely hit a snag when trying to duplicate my example of a table set to 50 percent of the browser window's height. Never fear—there is an explanation for this problem, and it lies in how the browser actually defines what 100 percent of the height is.

You see, when you specify that the table should be 50 percent, the browser reads that as "50% of the parent object." In this case, the parent object is the HTML page itself. Because HTML pages aren't block-level elements, they don't automatically fill all the available space. This causes a dilemma if you want your table to fill half the screen, especially when the browser thinks the "screen" stops as soon as your page content does.

The solution is to add a simple bit of code to your style sheet to force the browser to behave like a block-level element, or rather to fill the entire browser window, regardless of the amount of content visible.

(continued)

```
html, body {
    height:100%;
    margin: 0;
    padding: 0;
    border: none;
    }
```

Once you've done that, the `height:50%` declaration will actually work on your `table` tag!

Basic Alignment

As discussed in the previous module on images, you can use the float property to cause a table to be aligned to the right or left of any surrounding text. If only one table existed on the page, you can even use the `table` tag as your selector, like that presented next:

```
table {float: right;}
```

The following illustration shows our tic-tac-toe table aligned to the right of the window, with text flowing around it on the left.

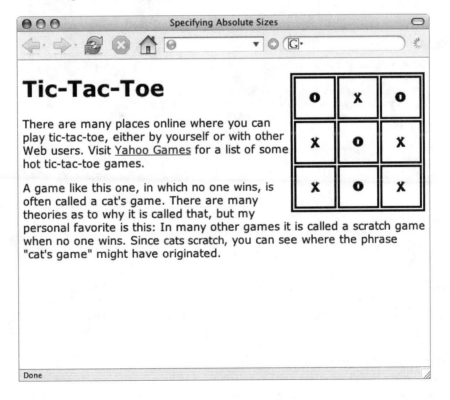

NOTE

You can also achieve a more complex alignment (such as placing a table in a specific location on the page and prohibiting it from moving) with style sheets. Module 12 discusses this more in depth.

Colors

To change the background color of an entire table, you can add the background-color property to your style sheet, using the `table` tag as the selector. The following example shows how this might look in an internal style sheet, supposing the table you're formatting is the only table on the page.

```
table {background-color: #999;}
```

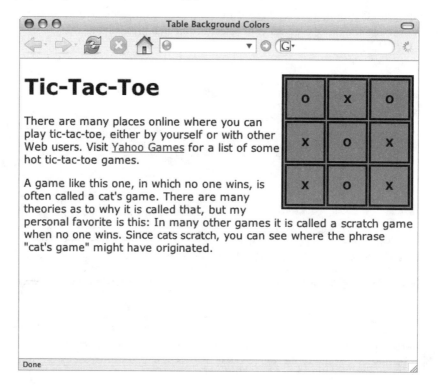

But what if you did have several tables on your page? Be aware that using the preceding code would cause all tables on the page to be rendered with the same background color. To create specific styles for each table on a page that included multiple tables, you might use classes:

```
.table1 {background-color: #999999;}
.table2 {background-color: #333333;}
```

Then, you'd reference the class name (without the period) from the opening `table` tag, as in:

```
<table class="table1">
```

Depending on which browser renders the table, the background color you specify may or may not appear within the borders. Be sure to test your pages in multiple browsers to be sure.

Background Images

The background-image property can be added to your style sheet to apply an image to the entire table background. The background-image property works the same when applied to a table as it does applied to other web page objects. This means it automatically repeats from left to right, top to bottom. However, you can use the other background properties discussed in Module 6 (such as background-repeat and background-attachment) to change the repeating options if desired.

Adding a background image is one way you could achieve a textured or patterned table background, as shown in Figure 9-1. This only requires a small repeating image, such as the following:

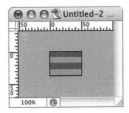

and a bit of code added to your style sheet:

```
table {background-image: url('images/stripes.gif');}
```

Captions

The `caption` tag enables you to specify captions for your tables. This isn't an attribute of the `table` tag; it's a standalone element used after the `table` tag, but before the first table row.

```
<table border="3" align="right" bgcolor="#999999">
<caption>This is a "cat's game" of tic-tac-toe.</caption>
<tr>
    <td>O</td>
    <td>X</td>
    <td>O</td>
</tr>
```

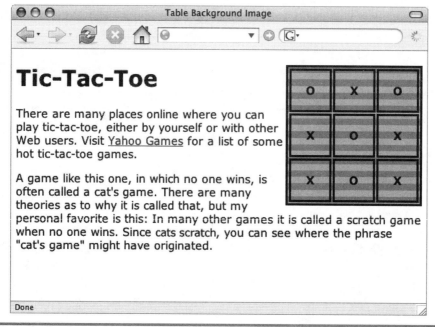

Figure 9-1 The background-image property can be added to the table to produce a patterned effect.

Opening and closing `caption` tags surround the actual text you want to display as a caption for the table. By default, the caption is aligned at the top-center of the table. Two CSS properties are useful in changing the caption alignment:

- **text-align** Use this to adjust whether the text is aligned left, right, or center on whichever side it is placed.

- **caption-side** Use this to specify on which side the caption should be placed (top, right, bottom, or left).

With those properties in mind, can you figure out how to align a caption along the bottom edge of a table, and then set the text to be right-aligned along that edge? Figure 9-2 shows a visual example, and the following code provides the answer.

```
caption {text-align: right;    caption-side: bottom;}
```

TIP

You can also use additional formatting properties to draw more attention to a caption, such as making it bold or different colors.

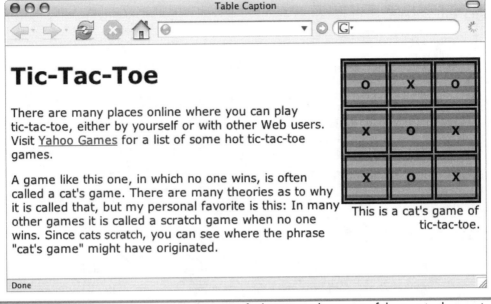

Figure 9-2 The `caption` tag is styled to specify the exact alignment of the text in the caption.

Project 9-1 Create a Basic Table

Chop Point Summer Camp keeps a table of its adventure trips to provide parents and campers with an easy way to see which trips are offered each session. You'll use the skills you just learned to add such a table to a web page. Goals for this project include

- Creating a basic table structure
- Adding text content to the table structure
- Formatting the table

NOTE

All the files needed to complete the projects in this book for Chop Point can be downloaded from **www.osborne.com** or **www.wendywillard.com**. In addition, you can view my version of the web site anytime by visiting **www.choppoint.org**. If you aren't using the Chop Point site, you can tailor the project to your particular needs.

(continued)

Step by Step

1. Open your text or HTML editor and create a new file entitled **trips-2006.html**.

2. Type all the HTML tags needed for a basic web page.

3. In your style sheet, specify the background, text, and link colors of your choice.

4. Create a table on the page, using the following table as a guideline. Note the first row is a table header row. (This text is also included in the Module09.zip file.)

Session 1	Session 2	Trip Type	Trip Duration	Trip Location
X		Canoeing	2 days	Kennebec River
X		Canoeing	4–5 days	Allagash River
	X	Canoeing	4 days	Moose River
X	X	Kayaking	2 days	Kennebec River
X	X	White Water Rafting	1 day	Kennebec River
X		Biking	3 days	Acadia National Park
	X	Mountain Biking	3 days	Carrabasset Valley
	X	Hiking	3 days	Baxter State Park
X		Hiking	3 days	Mount Washington
X	X	Sightseeing	3 days	Quebec City
X	X	Fishing	1 day	Maine Coast
	X	Whale Watching	1 day	Maine Coast
X	X	Sailing	2 days	Maine Coast

5. Specify a border size of 1.

6. Add the following Level 1 headline above the table: **Optional Adventure Trips - 2006**.

7. Add the following paragraph between the table and the headline:

> **Each summer, we schedule several optional adventure trips that campers find exciting and rewarding. The trips always provide memorable experiences. You can participate in as many or as few trips as you'd like, as long as none conflict with each other. Trips vary in length and are planned for the abilities of the participating campers.**

8. Save the file.

9. Open your web browser and choose File | Open Page (or Open File or Open, depending on the browser you're using). Locate the file you just saved. Make sure it appears as you want.

10. If you need to make changes, return to your text editor to do so. After making any changes, save the file and switch back to the browser. Choose Refresh or Reload to preview the changes you just made. If you're using the Chop Point site, you can compare your files to the following code and Figure 9-3.

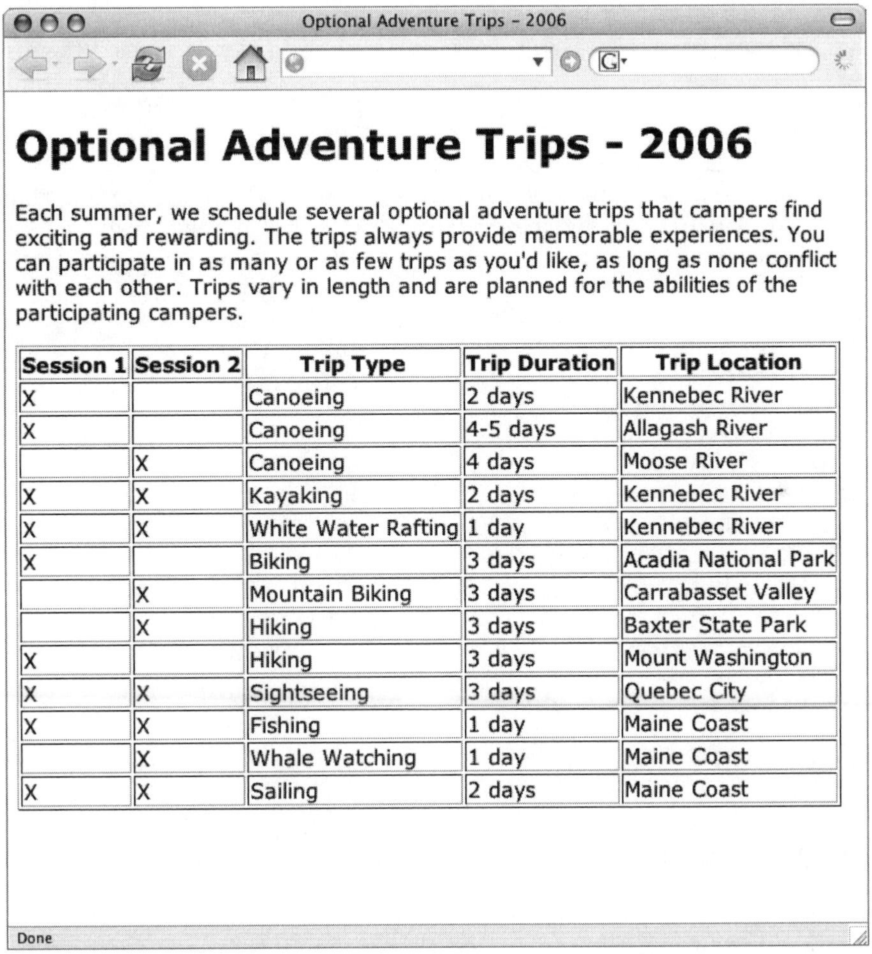

Session 1	Session 2	Trip Type	Trip Duration	Trip Location
X		Canoeing	2 days	Kennebec River
X		Canoeing	4-5 days	Allagash River
	X	Canoeing	4 days	Moose River
X	X	Kayaking	2 days	Kennebec River
X	X	White Water Rafting	1 day	Kennebec River
X		Biking	3 days	Acadia National Park
	X	Mountain Biking	3 days	Carrabasset Valley
	X	Hiking	3 days	Baxter State Park
X		Hiking	3 days	Mount Washington
X	X	Sightseeing	3 days	Quebec City
X	X	Fishing	1 day	Maine Coast
	X	Whale Watching	1 day	Maine Coast
X	X	Sailing	2 days	Maine Coast

Figure 9-3 Those using the Chop Point site should see a page similar to this one.

(continued)

NOTE

Is your table missing when you try to view the page? If so, check to make sure you have closed your `table` tag (`</table>`). For more tips, see Appendix C.

```
<!DOCTYPE html PUBLIC "-//W3C//DTD XHTML 1.0 Transitional//EN"
"http://www.w3.org/TR/xhtml1/DTD/transitional.dtd">
<html>
<head>
<title> Optional Adventure Trips - 2006  </title>
<style type="text/css">
body {font-family: verdana;
    background-color: white;}
</style>
</head>
<body>
<h1>Optional Adventure Trips - 2006</h1>
<p>Each summer, we schedule several optional adventure trips that
campers find exciting and rewarding. The trips always provide
memorable experiences. You can participate in as many or as few trips
as you'd like, as long as none conflict with each other. Trips vary in
length and are planned for the abilities of the participating
campers.</p>
<table border="1">
<tr><th>Session 1</td>
    <th>Session 2</td>
    <th>Trip Type</td>
    <th>Trip Duration</td>
    <th>Trip Location</td>
</tr>
<tr><td>X</td>
    <td></td>
    <td>Canoeing</td>
    <td>2 days</td>
    <td>Kennebec River</td>
    </tr>
<tr><td>X</td>
    <td></td>
    <td>Canoeing</td>
    <td>4-5 days</td>
    <td>Allagash River</td>
    </tr>
<tr><td></td>
    <td>X</td>
```

```
            <td>Canoeing</td>
            <td>4 days</td>
            <td>Moose River</td>
            </tr>
<tr><td>X</td>
            <td>X</td>
            <td>Kayaking</td>
            <td>2 days</td>
            <td>Kennebec River</td>
            </tr>
<tr><td>X</td>
            <td>X</td>
            <td>White Water Rafting</td>
            <td>1 day</td>
            <td>Kennebec River</td>
            </tr>
<tr><td>X</td>
            <td></td>
            <td>Biking</td>
            <td>3 days</td>
            <td>Acadia National Park</td>
            </tr>
<tr><td></td>
            <td>X</td>
            <td>Mountain Biking</td>
            <td>3 days</td>
            <td>Carrabasset Valley</td>
            </tr>
<tr><td></td>
            <td>X</td>
            <td>Hiking</td>
            <td>3 days</td>
            <td>Baxter State Park</td>
            </tr>
<tr><td>X</td>
            <td></td>
            <td>Hiking</td>
            <td>3 days</td>
            <td>Mount Washington</td>
            </tr>
<tr><td>X</td>
            <td>X</td>
            <td>Sightseeing</td>
```

(continued)

```
            <td>3 days</td>
            <td>Quebec City</td>
            </tr>
         <tr><td>X</td>
            <td>X</td>
            <td>Fishing</td>
            <td>1 day</td>
            <td>Maine Coast</td>
            </tr>
         <tr><td></td>
            <td>X</td>
            <td>Whale Watching</td>
            <td>1 day</td>
            <td>Maine Coast</td>
            </tr>
         <tr><td>X</td>
            <td>X</td>
            <td>Sailing</td>
            <td>2 days</td>
            <td>Maine Coast</td>
            </tr>
         </table>
         </body>
         </html>
```

Project Summary

Tables are used in a wide variety of ways throughout the digital and print industries. This project gave you practice creating a basic table structure, using trip details for Chop Point Summer Camp.

Progress Check

1. What tag is used to designate a new table row?

2. What tag encloses the content in a particular cell?

1. <tr>
2. <td>

Using Tables

CRITICAL SKILL
9.4 # Format Content Within Table Cells

Just as you can format the entire table, you can format each of the individual cells within the table. This means changing the alignment, width, height, and background colors, as well as restricting line breaks and spanning content across multiple columns or rows.

Alignment

If you refer to the table you created in Project 9-1, or to Figure 9-3, you may notice the alignment appears differently for some of the cells depending on how wide the browser window is open. For example, in Figure 9-3, the cells in the first row contain text that is centered, while the remaining cells in the other rows are left-aligned.

To change vertical and horizontal alignment, you can add the text-align property for horizontal alignment or the vertical-align property for vertical alignment to the `tr`, `th`, or `td` tags.

- **`tr`** Adding the text-align or vertical-align properties to the `tr` tag causes the alignment you specify to take effect for all the cells in that row.

- **`td`, `th`** Adding the text-align or vertical-align properties to the `td` or `th` tag causes the alignment you specify to take effect for only that cell.

The following table lists the possible values for these two properties when used in tables.

Property	Possible Values
text-align	left right center *string* (for example, text-align: '.' would tell the browser to align along the period, which could be useful for a column of monetary values)
vertical-align	baseline (aligns baselines of element and parent) sub (subscript) super (superscript) top (aligns top of element with tallest part of the line) text-top (aligns top of element with parent's font) text-bottom (aligns top of element with parent's bottom) bottom (aligns bottom of element with lowest part of the line) middle (aligns midpoint of element with baseline plus half the height of the letter "x" of the parent) *percentage* (relative to the element's line-height value)

NOTE

The default values for the text-align and vertical-align properties are left and middle, respectively. For header cells (using the `th` tag), however, the horizontal alignment defaults to center instead of left.

If you want to align all the cells in your table in a similar manner, it's easy to use the `td` tag as the selector in your style sheet in the following manner:

```
td {text-align: center;}
```

But what if you wanted each column of cells to be aligned differently? You could create three classes:

```
.left {text-align: left; vertical-align: top;}
.right {text-align: right; vertical-align: bottom;}
.center {text-align: center; vertical-align: middle;}
```

and then reference each class from within the appropriate `td` tag. Figure 9-4 shows the result of this type of style sheet when applied to our tic-tac-toe board.

```
<tr>
    <td class="left">O</td>
    <td class="center">X</td>
    <td class="right">O</td>
</tr>
```

Width and Height

Earlier in the module, you used the width and height properties to identify the size of the entire table. You can also specify the size of individual cells by adding those properties to your `td` or `th` tags.

TIP

This can be particularly useful if you want to have columns that are the same size, because most browsers won't make columns the same size when the width is left unspecified.

You may remember that the value of these two attributes can be either a pixel value or a percentage. This is the same regardless of what element is being sized. However, use caution when mixing pixel values with percentages because you might get unpredictable results in different browsers.

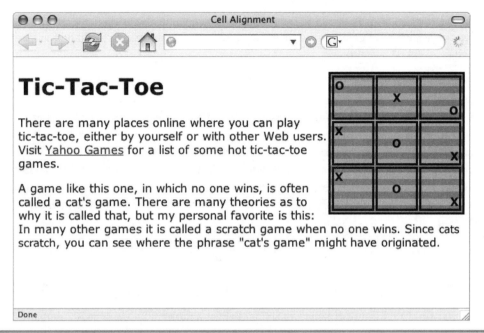

Figure 9-4 Three different classes were created to align the cells of this table in three different ways.

Look at the table in the following example. Although the table itself has a width set to 100 percent of the window opening, none of the cells have width dimensions. This leaves the decision about how wide each cell should be up to the browser.

If I want to make all three of the columns the same width, regardless of what size the browser window is, I could specify in my style sheet that each th tag should be one-third of the overall table width:

```
th {width: 33%;}
```

Then, each of the following cells in that column will have the same width (and/or height). An exception to this rule might be when one cell contains an extremely long string of text without spaces, such as "abcdefghijklmnopqrstuvwxyz". In this case, the browser may have to make that cell larger, as necessary, to accommodate the long string of text. It isn't necessary to place width properties in every cell in a column—only the first one. Again, I recommend testing your pages in multiple browsers to verify that the table appears as you intended.

Age	Height	Weight
Birth	19.5"	7 lbs. 9 oz.
6 months	25"	17 lbs. 8 oz
12 months	29.5"	22 lbs. 5 oz.

A Word About Cell Widths and Padding

One additional comment about width—while table cells don't have margins (at least not by CSS standards), they do have padding. This means if you want to have some buffer space around the content of your cells (padding), you'll need to take that into account when setting the cell widths. So, say you had enough content in one column to fill about 100 pixels in width, and you also wanted a 10-pixel padding on each side. Then you'd actually set the width of your column to 120 pixels (100 pixels of content, plus 10 pixels of padding on the left and 10 pixels of padding on the right). The style sheet might look like this:

```
td {width: 120px;
    padding: 10px;}
```

Colors

While adding the background-color property to a table style declaration lets you change the color for the entire table, using this property with the `tr`, `td`, or `th` tags lets you specify the color of a single row or cell.

```
tr {background-color: green;}
```

Coloring rows or columns in a table with different hues can be a great way to make the table more readable, particularly if it's a long table. Style sheets make it easy to create such patterns, through the use of classes. Consider the table shown in Figure 9-5. If you had to add the style declarations to each row in the table, it could become quite cumbersome as the table grew to include more rows. Instead, create the two classes in your internal or external style sheet:

```
.hilite {background-color: #ccc;}
.lolite {background-color: #999;}
```

and then reference each one in alternating rows of your table.

TIP

When naming classes, stick with names that reference the purpose of the class, as opposed to the style of the class. For example, avoid a name like "bluerow" and "orangerow" because these would become confusing if you ended up changing the colors of the rows. Instead, try "hilight" and "lolite" for alternating color rows like these.

Age	Height	Weight
Birth	19.5"	7 lbs. 9 oz.
6 months	25"	17 lbs. 8 oz
12 months	29.5"	22 lbs. 5 oz.

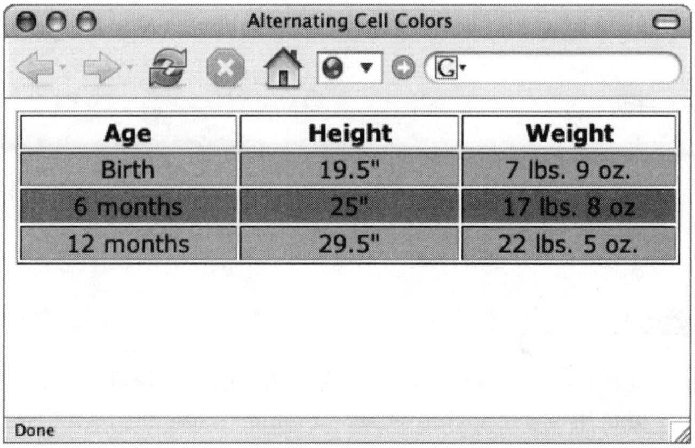

Figure 9-5 Style sheets and classes make it easy to create alternating color rows like these.

```
<tr class="hilite"><td>Birth</td>
   <td>19.5"</td>
   <td>7 lbs. 9 oz.</td>
   </tr>
<tr class="lolite"><td>6 months</td>
   <td>25"</td>
   <td>17 lbs. 8 oz</td>
   </tr>
<tr class="hilite"><td>12 months</td>
   <td>29.5"</td>
   <td>22 lbs. 5 oz.</td>
   </tr>
```

NOTE

When you include background colors for both individual cells and the entire table, the background color of the table may also show through in between the cells (in the border). However, this does vary somewhat from browser to browser. My advice to you on this topic is to test your pages in a wide number of settings to make sure you're happy with how they look under each different browser.

Prohibit Line Breaks

At times, you might have content in a cell that needs to be kept on a single line. In cases like this, you can use the white-space property with a value of "nowrap" to tell the browser to try and keep all the content in that cell on a single line if possible. (This might not be possible if the browser window is so small that the content cannot be rendered across a single line.) The style sheet might look like the following:

```
td.nowrap {
     white-space: nowrap;}
```

while the only change to the HTML table is the addition of the class reference.

```
<td class="nowrap">This content won't wrap.</td>
```

Spanning Columns

So far in this module, you have only worked with tables in a grid-like fashion where an equal number of cells are in each row and column. While this is the default, you can add an attribute to a `td` or `th` tag to cause it to merge with another cell below it (see the next illustration).

	3
These two cells have been merged so the content from the first cell flows into the second.	
4	5	6

To accomplish this, use the `colspan` attribute. By default, each cell is set to *span*, or to go across, only one column. Using the `colspan` attribute enables you to change that, so a cell spans two or more columns. The following HTML shows how you might code the previous table.

```
<table border="1">
<tr>
    <td colspan="2">These two cells have been merged so the content
from the first cell flows into the second.</td>
    <td>3</td>
</tr>
<tr>
    <td>4</td>
    <td>5</td>
    <td>6</td>
</tr>
</table>
```

Span Rows

Just as you can merge cells across two or more columns, you can merge cells across two or more rows. The attribute used to do so is `rowspan`.

If you take the table used in the previous section and merge the two cells on the right (#3 and #6) into one, the table might look like that shown next.

These two cells have been merged so the content from the first cell flows into the second.		These two cells have been merged so the content from the top one flows into the bottom one.
4	5	

Here you have two cells in the first row merged, while the third cell from the first row is merged with the third cell from the second row. The HTML used to create this table is shown in the following.

```
<table border="1">
<tr>
    <td colspan="2">These two cells have been merged so the content
from the first cell flows into the second.</td>
    <td rowspan="2">These two cells have been merged so the content
from the top one flows into the bottom one.</td>
</tr>
<tr>
    <td>4</td>
    <td>5</td>
</tr>
</table>
```

The rowspan attribute can be used by itself in a td tag to cause a cell to merge with the cell below it, or it can be combined with the colspan attribute to cause a cell to merge with both the cell below it and the one next to it.

Although the colspan and rowspan attributes give web developers a lot of power to build creative table structures, they add a degree of complexity to tables that's often difficult to grasp. Don't worry—everyone struggles with these concepts at first. If you have trouble, go back to using your pencil and paper to plan out your table structure before you type a single key.

TIP

If you have a picture in your mind of the final output of your table, draw that first. Then, go back and add the table or grid structure around the picture, placing each piece into a cell or a group of cells. This is also one of the places where a WYSIWYG HTML editor may come in handy because it enables you to see the table while you're creating it.

NOTE

CSS also gives you the ability to control columns and rows with two style sheet properties: column-span and row-span. They work quite similarly to the colspan and rowspan HTML attributes.

Progress Check

1. What style sheet property can you use to prohibit a line break in a cell?

2. Which attribute is used to merge cells across multiple columns?

Additional Formatting Techniques

HTML has additional tags geared toward helping web developers build more user-friendly tables. These tags and attributes enable you to group rows and/or columns so the browser more clearly understands the purposes of each element.

Group and Align Rows

Three tags in particular are used to group rows within tables.

- **thead** table header
- **tfoot** table footer
- **tbody** table body

When you use these tags, the browser is able to differentiate between the header and footer information, and the main content of the page. The benefit here is, when a user views a page containing a long table, the header information is repeated at the top of each page or screen view of the table, even if the table is printed. This helps users avoid wondering what column three was supposed to hold, when they are looking at page four, and the title of column three was only listed on page one.

While these three tags are never required, when they are used, each must contain at least one table row, as defined by the tr tag. In addition, if you include a thead and/or a tfoot, you must also include at least one tbody. So, a table layout using these three tags might look like this:

```
<table>
<thead>
<tr>
```

---

1. white-space: nowrap
2. colspan

```
        <th>Age</th>
        <th>Height</th>
        <th>Weight</th>
    </tr>
    </thead>
    <tfoot>
    <tr>
        <td colspan="3">Data taken from the Corinna Research Society</td>
    </tr>
    </tfoot>
    <tbody>
    <tr>
        <td>Birth</td>
        <td>19.5 inches</td>
        <td>7 lbs. 9 oz.</td>
    </tr>
    <tr>
        <td>6 m.</td>
        <td>25 inches</td>
        <td>17 lbs. 8 oz.</td>
    </tr>
    <tr>
        <td>12 m.</td>
        <td>29.5 inches</td>
        <td>22 lbs. 5 oz.</td>
    </tr>
    </tbody>
    </table>
```

An additional benefit of using these tags is that it helps make styling the table easier. For example, suppose you wanted to format the data rows of your table in one way, the header in a different way, and the footer in yet another fashion. As long as the `thead`, `tbody`, and `tfoot` tags are in place, you only need to reference those tags in your style sheet to do so. Figure 9-6 shows how the previous code would be viewed in a browser when the following style sheet is also included:

```
body {font-family: verdana;}
thead {background-color: black;
    color: white;}
tbody {background-color: #ccc;}
tfoot {font-size: 10pt;
    font-style: italic;}
```

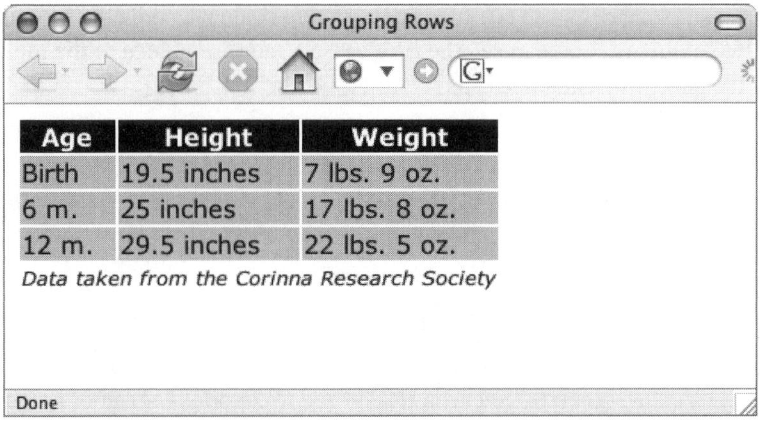

Age	Height	Weight
Birth	19.5 inches	7 lbs. 9 oz.
6 m.	25 inches	17 lbs. 8 oz.
12 m.	29.5 inches	22 lbs. 5 oz.

Data taken from the Corinna Research Society

Figure 9-6 When you use the `thead`, `tbody`, and `tfoot` tags, styling table rows becomes a snap.

Group and Align Columns

Along the same lines, you can group columns together with the `col` and `colgroup` elements. Browsers that understand these tags can then render the table incrementally, instead of all at once. This causes long tables to load more quickly than they might otherwise. In addition, using `colgroups` enables you to apply styles and characteristics to entire sections of columns, as opposed to doing so individually.

TIP

Simply stated, the `colgroup` and `col` tags are ways to pass information about structure and style on to the browser in the beginning of the table in order to help render it.

The opening and closing `colgroup` tags enclose one or more columns in the group, and can dictate how those columns should be rendered. This means you can use the `colgroup` tag as a selector in your style sheet to format all the columns in that group the same way. You can also add the `span` attribute to this tag to tell the browser how many columns should be included in the group.

NOTE

If you had both `colgroups` and `theads`, the `colgroups` would be placed before the `theads` in your table structure.

In this example, the first `colgroup` contains five columns, while the second `colgroup` contains two columns. You can see the `colgroup` tags are placed at the top of the table, before all the table rows and table cells.

```
<table border="1">
<colgroup span="5" id="group1"></colgroup>
<colgroup span="2" id="group2"></colgroup>
<tr>
    <td>
```

Each `colgroup` in this example also has an ID assigned: group1 and group2. If you make formatting specifications in the corresponding ID style declaration, they take effect for all the columns in that group. If you need to alter the width or alignment of specific columns in the group, you then only have to make the change once in the style sheet. The following shows what a style sheet might look like to make all the columns in group1 be 50 pixels in width, while those in group2 are 25 pixels wide.

```
colgroup#group1 {width:50px;}
colgroup#group2 {width:25px}
```

This tells the browser to look for a `colgroup` with an ID name of group1, and then apply the corresponding style to it.

In the following example, the group of five columns has each column set to be 75 pixels wide. However, the fourth column (denoted with the `class="col4"` attribute) has that width overridden and reset to 25 pixels. By default, text alignment is left. The last column (col5) is the only one to have a background color.

```
<style type="text/css">
colgroup#tuition {width: 75px;}
colgroup col#books {width: 25px;}
colgroup col#total {background-color: yellow;}
</style>
</head>
<body>
<table border=1>
<colgroup span="5" id="tuition">
    <col id="year"></col>
    <col id="base"></col>
    <col id="roomboard"></col>
    <col id="books">
    <col id="total">
</colgroup>
<tr>
    <td>
```

NOTE

As of this writing (CSS 2.1), the only aspects of `cols` or `colgroups` that can be styled are borders, background, width, and visibility. Unfortunately, this means you can't use a `colgroup` to adjust the alignment of all the cells in that column (wouldn't that be nice!). The only way to do that is to add a class to each cell you want to style, and then use the text-align property with that class in your style sheet.

Whether used in the `colgroup` or `col` tag, column width can be specified as demonstrated in the following table.

Value	Description	Example
pixels	Sets the width of each column in pixel dimensions	colgroup {width: 50px;} col {width: 20px;}
percentages	Sets the width of each column in percentages, relative to the size of the entire table	colgroup {width: 50%;} col {width: 10%;}

Project 9-2 Format Cell Content

Returning to the timeline.html page you began in Project 9-1, let's format some of the individual cells and add a horizontal rule that spans the entire width of the table. Goals for this project include

- Changing the alignment of content within table cells
- Causing a cell to span across multiple columns

NOTE

All the files needed to complete the projects in this book for Chop Point can be downloaded from **www.osborne.com** or **www.wendywillard.com**. In addition, you can view my version of the web site anytime by visiting **www.choppoint.org**. Those of you who aren't using the Chop Point site can tailor the project to your particular needs.

Step by Step

1. Open your text or HTML editor and open the file trips-2006.html created in Project 9-1.

2. Add a new row at the very top of the table.

(continued)

3. Add **Sessions** and **Trip Details** to the first row and format it to display like the following:

SESSIONS		TRIP DETAILS		
1st	2nd	Type	Duration	Location

4. Add a background color behind the first two rows (whichever color you choose).

5. Create two column groups—one for the first two columns, and one for the last three columns.

6. Assign IDs to each column so you can reference them from your style sheet.

7. Style the first column to have a colored background.

8. Style the second column to have a different colored background.

9. Style the table header rows to have a very dark background color with white (or very light) text.

10. Add a four-pixel padding to the table cells for a bit of buffer space around the content.

11. Adjust the border to display only the outside box around the table, and the horizontal lines between each row (but not the vertical lines between the columns).

12. Save the file.

13. Open your web browser and choose File | Open Page (or Open File or Open, depending on the browser you're using). Locate the file you just saved. Make sure the file appears as you intended it.

14. If you need to make changes, return to your text editor to do so. After making any changes, save the file and switch back to the browser. Choose Refresh or Reload to preview the changes you just made. If you're using the Chop Point site, you can compare your files to the following code and Figure 9-7.

NOTE

Feel free to experiment with other types of formatting as you see fit for your particular table design.

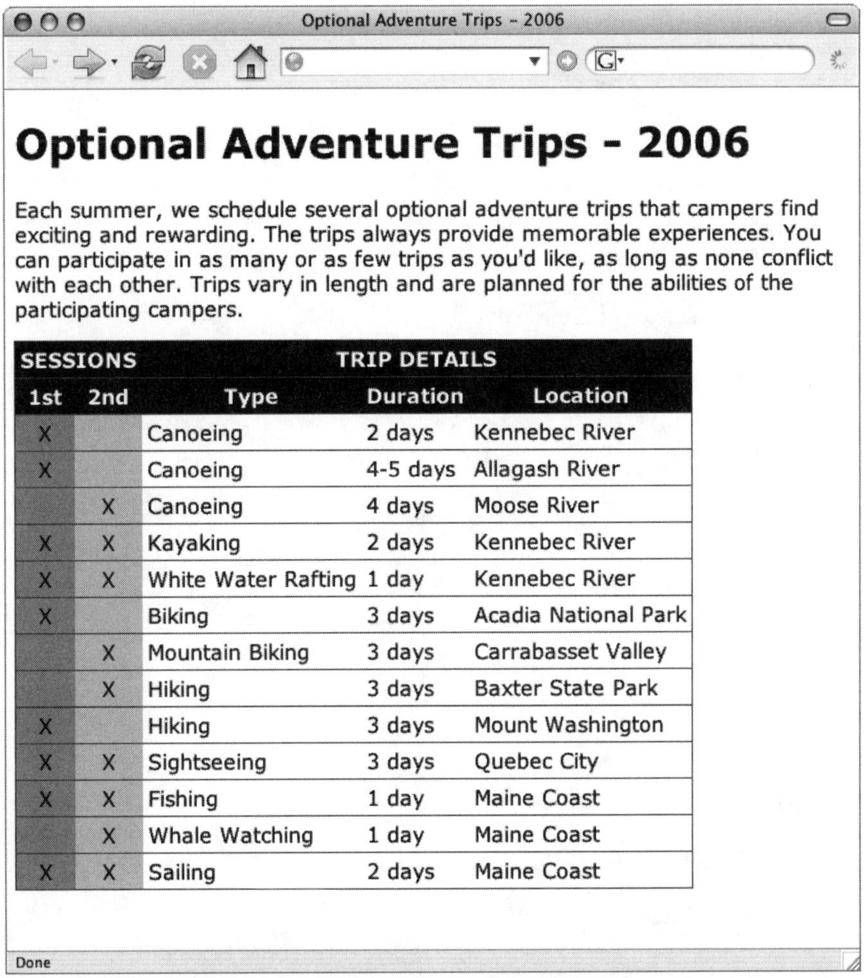

Optional Adventure Trips - 2006

Each summer, we schedule several optional adventure trips that campers find exciting and rewarding. The trips always provide memorable experiences. You can participate in as many or as few trips as you'd like, as long as none conflict with each other. Trips vary in length and are planned for the abilities of the participating campers.

SESSIONS		TRIP DETAILS		
1st	2nd	Type	Duration	Location
X		Canoeing	2 days	Kennebec River
X		Canoeing	4-5 days	Allagash River
	X	Canoeing	4 days	Moose River
X	X	Kayaking	2 days	Kennebec River
X	X	White Water Rafting	1 day	Kennebec River
X		Biking	3 days	Acadia National Park
	X	Mountain Biking	3 days	Carrabasset Valley
	X	Hiking	3 days	Baxter State Park
X		Hiking	3 days	Mount Washington
X	X	Sightseeing	3 days	Quebec City
X	X	Fishing	1 day	Maine Coast
	X	Whale Watching	1 day	Maine Coast
X	X	Sailing	2 days	Maine Coast

Done

Figure 9-7 If you're working on the Optional Adventure Trips page for Chop Point, it might display like this one in the Firefox browser. (IE and other browsers sometimes display the `frame` and `rules` attribute values differently.)

```
<!DOCTYPE html PUBLIC "-//W3C//DTD XHTML 1.0 Transitional//EN"
"http://www.w3.org/TR/xhtml1/DTD/transitional.dtd">
<html>
<head>
```

(continued)

```
<title> Optional Adventure Trips - 2006  </title>
<style type="text/css">
body {font-family: verdana;
    background-color: white;}
th {background-color: black;
    color: white;
    padding: 4px;}
td {padding: 4px;}
#first {background-color: #999;}
#second {background-color: #ccc;}
.center {text-align: center;}
.uppercase {text-transform: uppercase;}
</style>
</head>
<body>
<h1>Optional Adventure Trips - 2006</h1>
<p>Each summer, we schedule several optional adventure trips that
campers find exciting and rewarding. The trips always provide
memorable experiences. You can participate in as many or as few trips
as you'd like, as long as none conflict with each other. Trips vary in
length and are planned for the abilities of the participating
campers.</p>

<table rules="rows" frame="box">
<colgroup id="sessions">
    <col id="first"></col>
    <col id="second"></col>
</colgroup>
<colgroup id="trip-details">
    <col id="type"></col>
    <col id="duration"></col>
    <col id="location"></col>
<tr class="uppercase"><th colspan="2">Sessions</th>
    <th colspan="3">Trip Details</th>
    </tr>
<tr><th>1st</td>
    <th>2nd</td>
    <th>Type</td>
    <th>Duration</td>
    <th>Location</td>
</tr>
<tr><td class="center">X</td>
    <td class="center"></td>
    <td>Canoeing</td>
    <td>2 days</td>
    <td>Kennebec River</td>
```

```
</tr>
<tr><td class="center">X</td>
    <td class="center"></td>
    <td>Canoeing</td>
    <td>4-5 days</td>
    <td>Allagash River</td>
</tr>
<tr><td class="center"></td>
    <td class="center">X</td>
    <td>Canoeing</td>
    <td>4 days</td>
    <td>Moose River</td>
</tr>
<tr><td class="center">X</td>
    <td class="center">X</td>
    <td>Kayaking</td>
    <td>2 days</td>
    <td>Kennebec River</td>
</tr>
<tr><td class="center">X</td>
    <td class="center">X</td>
    <td>White Water Rafting</td>
    <td>1 day</td>
    <td>Kennebec River</td>
</tr>
<tr><td class="center">X</td>
    <td class="center"></td>
    <td>Biking</td>
    <td>3 days</td>
    <td>Acadia National Park</td>
</tr>
<tr><td class="center"></td>
    <td class="center">X</td>
    <td>Mountain Biking</td>
    <td>3 days</td>
    <td>Carrabasset Valley</td>
</tr>
<tr><td class="center"></td>
    <td class="center">X</td>
    <td>Hiking</td>
    <td>3 days</td>
    <td>Baxter State Park</td>
</tr>
<tr><td class="center">X</td>
    <td class="center"></td>
    <td>Hiking</td>
```

(continued)

```
        <td>3 days</td>
        <td>Mount Washington</td>
   </tr>
   <tr><td class="center">X</td>
       <td class="center">X</td>
       <td>Sightseeing</td>
       <td>3 days</td>
       <td>Quebec City</td>
   </tr>
   <tr><td class="center">X</td>
       <td class="center">X</td>
       <td>Fishing</td>
       <td>1 day</td>
       <td>Maine Coast</td>
   </tr>
   <tr><td class="center"></td>
       <td class="center">X</td>
       <td>Whale Watching</td>
       <td>1 day</td>
       <td>Maine Coast</td>
   </tr>
   <tr><td class="center">X</td>
       <td class="center">X</td>
       <td>Sailing</td>
       <td>2 days</td>
       <td>Maine Coast</td>
   </tr>
   </table>
   </body>
   </html>
```

Project Summary

Although somewhat complex in nature, the `colspan` and `rowspan` attributes enable you to build more creative tables than might otherwise have been possible. In addition, formatting techniques such as adjusting alignment, colors, and sizes are ways to draw attention to cell content. This project gave you practice working with many of these features.

✓

Module 9 Mastery Check

1. What is the difference between the `td` and `th` tags?

2. The `td` and `th` tags are contained within which other table tag (aside from the `table` tag itself)?

3. How do you force a cell's contents to display along a single line?

4. What is the most widely supported way to make all internal and external borders of a table invisible?

5. True/False: You cannot use other HTML tags between opening and closing `td` tags.

6. Which attribute affects the appearance of the internal table borders only, not external borders?

7. Fill in the blank: The _____ attribute affects the space in between each of the individual table cells.

8. Fix the following code.

```
<table>
<td>HTML</td>
<td>Hypertext Markup Language is the authoring language used to
create documents for the World Wide Web.</td>
</table>
```

9. What are two types of measurements you can use to identify a table's width?

10. Add the appropriate code to cause this table to fill the entire browser window, regardless of the user's screen size.

```
<html>
<head>
   <title>A Big Table</title>
<style type="text/css">

</style>
</head>
```

```
<body>
<table>
<tr
  <td>X</td>
  <td>X</td>
  <td>O</td>
</tr>
</table>
</body>
</html>
```

11. Fill in the blank: You can add the _____ property to your style sheet to change the background color of the whole table.

12. True/False: To add a caption to a table, you use the `caption` attribute in the opening `table` tag.

13. If you include a `thead` or a `tfoot` group in your table, you must also include which other group?

14. Which CSS property (and value) is used to align all the text in a cell to the right?

15. True/False: If you had both `colgroups` and `theads` in a single table, the `colgroups` would be placed before the `theads` in your table structure.

Module 10

Developing Frames

Have you ever visited a web site, clicked a link within that site, and noticed after doing so that only a portion of the page changed? This type of web site may have been created using frames to let you see two different web pages at the same time. Module 10 walks you through understanding what frames are and how they can be used in a web site, as well as how to format frames for your needs.

CRITICAL SKILL
10.1
Understand the Concept and Uses of Frames in Web Pages

The use of frames on a web site is similar to a television set with picture-in-picture. While picture-in-picture enables you to watch two television programs at one time, frames in a web site enable you to view two (or more) separate HTML pages at the same time.

You, as the web developer, can specify where the additional pages appear on the screen—in columns, rows, or a combination of each. For example, you might choose to load your site's

Ask the Expert

Q: Before we start... I heard frames are no longer used by *professional* web designers. Is this true? If so, why do you include it in this book?

A: I guess there's really no way to beat around this bush... yes, it's true. Frames have always received mixed reviews in the web community. And now that you can achieve the same results by separating content into divs and then formatting them with style sheets, the majority of web developers steer away from frames.

Even though frames are still valid in the XHTML specification, they can be difficult to style. This is because there's no "legal" or official way to turn off all of the frame borders... something most designers want to do to achieve that seamless look.

While revising this book for its third edition, I decided to leave a somewhat scaled-down discussion on frames in the book for those who have a real need for true frames. Until frames are dropped by the W3C officially, I see no reason why they can't be used for sites in which CSS either doesn't make sense or isn't a viable way to achieve the desired results.

Having said that, keep in mind that frames may cause some trouble for users who wish to bookmark your site, and also for those entering your site through a search engine (they may not see all the "frames" if they come to a single page from a search engine). I encourage you to review this module's information, as well as alternative methods (such as those discussed in Module 12), to determine the best solution for your particular needs.

links in a column on the left side of the screen, and then load the actual pages of content in another frame on the right side of the screen. This group of frames is called a *frameset*.

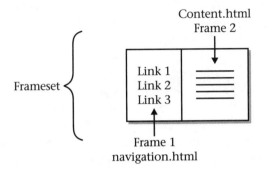

TIP

Just as with tables, I find it useful to map out my frames on paper before beginning.

Each frame in the frameset displays a different HTML page, just as each picture on the television displays a different channel. What can sometimes become confusing is the process of keeping track of which page is displayed in which frame, as well as updating each of those pages—sort of like trying to watch two television programs at the same time. Throughout this module, I give tips on streamlining this process and keeping track of your frames.

In addition, this module addresses two different types of frames:

- Standard (anchored) frames
- Inline (floating) frames

Whenever you see a reference to the term *frames*, you can assume I'm talking about standard frames. When I delve into *inline frames* toward the end of the module, I always call them by that name to avoid confusion.

Browser Support for Frames

Just as certain types of television sets are capable of displaying picture-in-picture, certain browsers can handle frames. Netscape 2.0 was the first to introduce and support frames, but Microsoft quickly added support in its Internet Explorer 3.0 browser. But frames didn't become an official part of the W3C's HTML specifications until version 4.0, which meant not many other browsers supported frames at first. However, all current browsers not only support standard frames, but floating inline frames as well.

The major exception to this is browsers for handheld PDAs and web-enabled phones. These types of browsers have difficulty displaying frames-based sites, as well as any other site that relies on the display of lots of information at once. So if you do use frames on your site, you should still provide alternative versions of your web site for those people visiting with a non-frames-capable browser. You'll learn how to do that at the end of this module.

CRITICAL SKILL
10.2 Create a Basic Frameset

There's a special type of HTML file for a frameset. Unlike the pages discussed so far in this book, a frameset page doesn't have a body tag. This is because a frameset HTML file contains a set of instructions for the browser regarding how the browser window is broken up and which pages are loaded into each frame, or section, of the window. The following is an example of what a typical frameset looks like.

```
<!DOCTYPE HTML PUBLIC "-//W3C//DTD HTML 4.01 Frameset//EN"
 "http://www.w3.org/TR/html4/frameset.dtd">     ◄——— The DOCTYPE identifier is a bit
<html>                                                    different for frameset documents
<head>
    <title>Frameset Number 1</title>
</head>
                                   frame is a tag used for referencing the
                                   HTML page that should appear in the frame
<frameset>                         (you can add a space and a forward slash to
    <frame />  ◄——————             make it XHTML-compliant)
    <frame />
</frameset>  ◄——————— You must always close the frameset tag

</html>
```

Instead of a body tag, frameset documents have opening and closing frameset tags that enclose the rest of the tags on the page. The difference is that frameset tags don't enclose text, images, or other types of content as the body tag does. frameset tags only contain references to the individual parts that make up the frameset, using frame tags.

Several attributes are used with the frameset and frame tags that enable you to identify the content for the frames and customize the look of them.

Columns and Rows

You add the cols and rows attributes to the opening frameset tag to specify the size and location of each of the frames. Depending on the layout you intend to create, you might use the cols attribute only (for vertical frames), the rows attribute only (for horizontal frames), or both the cols and rows attributes for a mixed layout.

TIP

You cannot test your framesets without specifying pages to load in each frame. If you're not ready to load real pages yet and only want to experiment with your columns and rows, create a blank HTML page called blank.html and use that as the content for each frame during testing.

This tells the browser the first frame should be 200 pixels wide

This tells the browser the second frame should be whatever space is left over in the browser window

```
<frameset cols="200,*">
    <frame src="blank.html" />
    <frame src="blank.html" />
</frameset>
```

The src attribute of the frame tag tells the browser which HTML page to load in that frame

Regardless of whether you're using the cols or rows attribute, the value of each is specified as a pixel value, a percentage, or a variable (*). The first size (in this case, 200) corresponds to the first frame tag, the second size (in this instance, *) corresponds to the second frame tag, and so on.

When you use the asterisk to represent a variable frame size, the browser considers the total width of the browser window before subtracting any absolute frame sizes (which are expressed by pixels) to determine the variable frame's size.

In the previous example, the first frame is set to an absolute size of 200 pixels wide, while the second frame is variable (as denoted by the asterisk). If the browser window were open to 600 pixels wide, the size of that variable frame would be 400 pixels (600 – 200 = 400).

TIP

As with tables, relative sizing (using percentages or variables) is preferred over absolute sizing if you're trying to create a layout that expands to fill a variety of window sizes. Not all the frames need to be variable in size, though. You can mix fixed- and variable-sized frames by using one or more columns of fixed size and one set of variable (*) size that can expand and contract to fill the available space.

Columns Only

Using the cols attribute without the rows attribute will achieve a frames setup with columns, like the following.

```
<frameset cols="200,*">
    <frame src="page1.html" />
```

```
        <frame src="page2.html" />
    </frameset>
```

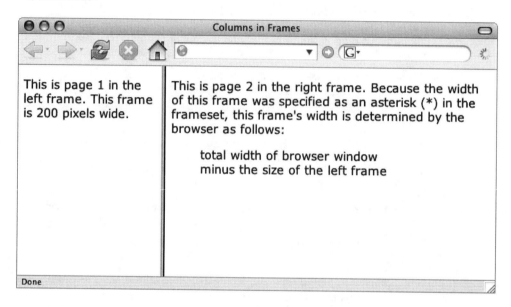

You can easily see the outline of each frame in this example because a border separates the two-framed columns. To add a third column to this frameset, you must add another width to the `cols` value in the `frameset` tag.

```
<frameset cols="200,*,50">
```
← Adding another comma and the value 50 would tell the browser to add a third frame after the second one, 50 pixels

Rows Only

Using the `rows` attribute without the `cols` attribute will achieve a frames setup with horizontal rows, like the following.

```
<frameset rows="75,*">
    <frame src="page3.html" />
    <frame src="page4.html" />
</frameset>
```

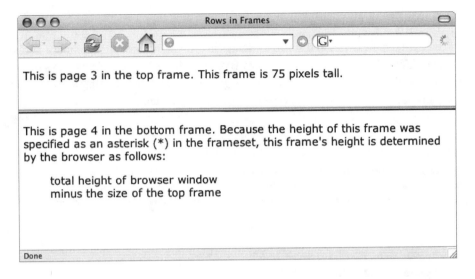

To add another row, the process is the same as adding another column. Commas separate the sizes of the columns and/or rows, and there is one size for each column or row.

A layout with four equal-sized rows might be expressed like that shown next:

```
<frameset rows="*,*,*,*">
```

or like the following:

```
<frameset rows="25%,25%,25%,25%">
```

In both cases, the window is separated into four equal horizontal frames.

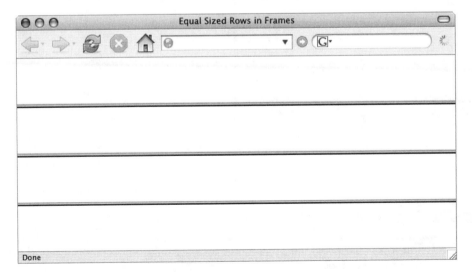

Mixed Layouts

You can use both the `cols` and `rows` attributes in a single frameset to combine a horizontal and vertical layout. The structure of a mixed layout can become tricky, but always remember you begin at the top and move from left to right, top to bottom, creating a grid of frames. Here's an example with four frames, created from two rows and two columns:

NOTE

When you mix columns and rows in a frameset, you are limited to the same number of columns as rows. If you want to have a different number of columns than rows in your layout, you must nest `frameset` tags, as discussed later in this module in the section titled "Nest Framesets".

```
<frameset rows="*,*" cols="*,*">
    <frame src="blank.html" />
    <frame src="blank.html" />
    <frame src="blank.html" />
    <frame src="blank.html" />
</frameset>
```

Because all the rows and columns are variable (denoted by an asterisk as the size), the frames in Figure 10-1 are all the same size.

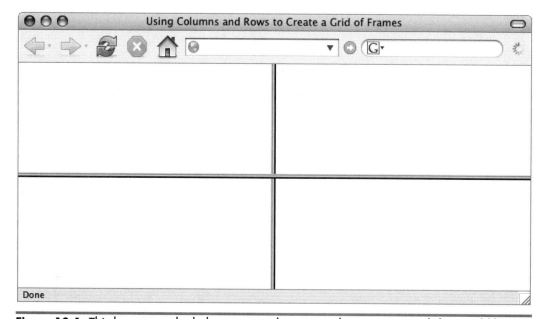

Figure 10-1 This layout uses both the `cols` and `rows` attributes to accomplish a grid-like structure of frames.

Identify Frame Content

Once you have the structure of your frameset identified, you need to tell the browser which pages to load in each of the frames. Use the `src` attribute in the `frame` tag to do so, but remember, the top-left frame must be defined before moving to the right and down the page.

In this example, I took the mixed layout from Figure 10-1 and reproduced it in an illustration to help determine which frames correspond to which HTML pages.

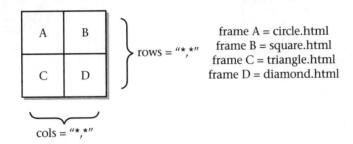

frame A = circle.html
frame B = square.html
frame C = triangle.html
frame D = diamond.html

This type of preparation can help when I code the frameset, working top to bottom, left to right.

```
<frameset rows="*,*" cols="*,*">
    <frame src="circle.html" />
    <frame src="square.html" />
    <frame src="triangle.html" />
    <frame src="diamond.html" />
</frameset>
```

The final output, shown in Figure 10-2, has each of the HTML pages appearing in the appropriate frame of the window, based on my illustration.

TIP

To view the source of a specific frame, first click inside the frame you are interested in, and then choose View | Frame Source or View | Source depending on your browser.

When you look at this page in the browser, whose filename is frameset_shapes.html, it's easy to forget that this screen (Figure 10-2) was created with five different HTML files (one

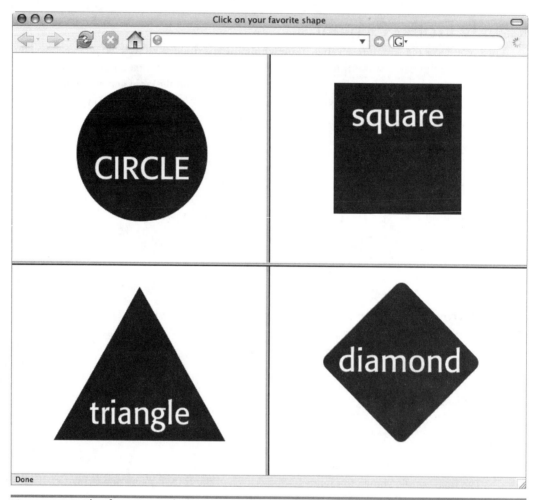

Figure 10-2 This frameset includes two rows and two columns, creating a grid of four frames. Each one contains a different HTML page.

for the frameset and four for the individual pages). If you need to make a change to any of these pages, however, you must

1. Open the specific HTML file in question.

2. Make your change(s) and save the file.

3. Return to the browser and click Reload or Refresh. If the change you made isn't readily apparent, try choosing File | Open or File | Open Page instead of Reload or Refresh.

CRITICAL SKILL
10.3 Format Frames Within a Frameset

Now that you know how to define the structure of a frameset and identify the page content for each frame, let's discuss how you can customize the look of the frames using several attributes of the `frameset` or `frame` tags.

Naming

The first attribute I discuss enables you to identify your frames with a name. This is important so that later, when you need to add a link to a page in one of the frames, you can tell the browser in which frame to load that link.

To name your frames, add the `name` attribute to each of your `frame` tags and specify a name that relates to the content of the frame. For example, if you used the left frame in a two-column frameset for all your links, you might name that frame "links."

```
<frameset cols="150,*">
    <frame src="links.html" name="links" />
```

Then, if the right frame contains an introduction about your company, you might call that frame the "intro."

```
<frame src="intro.html" name="intro" />
</frameset>
```

The concept used here is the same as when you link to sections within the same web page (discussed in Module 5). Before you can set up any links to it, you must first give the place you're linking to a name. The process of creating links to these frames is discussed toward the end of this module, in the section titled *Create Links Between Frames*.

Borders

If you refer to Figure 10-1 or 10-2, you can see, by default, that the browser separates each frame in a frameset with a gray border. At times, making those borders invisible might be necessary, giving the appearance of borderless or seamless frames. Turning the borders of frames off is similar to getting bifocal glasses that don't have a line in between the two different types of glass—the frames are still there, but you can no longer see the edges.

HTML 4.01 includes the `frameborder` attribute to alter the borders between frames. Setting this attribute to 0 tells the browser not to display the borders between the frames. The default value is 1, which tells the browser to go ahead and display the borders between the frame in question and any adjoining frames.

```
<frameset cols="150,*">
    <frame src="links.html" name="links" frameborder="0" />
    <frame src="intro.html" name="intro" frameborder="0" />
</frameset>
```

The problem with this attribute is that some browsers don't turn off all the border space when the `frameborder` is set to 0. Sometimes it may leave a gray or blank space in between the two frames.

To eliminate the three-dimensional borders, as well as that leftover space (as shown in Figure 10-3), many developers use the `border` attribute, with a value of 0 in your `frameset` tag. Keeping the `frameborder` attribute in your `frame` tags helps to ensure your frames are border-free in the largest number of browsers.

The only drawback in using the `border` attribute in the `frameset` tag is this: it is not part of the official W3C specifications, which means your page won't "validate" against those standards. However, in some circumstances it may be more important that your frames appear seamless than it is that they validate. As of this writing, though, there was no way to accomplish this task with CSS. In the end, you'll need to weigh these odds and determine how best to proceed.

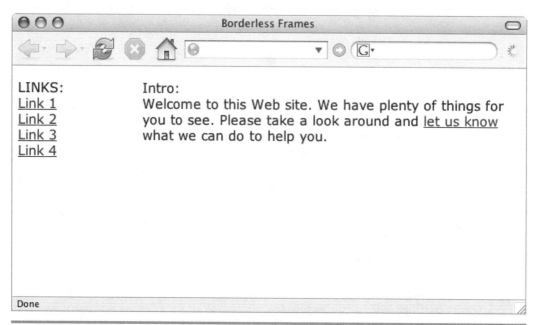

Figure 10-3 The best way to turn off the space completely between the frames is to set both the `border` and `frameborder` attributes to 0.

```
<frameset cols="150,*" border="0">
    <frame src="links.html" name="links" frameborder="0" />
    <frame src="intro.html" name="intro" frameborder="0" />
</frameset>
```

NOTE

While the `frameborder` attribute is supposed to be used only in the `frame` tag (as shown in the previous example), most browsers also recognize it when used in the `frameset` tag. This means you could use it once in the `frameset` tag instead of having to use it twice in each `frame` tag. Remember, this will not validate because it isn't part of the official XHTML specifications.

Margin Height and Width

In the previous module, you learned how to adjust the space in between content in table cells and the edges of those cells using the `cellpadding` attribute. You can use the `marginheight` and `marginwidth` attributes of the `frame` tag to do something similar.

- **marginheight**   Adjusts the space between the content of a frame and the top and bottom edges of that frame
- **marginwidth**   Adjusts the space between the content of a frame and the left and right edges of that frame

Because most common browsers use a default margin size of about eight pixels, the text in each frame is indented that much from the edges of the browser. To see what I mean, compare any of the previous figures in this module with Figure 10-4, in which I changed the sizes of both the height and width of the frame margins. The code used to create Figure 10-4 is shown next.

The left frame has a side margin of 0, causing the text to butt up against that edge. The top margin of the left frame is 20 pixels

```
<frameset cols="150,*">
  <frame src="links.html" name="links" marginheight="20" marginwidth="0" />
  <frame src="intro.html" name="intro" marginheight="0" marginwidth="20" />
</frameset>
```

In the right frame, these values are switched

You can also use style sheets to format the spacing and borders around frames. In particular, three CSS properties that we've already discussed can be used—padding, margin, and border-style. (See Module 4 for details about each of these properties.) In the following example, both the `frame` and `frameset` tags are used as CSS selectors, to apply the `padding`, `margin`, and `border` attributes to both tags on the page.

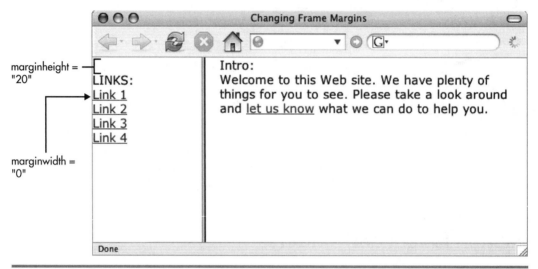

marginheight = "20"

marginwidth = "0"

Figure 10-4 The marginheight and marginwidth attributes can be used to change the amount of indent in each of the frames.

```
frame, frameset {padding: 0px;
                 margin: 0px;
                 border-style: none;}
```

TIP

While this will turn off the margins in and around the frames, there will still be margins and padding for the individual frames. To turn those off as well, add these properties to the style sheet affecting the individual pages displayed in each of the frames.

Scrolling

Whenever a page contains information that is longer than the current window, the browser includes a vertical scroll bar along the right side of the screen. Likewise, when information is wider than can be displayed, the browser includes a horizontal scroll bar across the bottom of the screen.

TIP

The scroll bar will be between 10 and 15 pixels in width, depending on the browser. Remember to allow room for scroll bars when allotting sizes for frames.

Using the scrolling attribute in the frame tag, you can force the browser to display or not display the scroll bars for each frame. Table 10-1 lists the possible choices for this attribute.

Attribute and Value	Description
scrolling="yes"	Tells the browser to display the scroll bars for the frame.
scrolling="no"	Tells the browser never to display the scroll bars for the frame.
scrolling="auto"	Tells the browser only to provide the scroll bars when necessary, based on the content of the frame. (This is the default for each frame.)

Table 10-1 Values of the `scrolling` Attribute

Resizing

By default, browsers give users the capability to resize variable- or relative-sized frames as needed. This is accomplished by clicking-and-dragging on a visible border in between the frames.

NOTE

Users cannot resize frames where the border is turned off, or on those that have absolute sizes.

You can click-and-drag the border to the left and right (if it's a vertical border), or up and down (if it's a horizontal border). When you do so, the mouse cursor changes to look like two little arrows pulling away from each other.

While this is a useful technique for many web sites, at times you might want to restrict users from being able to resize your frames. To do so, add the `noresize` attribute to the `frame` tag.

```
<frame src="links.html" name="links" marginheight="20" marginwidth="0"
noresize="noresize" />
```

Progress Check

1. Which attribute is added to the `frameset` tag to set up a frame structure with frames in columns?

2. What character is used to denote that the size of a frame is variable?

---

1. cols

2. *

CRITICAL SKILL

10.4 Create Links Between Frames

Whenever you use frames on a web site, you have to deal with the issue of linking between them. By default, whenever a user clicks a link within a frame, the page loads within that same frame. Sometimes it becomes necessary to load a linked page within *another* frame.

Before you can link to another frame, it must have a name. Earlier in this module, you learned how to use the `name` attribute with the `frame` tag to identify a frame by name:

```
<frameset cols="150,*">
    <frame src="links.html" name="links" />
    <frame src="intro.html" name="intro" />
</frameset>
```

Once the frame has been given a name, you only need to add the `target` attribute to the link.

Targets

Imagine you have an HTML page for a frameset with two columns, called frameset_cols.html. The frames in this structure are named "links" on the left and "intro" on the right. When a user clicks the words "About Us" in the left frame, you want the "About Us" page to load in the right frame.

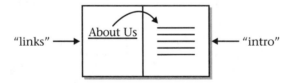

Accomplishing this task requires two steps.

1. Make sure the frame is named (using the `name` attribute), as in `<frame src="intro.html" name="intro" />` in the frameset HTML document.

2. Then, in the HTML page containing the link, use the `target` attribute in the a tag to specify in which frame the link should load. For example, `<a href="page3.html" target="intro">`.

NOTE

This is different from all the other attributes discussed so far in this module because this requires editing the HTML pages within the frames, as opposed to the HTML page for the frameset.

To change the target window of the "About Us" link, you have to edit the HTML page containing that link. In this case, the page you edit is saved as links.html.

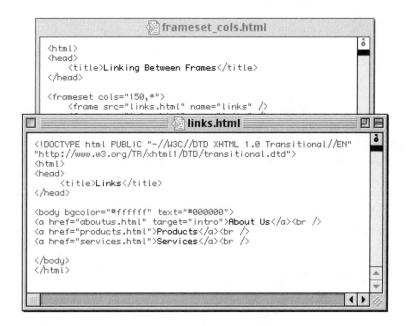

```
frameset_cols.html
<html>
<head>
    <title>Linking Between Frames</title>
</head>

<frameset cols="150,*">
    <frame src="links.html" name="links" />
```

```
links.html
<!DOCTYPE html PUBLIC "-//W3C//DTD XHTML 1.0 Transitional//EN"
"http://www.w3.org/TR/xhtml1/DTD/transitional.dtd">
<html>
<head>
    <title>Links</title>
</head>

<body bgcolor="#ffffff" text="#000000">
<a href="aboutus.html" target="intro">About Us</a><br />
<a href="products.html">Products</a><br />
<a href="services.html">Services</a><br />

</body>
</html>
```

As shown in the illustration, add `target="value"`, where *value* is the name you gave to the frame in which you want the link to load.

```
<a href="aboutus.html" target="intro">About Us</a>
```

This attribute would then cause the aboutus.html page to appear in the *intro* frame (the one on the right) instead of in the *links* frame.

There are also several standard frame names, each of which begins with an underscore (_):

- **target="_blank"** causes a link to be opened in a new unnamed browser window.

- **target="_self"** causes a link to be opened in the same window that is currently being used.

- **target="_top"** causes a link to be opened in the full, original window, without any frames.

- **target="_parent"** causes a link to be opened in the frameset of the current frame, thereby removing the current set of frames (but leaving any other frames that may exist if the current set of frames is nested inside another one).

Base Targets

If you want all the links on this page to load in the intro frame, you can use the base tag to simplify things.

```
<head>
    <title>Links</title>
    <base target="intro">
</head>
```

The base tag goes in between the opening and closing head tags, usually below the title tags, as shown in the previous example. By using the target attribute in the base tag instead of the individual links, you can avoid typing target="intro" (or whatever the name of your frame was) after every single link on your page.

If you do want one link to load in a frame other than the one specified in your base tag, just add the target attribute to that individual link. A target attribute in the a tag overrides any in the base tag.

CRITICAL SKILL
10.5 Nest Framesets

In the beginning of this module, I mentioned that with a single frameset an equal number of columns and rows must exist. If you want to create a frame structure with an irregular structure of columns and rows, you need to nest two or more framesets.

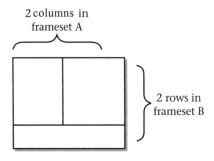

For example, in this case, you need to create two framesets. Frameset A contains two vertical columns, while frameset B contains two horizontal rows. While, initially, it may appear these could be contained in a single frameset, this isn't possible because both of the columns (in frameset A) are located within a single row of frameset B. This cannot be accomplished with a single frameset.

The actual HTML for nested frames takes on the same structure as any other nested tags. First, think about the overall structure of the frameset and decide which one contains the other. In this case, we already established that frameset B—specifically, the first row in that frameset—contains frameset A. The HTML is coded as such (see Figure 10-5 for a visual representation).

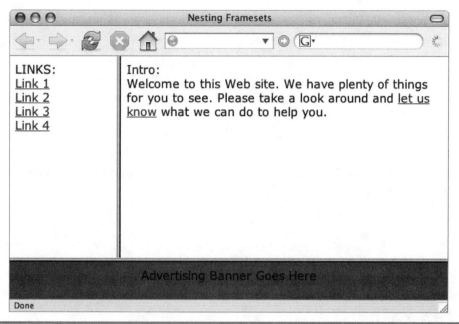

Figure 10-5 You could use a nested frameset to create irregularly shaped frame structures.

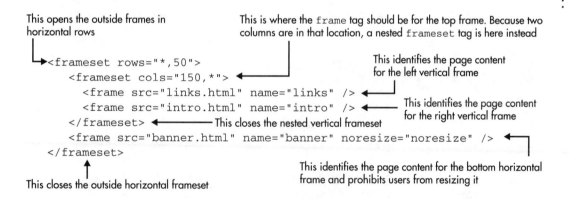

This opens the outside frames in horizontal rows

This is where the `frame` tag should be for the top frame. Because two columns are in that location, a nested `frameset` tag is here instead

This identifies the page content for the left vertical frame

This identifies the page content for the right vertical frame

```
<frameset rows="*,50">
    <frameset cols="150,*">
        <frame src="links.html" name="links" />
        <frame src="intro.html" name="intro" />
    </frameset>
    <frame src="banner.html" name="banner" noresize="noresize" />
</frameset>
```

This closes the nested vertical frameset

This closes the outside horizontal frameset

This identifies the page content for the bottom horizontal frame and prohibits users from resizing it

You can easily become confused when you nest any tags, but it's particularly confusing with frames. The most recently opened table must be closed first, so you work from the inside out. (Remember the semicircles that didn't touch in Module 2?)

Another way to deal with irregularly shaped frames structures avoids nesting. In this technique, you reference another HTML file with frames, instead of embedding those frames in the current HTML file. For example, here's how the previous code might be changed to avoid using nested framesets.

> Instead of embedding another frameset here, as in the previous example, that frameset is contained in its own HTML file and simply referenced here as a single frame

```
<frameset rows="*,50">
    <frame src="frameset-A.html" name="columns" />
    <frame src="banner.html" name="banner" noresize="noresize" />
</frameset>
```

If you used this HTML code instead of the nested frameset example, you also must create frameset-A.html to contain the frameset with columns.

```
<frameset cols="150,*">
    <frame src="links.html" name="links" />
    <frame src="intro.html" name="intro" />
</frameset>
```

— frameset-A.html

Progress Check

1. What must you do before you can load links into another frame?

2. Which tag and attribute are used to change the target frame for all links within a page?

CRITICAL SKILL
10.6 Create Inline Frames

Sometimes you may want to include an entire web page within another one. While you can use the `object` tag to do this (discussed in Module 7), HTML 4.01 also enables you to use the `iframe` tag for the same purpose.

The biggest advantage of inline frames is their flexibility: they can be included anywhere on a web page, much like an image or multimedia component. For example, Figure 10-6 shows a web page with an inline frame using the following code:

```
<iframe src="photo-bball.html" name="photos" width="230" height="230"
style="float:right;"><strong>Unfortunately, these photos are visible
only with an up-to-date browser.</strong></iframe>
```

---

1. Use the name attribute to identify that frame.
2. `<base target="framename">`

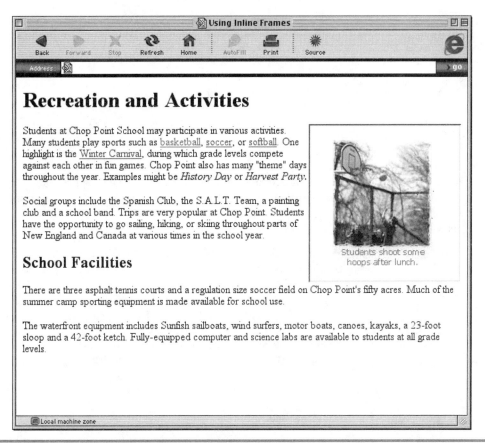

Figure 10-6 Inline frames can "float" anywhere you wish to place them on the page.

TIP

You can also use style sheets to further format inline frames. In this case, I only included an inline style to float the frame to the right of the text, but you could also use styles to adjust the frame's borders, margins, and so on.

Each of the links in the paragraph next to the inline frame is loaded into that frame, by referencing the iframe's name:

```
<p>Students at Chop Point School may participate in various activities. Many
students play sports such as <a href="photo-bball.html"
target="photos">basketball</a>, <a href="photo-soccer.html"
target="photos">soccer</a>, or <a href="photo-softball.html"
target="photos">softball</a>. One highlight is the <a
```

```
href="photo-carnival.html" target="photos">Winter Carnival</a>, during which
grade levels compete against each other in fun games. Chop Point also has many
"theme" days throughout the year. Examples might be <i>History Day</i> or
<i>Harvest Party.</i></p>
```

Remember these additional things about inline frames.

● Include alternative text in between the opening and closing iframe tags for browsers not supporting inline frames.

● Browsers that don't support inline frames may launch a new browser window when loading the links that were supposed to load in the inline frame. This happens because that frame was given a name that doesn't exist for browsers not supporting inline frames. When trying to load a link within a named frame it cannot find, the browser usually launches a new browser window, giving it that name.

● Attributes that can be used in the iframe tag include those listed in Table 10-2.

TIP

Most HTML tags can be used within the alternative text, but be wary of using the p tag there. In my testing, this tag caused the alternative text to be visible even in some browsers that do support inline frames—the text appeared next to the inline frame.

Attribute and Value(s)	Description
src="filename.html"	Identifies the HTML page to be included.
name="frame name"	Gives the frame a name so that links can be loaded into it.
width="#"	Specifies a width for the frame in pixel dimensions.
height="#"	Specifies a height for the frame in pixel dimensions.
marginwidth="#"	Specifies the amount of blank space between the frame's content and its horizontal borders.
marginheight="#"	Specifies the amount of blank space between the frame's content and its vertical borders.
scrolling="value"	Defines whether scroll bars are visible for the frame. Possible values are yes, no, and auto.
frameborder="#"	Specifies whether the frame has a visible border. Possible values are 0 (turns the border off) and 1 (turns the border on).

Table 10-2 Attributes for the iframe Tag

CRITICAL SKILL
10.7 Accommodate Non-Frames-
Capable Browsers

You need one final piece of information before you create HTML frames. Because some browsers don't support frames, particularly those on handheld devices, you need to include alternative content for those unable to see the content of your frames. This is accomplished through use of the noframes tag.

NOTE

If you don't include the noframes tag, those who visit your page using a non-frames-capable browser will see only a blank page.

The noframes tag—placed in the HTML document after the frame tags, but before the closing frameset tag—is best used to link visitors to your individual HTML pages outside the frameset. For example, in the following code the noframes tag provides visitors with a link to an alternative HTML page containing all the important information from the frame documents.

```
<frameset cols="50%,50%">
    <frame src="links.html" name="links" />
    <frame src="intro.html" name="intro" />
    <noframes>
<p>This site uses frames to display its content but, unfortunately,
your Web browser is not capable of displaying frames. We have created
an <a href="noframes.html">alternative page</a> with all the same
content for you.</p>
    </noframes>
</frameset>
```

You can also add the noframes tag to regular HTML pages, particularly the ones you plan to load within a frames structure. The content of the noframes tag would then only be displayed when the page was not viewed within the context of a frameset.

NOTE

This is especially important for those coming to your web site from a search engine because most search engines index the pages referenced by the frames, as well as the frames document.

For example, if you have a web site where the links for the site were included in a second frame, visitors who viewed the content pages outside the frame wouldn't see the links. By including those links within a `noframes` tag on every page of your web site, you can be assured all viewers will have access to the links, even if they view the pages without the frames.

Project 10-1 Creating a Basic Frameset

One common use of frames occurs when a site offers links to other web sites, but also wants to provide the user with a hook, or a quick way to get back to the original page. This project walks you through the steps in creating just such a frameset for the Chop Point site. Goals for this project include

● Creating a basic frameset

● Formatting the frames within the frameset

NOTE

All the files needed to complete the projects in this book for Chop Point can be downloaded from **www.osborne.com** or **www.wendywillard.com**. In addition, you can view my version of the web site anytime by visiting **www.choppoint.org**. Those of you who aren't using the Chop Point site can tailor the project to your particular needs.

Step by Step

1. Open your text or HTML editor and create a new file entitled **frameset.html**.

2. Type all the HTML tags needed for a basic frameset page containing two horizontal rows.

3. Format the top frame to be 25 pixels tall and the second frame to take up the remaining space.

4. Name the top frame "**hook**" and the bottom frame "**links**".

5. Set the margin height and width of the top frame each to have a value of 2.

6. Use `http://www.acacamps.org` as the source for the top frame, to simulate how the page might display if a user really had clicked a link from the Chop Point page.

7. Create a new page for the source of the top frame, called **hook.html**.

   ● Include all the HTML tags needed for a basic HTML page, as well as the following link:

   `< Return to the Chop Point Summer Camp Site`

- The link should be directed toward the index.html page you created, and should load so as to fill the page and remove the frames.
- Give this page the background color of your choice, making sure your link color stands out against the background. Select whichever font style you prefer, making sure the text is small enough to fit in the space allowed without forcing a scroll bar.

8. Include alternative text in the `noframes` tag of framset.html to link to the index.html page for non-frames-capable browsers.

9. Save the files.

10. Open your web browser and choose File | Open Page (or Open File or Open, depending on the browser you're using). Locate the file frameset.html you just saved. Make sure the file appears as you intended.

11. If you need to make changes, return to your text editor to do so. After making any changes, save the file, and then switch back to the browser. Choose Refresh or Reload to preview the changes you just made.

TIP

Does your screen appear blank? If so, check to make sure you closed your `frameset` tag (`</frameset>`). For more tips, see Appendix C.

If you're using the Chop Point site, you can compare your files to the following code and Figure 10-7.

frameset.html

```
<!DOCTYPE HTML PUBLIC "-//W3C//DTD HTML 4.01 Frameset//EN"
 "http://www.w3.org/TR/html4/frameset.dtd">
<html>
<head>
    <title>Links from the Chop Point Summer Camp</title>
</head>

<frameset rows="25,*">
    <frame src="hook.html" name="hook" marginheight="2" marginwidth="2" />
    <frame src="http://www.acacamps.org" name="links" />
    <noframes>Since your browser does not understand Web documents created with
frames, please use our <a href="index.html">page without frames</a>.</noframes>
</frameset>
</html>
```

(continued)

Figure 10-7 Sites commonly use hooks like this to provide users with a quick way back to the original page.

hook.html

```
<!DOCTYPE html PUBLIC "-//W3C//DTD XHTML 1.0 Transitional//EN"
 "http://www.w3.org/TR/xhtml1/DTD/transitional.dtd">
<html>
<head>
    <title>Chop Point Hook</title>
<style type="text/css">
body {background-color: yellow;
     font-size: 10px;
     font-family: verdana;}
```

```
</style>
</head>
<body>
&lt; Return to the <a href="index.html" target="_top">Chop Point Summer Camp</a> site
</body>
</html>
```

Project Summary

Frames can offer additional layout possibilities to web developers when used properly and with the web site user in mind. This project gave you practice creating a basic frameset for a hook bar, which is a typical use of frames on the Web.

✓ *Module 10 Mastery Check*

1. Fill in the blank: A group of frames is called a _____.

2. Which basic structure tag of most HTML pages is not included in a frameset page?

3. How do you tell the browser that a frame should fill whatever space is left over in the browser window after all other frames are placed?

4. To load a link in a particular frame, you must first do what in the `frame` tag?

5. True/False: To turn the frame borders completely off in the majority of browsers, add `frameborder="0"` to the opening `frameset` tag.

6. What is the default value of the `scrolling` attribute for frames?

7. Fill in the blank: The _____ attribute adjusts the space between the content of a frame and the top and bottom edges of that frame.

8. Fix the following code.

```
<frame cols="20%,80%">
  <frameset src="top.html">
  <frameset src="navigation.html">
</frame>
```

9. Which two tags embed an inline frame within a web page?

10. Add the appropriate code to create a frameset with two vertical frames—the first frame is 250 pixels wide, and the second takes up the rest of the browser window. Fill the first frame with navigation.html and the second frame with content.html.

```
<html>
<head>
  <title>Frames</title>
</head>


</html>
```

11. Fill in the blank: Use the _____ tag and _____ attribute to force all the links on a page to load in a particular frame.

12. True/False: By default, relative-width frames are resizable.

13. Which tag displays content for non-frames-capable browsers?

14. Which attribute should you add to the frameset tag to create two horizontal frames on the page?

15. Fill in the blank: The _____ attribute of the frame tag tells the browser which HTML page to load into that frame.

Module 11

Employing Forms

289

One of the best features of the Web is its capability to enable new forms of communication and have them connect with other methods already in existence. Online forms are popular ways of facilitating such communications. For example, forms allow web site visitors to comment on a site, order a product, add a post to a bulletin board, sign a guest book, and register for a service. This module discusses how to create forms such as these and use them effectively on your web site.

CRITICAL SKILL
11.1 # Understand the Concept and Uses of Forms in Web Pages

The most basic purpose of any form is to collect information. When you register to vote, you fill out a form specifying your name, address, birth date, and political party affiliation. The form is collected and processed. The same basic concept holds true with online forms—they are filled out, collected, and processed.

For example, Figure 11-1 shows a page with a form for customers to send an inquiry to their bank.

Just as paper forms must have once been written, typed, or otherwise created, online forms need to be coded. This can be accomplished with HTML alone or by combining HTML with other technologies. For the purposes of this module, we will use HTML to create our forms.

CRITICAL SKILL
11.2 # Create a Basic Form

Even the most basic forms have the same structure. This includes opening and closing `form` tags, input controls, and processing methods. The `form` tags surround the entire form, just as `html` tags surround the entire HTML document.

```
<form>
 ... content goes here ...
</form>
```

First, let's discuss *input controls*, or ways for users to enter data. For example, for you to enter your name on a form, there must be a space for you to do so. This space is what I'm referring to when I use the phrase *input control* or simply "control." Figure 11-1 contains some input controls (listed next) that are labeled for you.

- Text inputs
- Check boxes
- Radio buttons

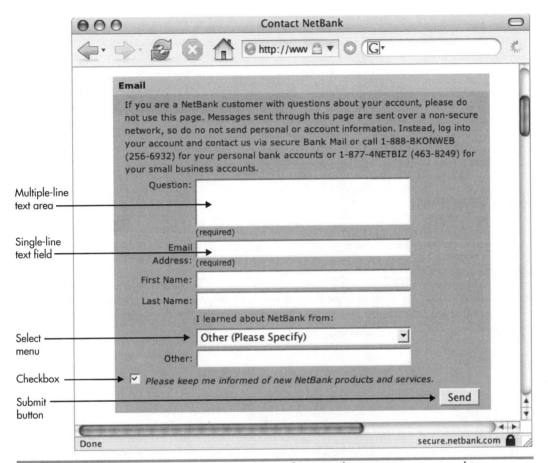

Multiple-line
text area

Single-line
text field

Select
menu

Checkbox

Submit
button

Figure 11-1 Online forms have a variety of uses, from sending messages to searching
for keywords.

- Select menus

- File selects

- Buttons (submit buttons, reset buttons, and push buttons)

- Hidden controls

NOTE

You can also use the `object` tag (discussed in Module 7) to embed objects within
forms. These are called object controls.

Because the majority of these controls are created with an `input` tag, the actual description of which control you want to include is made through the `type` attribute, as in the following example:

```
<form>
    <input type="text" />
</form>
```

The next sections explain the specific types of controls created with the `input` tag, as well as a few others that aren't created by it.

Text Input

Two types of text input are afforded in HTML: single-line text boxes (called *text fields*) and multiple-line text areas.

Single-Line Text Fields

The most basic type of input control is the single-line text field. This control is a space, resembling a box, that can contain a single line of text. Usually, text fields are preceded by descriptive text telling the user what to enter in the box. For example:

```
<form>
    Please enter your first name: <input type="text" /><br />
    Please enter your last name: <input type="text" />
</form>
```

As the following illustration shows, text fields are single-line white spaces that appear slightly indented into the page. Unless you specify otherwise with the `size` attribute, text fields are usually 20 characters in length.

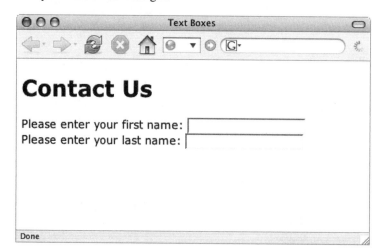

NOTE

The sizes of text fields are specified in characters. However, it ultimately depends on the default font size in the viewer's browser. This means even though you might specify a text field to be 25 characters in length, it may appear larger or smaller on someone else's system, depending on how that person's browser is set up.

Any of the attributes listed in Table 11-1 can be added to this input tag to customize the text field. Of those attributes, perhaps the most important one is name. To process all the controls in your form, each one must be identified with a name. For example, when the form is processed, you could tell it to take whatever the user entered in the control you named "FirstName" and print that text at the top of an e-mail message.

TIP

Blank spaces in between words in the value of some attributes can cause problems in HTML and other coding methods. To avoid such problems when using the name attribute, many developers like to run any phrases together, capitalizing the first letter in each word. For example, instead of using "Middle Initial" as the value of your name attribute, use "MiddleInitial". Just remember, these values are case-sensitive, which means whenever you reference that control later, you must also capitalize the first letter of each word. In addition, be sure to use unique names to avoid confusion when the form is processed.

```
<form>
   Please enter your first name: <input type="text" name="FirstName" /><br />
   Please enter your last name: <input type="text" name="LastName" />
</form>
```

Attribute	Value(s)	Description
name	Name	Identifies the control so that it's correctly handled when the form is processed. This information isn't displayed when the form is viewed through a browser.
size	Number	Specifies the length of the text field in characters.
maxlength	Number	Specifies the maximum number of characters that can be entered in the text field by the user.
value	Value	Defines what text, if any, should be present within the text field when it's initially displayed on the page.

Table 11-1 Attributes for Text Fields

The other three attributes—size, maxlength, and value—are optional. You can use the size attribute to specify the length of the text field in characters, while the maxlength attribute enables you to limit the number of characters that can be entered in that box. For example, if you created a text field where users can enter their birthdays in the following format: mm-dd-yy, you could specify a maxlength of eight characters.

Every control has an initial value and a current value. An *initial value* is an optional value you specify for a control when you code the form, while a *current value* is whatever the user entered that is then processed with the form. For example, instead of giving directions in the space before a text field, you might use the value attribute to place the directions within the text field. If you do, and the user doesn't enter any data, then the initial value you entered is sent along when the form is processed.

```
<form>
 <input type="text" name="FirstName" value="Enter First Name" /><br />
 <input type="text" name="LastName" value="Enter Last Name" size="20" />
</form>
```

When the page is viewed, however, users may have to erase the phrase before entering their information.

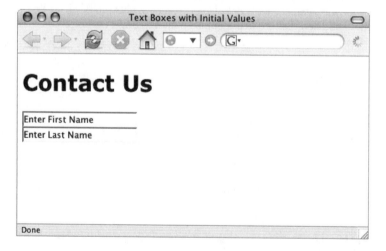

Text Fields for Passwords

HTML enables you to create two types of text fields: one for regular text (as you just learned) and a second for passwords. The main difference between the two is that password text fields show text that's entered as bullets instead of straight text.

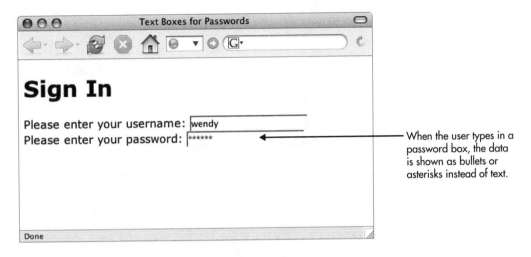

When the user types in a password box, the data is shown as bullets or asterisks instead of text.

You use `password` as the value of the `type` attribute in your `input` tag to create this type of control. The following is an example of the code for the previous illustration:

```
<form>
    Please enter your username: <input type="text" name="UserName"><br />
    Please enter your password: <input type="password" name="Password">
</form>
```

Although this may seem as if it adds a level of security to your page, it's merely a way to prevent those looking over the user's shoulder from seeing a password. The actual password is not encrypted in any way when the form is processed, and therefore, this control shouldn't be implemented as the only means of security for pages with passwords.

Multiple-Line Text Areas

When it's necessary to allow your web site visitors to enter more than a single link of text, use a text area instead of a text field. Unlike most other form input controls, a *text area* uses the `textarea` tag instead of the `input` tag.

```
<form>
    We welcome your thoughts and opinions about our products.<br />
    <textarea name="Comments"></textarea>
</form>
```

To specify the size of the text area, use the `cols` and `rows` attributes.

● The `cols` attribute identifies the visible width of the text area, based on an average character width.

- The `rows` attribute identifies the visible height of the text area, based on the number of text lines.

Because the sizes of the `rows` and `cols` attributes relate to the character width in the browser, the actual size of the text area may differ, depending on the user's settings. Scroll bars may appear when users attempt to enter more data than can be displayed in the visible text area.

You don't use the `value` attribute in this tag to create an initial value that prints within the text area. Instead, include any text you want to print within the text area between the opening and closing `textarea` tags. Figure 11-2 shows how the following code might be displayed in a browser.

```
<form>
    We welcome your thoughts and opinions about our products.<br />
    <textarea name="Comments" cols="30" rows="5">Type your comments here.</textarea>
</form>
```

TIP

You can control whether scroll bars appear on your text area with the CSS overflow property. For example, setting `overflow: scroll` forces scroll bars to appear, while `overflow: auto` leaves it up to the browser to decide based on the amount of text entered.

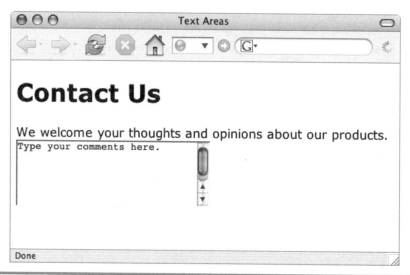

Figure 11-2 Text areas enable users to enter more than a single line of text. Any text you enter between the opening and closing `textarea` tags is used as the initial value of the text area.

Radio Buttons

Radio buttons are small, round buttons that enable users to select a single option from a list of choices. This is accomplished with the `input` tag and a value of `"radio"` in the `type` attribute. You might use radio buttons to allow those interested in receiving more information the option of choosing to do so via e-mail, phone, fax, or regular mail. When the user selects one of the options by pressing the radio button, the circle is filled in with a black dot.

TIP

Radio buttons are particularly useful for questions requiring a yes or no answer.

The `name` and `value` attributes are especially important to radio buttons because they help to make sure the data is processed correctly. Consider the following HTML code used to create the illustration shown next.

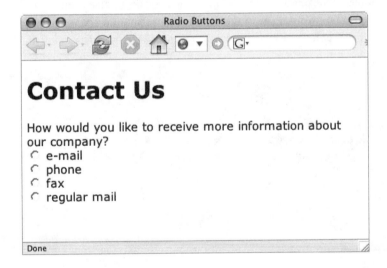

```
<form>
    How would you like to receive more information about our company?<br />
    <input type="radio" name="ContactMe" value="e-mail"> e-mail<br />
    <input type="radio" name="ContactMe" value="phone"> phone<br />
    <input type="radio" name="ContactMe" value="fax"> fax<br />
    <input type="radio" name="ContactMe" value="mail"> regular mail<br />
</form>
```

Notice the `name` attributes contain the same value for all four options. This ensures these four controls are linked together when the form is processed. Because the type of control is "radio," the browser knows only one option can be selected.

When the form is processed, it locates the selected option (meaning it looks for whichever radio button the user pressed) and transmits that option's `value` along with its `name`. If I pressed the radio button next to the word "fax," the appropriate name and value would be transmitted: ContactMe - fax. You can see how using words and phrases that actually mean something can be important.

If you want to set one of the radio buttons to be selected by default when the page is initially loaded, use the checked attribute in the `input` tag. Users can select a different option if they want.

```
<input type="radio" name="ContactMe" value="fax" checked="checked"> fax<br />
```

Check Boxes

Check boxes are similar to radio buttons in that they don't let users enter any data; they can only be clicked on or off. However, check boxes let the user select more than one choice from a list of options. For example, you might use check boxes to give users the option to select which services they would like to receive more information about. When a check box is pressed, a small *x* or a check mark typically appears in the box, depending on the browser.

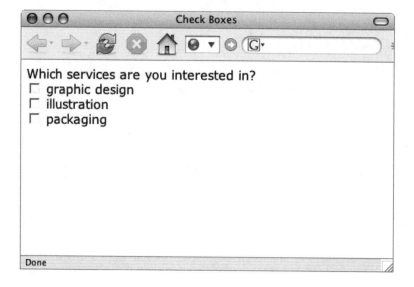

To include a check box in your online form, use the `input` tag and `type` attribute with a value of `checkbox` (note that check box is one word when used as an HTML value). Just as with radio buttons, the values of the name attributes for all the options should be the same. Use the value attribute to identify what is different about each option, as in the following example:

```
<form>
    Which services are you interested in?<br />
    <input type="checkbox" name="Services" value="graphic design"> graphic design<br />
    <input type="checkbox" name="Services" value="illustration"> illustration<br />
    <input type="checkbox" name="Services" value="packaging"> packaging
</form>
```

When the form is processed, the values of any check boxes pressed by the user will be transmitted to the server along with the value of the name attribute. So, in the previous example, if I pressed the check boxes next to "graphic design" and "illustration," the appropriate name and values would be transmitted: Services - graphic design, illustration.

Use the checked attribute any time you want a check box to be selected by default when the page is loaded. Users can uncheck that box if they want.

```
<input type="checkbox" name="Services" value="packaging" checked="checked"> packaging
```

Select Menus

Whenever you want to let users select from a long list of options, you might consider using a select menu instead of check boxes or radio buttons. Select menus are lists that have been compressed into one or more visible options, similar to those menus you find at the top of other software applications.

NOTE

Menus may appear differently depending on which browser or computer system is used. These examples show menus from both Macintosh and Windows systems.

Also called *drop-down menus*, this type of menu enables users to click an option initially visible, and then pull down to reveal additional options. Unless a number greater than 1 is specified in the size attribute, only a single option is visible when the page loads. This option is accompanied by a small arrow, signifying that the menu expands. When the size attribute is 2 or more, that number of choices is visible in a scrollable list. Figure 11-3 shows two select menus. The first one uses the default size of 1, while the second is set to size=3.

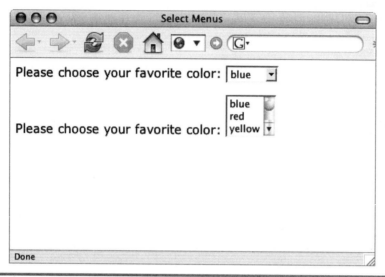

Figure 11-3 The `size` attribute enables you to specify how many options in your select menu are visible at once.

The `select` element is used to create the menu initially, while `option` tags surround each item in the menu. A menu asking users to choose their favorite color might be coded like the following:

```
<form>
Please choose your favorite color:
<select name="FavoriteColor" size="3">
    <option value="blue">blue</option>
    <option value="red">red</option>
    <option value="yellow">yellow</option>
    <option value="green">green</option>
    <option value="other">other</option>
</select>
</form>
```

NOTE

If you don't use the `value` attribute with each `option` tag, the text displayed in the menu will be transmitted as the option's value when the form is processed. Based on my experience, I recommend using the `value` attribute whenever possible to avoid confusion when the form is processed.

By default, users can select one item from the list. If you'd like them to be able to choose more than one option, add the `multiple` attribute to your opening `select` tag. The way users select more than one menu item depends on their computer system. For example, Macintosh users hold down the COMMAND key when clicking, while Windows users hold down the SHIFT key, or the CONTROL key, to select noncontiguous choices in the list, and click.

```
<select name="FavoriteColors" size="3" multiple="multiple">
```

In addition, you can specify any item to be already selected when the page is loaded by adding the `selected` attribute to that item's opening `option` tag. Users can select a different menu item if they choose.

NOTE
Don't specify more than one item as `selected`, unless you also let users choose more than one option by adding the `multiple` attribute to the `select` tag.

```
<option value="red" selected="selected">red</option>
```

Submenus

The `optgroup` element is used to divide long menus into categories of submenus. The `label` attribute is employed along with the `optgroup` element to give the submenu a name. The following is an example of how to create submenus with `optgroup` tags, followed by a visual representation of how one browser displays them.

```
<form>
Please choose the time and day that is best to reach you.
<select name="TimeDay">
<optgroup label="Monday">
    <option value="Monday AM">Monday AM</option>
    <option value="Monday PM">Monday PM</option>
</optgroup>
<optgroup label="Tuesday">
    <option value="Tuesday AM">Tuesday AM</option>
    <option value="Tuesday PM">Tuesday PM</option>
</optgroup>
</select>
</form>
```

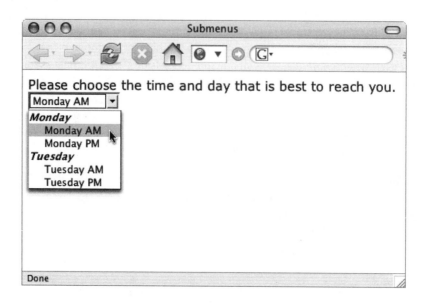

File Uploads

Some online forms might require that a file be transmitted along with any data from the form. For example, you might provide the option for potential employees to submit a photo along with a job application being filled out online. This can be accomplished by using type="file" with the input tag.

```
<form>
    <input type="file" name="PhotoUpload" />
</form>
```

By giving your control a name, you can reference it when the form is processed

This tells the browser to expect a file input from the user

NOTE

Check with your site's system administrator before adding file uploads to your web form because some hosts do not permit users to upload files through the web browser for security reasons. In addition, even if file uploads are permitted on your site's system, some adjustments to the host computer may need to be made.

For document uploads, most browsers display a text field followed by a button typically labeled Browse... By clicking the button, users can locate the file they want to send with the form on their computers (see Figure 11-4). After doing so, the browser prints the location and name of the file in the text field provided (see Figure 11-5).

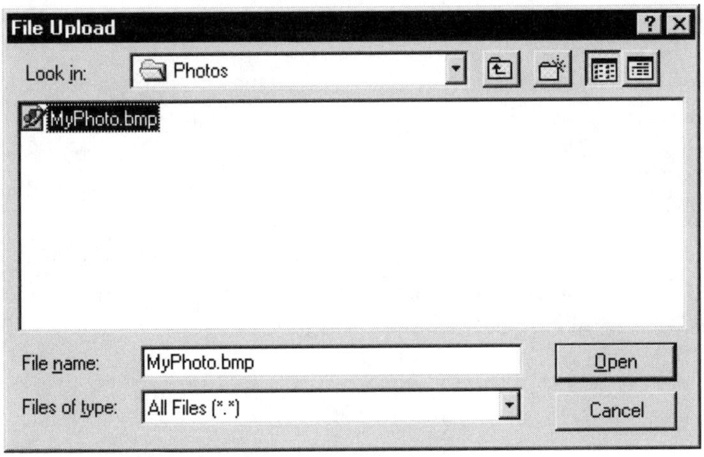

Figure 11-4 Users can locate the file they want to upload on their computers after clicking the button labeled Browse...

You can increase the size of the text field by adding the `size` attribute to the `input` tag. Because many file locations may be long, you might want to specify a size of 30–40 characters.

```
<input type="file" name="PhotoUpload" size="40" />
```

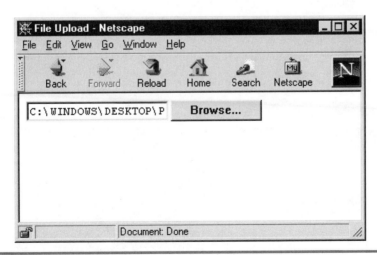

Figure 11-5 After locating the file to be uploaded, the browser prints its name and location in the text field provided.

Hidden Fields

Depending on the type of form you are creating, you may need to include a hidden field. For example, many teachers create several versions of a test to avoid having students look over their classmate's shoulder and cheat. In cases like this, you might make a special mark on the test identifying to which answer key it belongs. On web forms, these special marks are called *hidden fields*.

A hidden field is data attached to, and processed with, a form that cannot be seen or changed by the user. You can use as many hidden fields in your form as you'd like, using `input` tags with `type` attributes set to `hidden`.

```
<input type="hidden" name="TestVersion" value="3" />
<input type="hidden" name="Creator" value="Wendy Willard" />
```

TIP

This is also how you pass information from one form to the next when you start to build multipage forms.

Buttons

Buttons enable users to interact with a form. For example, to tell the browser you're finished filling out a form and are ready to process it, you might click a button labeled *Submit*. You can create three types of buttons with HTML:

- **Submit buttons** Used to process a form
- **Reset buttons** Used to reset a form
- **Other buttons** Serving any alternative needs for buttons in a form

You can use the `input` or `button` tag to create any of these buttons. Although the `input` tag is supported by many versions of both Internet Explorer and Netscape as a way to add buttons to your page, the `button` tag wasn't supported until version 4 of Internet Explorer and version 6 of Netscape.

In either case, add the `type` attribute and appropriate `value` to identify which button you are creating (see Table 11-2).

Type of Button	Description	HTML	Browser View
Submit	When pressed, this button processes the form.	`<input type="submit" value="Submit" />` or `<button type="submit">Submit </button>`	Submit
Reset	When pressed, this button resets all the form's fields back to their initial values.	`<input type="reset" value="Reset" />` or `<button type="reset">Reset</ button`	Reset
Button	When pressed, an action or event is triggered, based on a predefined script or function. (This usually involves some scripting language such as JavaScript. For more information, see Module 15.)	`<input type="button" value="Verify Data" />` or `<button type="button">Verify Data</button>`	Verify Data

Table 11-2 Types of Buttons

NOTE

On the PC, these buttons are displayed as rectangles with squared-off edges.
On the Mac, these buttons have rounded edges.

Formatting with the button Tag

You may be wondering why I'd even mention the `button` tag when the `input` tag appears to be better supported. Well. . . while the `input` and `button` tags both create a basic gray button with text inside, the `button` tag has additional formatting possibilities. You may have noticed in Table 11-2 that, unlike the `input` tag, which doesn't have a closing version, the `button` element has both opening and closing tags. This enables you to enter text, images, and other HTML that will be placed on the button when viewed in the browser.

For example, if I include an `img` tag in between the opening and closing `button` tags, that image would be displayed in the center of the button when viewed in the browser.

```
<button type="submit" name="Submit" value="Submit">
<img src="sendmessage.gif" width="100" height="68" alt="Send Message">
</button>
```

When viewed in a browser supporting the `button` tag, such as Internet Explorer 5.0, that button might look like the following:

TIP

Remember, all buttons have gray background colors by default. If you want your images to appear seamlessly on the button, use that same gray as your image's background color or make the image's background transparent. For more tips on creating web graphics, see Module 13.

Graphical Buttons with the input Tag

You can also use an image as a button with the `input` tag by changing the type to `image`, as in the following example. The `src` attribute is then required to specify where to find the image. Likewise, you also should add the `alt` attribute to allow for a text description to display when the image does not.

```
<input type="image" src="sendmessage.gif" name="Submit" alt="Send Message" />
```

Graphical buttons created with the `input` tag are different from those created with the `button` tag because they aren't placed on a button in the browser. Instead, they're surrounded by a border, just like what's around any other linked image by default. You can use style sheets, as needed, to turn off that border.

To turn off the border, add ———▶
`border = "0"` to the input tag

Project 11-1 Create a Basic Form

All web sites should contain some way for visitors to contact the business or organization. Otherwise, it's like having an advertisement in the phone book that doesn't list your phone number! This could be accomplished through a simple e-mail link, a listed phone number, or even a *Contact Us* form. In this project, you create a *Contact Us* form for Chop Point. The goals for this project include

- Creating a basic form

- Using several different input controls in the form

- Creating submit and reset buttons

NOTE

All the files needed to complete the projects in this book can be downloaded from **www.osborne.com** or **www.wendywillard.com**. In addition, you can view my version of the web site anytime by visiting **www.choppoint.org**. If you aren't using the Chop Point site, you can tailor the project to your particular needs.

Step by Step

1. Open your text or HTML editor and create a new file entitled **contactus.html**.

2. Type all the HTML tags needed for a basic HTML page.

3. Type opening and closing `form` tags.

4. Using Figure 11-6 as your guide, type the HTML tags needed to create the form. (The text is also included in the .zip file for this module.)

5. Save the file.

6. Open your web browser and choose File | Open Page (or Open File or Open, depending on the browser you're using). Locate the file contactus.html, which you just saved. Make sure the file appears as you intended it. Note: Nothing will happen when you try to "submit" your form, but don't worry—we address processing forms in the next section. For now, we're focusing on creating the form itself.

7. If you need to make changes, return to your text editor to make changes. After making any changes, save the file and switch back to the browser. Choose Refresh or Reload to preview the changes you just made.

TIP

Do your text fields, select menus, and other controls appear? If not, check to make sure you closed your `form` tag (`</form>`). For more tips, see Appendix C.

(continued)

8. If you're using the Chop Point site, you can compare your files to the following code and Figure 11-6.

```
<!DOCTYPE html PUBLIC "-//W3C//DTD XHTML 1.0 Transitional//EN"
"http://www.w3.org/TR/xhtml1/DTD/transitional.dtd">
<html>
<head>
<title> Email a Camper </title>
</head>
<body>
<h1>Email a Camper</h1>
<p>You can use this form to send email to the camper or staff member of your
choice. You are required to enter your name and email address, in case the person
you're writing would like to reply. Enter your phone number if you want the person
to respond by phone.</p>
<p>Email is downloaded each evening and given to the recipients each morning at
breakfast. Camp activities keep everyone quite busy, and it is normal for emails to
go unanswered for a few days.</p>
<form>
<p>Your Name: <input type="text" size="25" name="author" /></p>
<p>Your E-mail: <input type="text" size="25" name="email" /></p>
<p>Your Phone: <input type="text" size="25" name="phone" /></p>
<p>Who is this message for?<br />
<select name="who">
<option value="">Please Select</option>
<option value="Camper:">Camper:</option>
<option value="Counselor:">Counselor:</option>
<option value="Senior Staff:">Senior Staff:</option>
</select> <input type="text" size="25" name="recipient" /></p>
<p>Your Message:<br />
<textarea rows="10" cols="50" name="message"></textarea></p>
<p>Would you like a response?<br />
<input type="radio" name="response" value="none" />No response necessary,
just have fun!<br />
<input type="radio" name="response" value="email" />E-mail me back, please<br />
<input type="radio" name="response" value="phone" />Give me a call when you can</p>
<input type="submit" name="submit" value="Send Message" />
</form>
</body>
</html>
```

Project Summary

Online forms are a great way to get customer feedback. In addition, forms make it easy for your visitors to ask questions about products and services. This project gave you practice working on a basic form.

Figure 11-6 Using this as your guide, create a form allowing visitors to e-mail campers (or staff members).

Progress Check

1. What tag is used to create spaces where users can enter multiple lines of text?

2. Radio buttons enable users to select how many choices?

11.3 Provide a Way for Your Form to Be Processed

The phrase *processing method* refers to what happens to the form after the user enters all the data and presses the Submit button. Is it e-mailed to the site's administrator or stored in a database? Or perhaps it's written to another web page on the site, such as what occurs with a guest book or bulletin board. Many possibilities exist, which ultimately depend on the purpose of the form.

Inside the opening `form` tag, you need to tell the browser how to process your form. This is accomplished through the `action` attribute (which is required), as well as the `method` and `enctype` attributes (which are optional).

The action Attribute

The `action` attribute gives the location where the form's information should be sent. This can be in either the form of an e-mail address

```
<form action="mailto:name@emailaddress.com">
```

or the URL of a CGI script.

```
<form action="../cgi-bin/form.cgi">
```

While the easiest way to process a form is to have the data sent to an e-mail address, I don't recommend this method. Because no official specification exists for using e-mail to process forms in HTML, the results achieved with this method vary according to the browser. In fact, many browsers don't support this method at all. Perhaps the best use of this might be testing your forms before implementing a CGI script.

---

1. `<textarea>`
2. One

TIP

You might think of a CGI program as being similar to the mail carrier for your post office. This person picks up your mail and transports it to and from the post office. Some mail carriers drive trucks, while others drive cars or walk. Regardless of how they get there, they all take mail to the post office and bring mail back to you. In like manner, CGI scripts, regardless of which language they are written in, transfer information to and from the server.

CGI stands for *Common Gateway Interface* and refers to a program that sends information to and from the server. This program, also called a *script*, can be written in several different computer languages such as Visual Basic, C++, and Java. The most common of these languages is Perl, because of its ease of use and the large number of people who are able to write it.

CGI scripts must reside on your server (the computer hosting your web pages for everyone on the Web to access) in directories with special settings that allow them to be *executed* or run. For this reason, using a CGI script requires you to talk to the company that hosts your web site about whether it supports CGI scripts and, if it does, how to implement them. Most hosting companies receive questions about CGI scripts quite often and have pages of information on their web sites dedicated to the subject. When in doubt, visit your host company's web site or call to see what your next step should be.

NOTE

One reason some hosting providers don't allow CGI scripts on their servers is that they can infringe on the site's security. If your hosting provider doesn't let you use a CGI script, don't worry. Several services are set up to host these scripts and process your forms for you. Check with your own hosting provider for referrals, or visit **http://dir.yahoo.com/Computers_and_Internet/Internet/World_Wide_Web/Programming/Forms/** for a list of companies providing these types of services.

What Does a CGI Script Look Like?

Just because a CGI script cannot be written in HTML doesn't mean you can't learn how to write one. As I mentioned before, I don't consider myself a computer programmer and I didn't study computer science in school. I can understand and write basic Perl scripts to process my HTML forms, though.

While creating CGI scripts (whether in Perl or another language) is beyond the scope of this book, Figure 11-7 shows what a CGI script written in Perl looks like. By showing this, I hope to give you an idea of what happens to the form data after a user clicks the Submit button.

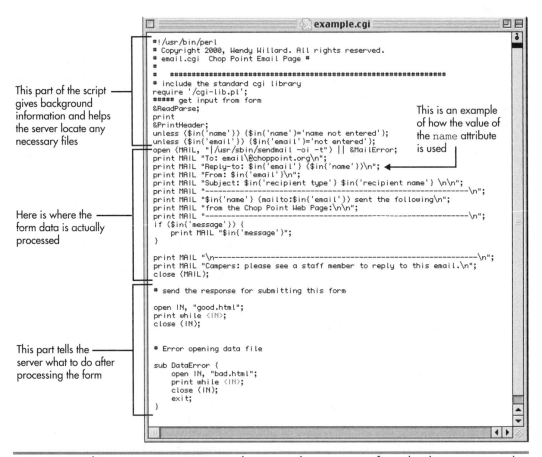

This part of the script gives background information and helps the server locate any necessary files

This is an example of how the value of the name attribute is used

Here is where the form data is actually processed

This part tells the server what to do after processing the form

```
#!/usr/bin/perl
# Copyright 2000, Wendy Willard. All rights reserved.
# email.cgi   Chop Point Email Page #
#
# ############################################################
# include the standard cgi library
require '/cgi-lib.pl';
##### get input from form
&ReadParse;
print
&PrintHeader;
unless ($in{'name'}) ($in{'name'}='name not entered');
unless ($in{'email'}) ($in{'email'}='not entered');
open (MAIL, "|/usr/sbin/sendmail -oi -t") || &MailError;
print MAIL "To: email\@choppoint.org\n";
print MAIL "Reply-to: $in{'email'} ($in{'name'})\n";
print MAIL "From: $in{'email'}\n";
print MAIL "Subject: $in{'recipient type'} $in{'recipient name'} \n\n";
print MAIL "------------------------------------------------\n";
print MAIL "$in{'name'} (mailto:$in{'email'}) sent the following\n";
print MAIL "from the Chop Point Web Page:\n\n";
print MAIL "------------------------------------------------\n";
if ($in{'message'}) {
    print MAIL "$in{'message'}";
}

print MAIL "\n-----------------------------------------------\n";
print MAIL "Campers: please see a staff member to reply to this email.\n";
close (MAIL);

# send the response for submitting this form

open IN, "good.html";
print while <IN>;
close (IN);

# Error opening data file

sub DataError {
    open IN, "bad.html";
    print while <IN>;
    close (IN);
    exit;
}
```

Figure 11-7 This CGI script, written in Perl, was used to process a form that lets parents and friends e-mail kids at camp.

Where Can I Get a CGI Script?

Literally thousands of free CGI scripts are available on the Web, and thousands of others are available for small fees. First, check with your hosting provider for referrals. Your provider might even have some scripts on hand for you to use, which are already set up to work on their systems.

If you need to find your own scripts, try looking at some of these sites:

- **Matt's Script Archive**   www.scriptarchive.com

- **HotScripts.com**   www.hotscripts.com

- **The CGI Resource Index**   www.cgi-resources.com

Pay attention to the documentation offered with each script because it should tell you how to customize the script for your needs and how to install it on your server.

The method and enctype Attributes

The two other attributes you'll probably use in the opening form tag are method and enctype. The method attribute tells the browser how to send the data to the server. There are two possible values for this attribute: get and post.

TIP

For help deciding which method or enctype to use, consult your hosting provider or the creator of your CGI script.

The get method takes all the data submitted with the form and sends it to the server attached to the end of the URL. For example, say the script location is **http://www.yoursite.com/cgi-bin/form.cgi**, and the only data from the form is the user's name (in this case, we'll use wendy). If the method was set to get, here's what would be sent to the server when the user clicked the Submit button:

```
http://www.yoursite.com/cgi-form.cgi?name=wendy
```

This method works best for searches where a small amount of information must be transferred to the server, such as the keywords you are searching for. For more comprehensive forms, the post method can be used. Instead of attaching the information to the URL of the script, the information is sent directly to the location of the script file.

The enctype attribute, short for *encoding type*, tells the browser how to format the data when the method attribute is set to post. The default value is application/x-www-form-urlencoded. Because this should work for most of your forms, you needn't include the enctype attribute in your form tag unless you want to change the value.

For example, if you are allowing users to upload files with your form, you need to change the enctype to multipart/form-data, as in the following example.

```
<form action="myscript.cgi" method="post" enctype="multipart/form-data">
```

CRITICAL SKILL
11.4 Use Additional Formatting Techniques for Forms

You can use many of the formatting techniques discussed in previous modules to format your forms. For example, to make the label of a text field bold, you could simply add the b or strong tags around the text.

```
<b>First Name:</b> <input type="text" name="FirstName">
```

If you refer to Figure 11-7 in the preceding project, you'll notice the text fields are scattered through the page. If, instead, you want to have all the text fields lined up in a column, you could use a table to format your form.

Tables

When using a table to lay out a form, you will probably place each individual element in its own table cell. Perhaps the labels for the form (telling people what information to enter) might be placed in cells in the first column, while the input controls (text fields, and so forth) might be placed in the second column.

```
<form action="..." method="post">
<table>
<tr>                              This text label is in a cell by
    <td>First Name</td> ←——— itself in the first column
    <td><input type="text" name="FirstName" /></td>
</tr>
                          This cell in the second column contains only
<tr>                      the input control for the user's first name
    <td>Last Name</td>
    <td><input type="text" name="LastName" /></td>
</tr>
<tr>
    <td>Mailing Address</td>
    <td><input type="text" name="AddressLine1" /></td>
</tr>                                          This text field is a second
<tr>                                          line for users to enter their
    <td> </td> ←——This cell is empty      mailing addresses
    <td><input type="text" name="AddressLine2" /></td> ←
</tr>        ┌── The two columns are merged for this row to allow the Submit
            │    and Reset buttons to flow freely at the bottom of the table
<tr>        ↓
    <td colspan="2"><input type="submit" value="Send Form"
 /><input type="reset" value="Start Over" /></td>
</tr>
</table>
</form>
```

Using a table like this enables you to achieve a more uniform look in your forms. Notice in the following illustration how all of the text fields line up vertically, regardless of how long or short the preceding text is.

```
 ⊖ ⊖ ⊖            Tables and Forms            ⬭

  ⇐ ·  ⇒ ·  🔃  ⊗  🏠 [◉ ▾] ◉  (G·

   First Name      [                        ]
   Last Name       [                        ]
   Mailing Address [                        ]
                   [                        ]

     [ Send Form ] [ Start Over ]




  Done                                       ◢
```

TIP

Because determining where each text label and input control should be placed can initially be confusing, I recommend you first create the form itself before placing it into a table. As with any table, it may help to plan the form on paper before coding.

Tab Order and Keyboard Shortcuts

Module 5 discussed changing the tab order and adding keyboard shortcuts for links using the `tabindex` and `accesskey` attributes. You can also use these attributes to format input controls in a form. Remember, the tab index begins at 0, not 1.

⎡ This attribute causes the text field to become
  active after the user clicks the tab key three times

```
Enter your first name (alt-f):
<input type="text" name="FirstName" tabindex="2" accesskey="f"> ⬅
```

This allows the text field to become active when the user types
F and another key (ALT on the PC, COMMAND on the Mac)

Refer to Module 5 for details on using either of these two attributes.

Ask the Expert

Q: I used a table to lay out my web page and placed a form for searching in one cell. However, when I did so, I noticed a lot of extra space in that cell, which I can't seem to delete by adjusting the padding or margins. What's going on?

A: Unfortunately, this is a common problem. The root of the problem lies in understanding what kind of tag the form tag is. Tags in HTML usually fall into one of two categories: block elements or inline elements. *Block elements*, like the form tag and the table tag, are used for structure and layout on a page, while inline elements are employed to alter the appearance of text. For example, the b tag, an inline element, is used to make text bold, but it doesn't alter the location of the text.

Block elements do alter the location of text or other items on a page, and, by default, many of them force a line break within the page. This means that wherever you place the form tag, a blank line is also inserted.

Q: Yes, but isn't there any way around that?

A: You can try to fix this by moving your form tag to another location where the space is less obvious, but remember, you cannot nest forms. So, if you have more than one form on your page, each of their opening and closing tags must not overlap.

If this is a big problem on your page, a better option is to use style sheets instead of tables to lay out your form. This is discussed more in the later part of this module, in the section titled "Use Styles and Fieldsets to Eliminate the Table Layout."

Labels

Whenever you include descriptive text before an input control, you are labeling it for users, helping them to understand what type of information they should enter. To link the label and the associating control formally, you can use the label tag and the id attribute. Each label can only be attached to one control.

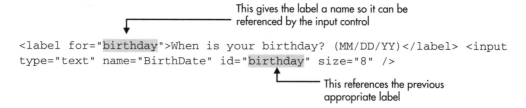

This gives the label a name so it can be
referenced by the input control

```
<label for="birthday">When is your birthday? (MM/DD/YY)</label> <input
type="text" name="BirthDate" id="birthday" size="8" />
```

This references the previous
appropriate label

NOTE

At press time, the use of either the `label` tag or the `id` attribute doesn't change the way the page appears in a graphical browser.

This formal labeling process was new to HTML in version 4.01. As this process has gained support, it's become an important technique for linking labels and controls, particularly to ensure your page is accessible to all users. The reason for this is, when tables are used, controls and their labels are often separated across table cells. This can be especially troublesome for nonvisual browsers when they try to link controls with the appropriate label.

```
<form action="..." method="post">
<table>
<tr>
    <td><label for="fname">First Name</label></td>
    <td><input type="text" name="FirstName" id="fname" /></td>
</tr>
<tr>
    <td><label for="lname">Last Name</label></td>
    <td><input type="text" name="LastName" id="lname" /></td>
</tr>
</table>
</form>
```

Groups

While the `label` attribute is used to attach names to controls formally, the `fieldset` attribute enables you to group sets of labels and controls. For example, if you had an employee application form with three distinct sections, such as Schooling, Work Experience, and Skills, you could use the `fieldset` attribute to group all the labels and controls under these headings. The `legend` attribute then gives a caption to the group, if you want to include one.

```
<form action="..." method="post">
<fieldset>
  <legend>Schooling</legend>
  <p>
  High School: <input type="text" name="HighSchool" /><br />
  College: <input type="text" name="College" />
  </p>
</fieldset>
<fieldset>
```

```
 <legend>Work Experience</legend>
 <p>
 Current Job: <input type="text" name="CurrentJob" /><br />
 Previous Job: <input type="text" name="PreviousJob1" /><br />
   Previous Job: <input type="text" name="PreviousJob2" />
 </p>
</fieldset>
<fieldset>
  <legend>Skills</legend>
  <p>
  Skill 1: <input type="text" name="Skill1" /><br />
  Skill 2: <input type="text" name="Skill2" /><br />
  Skill 3: <input type="text" name="Skill3" />
  </p>
</fieldset>
</form>
```

Most browsers supporting the `fieldset` tag add boxes around each group and place the caption from the `legend` tag in the outline of the box as a headline.

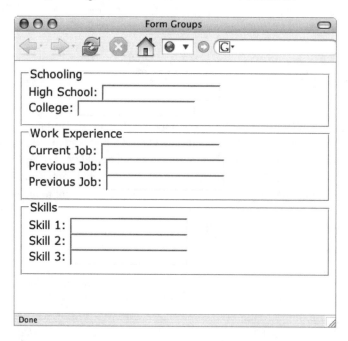

Disable Form Elements

When you want to restrict a user's input for a specific element, you might use one of two attributes:

```
readonly
disabled
```

NOTE

These two attributes weren't supported by browsers prior to IE 5 and Netscape 6.

The `readonly` attribute can be added to input controls so users cannot change the values. For example, in the following code, the phrase ww1234 is displayed in the text field but cannot be changed by the user. If you try to type in a text field that has been set to `readonly`, an alert is displayed or heard, but otherwise, no change exists in the appearance of the box.

```
Your username: <input type="text" value="ww1234" name="UserName" readonly="readonly" />
```

The `disabled` attribute works essentially the same way, except input controls that are disabled also appear in gray or faded text to reduce their importance in the form. You cannot click in a text field that has been set to `disabled`.

```
Your username: <input type="text" value="ww1234" name="UserName" disabled="disabled" />
```

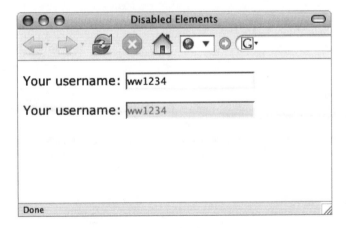

CRITICAL SKILL
11.5 Style Forms

Most of the `form` tags you just learned can also be altered with style sheets. This means you could quite easily turn all of your text boxes green if you wanted to. It also means you can finally do away with those boring white and gray form elements! And because the `form` tag is a block-level element (just like the `p` tag), you can even style your entire form to have a particular background color or border.

To further illustrate this point, consider Figures 11-8 and 11-9. The first figure shows a basic HTML form (created with the tags discussed in this module) that has been placed in a table. The HTML used to create this form is shown next.

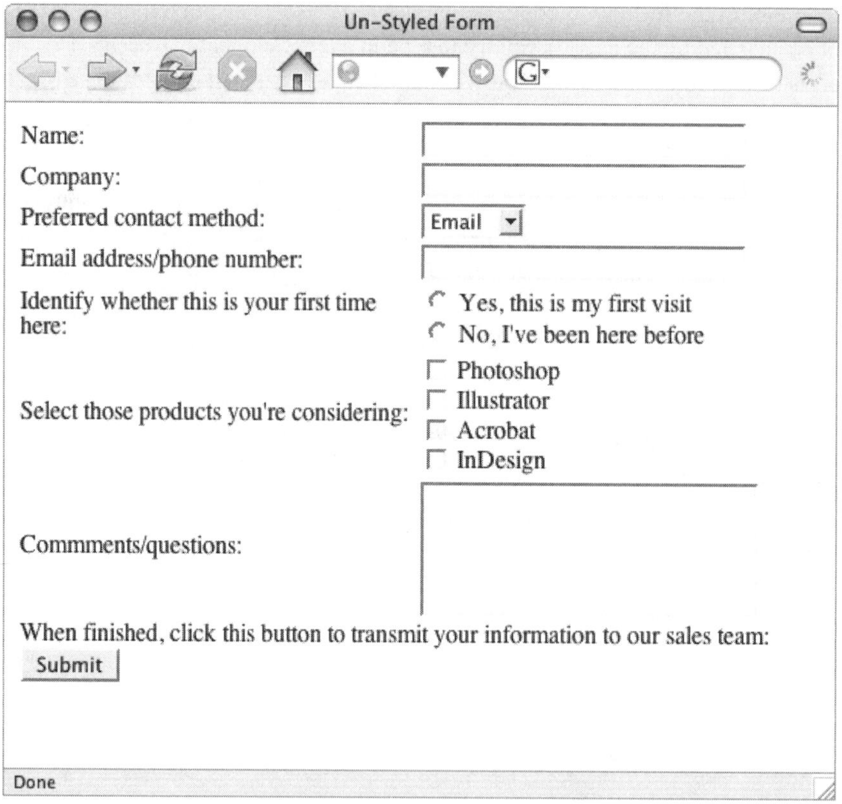

Figure 11-8 This is our very basic HTML form (inside a table) before CSS.

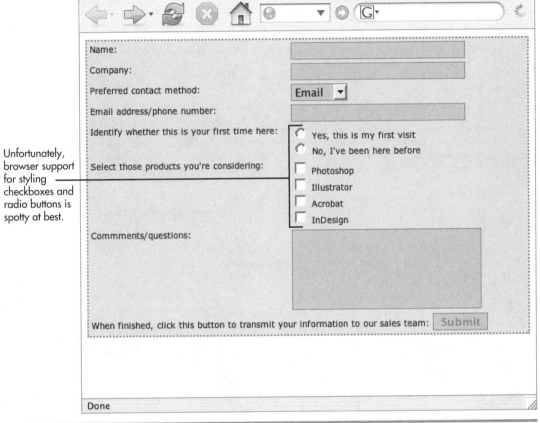

Unfortunately, browser support for styling checkboxes and radio buttons is spotty at best.

Figure 11-9 This is the same HTML code, with a style sheet applied.

```
<form action="..." method="post" id="salesform">
<table>
<tr><td width="50%">Name:</td>
<td width="50%"><input name="name" type="text" size="25" /></td>
</tr>
 <tr><td>Company:</td>
<td><input name="company" type="text" size="25" /></td>
</tr>
<tr><td>Preferred contact method:</td>
<td><select name="contact-type"><option value="Email">Email</option>
<option value="Phone">Phone</option></select></td>
```

```
</tr>
<tr><td>Email address/phone number:</td>
<td><input type="text" size="25" name="contact-method" /></td>
</tr>
<tr><td>Identify whether this is your first time here:</td>
<td><input type="radio" name="first-visit" value="yes" class="radio">
Yes, this is my first visit<br />
<input type="radio" name="first-visit" value="no" class="radio"> No, I've been
here before</td>
</tr>
<tr><td>Select those products you're considering:</td>
<td><input type="checkbox" name="products" value="Photoshop"> Photoshop<br />
<input type="checkbox" name="products" value="Illustrator"> Illustrator<br />
<input type="checkbox" name="products" value="Acrobat"> Acrobat<br />
<input type="checkbox" name="products" value="InDesign"> InDesign</td>
</tr>
<tr><td>Commments/questions:</td>
<td><textarea cols="25" rows="5" name="comments"></textarea></td>
</tr>
<tr>
  <td colspan="2">When finished, click this button to transmit your information
to our sales team: <input type="submit" name="Submit" value="Submit"
id="submit" /></td>
  </tr>
    </table></form>
```

Figure 11-9, however, adds a style sheet to customize the design of both the form elements and the table. Notice the HTML code has not changed at all—the only addition is the following internal style sheet:

```
<style type="text/css">
body {
    font-family: verdana;
    font-size: 10px;
}
form#salesform {
    border: 2px dotted #F60;
    background-color: #fde6a2;
}
input, select, textarea {
    border: 1px solid #F60;
    background-color: #FC3;
}
textarea {
    overflow: auto;
    padding: 5px;
}
td {
    vertical-align: top;
}
```

```
input#submit {
    color: #F60;
    font-weight: bold;
}
</style>
```

TIP

The key to styling forms (or any other page element for that matter) is in properly preparing the HTML code before you even begin the style sheet. Depending on your needs, this may mean adding ID attributes to each form element so they can be referenced later. Or perhaps using the `colgroup` tag to enable easy access to each column (for styling purposes).

Use Styles and Fieldsets to Eliminate the Table Layout

What if you wanted to take your style sheet one step further, and use it to lay out the entire form, and even eliminate the need to use a table for layout. Not only is this a great option, it actually can make the design and maintenance of forms much easier. Consider the same form used in the previous section, this time coded without any table tags:

```
<form action="..." method="post" id="salesform">
<fieldset>
<legend>Contact Information</legend>
<label for="name">Name:</label> <input name="name" type="text" size="25" id="name" />
<label for="company">Company:</label> <input name="company" type="text" size="25"
id="company" />
<label for="contact-type">Preferred contact method:</label> <select name="contact-type"
id="contact-type"><option value="Email">Email</option><option
value="Phone">Phone</option></select><label for="contact-method">Email address/phone
number:</label><input type="text" size="25" name="contact-method" id="contact-method" />
</fieldset>

<fieldset>
<legend>New Customer?</legend>
<label for="first-visit">Identify whether this is your first time here:</label>
<input type="radio" name="first-visit" value="yes" class="radio"> Yes, this is my first
visit<br />
<input type="radio" name="first-visit" value="no" class="radio"> No, I've been here
before
</fieldset>

<fieldset>
<legend>Product Interest</legend>
<label for="products">Select those products you're considering:</label>
<input type="checkbox" name="products" value="Photoshop"> Photoshop<br />
<input type="checkbox" name="products" value="Illustrator"> Illustrator<br />
<input type="checkbox" name="products" value="Acrobat"> Acrobat<br />
<input type="checkbox" name="products" value="InDesign"> InDesign
```

```
</fieldset>

<fieldset>
<legend>Message</legend>
<label for"comments">Please enter your comments/questions here:</label>
<textarea cols="25" rows="5" name="comments"></textarea>
</fieldset>

<label for="Submit">When finished, click this button to transmit your information to our
sales team:</label>
<input type="submit" name="Submit" value="Submit" id="Submit" />
</form>
```

Figure 11-10 shows the preceding table as coded, without any styling. While there is a little bit of structure, just from the `fieldset` tags, much of the content runs together across

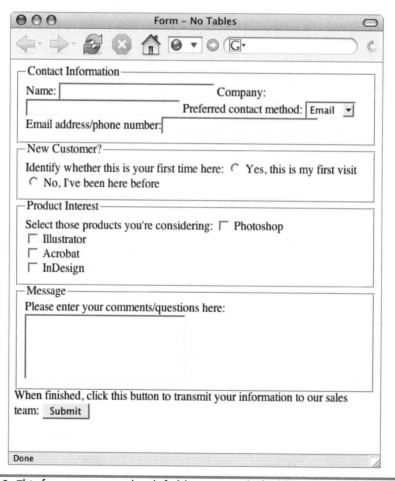

Figure 11-10 This form was created with fieldsets instead of tables. Even though it's a bit jumbled now, a style sheet will make this form shine.

the screen. To prevent this, you could specify that the labels for each form element be displayed as block elements. You might remember this causes the browser to fill the screen horizontally with the element in question. So in the case of our form field labels, it forces the form field after each label to drop down to the line below. Take a look at Figure 11-11 to see what I mean. The following is the complete style sheet used to display the styled form.

```
<style type="text/css">
body {
    font-family: verdana;
    font-size: 10px;
}
form#salesform {
    border: 2px dotted #F60;
    background-color: #fde6a2;
    padding: 10px;
}
input, select, textarea {
    border: 1px solid #F60;
    background-color: #FC3;
    clear: both;
}
textarea {
    overflow: auto;
    padding: 5px;
}
input#submit {
    color: #F60;
    font-weight: bold;
}
label {
    padding-top: 10px;
    display: block;
    font-weight: bold;
}
legend {
    font-size: 14pt;
    font-weight: bold;
    color: #F60;
}
fieldset {
    border-width: 1px 0px 0px 0px;
    border-style: solid none none none;
    border-color: #F60;
    margin-bottom: 10px;
}
</style>
```

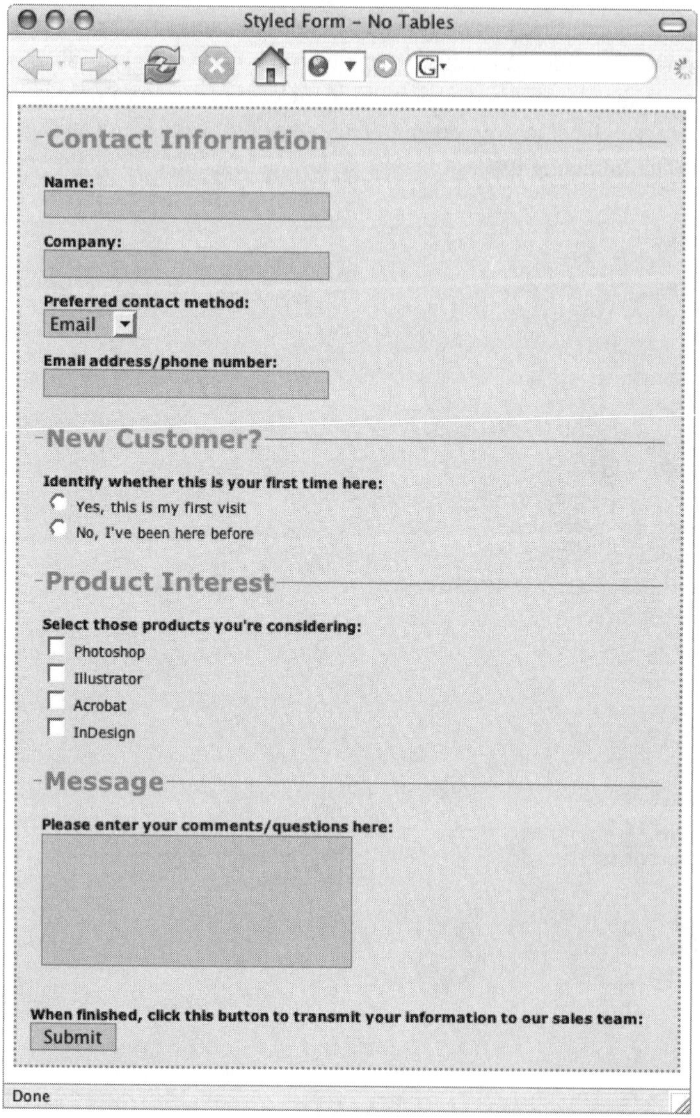

Figure 11-11 After the style sheet is added to this form, the content becomes more legible and organized.

As you can see, by comparing the table-based form with the fieldset/style-based form, you can achieve somewhat similar results with the two different types of coding methods.

However, the latter—when combined with style sheets—is easy to code and maintain, and offers significantly more customization options.

Project 11-2 Format the Form

Returning to the Contact Us page created in Project 11-1, use additional formatting techniques to achieve a more uniform appearance of the labels and controls. Goals for this project include

- Grouping form elements with the `fieldset` and `legend` tags
- Styling the form
- Referencing a CGI script in the `action` attribute of the `form` tag

Step by Step

1. Open your text or HTML editor and open the file entitled contactus.html from Project 11-1.

2. Group the first three controls into a fieldset labeled **Your Contact Information**. Group the recipient and message into a fieldset called **Your Message** and place the remaining control into its own fieldset labeled **Your Response**.

3. Use `label` tags to associate each form control with its text description.

4. Add a style sheet to format the page in a similar fashion as was discussed previously, in Figure 11-11. (Feel free to adjust the colors, fonts, and so on, according to your tastes.)

5. Add the `action` and `method` attributes to the opening `form` tag. For testing purposes, you can have the results mailed to your e-mail address or simply use a fake address for a CGI script. Set the `method` to `post`.

6. Save the file.

7. Open your web browser and choose File | Open Page (or Open File or Open, depending on the browser you're using). Locate the file contactus.html you just saved. Make sure the file appears as you intended it.

8. If you need to make changes, return to your text editor to do so. After making any changes, save the file and switch back to the browser. Choose Refresh or Reload to preview the changes you just made.

9. If you're using the Chop Point site, you can compare your files to the following code and Figure 11-12.

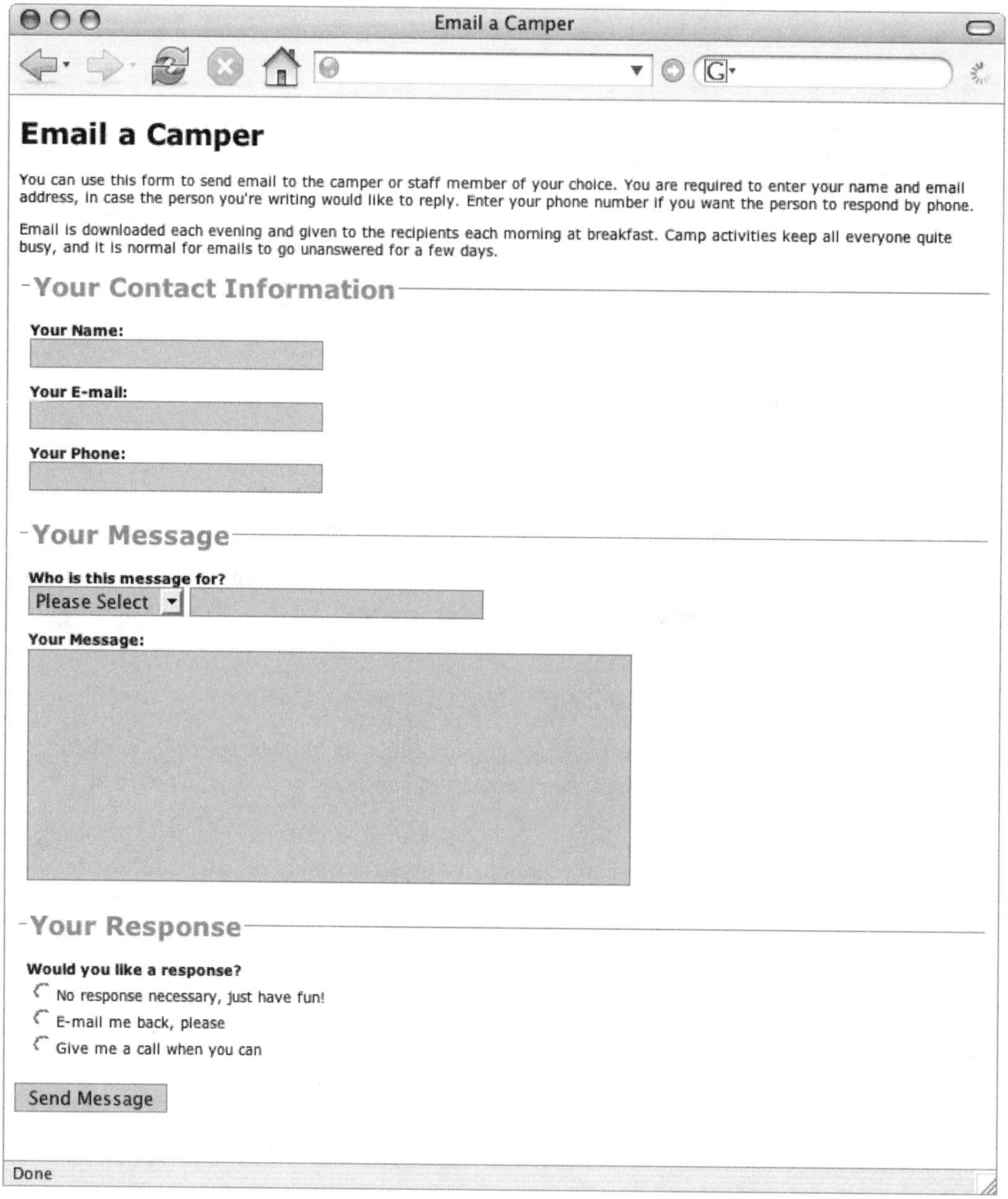

Figure 11-12 Those using the Chop Point site may end up with a page similar to this one.

```
<!DOCTYPE html PUBLIC "-//W3C//DTD XHTML 1.0 Transitional//EN"
"http://www.w3.org/TR/xhtml1/DTD/transitional.dtd">
<html>
<head>
<title> Email a Camper </title>
<style type="text/css">
body {
    font-family: verdana;
    font-size: 10px;
}
input, select, textarea {
    border: 1px solid #F60;
    background-color: #FC3;
    clear: both;
}
textarea {
    overflow: auto;
    padding: 5px;
}
input#submit {
    color: #F60;
    font-weight: bold;
}
label {
    padding-top: 10px;
    display: block;
    font-weight: bold;
}
    legend {
    font-size: 14pt;
    font-weight: bold;
    color: #F60;
}
fieldset {
    border-width: 1px 0px 0px 0px;
    border-style: solid none none none;
    border-color: #F60;
    margin-bottom: 10px;
}
</style>
</head>
<body>
<h1>Email a Camper</h1>
<p>You can use this form to send email to the camper or staff member of your
choice. You are required to enter your name and email address, in case the person
you're writing would like to reply. Enter your phone number if you want the person to
respond by phone.</p>
<p>Email is downloaded each evening and given to the recipients each morning at
breakfast. Camp activities keep everyone quite busy, and it is normal for emails to
go unanswered for a few days.</p>
```

```
<form>
<fieldset>
<legend>Your Contact Information</legend>
<label for="author">Your Name: </label><input type="text" size="25" name="author" />
<label for="email">Your E-mail: </label><input type="text" size="25" name="email" />
<label for="phone">Your Phone: </label><input type="text" size="25" name="phone" />
</fieldset>
<fieldset>
  <legend>Your Message</legend>
    <label for="who">Who is this message for?</label>
    <select name="who">
      <option value="">Please Select</option>
      <option value="Camper:">Camper:</option>
      <option value="Counselor:">Counselor:</option>
      <option value="Senior Staff:">Senior Staff:</option>
    </select> <input type="text" size="25" name="recipient" />
  <label for="message">Your Message:</label>
    <textarea rows="10" cols="50" name="message"></textarea>
</fieldset>
<fieldset>
  <legend>Your Response</legend>
  <label for="response">Would you like a response?</label>
    <input type="radio" name="response" value="none" />No response necessary, just have
fun!<br />
    <input type="radio" name="response" value="email" />E-mail me back, please<br />
    <input type="radio" name="response" value="phone" />Give me a call when you can</p>
</fieldset>
<input type="submit" name="submit" value="Send Message" />
</form>
</body>
</html>
```

Project Summary

Many of the additional formatting techniques used with forms help to make them more
efficient and accessible. This project gave you practice using some of those techniques to
make an existing form more user-friendly.

Module 11 Mastery Check

1. Fill in the blank: _____ tags must surround all web forms.

2. What are two types of text input in HTML web forms?

3. Which attribute identifies an input control so that it's correctly handled when the form is processed?

4. Which input control is most useful for questions requiring a simple yes or no answer?

5. True/False: Radio buttons are small, round buttons that enable users to select a single option from a list of choices.

6. Which attribute can prohibit text in a text area from being continued across long lines out of the visible window?

7. Fill in the blank: The _____ attribute identifies the visible width of a text area based on an average character width.

8. Fix the following code so that users can enter multiple lines of data into the comment box, which should measure 30 characters wide by five lines tall.

```
Enter your comments here:
  <input size="30,5"></input>
```

9. How do you cause three options in a select menu to be visible at once?

10. Add the appropriate code to create a single-line text field in which, upon entry of data, all contents are displayed as bullets or asterisks in the browser. Name the field "secret" and make it XHTML-compliant.

```
Please enter your secret word:
<                                    >
```

11. Fill in the blank: _____ tags surround each item in a select menu.

12. True/False: The `fieldset` tag is used to divide long select menus into categories of submenus.

13. Add the appropriate code to create a place where users can upload a graphic file from their personal computers to the web server. Name the field "upload" and make it XHTML-compliant.

```
Please select the file to upload:
<                                    >
```

14. Which attribute is added to the `form` tag to give the location where the form's information should be sent?

15. Which attribute and value are added to the `form` tag to tell the browser to take all the data submitted with the form and send it to the server attached to the end of the file's URL?

Module 12

Positioning Page Elements

In the first two editions of this book, I suggested using tables for the bulk of your page layout. This meant the module teaching tables were double their current size, and detailed some very complicated coding to create seemingly invisible tables for page layout. Thankfully, all that's in the past! In fact, a key reason for revising this book was to remove the outdated table discussions in order to make way for more current forms of page layout—with style sheets.

CRITICAL SKILL

12.1 Understand the Concept and Uses of Style Sheets for Page Layout

Thus far in the book, you've learned how to format various types of content, from bits of text to images, multimedia, and response forms. This section of the book seeks to close the loop, so to speak, by discussing how to pull it all together into effective, user-friendly web pages. Thus, in this module, it's all about the layout.

To summarize my earlier discussions on CSS, style sheets were created to provide a way to separate the content of a web site from the design. The theory is that content is king (which it should be, in most cases), and so anything else is simply icing on the proverbial cake. So we keep the content in the main HTML document, and pull the design aspects into the style sheet.

The most striking benefit to this arrangement is in maintenance of the web site. In the past, if you wanted to change the color of the links on all the pages of your site, for example, you had to edit every body tag on every page. But now, if that information is contained in a single style sheet, which is then linked from each page on the site, you need only make a single change to alter the link colors for the entire web site.

This also holds true for the overall page layout. It used to be an expensive and exhaustive process for businesses to redesign their web sites every few years. If the content is separated from the design with style sheets, the site can be redesigned much more quickly, at a mere fraction of the cost. The reason is simple—instead of recoding every page on the site, the developer only has to recode the site style sheet.

TIP

Remember the CSS Zen Garden mentioned in a previous section? That web site is a perfect example of this concept. Refer to **www.csszengarden.com** to see how the entire look and feel of the site is completely altered, after changing only a single style sheet.

CRITICAL SKILL

12.2 Create a Single-Column, Centered, Fluid Page Layout

So now that you understand the key reason for using style sheets to lay out your web pages, let's get to it! When tables ruled for page layout, a centered "box" became the standard design.

Because screen sizes varied from very small (640×480) to much larger (1024×768), that box was often a fixed width so as not to hide any of the content from those using small monitors.

Thankfully, times have changed and there is no longer a need to design for 640×480 monitors. In fact, the average screen size, as of this writing, is somewhere between 800×600 and 1024×768, with more and more people getting larger monitors. I still advocate limiting the horizontal size of graphics, however, so you don't end up forcing the user to scroll horizontally just to see the rest of the content. But with that said, I see no reason why the text content of your page can't be fluid so as to grow and shrink according to the size of the browser window.

Many other designers agree, and the centered, fluid page layout is quite popular, whether used with one or more columns of content. For our first page layout with style sheets, I decided to keep it simple and create a single-column, centered, fluid page design. Compare Figures 12-1 and 12-2 to see how this layout grows according to the size of the browser window.

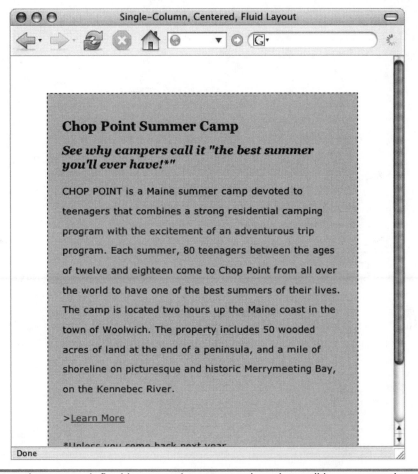

Figure 12-1 The centered, fluid layout is shown in a relatively small browser window.

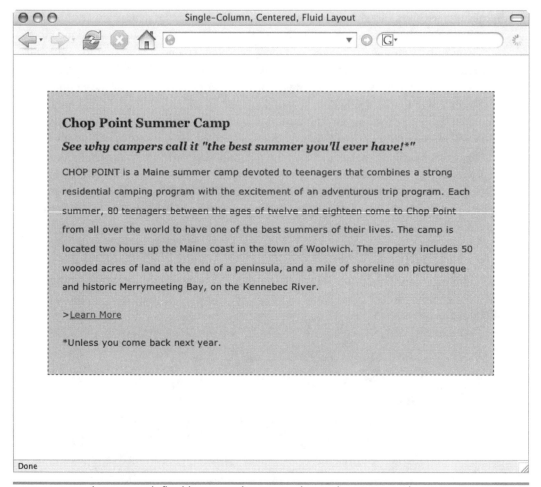

Figure 12-2 The centered, fluid layout is shown in a larger browser window.

The style sheet for this layout is quite simple. In fact, the layout portion includes only the following declarations to style the body tag and the content division labeled "content":

```
body {
    margin: 0px;
    padding: 0px;
}
#content {
    margin: 50px;
    padding: 20px;
```

```
   background-color: #ccc;
   border:1px dashed black;
}
```

Break Down the Code

Even though the styles used for positioning this layout are relatively simple, it helps to break each section down to really understand how each style sheet property works. So let's look at the properties applied to the body tag.

```
body {
    margin: 0px;
    padding: 0px;
}
```

Whenever you set out to use style sheets to position elements on the page, it's best to get off to a good start. That usually means letting all the browsers know exactly where to begin displaying your content, because some browsers have different default "starting points" than others. If you remember to think of the available space within the browser window as a big box, the "starting point" identifies any margins outside that box, and the padding inside of it.

For the purposes of this layout, we're essentially turning off all margins and padding. This means we can place content all the way up to the edge of the browser window if we choose, and it gives us the flexibility to design accordingly.

#content

The main content area (outlined with a dotted line in Figures 12-1 and 12-2) is contained within a division called "content" using code like this:

```
<div id="content"> Content goes here </div>
```

All of the formatting of that content is achieved by adding properties to the style sheet declaration for that section.

```
#content {
    margin: 50px;
    padding: 20px;
    background-color: #ccc;
    border:1px dashed black;
}
```

The margin property adds a 50-pixel margin around all sides of the content box. Because div tags are block-level elements in HTML, the content box fills the remaining available space. And, because there is an equal amount of space around all four sides, the content box becomes centered in the browser window. Voila!

To create some empty space between the edge of the box and the content inside, the `padding` property is added. This makes a 20-pixel buffer zone along all internal edges of the box. The `background-color` and `border` properties aren't used for positioning but to add character to the box itself.

Pull It All Together

The complete code used to create this layout, as shown previously in Figures 12-1 and 12-2, is as follows:

```
<!DOCTYPE html PUBLIC "-//W3C//DTD XHTML 1.0 Transitional//EN"
"http://www.w3.org/TR/xhtml1/DTD/transitional.dtd">
<html>
<head>
<title> Single-Column, Centered, Fluid Layout </title>
<style type="text/css">
body {
    margin: 0px;
    padding: 0px;
}
#content {
    margin: 50px;
    padding: 20px;
    color: black;
    background-color: #ccc;
    border:1px dashed black;
}
p {
    font-size: 10pt;
    line-height: 20pt;
    font-family: verdana, arial, helvetica, sans-serif;
    margin: 0px 0px 12px 0px;
}
h1 {
    font-size: 14pt;
    font-family: georgia;
}
h2 {
    font-size: 12pt;
    font-family: georgia;
    font-style: italic;
}
```

```
</style>
</head>
<body>
<div id="content">
<h1>Chop Point Summer Camp</h1>
<h2>See why campers call it "the best summer you'll ever have!*"</h2>
<p>CHOP POINT is a Maine summer camp devoted to teenagers that
combines a strong residential camping program with the excitement of
an adventurous trip program. Each summer, 80 teenagers between the
ages of twelve and eighteen come to Chop Point from all over the world
to have one of the best summers of their lives. The camp is located
two hours up the Maine coast in the town of Woolwich. The property
includes 50 wooded acres of land at the end of a peninsula, and a mile
of shoreline on picturesque and historic Merrymeeting Bay, on the
Kennebec River.</p>
<p>&gt;<a href="">Learn More</a></p>
<p>*Unless you come back next year.</p></div>
</body>
</html>
```

TIP

I always show internal style sheets in my examples, because it's easier when teaching in
a book. However, if you're adding these layouts to multiple pages, it makes much more
sense to save the style sheet as an external style sheet, and simply reference it from each
page. The final section in this module discusses several ways to accomplish this task.

Browser Support

This style sheet layout actually enjoys wide support among the popular browsers. It is simple
enough in concept that there really aren't any offending properties or values used. But with
any CSS page layout, it's important to test your page in as many browsers as possible. This
becomes even more important if you customize this layout to add additional columns.

CRITICAL SKILL
12.3 Create a Multicolumn Fluid Page Layout

Probably the most widely used web page layout is one with three columns, one or more of
which grow according to the size of the browser window. Typically, the site's navigation
is placed in the left column, while ads or other supplemental information is added to the far
right column.

This leaves the center column for the real meat of the site—its text content. In situations
like this, the left and right columns remain static in size, while the center column grows or

shrinks according to the width of the browser window. There may also be a header and a footer area, to complete the layout, as shown in the following example.

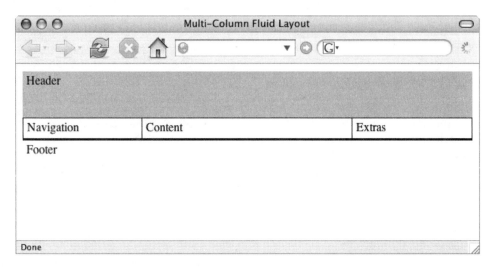

Continuing with our three-column fluid page layout, the following shows what the style sheet might look like:

```
body {
    margin: 10px 10px 0px 10px;
    padding: 0px;
}
#header {
    height: 50px;
    background-color: #ccc;
    padding: 5px;
}
#navigation {
    position: absolute;
    left: 10px;
    top: 70px;
    width: 150px;
    border: 1px solid #000;
    padding: 5px;
}
#extras {
    position: absolute;
    right: 10px;
    top: 70px;
    width: 150px;
```

```
    border: 1px solid #000;
    padding: 5px;
}
#content {
    background-color: #999;
    margin-left: 162px;
    margin-right: 162px;
    padding: 5px;
}
#footer {
    border-top: 2px solid #000;
    padding: 5px;
}
```

And the corresponding HTML is quite simple in this case:

```
<div id="header">Header</div>
<div id="content">Content</div>
<div id="navigation">Navigation</div>
<div id="extras">Extras</div>
<div id="footer">Footer</div>
```

TIP

Notice how the content section is placed before the navigation section in the HTML code, but appears to the right of it in the browser view? That's intentional, and very important. Search engines and other tools that "read" the code need to "see" the real meat of the site as soon as possible. CSS enables us to place that content before other less important aspects, such as the navigation, because the actual placement of the content is done in the style sheet instead of the HTML code. This means Braille readers, for example, can access the content quicker. In fact, many search engines give more weight to keywords found in the first part of the code than in the latter.

Break Down the Code

To really understand what's happening in this style sheet in order to position the elements appropriately on the page, let's break it down a bit. First, take a look at the style sheet declaration for the body tag:

```
body {
    margin: 10px 10px 0px 10px;
    padding: 0px;
}
```

This particular layout allows for a ten-pixel margin around the top, right, and left edges, but no margin along the bottom edge. Internally, the style sheet turns off padding on all four sides. The following is a graphical representation of what we've created thus far:

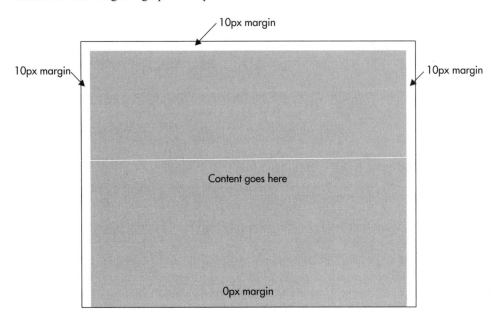

#header

Next, consider the division called "header" by looking at its portion of the style sheet.

```
#header {
    height: 50px;
    background-color: #ccc;
    padding: 5px;
}
```

This element's style declaration is very basic, specifying only its height, background color, and padding size. Even so, there are a couple of important aspects to this element. First, even though the header's height is 50 pixels, it will actually be 60 pixels from the top edge of the available window space, as shown graphically in the following illustration.

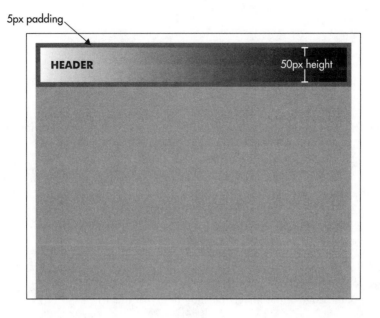

Why? Because we must remember that according to the W3C specifications, padding is *added to* the width or height. This means our header takes up 50 pixels in content height, plus five pixels of padding along the top edge and five pixels of padding along the bottom edge, for a total of 60 pixels in height. Keep that in mind as we move on to the navigation box.

NOTE

Wondering how the browser knew to draw the header box all the way across the width of the screen even though we didn't specify a width? The answer lies in the fact that the header is contained within a `div` tag, which is a block-level element in HTML. By default, the browser normally displays block-level items one after the other, from top to bottom on the page, and fills the available space horizontally. Thus, our header division will automatically span across the entire width of the browser window.

#navigation

Now that we have our header positioned, let's consider the first column in our multicolumn layout—the navigation.

```
#navigation {
    position: absolute;
```

```
        left: 10px;
        top: 70px;
        width: 150px;
        border: 1px solid #000;
        padding: 5px;
    }
```

Right off the bat we have a new style sheet property to consider: position. Possible values for the position property include

- **static**   This is the default normal flow of a document that results with standard HTML. In many ways, you might consider this to be no positioning at all, because a declaration of position: static ultimately leaves the browser to determine where an element is placed.

- **relative**   This is actually a way to adjust an element's position on the page, relative to itself. So, for example, to move an image 50 pixels up from where it normally sits on the page, you'd use position: relative and bottom: 50px (thus adding 50 pixels to the bottom edge of the image, pushing it up that much).

- **absolute**   Absolute positioning is used to precisely place elements on the page, thereby taking them out of the normal flow. This means an absolute positioning element could, in fact, be placed on top of another element. One additional note about absolute positioning is this: items are positioned absolutely, in relation to their *parent* element, or rather the object in which they are contained.

Progress Check

1. Which CSS property is used to specify how an element will be positioned on the page?

2. Which value for that property is the default value?

So in the case of our navigation column, we're absolutely positioning it in a specific spot on the page. Because it is not contained within any other HTML element, the browser window

---

1. position
2. static

Ask the Expert

Q: Wait, I'm confused. You said absolute positioning places items precisely on the page, but then you said those items are placed in relation to something else? How is that *absolute*?

A: To absolutely position an element, you specify its exact location with the top, bottom, left, and right properties. The potentially tricky part is this: the element is then placed *relative* to its container block. So, yes, even though you're specifying an item's location, you must do so in relation to the positioned block that contains the object. In many cases, where there isn't any such positioned "ancestor," this ends up being the actual body of your page, so the element is positioned in relation to the *browser window*.

However, suppose you want to absolutely position an image contained within a news story on your page. Here's where the mix of relative and absolute positioning comes into play. By placing the news story in a div, whose positioning is set to relative but not further altered), you've achieved your goal: you can absolutely position the image within the context of the news story division since the news story division now functions as the image's positioned container.

is the parent object relative to which our first column is being positioned. Let's look at the code again to see exactly where it's being positioned:

```
#navigation {
    position: absolute;
    left: 10px;
    top: 70px;
    width: 150px;
    border: 1px solid #000;
    padding: 5px;
}
```

The left property specifies where the left edge of the column will be placed (in relation to the browser window). The tricky part is that even though we specified that the column should be ten pixels from the edge of the browser window, we must also consider any style sheet properties already attached to the browser window. With that in mind, can you figure out where the left edge of the navigation column will actually be placed?

The left edge of the navigation column will begin 10 pixels from the edge of the browser window, so it sits just below the header area above.

Here's another brainteaser for you... can you determine how I even came up with the value of 70 for the `top` property? To answer this question, you might need to refer back to the `#header` code:

```
#header {
    height: 50px;
    background-color: #ccc;
    padding: 5px;
}
```

The navigation column needed to be positioned below the header. We already determined the header takes up 60 pixels of vertical space (50px + 5px padding on top + 5px padding on bottom). So, to place our navigation column right below the header, I added 60 to the 10-pixel top margin, and used a value of 70 for the `top` property.

The remaining pieces of the style sheet declaration for the navigation column determine the column's width (150px), border style, and padding (5px around all internal sides). The following graphic helps visualize what we've achieved thus far.

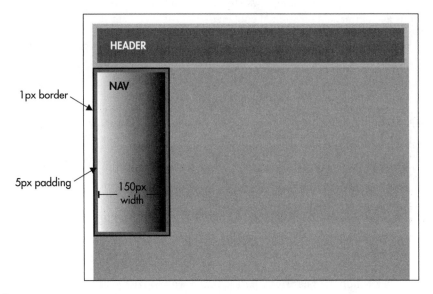

TIP

Want to see an example of someone pushing the envelope of page layout with CSS? Style sheet guru Eric Meyer has created CSS/edge for that very purpose. Check it out at **www.meyerweb.com/eric/css/edge**.

#extras

The column to the far right in the layout is very similar to the navigation column. I've labeled this column "extras" because it is typically used to house bonus elements not integral to the content of the page. For example, you might include advertisements or links to related information in that area.

A review of the style declaration for the extras column shows just how similar it is to the navigation column. In fact, the only difference is this column is placed ten pixels from the *right* edge of the browser, while the navigation column was placed ten pixels from the *left* edge.

```
#extras {
    position: absolute;
    right: 10px;
    top: 70px;
    width: 150px;
    border: 1px solid #000;
    padding: 5px;
}
```

This means our graphical representation now includes two of the three columns we're trying to create, and I've updated the graphical representation accordingly.

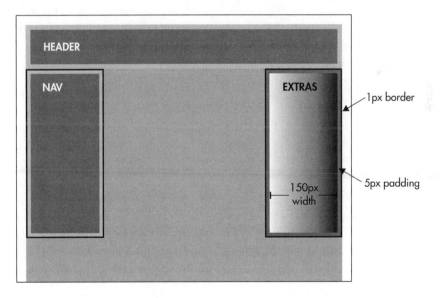

#content

While the navigation and extras sections were absolutely positioned, the middle content column is designed to fit within the normal (static) flow of the document. However, that doesn't mean we can't specify where the element should sit on the page. Refer to the style declaration to see what I mean.

```
#content {
    background-color: #999;
    margin-left: 162px;
    margin-right: 162px;
    padding: 5px;
}
```

First, we don't need to specify how far down on the page the column will display, because it will sit below the header by default. (If we wanted to allow for space between the header and this section, we would have to use the margin-top property to push the element down a bit.) But if we leave all four edges of the center column to chance, it will end up overlapping the navigation column. By adding margins to either side of the column, I am essentially telling the browser how much space to leave on those two sides, which means the element will fill the space left over in the middle of the two absolutely positioned columns.

This trick is figuring out just how much space to allow on either side of the element, so it sits perfectly in the middle. In this particular example, I first needed to consider the total horizontal space covered by the navigation column, because it lies to the left of the main content area I'm currently positioning. The result was 162 pixels (150px width + 5px left padding + 5px right padding + 1px left border + 1px right border).

TIP

Specifying a left margin of 162 pixels places the center content exactly next to the navigation column. If you wanted to leave some blank space between the two, simply increase the size of the left margin.

The right margin needs to be the same size as the horizontal space used by the extras column. Just like the navigation column, the result is 162 pixels (150px width + 5px left padding + 5px right padding + 1px left border + 1px right border).

Finally, a five-pixel padding ensures the text in this column doesn't smash right up against the borders of the other columns. The following shows how the center column fits in our graphical representation:

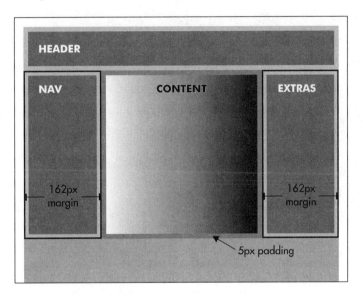

#footer

The final piece in our multicolumn fluid layout is the bottom footer. This could hold something as simple as a copyright notice, or additional content such as text links and supplemental graphics. The style sheet declaration reflects the simplicity of this content area.

```
#footer {
    border-top: 2px solid #000;
    padding: 5px;
}
```

As with the header division, this section will automatically fill the horizontal space in the browser window. Unless we specify otherwise, the height will be determined by the amount of content placed within the footer division. In fact, in my style sheet, I only added a five-pixel border to allow some buffer space around the content, and a two-pixel border along the top edge to help separate the footer from the content above. The following illustration finalizes our graphical representation of this layout.

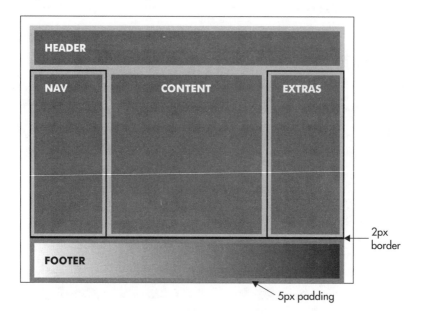

Pull It Back Together

Viewing this very layout in a browser gives us a real glimpse as to just how fluid and flexible it is. Compare Figures 12-3 and 12-4 to see the layout at different browser window sizes.

Browser Support

What would a layout example be without a few caveats? Anytime style sheets are involved, there are questions about compatibility (whether the style sheet properties are supported the same in the popular browsers) and degradation (what happens to the elements when certain properties are not supported). So on that note, I have good news and bad.

The good news is that style sheet support among browsers has come a long way over the past few years. The biggest culprit, with regard to poor style sheet support, is Internet Explorer (IE) 5. But as of this writing, IE 5 comprises as little as 1 percent of the browser market, and no more than 5 percent, by most accounts.

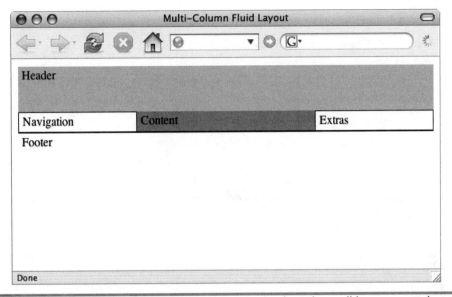

Figure 12-3 The multicolumn fluid layout is shown in a relatively small browser window.

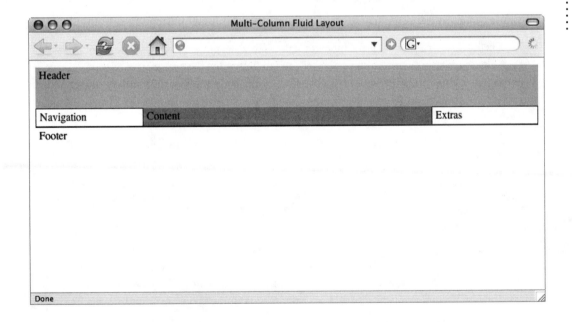

Figure 12-4 The multicolumn fluid layout is shown in a bit larger browser window.

NOTE

I confirmed this statistic by reviewing the web logs for Chop Point's site. In one month, there were just over 2000 requests made by IE 5 browsers, out of more than 200,000 total requests.

The most popular browser, as of this writing, is IE 6, which comprises just over 80 percent of the browser market worldwide. Firefox has the largest user-base beyond IE, with Netscape, Opera, Safari, and AOL being the only other browsers with substantial numbers of users.

So what does all this mean to you if you use our multicolumn fluid layout? This layout displays appropriately in IE 6 and all other modern versions of popular browsers. However, it will not display properly in IE 5 or other older browsers. When the number of IE 5 users was higher, most web developers used tricky "hacks" to try and make their style sheet layouts work in IE 5 and other older browsers.

NOTE

This layout also "breaks" if you shrink the browser window below about 400 pixels in width. This is important because it means you should offer a different style sheet for users of handheld, web-enabled devices, if those types of users are a large part of your target audience.

The hacks can be both confusing and frustrating to developers, because they require more code and more time to test. In the end, you need to determine the best course of action for your particular audience. For personal web sites, this will likely mean you simply ignore the older browsers, provided you aren't one of those using such a browser!

TIP

Search for CSS Hacks online and you will find thousands of articles written about this topic. One such primer that clearly explains the problem, as well as several solutions, is **www.communitymx.com/content/article.cfm?cid=E0989953B6F20B41**.

If you're developing a site for a business and determine that IE 5 (or another older browser) is common among your target audience, consider using one of the workarounds to make your page layouts work properly. The moral of this story is to test, test, and test some more, until you're satisfied with the results in the browsers used by your target audience.

Other CSS Page Layouts

The preceding two sections listed two sample CSS page layouts, a very basic one and another one that's a bit more complex. These are really just the tip of the iceberg when it comes to CSS page layout, and are meant to simply show you examples of what's possible.

One of the wonderful aspects of the Web itself is its open-source nature. If you see a page layout that inspires you, choose View | Source in your browser to *learn* from the site's author. (Of course, I'm not advocating plagiarizing at all—please contact the author to request permission if you want to copy the code explicitly.)

The following list provides additional online resources for CSS page layout.

- **www.meyerweb.com/eric/css/edge**

- **www.alistapart.com**

- **www.mezzoblue.com**

- **www.whatdoiknow.org**

- **friendlybit.com/css/beginners-guide-to-css-and-standards**

- **glish.com/css**

CRITICAL SKILL
12.4 Layer Content Within a Layout

If you've ever played with a graphics program like Adobe Photoshop, you know the power of layers. I like to explain layers like this... imagine if you had two transparencies (you know, like the ones your teachers used with overhead projectors in school), each of which had different pictures on them. If you put one transparency behind the other, the front image would block portions of the back image. If you reversed them, the back image would now block part of the front image.

Using layers on a web page is quite similar. In the previous section, I discussed how the center content area of the layout would overlap the navigation if the correct left margin weren't specified. That is true, but what I haven't yet mentioned is that you can actually control which content area is "on top" whenever multiple sections do overlap. In fact, you can control the entire stacking order with the z-index property.

NOTE

The z-index property only works on elements that are positioned (in other words, those that have the position property set to either relative or absolute).

To help explain this concept, let's compare apples to oranges. The following code creates two boxes on the screen. The first one, labeled "Apples," is absolutely positioned 20 pixels from the top and left edges of the browser window. The second box, labeled "Oranges," is relatively positioned. This means it is allowed to flow relative to any other elements on the page. However, because absolutely positioned elements are *removed* from the normal page flow, there are no other elements for the Oranges box to flow around! So the Oranges box is simply placed in the upper-left corner of the screen, as shown in Figure 12-5.

```
<html>
<head>
<title> Layers </title>
<style type="text/css">
body {
    font-family: verdana;
}
#apples {
    position: absolute;
    top: 20px;
    left: 20px;
    width: 200px;
    padding: 10px;
    text-align: center;
    background-color: #ccc;
    border:1px dashed black;
}
#oranges {
    position: relative;
    width: 200px;
    padding: 10px;
    text-align: center;
    background-color: #333;
    color: #fff;
    border: 3px solid #999;}
</style>
</head>
<body>
<div id="apples">APPLES</div>
<div id="oranges">ORANGES</div>
</body>
</html>
```

What if you didn't mind the fact that these were overlapping, but just wanted the Apples layer to be in front of the Oranges layer? One way to accomplish this is to use the z-index property. Compare Figures 12-5 and 12-6 to see the effects. In Figure 12-6, the content area

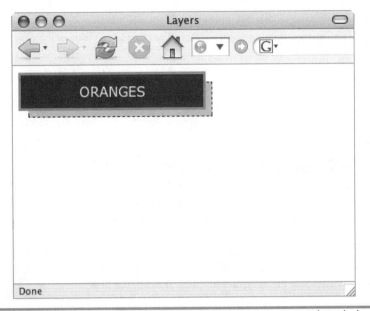

Figure 12-5 By default, the relatively positioned element (Oranges) is placed above the absolutely positioned element (Apples) in this layout.

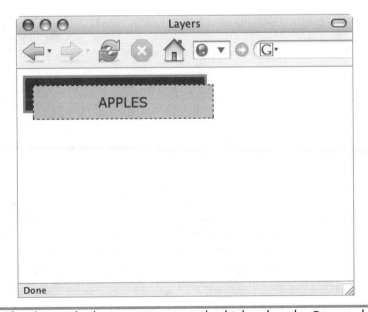

Figure 12-6 After the Apples layer is given a z-index higher than the Oranges layer, it becomes visible.

labeled "Apples" is given a z-index property of 2, while "Oranges" has a z-index property of 1. With this property, the element with the highest z-index value is the one "on top."

TIP

You can also use negative z-index values to force a layer to drop behind others.

Realistic Uses of Layers in Web Pages

While the apples and oranges comparison may not have been the most realistic web page layout scenario, it did help explain the concept of layers in web pages. So what are some more realistic uses for this powerful tool? The following are just a few:

● **Advertising**   Ever clicked a link in a banner ad, only to have that ad appear to grow larger without the actual web page changing? Very likely, the larger version of the ad was a *hidden* layer set to appear when you clicked that link.

● **Games**   While many online games use Flash for interactivity, some use a combination of JavaScript and CSS called Dynamic HTML. These games often place different elements on layers so they can be easily moved around on the page, independent of the other page content.

● **Navigation**   You've likely visited a web site and used navigation that had sub or drop-down menus. These types of navigation systems can be accomplished by placing the drop-down menu content into a layer that is "brought forward" or "made visible" with the click of a particular link.

TIP

A layer is hidden by setting the visibility property to "hidden" in the style sheet declaration.

You probably noticed that most realistic examples of layers within web pages involved some sort of interaction on the user's part, whether that's to make a layer visible or move a player in a game. Unfortunately, this interaction is not achieved through HTML or CSS alone, but involves the use of some sort of scripting, like JavaScript. While this is technically beyond the scope of this book, I wanted to give you an idea as to what was possible. Refer to Module 15 for a bit more information, as well as links to online references and other ways to learn more.

CRITICAL SKILL
12.5 Use External Style Sheets

The vast majority of style sheet examples in this book have been shown as internal or embedded styles, meaning they were placed within the actual web page they affected. But when you use style sheets for layout purposes, you're typically planning to use the same (or very similar) layout with other pages on your site. In such cases, using an internal style sheet would almost defeat the purpose of using style sheets altogether, because you'd have to edit each and every page to make a change to the layout.

A better solution is to create an external style sheet with the page layout information, and then reference that style sheet from each page it should affect. There are essentially two ways to reference an external style sheet—linking or importing.

TIP

When developing my site's style sheet, I usually create it as an internal style sheet within my test page. Then, after I'm satisfied with the results, I copy and paste it into an external style sheet, and add a reference to it from all of the pages it should affect.

Link to an External Style Sheet

The concept of linking to an external style sheet was introduced in an earlier module, but I want to reiterate it here where it's most appropriate. It's accomplished by using the `link` tag, as shown next:

```
<link rel="stylesheet" href="styles.css" />
```

The previous code simply tells the browser to use the content of `styles.css` when displaying the current page.

To take it one step further, you can add the `media` attribute to your `link` tag to specify to which medium the style sheet applies. This means you could link to multiple style sheets for multiple media. The following shows an example that specifies one style sheet to use when the page is displayed on the screen, and another when the page is sent to a printer.

```
<link rel="stylesheet" href="screen.css" media="screen" />
<link rel="stylesheet" href="print.css" media="print" />
```

Other possible values for the `media` attribute are as follows:

● `projection` (for projected presentations)

● `aural` (for speech synthesizers)

- braille (for presentation on Braille tactile feedback devices)

- tty (for display using a fixed-pitch font)

- tv (for televisions)

- all

TIP

If a particular linked style sheet applies to multiple media, separate them with a comma, as in media="screen,projection".

Import an External Style Sheet

Another way to reference an external style sheet is to import its styles into the current document. Instead of a separate HTML tag, this is accomplished with the @import statement in between the opening and closing style tags.

```
<style type="text/css" media="screen">
    @import "/layouts/screen.css";
</style>
```

Because the @import statement is placed in between the opening and closing style tags, you can actually mix internal and external style sheets with this method. This can be particularly useful if, perhaps, you want to use the same general layout on all the pages of your site (with an imported style sheet), but also want to include a few custom internal styles on certain pages.

Another important aspect of this method is the ability to import multiple style sheets. Say, for example, you had one style sheet for the layout of your pages, and another one for different design aspects (colors, fonts, and so on). This might be accomplished with code like the following:

```
<style type="text/css" media="screen">
    @import "/styles/layout.css";
    @import "/styles/design.css";
</style>
```

NOTE

Whenever you combine different style sheets, it's good to remember the rules of precedence. These state that styles are applied with the following order of importance: embedded styles take precedence over internal styles, which take precedence over external styles.

Project 12-1 Use CSS for Page Layout

So far, the project files you've completed have been mostly devoid of any real concrete page layout. In this project, you select one of the files you already created and apply a CSS page layout. The goals for this project include

- Using CSS for page layout
- Creating a style sheet that works in most modern browsers
- Using an external style sheet

NOTE

All the files needed to complete the projects in this book can be downloaded from **www.osborne.com** or **www.wendywillard.com**. In addition, you can view my version of the web site anytime by visiting **www.choppoint.org**. If you aren't using the Chop Point site, you can tailor the project to your particular needs.

Step by Step

1. Open your text or HTML editor and load any of the pages you've developed thus far.

2. Determine the type of layout that will work best on the page you selected. To get started, consider the following questions: *Does the page have content that easily fits into two or more columns? Or is it a page whose content flows best as a single column with perhaps a top header and a bottom footer for navigation, and so on?*

3. After selecting your layout, return to your HTML page and add the necessary div tags and IDs to divide the content into manageable sections.

TIP

Remember to use ID names that describe the content itself, as opposed to how you plan to style it. For example, if you plan to put a calendar of events in column three, and also want to give that column a yellow background, naming your ID "events" would be much better than "column3" or "yellowcolumn". Why? At some point, you may move the events to another column, or you may change the background color, but they will always be events.

(continued)

4. Work with your internal style sheet to add the appropriate CSS properties to lay out the page. Refer to the samples provided in this module, as well as the online resources I suggested.

5. Save the file and test it often in your favorite browser, as well as any others you can get your hands on.

TIP

Some online web sites offer the ability to display your site on multiple web browsers, so you can see how it looks without having to actually install those browsers on your machine. Siteviewer (**www.anybrowser.com/siteviewer.html**) offers a free compatibility tool to check a page's code against different HTML specifications used by browsers, while BrowserCam (**www.browsercam.com**) charges a monthly fee for its comprehensive browser viewing services.

6. When you're satisfied with the layout, copy and paste your internal style sheet (without the `style` tags) into a blank text document. Then save it as **style.css**.

7. Return to your HTML file and use the `link` tag or the `@import` statement to reference the external style sheet you just created. Save the file and switch back to the browser. Choose Refresh or Reload to preview the changes you just made and make sure your external style sheet works.

TIP

If your style sheet no longer works after you switched from internal to external, check the location of the external style sheet. Is it in the same folder as your HTML file? If not, be sure to add the folder path to your `link` tag or `@import` reference? For more tips, see Appendix C.

Project Summary

Cascading style sheets have come a long way, and now provide excellent page layout options for web designers. This project gave you practice developing your own layout using style sheets.

For added practice, perform this project again on other pages you developed while working through this book.

Module 12 Mastery Check

1. Fill in the blank: _____ positioning takes an element out of the normal page flow and positions it in a particular place on the page.

2. Which property determines whether a layer is hidden or visible?

3. Which two properties are set in the body tag to ensure all browsers use the same "starting point" for page layout?

4. According to the W3C specifications, if you had a box that was 150 pixels wide, with ten pixels of padding on all four sides, and a two-pixel border all the way around, what would be the total horizontal space used by the box?

5. Which version of Internet Explorer was the last one to not follow the W3C specifications for box and page layout?

6. Which HTML tag is used to create sections of content to be formatted with style sheets?

7. Fill in the blank: The _____ attribute identifies the medium for which a particular external style sheet should be used.

8. Add the appropriate code so the content area has a 20-pixel margin around the top, right, and left sides, but a five-pixel margin around the bottom.

   ```
   #content {

       }
   ```

9. Which HTML tag can be used to reference an external style sheet?

10. Add the appropriate code to import a style sheet called design.css.

    ```
    <style type="text/css">

    </style>
    ```

11. Fill in the blank: _____ positioning is the default type of positioning.

12. True/False: Relative positioning adjusts an element's location on the page relative to itself.

13. Add the appropriate code to place the content area 50 pixels from the left edge of the browser and 150 pixels from the top edge.

```
#content {



     }
```

14. Which property is used to specify an element's stacking order on the page?

15. True/False: When adjusting an element's stacking order on the page, lower values take precedence over higher values.

Part II

Beyond HTML

Module 13

Creating Your Own Web Graphics

Creating graphic images for a web site can be an enjoyable experience for anyone, regardless of artistic experience, but success in this area requires a bit of determination and creativity. This module gives a brief introduction to the issues involved in creating your own web graphics.

CRITICAL SKILL
13.1 Become Familiar with Graphics Software

If you walk down the software aisles of your local computer store, you might be surprised by the sheer volume of graphics-related software available. You can buy clip art and photography, fonts, scanning utilities, animation titles, photo editing programs, desktop publishing applications, drawing tools, and so forth.

NOTE

You'll hear the term *layers* used a lot when discussing graphics software. Using layers in a graphics program is similar to making a bed. You place sheets, blankets, and pillows over the mattress, but you can change any of those items freely if you decide you dislike one. The same is true with layers—you can paint on a layer, and then delete it later if you don't like it. Layers offer much flexibility in graphics programs.

For the purposes of this module, I focus on those software titles that offer you the best tools for creating web graphics. Two main categories of software titles exist: vector and bitmap.

Bitmap applications, also called *raster*, create graphics using tiny dots known as *bits*. These types of images are more difficult to resize because you must change each individual dot, but they have been around longer and enjoy more support from file formats. GIFs and JPEGs are bitmap images.

Vector applications, also called *object-oriented* applications, are based on mathematically calculated lines and curves that are easily changed and updated. Images created with vectors tend to be smaller in file size and, for that reason, are increasing in popularity on the Internet.

TIP

Can't decide which graphics program to purchase? All the products listed here have trial or demo versions available for free. Visit each company's web site for details.

The programs discussed in the following are by no means the only products available for creating web graphics. Given the scope of this book, though, I thought it best to limit the discussion to the most popular programs. If none of these tools suits your needs, try searching in Yahoo! (**www.yahoo.com**) or CNET's download center (**download.cnet.com**) for "web graphics," and perhaps you'll find one more suitable for your purposes.

One final note before I discuss the most popular programs—Microsoft has recently entered the digital imaging market with its Digital Image 2006 tools. Because it's so new to the market, as of this writing I'm not including it in my list of the top graphics tools. However, it may be worthwhile for you to consider if you aren't already hooked on Adobe or Macromedia products, and are using a Windows PC. They are also bundling this software with many of their other products, so if you've recently bought something from Microsoft, you might check for a bundled copy of Digital Image. To learn more, visit **www.microsoft.com/products/imaging**.

Adobe Photoshop

Adobe is the world leader in graphics and imaging software. It offers such renowned titles as Photoshop and Illustrator, which have been used in the printing and design industry for years.

TIP

Adobe's products are available for Windows and Macintosh systems. For more information, visit **www.adobe.com**.

Photoshop is a bitmap program, best known for image manipulation, using layers to allow for virtually limitless flexibility in design. In fact, if you've recently bought a new scanner, you might have acquired a scaled-back version of Photoshop with it. Illustrator, on the other hand, is a vector tool, more suited for freehand drawing and illustration. Both products can save and open web file formats.

In many design circles, Adobe's Photoshop is *the* product to use. For the typical home user, however, the price for the full version is a bit steep (around $600). If you're familiar with Adobe's products and enjoy them, I recommend sticking with Photoshop. Likewise, if you're interested in creating web graphics as well as editing images for printed publications, Photoshop is your best bet.

If you don't fall into either of those categories, you might be interested in Photoshop Elements (the scaled-back, but still fabulous, version), which costs under $100. While this version doesn't have all the high-powered image editing tools used by the professionals, it's more than capable of handling the needs of someone just starting, and it even has a few bells and whistles that the full version doesn't. Photoshop Elements, available for both the Mac and the PC, is a superb gateway graphics program for the typical home user.

TIP

If you are a student or are employed by an academic institution, remember to check into academic pricing for software like this since Adobe offers significant academic discounts.

Macromedia Fireworks

Macromedia was once best known for its animation title, Director. With the advent of the Web, Macromedia became a major player in the graphics industry. Fireworks is a web-specific tool for creating web graphics. I use the term *web-specific* because, unlike many other graphics software titles, Fireworks was created specifically for the Web.

NOTE

In 2006, Adobe purchased Macromedia. To learn more abut Fireworks, visit **www.adobe.com/fireworks**.

Fireworks offers such features as web animation, file optimization, image slicing, rollover creation, and web previewing. It also seamlessly integrates with Dreamweaver, a top-rated WYSIWYG tool for web authoring and page layout, making the two software titles a highly regarded and powerful web development suite.

Fireworks has a particularly strong following among web designers who never got hooked on Adobe's products. Although its learning curve is a bit steeper than that of Jasc's Paint Shop Pro (discussed at the end of this section), at $200–300 it remains a viable alternative for cost-conscious home users.

Macromedia also developed Flash, which is worth mentioning, even though it doesn't directly compete with any of the other products listed here. Flash is a vector application specifically designed for creating animations and interactive presentations on the Web.

Corel's Paint Shop Pro

The least expensive of these programs is Paint Shop Pro, which was recently purchased by Canadian graphics powerhouse Corel. Retailing for about $90, the latest version of this title offers much for that price. Features include animation, direct digital camera support, layers, filters, watermarks, special effects, and advanced text tools, such as text on a path.

NOTE

Paint Shop Pro is only available for Windows. For more information, visit **www.corel.com**.

Those of you interested in creating web graphics will be pleased to know that recent versions included image slicing, support for rollovers, and previewing capabilities in up to three web browsers. Image map tools and support for the PNG file format also put this title at the forefront of web graphics.

For the cost-conscious home user trying to create some web graphics, I recommend starting out with Paint Shop Pro. You may even decide you don't need anything else.

CRITICAL SKILL
13.2 Describe Issues that
Impact Design Decisions

Consider a printed magazine. Regardless of where the magazine is purchased, the images displayed inside look the same. In fact, only those who are color-blind or vision-impaired will encounter differences in printed graphics. This isn't the case with web graphics, because each person viewing a web site is doing so with a different set of experiences, affected by his or her computer, browser, monitor, lighting, and modem, to name a few.

When creating your own web graphics, several issues directly affect the outcome and must be considered. These issues include

- Platforms
- Target audience demographics
- HTML
- Browsers
- Color
- Bandwidth

While entire books are written on some of these topics, the next few sections give you a basic understanding of what to consider. At the end of this module is a section entitled "Learning More" that gives you a list of places to go for a more in-depth discussion on any of these topics.

Platforms

A person's web experience is affected by his or her platform, or the type of device being used to access the Web. While obvious differences exist between computers and telephones, both are used to view web pages. Furthermore, many differences exist between the types of computers used—for example, consider the differences among handheld computers, laptop computers, and desktop computers.

And among those different types of computers, Windows, Macintosh, UNIX, Linux, and many other operating systems are running. Many computers even enable you to surf the Web from your television. Undoubtedly, many more such devices are to come.

The most important thing to consider about platforms is that the one you're working on probably won't be the only one your visitors will use. The following are a few general things to remember when you're designing for more than one platform.

- Graphics generally look darker on a Windows PC than they do on a Mac, but Windows gamma (or brightness) can vary widely. A graphic that appears fine on one Windows PC might look much darker on another Windows PC with different settings.

- Software (such as browsers, plug-ins, and ActiveX controls) available for your platform might not be available for others.

- The size and settings of the viewing device (be it a 17-inch monitor, a 27-inch TV, or a two-inch handheld screen) used by your visitors will alter the appearance of your graphics.

The moral of this section is that you need to be aware of these differences and plan accordingly. In addition, test your web graphics on a variety on platforms to be sure you are achieving the results you want.

Target Audience Demographics

Module 1 contained a brief section on planning for web sites. This included identifying the target audience as a key step in the planning stages of web development. One reason that identifying the target audience is so important is because it directly affects how the graphics should be created.

TIP

Some online surveys about audience demographics might be of help to you in this category. Visit **http://dir.yahoo.com/Computers_and_Internet/Internet/ Statistics_and_Demographics/** for links to these resources.

For example, if you are creating a site for your company's private network, wherein the people on that network only use Windows PCs, you can safely rule out the need to test your pages on Macintosh computers. Likewise, if you know that everyone on your network uses 21-inch monitors, you can design at that size.

While these scenarios might not be the norm, knowing your target audience will help to identify the style you should develop. Consider that a site geared for 12–18-year-olds might use different colors than one geared toward those over age 63. In addition, a site for young children should use a color palette and graphics style different than one for teenagers.

Design for a Specific Size

Module 12 discussed using style sheets and divs for page layout in web pages. In that module, I mentioned that, whenever possible, it's best to create flexible tables that grow or shrink in proportion to the size of the browser window.

Even if you do design your pages to grow or shrink according to window size, remember, the smallest screen resolution for desktop and laptop computers is 640 by 480 pixels. If you take into consideration the scroll bars and edges of the browser window, that leaves you with about 600 pixels across for your graphics.

Vertically, you have to deal with the many buttons and toolbars in the browser. Depending on how many toolbars are visible at any given time, you may lose 100–200 pixels in height from the top of the screen and about 25 pixels at the bottom for the status bar. (Windows users who have their Start menu at the bottom of the screen may lose another 50–100 pixels.)

So, if you want your pages to display appropriately, even in the smallest of window sizes, make sure the most important information is in the top 600 (wide) by 300 (tall) pixels of the page. Figure 13-1 is an example of a viewable portion of the web page.

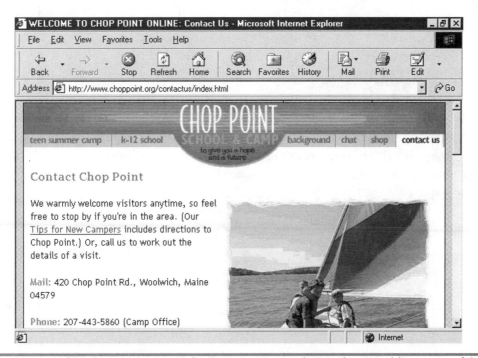

Figure 13-1 When this page is viewed at a 640×480 resolution, the viewable portion of the page is about 600×300 pixels.

HTML

As you've probably noticed by now, HTML has some restrictions and limitations that can affect the way graphics are used on a web page. For example, all graphics in a web page must be contained in a rectangular box, even if that box isn't readily apparent to viewers. Any text flowing around a graphic must either follow the rectangular shape of the box or be contained within the graphic.

Without understanding these limitations, it's hard to create web graphics that will work in an HTML page. This is especially true because graphics editors enable you to mix text and graphics. A layout like this one is entirely possible in a graphics editor.

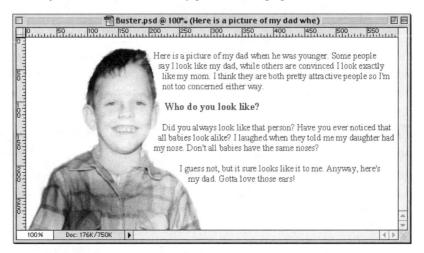

Those with HTML experience recognize this layout isn't possible in standard HTML, unless the text itself is contained within that graphic. A more suitable layout using the same text and graphic might be the following.

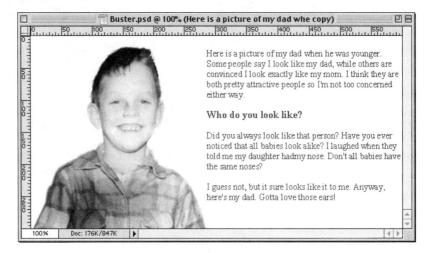

Whenever you create your own web graphics, it's important to remember the limitations and possibilities of HTML presented in this book.

Browsers

While the most popular browser might be Internet Explorer, many other browsers are in use by web surfers. Firefox in particular has gained significant ground in recent years. Web sites like CNET's **browsers.com** list lots of other browsers, such as Opera, NetCaptor, NetPositive, Lynx, iCab, and NeoPlanet. All told, **browsers.com** lists over 200 different versions of browsers, the vast majority of which are free to download.

What does this mean to you as a web developer? That depends. As I mentioned, knowing your audience affects more than just the marketing plan. It affects which browsers you build the site for and why. Because it's ultimately the browser creator's decision on which tags to support, you might find some browsers display your pages much differently than others.

In fact, some of the alternative browsers are text-only browsers, for systems incapable of displaying graphics. Anyone using these browsers won't be able to see the graphics you include on your web pages. Because of this, remember, if the most important information on your site is shown in graphics, alternative text-only versions should also be made available. Figure 13-2 shows different ways of handling cases where the page is viewed without the graphics.

The following are a few things to remember when designing web graphics for different browsers.

- **Use standard HTML tags**   Throughout this book, I mentioned some tags that might be introduced by a particular software developer that aren't supported by other browsers. While in some cases using these proprietary tags might be considered acceptable, you shouldn't do so if you are trying to reach the widest possible audience. Try to stick with standard XHTML tags recognized by the W3C (**www.w3.org**) and you'll be better suited to reach the most people.

- **Provide alternatives**   Whether this means coding your pages with the `alt` attributes for those who can't view images or including different ways of accessing the information, providing alternative means of navigating and viewing your site is important.

- **Test, test, test**   Don't settle for viewing your pages in only Internet Explorer on your personal computer. Go to your neighbor's house or your office computer and view the pages there. You'll undoubtedly find differences you may or may not appreciate.

For additional resources on browser differences, visit either of the following web sites.

- **www.browsers.com**

- **http://dir.yahoo.com/Computers_and_Internet/Software/Internet/ World_Wide_Web/Browsers/**

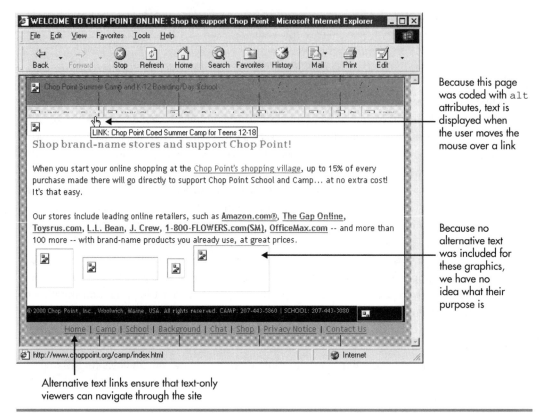

Because this page was coded with `alt` attributes, text is displayed when the user moves the mouse over a link

Because no alternative text was included for these graphics, we have no idea what their purpose is

Alternative text links ensure that text-only viewers can navigate through the site

Figure 13-2 When this page is viewed with graphics turned off in Internet Explorer, boxes appear where the graphics should have. Whenever alternative text is included using the `alt` attribute, users will have an idea of what the graphic displayed.

Color

A big consideration for those developing web graphics is color. While graphics created for the printed page look relatively the same to all who view them, web graphics may look vastly different from one computer to the next.

As discussed in Module 3 in the section "Using Web-Safe Colors," this variation in color can be caused by differences in system color palettes, as well as lighting and gamma issues related to the user's monitor. Whenever you need to render a specific color that needs to look exactly the same on as many systems as possible, stick with a web-safe color.

You can create a web-safe color in any graphics editor by altering the red, green, and blue values. To make things easier, you can also load pre-made web-safe color swatches into most graphics editors. These color swatches are often called *CLUTS*, short for *color lookup tables*. You can find several different CLUTS for use in many graphics programs on Visibone's web site at **www.visibone.com/swatches**.

Bandwidth

Another big difference between graphics created for the Web and those created for virtually any other medium is bandwidth. The term *bandwidth* refers to the speed at which web users access the Internet. Telephone modem users offer access at speeds of 28.8K to 56K, while cable modem or network users' speeds are double or triple that amount. Because people visiting your web site will probably be doing so from many different access speeds, you must design your graphics accordingly.

The biggest issue related to bandwidth is file size. If the graphics on your web pages are large in file size, they'll take longer to download. Whenever I ask my friends or family how long they're willing to wait for pages to download on the Internet, they usually give their answer in seconds as opposed to minutes. It's true that most of us are quick to click that mouse button and zoom off to a new web site if the current one takes more than a few seconds to capture our interest. This means the graphics on your web pages need to be quite small in file size.

Determining File Size

So, exactly how small is small? Let's use a 56-Kbps (the Kbps stands for kilobits per second) modem connection as our example. A 56-Kbps modem will download about 7000 keystrokes of information per second. That translates to about 2.5 single-spaced typewritten pages of text or about 6–7 kilobytes (K) of web content per second.

As you know, web pages consist of text and images. To estimate the size of a web page, you have to add together the sizes of the text (the HTML file) and the images (the GIFs and JPEGs). Using the previous approximation, a page totaling 30K in content might take five seconds to download on a 56-Kbps modem. Table 13-1 shows the best download speeds per second for the most common connection types.

Connection Type	Best Download Per Second
T1 network	200K
Cable modem/DSL	180K
56-Kbps modem	6–7K
33.6-Kbps modem	4–5K
28.8-Kbps modem	3–4K

Table 13-1   Best Download Speeds for Popular Connection Types

If you're creating web pages for the general public, a good rule of thumb is to limit your pages to no more than 40–60K in total size. HTML files usually weigh in at about 1–3K, so that leaves a mere 37–59K for other content such as graphics. In fact, this amount can often restrict you to using the most important and necessary graphics on a page.

TIP

To put things into perspective, consider that a floppy disk holds 1.4MB or about 1,400,000K of data.

You can determine the actual file size of an image in several ways. Many graphics editors display the file size and approximate download speed right within the program. For example, Figure 13-3 shows how the size of a web graphic is displayed within Photoshop's Save For Web feature.

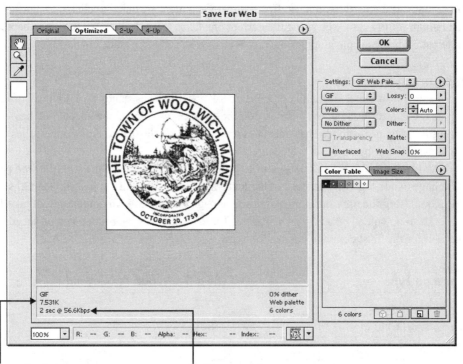

When saved with these settings, this file will be 7.531K in size

At this file size, it takes approximately two seconds to load the graphic on a 56-Kbps modem connection

Figure 13-3 In Photoshop's Save For Web feature, you can see the file's size and approximate download time.

With all this talk about best download speeds, I must warn you that many things might cause a connection to be slower at any given time. Just as detours can happen when you drive somewhere, detours can also occur in the route taken from your computer to the one housing a particular web site. So while you can use the numbers in Table 13-1 to give you an idea of how fast your page *might* download, remember, it could be significantly slower for some users.

Ways to Reduce File Sizes of Images

Two basic rules exist in reducing the file sizes of your images:

- Reduce the actual height and width

- Compress the image

When you reduce the height or width of an image, you make it smaller in physical size and in file size. This can be accomplished by shrinking the entire image or by cropping it to show only a portion of the original.

TIP

Another way to reduce your overall page size is to remove images altogether. In some cases, you may find a text solution works just as well, if not better.

Consider if the following photograph was used in a web page. At 275 by 350 pixels, this illustration is about 27K.

By simply cropping in on the most important part, I can cut the file size down to less than 5K.

If the file needed to remain at its original size, I could try compressing it instead. *File compression* refers to the way in which data is stored or packed. Just as different people can stuff more or less clothing into a single suitcase, different compression types can pack more or less data into a file.

Specific compression methods—GIFs, JPEGs, and PNGs—work best for web graphics. The next few sections of this module discuss these file formats, and their compression methods, in further detail.

Progress Check

1. How can a user's platform affect how she views a web page?

2. What are two ways to reduce a graphic's file size?

CRITICAL SKILL

13.3 Recognize Graphic File Formats for the Web

If you try to load a Windows Bitmap file (.bmp) or a Macintosh Picture File (PICT) into your web page, users will see a broken image symbol. This occurs because graphics in web pages

---

1. Graphics generally look darker on a Windows PC than they do on a Mac. Software available for your platform might not be available for others. The size and settings of the viewing device used by your visitors will alter the appearance of your graphics.

2. Reduce the actual height or width, and compress the image.

must be in a format understood by the web browser. The most popular graphics file formats recognized by web browsers are GIF, JPEG, and PNG.

Terminology

Before you dive into the actual file types, you need to learn a few terms that relate to web file formats.

Compression Methods

Web graphic file formats take your original image and compress it, to make it smaller for web and e-mail delivery. Two types of compression methods are used for web graphics.

- Lossy
- Lossless

Lossy compression requires data to be removed from the image to compress the file and make it smaller. The compression method attempts to remove the least important data first, to avoid making files unreadable. *Lossless* compression is the opposite of lossy, in that no data is lost when the file is compressed. In these cases, the actual data looks the same whether it's compressed or uncompressed.

Resolution

In a previous module, you learned about monitor resolution, but in this case I'm referring specifically to file resolution. Whenever you create or edit a file in a graphics editor, you need to specify a file resolution (see Figure 13-4). The standard file resolution for web graphics is 72 *dots per inch* (*dpi*).

Transparency

When you view an image and are able to *see through* parts of it, that image is said to have *transparency*. Some graphics editors show this transparency by displaying a gray and white checkerboard behind the image. Figure 13-5 shows an example of this in Paint Shop Pro.

When a web graphic contains transparency, the page's background color or background tile shows through in the transparent areas.

File types that support transparency fall into two categories: binary and variable. *Binary transparency* means any given pixel is either transparent or opaque. *Variable transparency*, also known as *alpha channel,* allows pixels to be partially transparent or partially opaque; therefore, it is capable of creating subtle gradations.

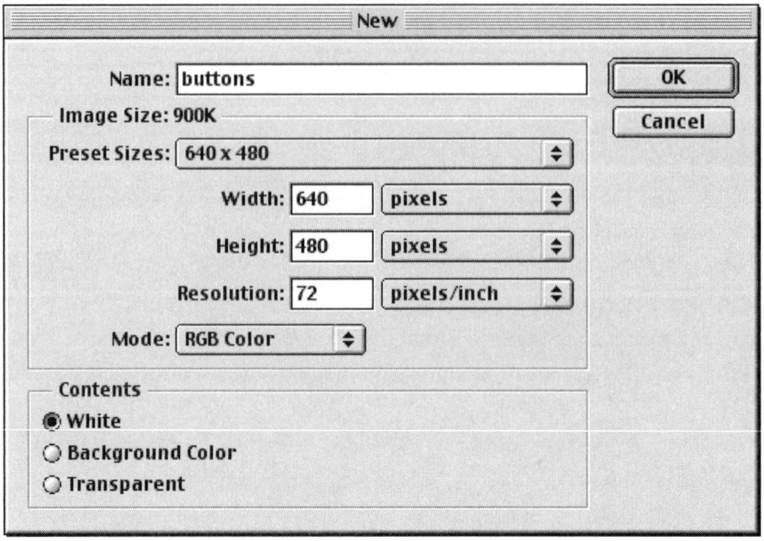

New

Name: buttons   OK

Image Size: 900K   Cancel

Preset Sizes: 640 x 480   ⇕

Width: 640   pixels   ⇕

Height: 480   pixels   ⇕

Resolution: 72   pixels/inch   ⇕

Mode: RGB Color   ⇕

Contents
◉ White
○ Background Color
○ Transparent

Figure 13-4 When working with web graphics, use a file resolution of 72 dpi.

Certain file types don't support transparency. If the image shown in Figure 13-5 were to be saved in a file format not supporting transparency, the areas shown in a checkerboard would be filled in with a solid color.

Buster.psd* [1:1] (Layer 1)

Figure 13-5 When a file with transparency is displayed in a graphics program, you typically see a gray and white checkerboard in the transparent areas of the image.

Interlacing

Have you ever viewed a web page and noticed that a web graphic first appeared blocky or fuzzy before gradually coming into focus? *Interlacing* is a process where the graphic is displayed at multiple levels of clarity, from blurry to clear.

When an interlaced JPEG is loaded in the browser, it first appears blotchy and blurry →

← Once it is fully loaded, the blurriness disappears

Noninterlaced images must be fully loaded before the browser displays them on a page. If you have a large image on a page, users may see only blank space if the graphic takes a while to download. If it takes too long, users may leave.

Because interlaced graphics appear more quickly, even if they appear fuzzy, users might be more willing to wait for the page to download fully. Ultimately, the choice in using interlaced or noninterlaced graphics depends on the size and style of the graphics on your page. I generally use interlacing for larger graphics that take up more space on the screen, as opposed to small buttons or icons that load quickly anyway.

Animation

Some web file formats support animation as well as still images. These animation files contain two or more individual files called *animation frames*. The following illustration shows three frames of an animation. Notice that the position of the rattle changes slightly from frame to frame.

When the file is played back through the browser, viewers watch the various frames of the animation appear, one after the other. The rate at which the frames change can vary between a speedy filmstrip and a slowly blinking button. In the preceding example, the rattle appears to shake.

The most common example of this type of animation—bitmap animation—is GIF animation. More robust animation tools are those that use vectors instead of bitmaps. This means the animation is sent as a series of instructions instead of actual pixel renderings. The result is much more fluid animation that downloads in a fraction of the time a similar bitmap animation would. Flash is the most common type of vector animation.

GIF

GIF is the acronym for *graphic interchange format*. Originally designed for online use in the 1980s, GIF uses a compression method that is well suited to certain types of web graphics. This method, called *LZW compression*, is lossless and doesn't cause a loss of file data. However, several characteristics of GIFs restrict the type of files capable of being saved as GIFs. Table 13-2 lists these and other characteristics of the GIF file type.

NOTE

According to its creator, GIF is officially pronounced with a soft g. Because the word is an acronym, though, many people pronounce it with a hard g.

Because of these characteristics, the following types of images lend themselves to being saved as GIFs. Notice all of these are limited in colors.

TIP

The g in GIF gives you a hint about what types of images are best saved as GIFs: graphics (as opposed to photographs).

Characteristic	Description
Color mode	Restricted to no more than 256 exact colors (8-bit)
Compression method	Lossless
Animation	Supported
Transparency	Supported (binary only)
Interlacing	Supported

Table 13-2 GIF File Format Characteristics

- Text
- Line drawings
- Cartoons
- Flat-color graphics

Save a GIF

When you save a file as a GIF in a graphics program, look for it to be called GIF, GIF87, GIF89, GIF89a, or even CompuServe GIF. In most cases, any of these options will work. If your file includes transparency or animation, use GIF89 or GIF89a.

You have the option of saving your image with or without dithering. GIF color palettes only have a limited number of colors, and the fewer colors present, the smaller the file size. When you want to reduce the number of colors in the palette, the program must know what to do with the areas in your image that contain the colors you're removing.

NOTE

You may recall the term "dithering" from Module 3, where it was discussed in reference to web-safe colors.

If you tell the program to use dithering (you can specify any amount of dithering between 0 and 100 percent), it may use multiple colors in a checkerboard pattern in those areas to give the appearance of the color you removed. If no dithering is used, the removed colors are replaced with another solid color (see Figure 13-6). Dithering can be useful in giving the appearance of gradations or subtle color shifts, but be forewarned, it adds to the file size.

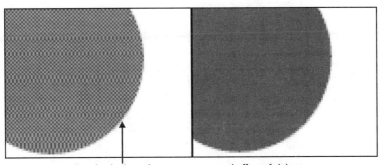

This checkerboard pattern is a typical effect of dithering

Figure 13-6 In this example, the graphic on the left is dithered, while the graphic on the right is not.

Ask the Expert

Q: I noticed photographs aren't on this list. I've seen plenty of photographs used on web pages—can't they be saved as GIFs?

A: Images with photographic content shouldn't usually be saved as GIFs, unless they're part of an animation or require transparency. Other file types are more capable of compressing photographs. In fact, the JPEG file format was created specifically for photographs and shouldn't be used for other types of images such as flat-color graphics and text.

TIP

Few images actually need all 256 colors available in a GIF color palette. Try reducing the number of colors all the way down to 8 or 16, and work your way back up as high as you need to go to make the image look acceptable. This assures that you reach the minimum colors more easily than if you try to work from the most colors on down. Remember, the fewer colors in the palette, the smaller the file size.

JPEG

The *JPEG* file format (pronounced *jay-peg*) was created by the *Joint Photographic Experts Group*, who sought to create a format more suitable for compressing photographic imagery. After reading Table 13-3, review Table 13-2 to compare JPEG's characteristics with those of GIFs.

Characteristic	Description
Color mode	Displayed in 24-bit color, also called millions of colors. If the user's monitor isn't set to view 24-bit color, the file is displayed with as many colors as are available
Compression method	Lossy
Animation	Not supported
Transparency	Not supported
Interlacing	Supported as progressive JPEGs

Table 13-3 JPEG File Format Characteristics

13

One major difference between GIFs and JPEGs is that JPEGs don't contain an exact set of colors. When you save a photograph as a JPEG, you might consider all the colors in the file to be *recommended*, because the lossy compression might require some colors to be altered. In addition, all web JPEG files must be in the RGB (Red, Green, Blue) color mode, as opposed to the print standard—CMYK (Cyan, Magenta, Yellow, Black).

Save a JPEG

When you save an image as a JPEG, you choose between several different quality levels. The highest-quality JPEG has the least amount of compression and, therefore, the least amount of data removed. The lowest-quality JPEG has the most amount of data removed and often looks blotchy, blurry, and rough. I usually save JPEG images with a medium quality. The decision is made based on how low in quality you can go without compromising the integrity of the file: the lower the quality level, the lower the file size.

NOTE

Don't bother making your JPEGs web-safe. Not only will they look terrible, but because you can't specify exact colors in the JPEG file format, the web-safe colors will quickly become un-web-safe.

PNG

PNG, which stands for *Portable Network Graphics* and is pronounced *ping*, is the newest and most flexible of these three graphics file formats. After looking at the list of characteristics for PNG in Table 13-4, you might think of PNG as being the best of both the GIF and JPEG formats.

Characteristic	Description
Color mode	Can be stored as 8-bit, 24-bit, or 32-bit
Compression method	Lossless
Animation	Not supported
Transparency	Supported (variable/alpha)
Interlacing	Supported (two-dimensional)

Table 13-4 PNG File Format Characteristics

TIP

The 32-bit color format is similar to 24-bit color because it also has millions of colors. However, 32-bit color also has a masking channel, which can be used for alpha transparency.

An additional benefit of PNG is its gamma correction. The PNG file format has the capability to correct for differences in how computers and monitors interpret color values. While all these characteristics make PNG well suited for almost any type of web graphic, there is one drawback that has limited its use for some people. Unfortunately, because it wasn't an original web file format, users of older browsers must download a plug-in to view web graphics saved in the PNG format.

Save a PNG

When saving a file as a PNG, you must first choose how many colors to include in its palette. Saving as a PNG-8 uses an exact palette of 256 colors or less. Transparency and dithering are available in the PNG-8 setting. PNG-24 and PNG-32 offer 24-bit (millions) and 32-bit (millions, plus an alpha channel) color modes, respectively.

Choose the Best File Format for the Job

Now that you know a little about the different web graphics file formats, you're probably wondering how you might select the best format for the job. While I wish I could give you a foolproof method, the answer, ultimately, lies in your own testing.

Luckily, many of the popular graphics programs make this testing easy. For example, Photoshop and Fireworks enable you to compare how a single image might look when saved in any of these file formats.

TIP

If the graphics program you're using doesn't allow you to compare and preview file types, save several different versions of the same file and preview each one in a browser. Compare their file size (download speed) and appearance to determine which file type and settings are the best.

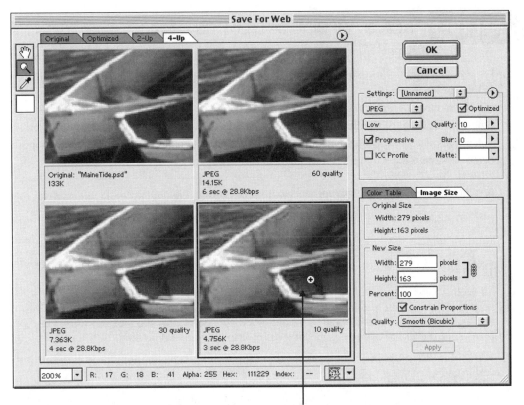

When magnified to 200 percent, you can better
see how the lower quality affects the image

In the preceding example, I used Photoshop's Save For Web feature to compare three different quality levels for the JPEG file format. The settings and file sizes are printed below each example to help decide which would work the best.

Choosing the best file format is like shopping—you are looking for the file format that looks the best, but costs the least. In this case, the cost comes in download time for web page visitors.

Project 13-1 Save Web Graphics

Designers often receive images for web pages on disc, via e-mail, or even in printed format. On receipt of these files, you need to put them in a web-ready format by saving them as GIFs, JPEGs, or PNGs.

If you have a graphics program, this project gives you a chance to practice saving different types of images in the appropriate web file format. If you don't already have a graphics program, you might visit the web sites listed in the beginning of this module to download trial copies or demo versions. Goals for this project include the following:

- Saving a photograph in an appropriate web file format

- Saving an illustration in an appropriate web file format

NOTE

All the files needed to complete the projects in this book for the Chop Point site can be downloaded from the Osborne web site (**www.osborne.com**). In addition, you can view my version of the web site anytime by visiting **www.choppoint.org**. Those of you who aren't using the Chop Point site can tailor the project to your particular needs.

Step by Step

1. Open your graphics editor and load the file called lighthouse.tif from the Module 13 folder.

2. Adjust the DPI and pixel dimensions to be more suited toward placement of this image in a web page.

3. Determine which file format is the most appropriate for this image, using any of the following techniques. If necessary, keep track of your progress by entering each file's setting in the following table. The first two rows give examples of how the table might be used.

   - Review the guidelines in this module.
   - If available, use the program's preview and compare features.
   - Save multiple versions of the file, using different settings in each one, and view them in a web browser.

4. Repeat this process for choppoint_logo.tif, also found in the Module 13 folder.

Filename	File Type	Colors/ Palette	Interlaced	Dithered	Quality	File Size
lighthouse.gif	GIF	128 Selective	Yes	85%	–	72K
lighthouse.jpg	JPEG	–	Yes	–	Medium (50%)	21K

5. Open your web browser and choose File | Open Page (or Open File or Open, depending on the browser you're using). Locate the graphics you just saved. Make sure the image appears as you intended.

6. If you need to make changes, return to your graphics editor to make changes. After making any changes, save the file and switch back to the browser. Choose Refresh or Reload to preview the changes you just made.

TIP

Do you see broken image symbols instead of your images? Make sure the filenames end in a three-letter extension (such as .gif or .jpg). If they don't, go back to your graphics editor and resave or re-export the file as a GIF, JPEG, or PNG. For more tips, see Appendix C.

Project Summary

Creating your own web graphics can be a great way to add your own personal style to your web pages. This project gave you a chance to practice saving files in formats viewable on the Web.

NOTE

For extra practice, try processing any of the additional files found in the Module 13 folder and including them in a web page. Then, embed the graphics you just saved into any of the Chop Point pages you already created.

Module 13 Mastery Check

1. Fill in the blank: _____ applications create graphics using tiny dots.

2. Name three key issues that affect web design decisions.

3. If you are designing web graphics to fit without scrolling in a 640×480 monitor, what should be the largest width of any such graphics?

   A. 640

   B. 600

   C. 540

   D. 500

   E. 480

   F. 400

4. What is a CLUT?

5. True/False: Graphics generally look lighter on a Windows PC than they do on a Mac.

6. Name two ways to reduce a graphic's file size.

7. Fill in the blank: The standard file resolution for web graphics is _____.

8. Which type of file compression requires data to be removed from the image to compress the file and make it smaller?

9. What is the difference between binary and variable transparency?

10. What is the color mode of GIF files?

11. Fill in the blank: _____ is a process in which a graphic is displayed at multiple levels of clarity, from blurry to clear.

12. True/False: The JPEG file format supports transparency.

13. In which file format should you save a photograph if it's going to be part of an animation?

14. In what color modes can PNG files be stored?

15. Fill in the blank: When saving a GIF, _____ can be used to give the appearance of gradations of subtle color shifts, but it adds to the file size.

Learn More

This module barely touched the surface of creating your own web graphics. If you found this is something you are interested in, I encourage you to consider any of the following sources of additional information.

- **Lynda Weinman**   Lynda was my teacher at Art Center College of Design, where she also became my friend and respected colleague. She is a renowned expert on the subject of web graphics, having written many excellent books on the subject. Lynda produces training videos and an informational web site, in addition to running her own courses on the subject in Ojai, California. Visit **www.lynda.com** for more information on any of Lynda's endeavors.

- **Jakob Nielsen**   Mr. Nielsen is an expert in web site usability, particularly helping developers create web sites that work. His books about web usability are must-reads for anyone creating web sites. His web site, **www.useit.com**, offers additional information about creating usable information technology.

- **WebMonkey**   This online magazine, located at **www.webmonkey.com**, is chock full of tips, techniques, and advice for web developers. Topics include Web Authoring (HTML, JavaScript, and so forth), Design (Graphics, Fonts, and so forth), Developing (Databases, Perl, and so on), E-Commerce, Multimedia, and Backend (Networks, Security, and other subjects).

Module 14

Web Content

Because the bulk of the information available on the Internet is in text format, you must take care to ensure users can locate and view this information in the quickest and most efficient manner possible. This module takes an introductory look at ways to do just that.

14.1 Ensure Onscreen Readability of Text

Reading extensive amounts of text on a screen is not only difficult on the eyes, it's also tiresome and inconvenient. Even so, many people use the same text content written for the printed page on their web sites. This repurposing of content detracts from a company's overall identity and can make reading the web site content quite difficult.

TIP

In an article entitled "Writing for the Web," usability expert Jakob Nielsen instructs, "write no more than 50 percent of the text you would have used in a hardcopy publication" (**www.useit.com/alertbox/9703b.html**). Even though this article was written a few years ago, the content is still relevant.

To make things easier on web readers, try following these guidelines.

- *Keep it short and concise.* Chances are good that most web readers won't last through more than a few screens of text on a web page. If you have a long article that needs to be made available to web surfers, try breaking it into several pages to avoid the super-long page-scroll. Remember, you only have a few seconds to grab a user's attention, and long-winded "speeches" (even if they're on the Web) rarely work.

- *Separate paragraphs with blank lines.* On the printed page, paragraphs are designated by an indent of the first sentence in each paragraph. On the screen, such paragraphs seem to run together. For easier onscreen reading, use paragraph tags (<p>) to leave a blank line in between paragraphs.

- *Limit column widths.* Ever wonder why newspaper columns are so short? One reason is it eases and speeds reading for the viewer. The same is true online, so be wary of 500-pixel-wide columns. I like to stay between 200–400 pixels.

- *Avoid underlining.* On the Web, underlined text signifies a link. When you use the u tag to give nonlinked text an underline, it's confusing to users.

- *When centering text, use moderation.* Avoid centering a whole section or paragraph of text, because more than a line or two of centered text is difficult to follow.

- *Do place emphasis on important text, but don't overemphasize.* While the b and i tags draw attention to important text, you can easily overdo it by bolding too much.

- *Avoid using all capital letters.* Consider which is used more on street and highway signs: all caps or a mix of lowercase and capital letters. You rarely see all caps used on street signs, because it's much easier to read words with a mix of uppercase and lowercase letters. In addition, the use of all capital letters is considered "screaming" in online communication.

- *Use lists and group-related information.* Lists improve the "scannability" of your page, making them easier to scan quickly in search of particular information. Headlines can also help differentiate between sections and offer users quick insight on the section's content.

- *Place the most important information at the top of the page.* If users have to scroll for it, you may lose them. Avoid pages that are too busy by limiting paragraphs to one main idea and pages to no more than seven main options or thoughts.

- *Make information easy to find.* Most studies show users don't click more than three times on a web site to try to find the information they want. Avoid burying content more than three levels deep if you expect anyone to find it. And, if you have a search engine on your site (which you should have if your site contains more than 100 pages), take care to ensure the titles of each page are descriptive.

Overall, remember most people scan web pages, as opposed to reading them. When you create a web page, put it away for a day or two and then look at it from a user's standpoint. If you had no idea what the purpose of the page was because you just stumbled on it, would you be able to pick out the main point(s) within ten seconds? If not, you might want to rework the content.

Or, ask a friend to look at the page and identify the first, second, and third things that pop out. If those three things aren't the most important things on the page, perhaps you need to reevaluate the page.

CRITICAL SKILL

14.2 Recognize Effective Links

The Web is all about links. If users cannot find the links on your page and successfully use them, that linked content might as well be deleted. One of the problems with so many web pages is what's commonly referred to as the "click here syndrome."

Discussed briefly in Module 5, this occurs when the phrase *click here* is used as a link's label text. Consider the following example:

Woolwich is a rural community on the east shore of the Kennebec River, opposite the historic city of Bath and approximately 12 miles from the Atlantic Ocean. First settled in the 1600s and incorporated in 1759, the town is named for Woolwich, England, which in like manner is situated on a large, navigable river. (Click here for information about Woolwich, England.)

The words *click here* that were underlined in the preceding example don't shed any light on exactly what you would find if you clicked that link. A better example might be the following:

Woolwich is a rural community on the east shore of the Kennebec River, opposite the historic city of Bath and approximately 12 miles from the Atlantic Ocean. First settled in the 1600s and incorporated in 1759, the town is named for <u>Woolwich, England</u>, which in like manner is situated on a large, navigable river.

Now, when you scan the paragraph, the words *Woolwich, England* jump out and you know more information about that place can be found by clicking the linked words.

Another common pitfall is using entire sentences as link labels. Compare the two links in the next paragraph. The shorter link at the end is easier to spot because you have to read the entire first sentence to understand the content of the link.

Woolwich is a rural community on the <u>east shore of the Kennebec River, opposite the historic city of Bath and approximately 12 miles from the Atlantic Ocean</u>. First settled in the 1600s and incorporated in 1759, the town is named for Woolwich, England, which in like manner is situated on a <u>large, navigable river</u>.

If you needed to place multiple links within a paragraph of text, it might be better to convert the paragraph into a list, where each link is at the beginning of the list item.

Woolwich is a rural Maine community on the east shore of the Kennebec River.

- <u>Historic Bath</u> is located opposite Woolwich
- <u>Atlantic Ocean</u> is approximately 12 miles down river
- <u>First settled</u> in the 1600s
- <u>Incorporated</u> in 1759
- <u>Woolwich, England</u>, gives the town its name

To summarize, it's important to scan over your web pages from the user's perspective to determine if your links are easy to spot and use. Short, meaningful words and phrases work better than lengthy marketing jargon.

Progress Check

1. Why should you avoid underlining text in a web page?

2. Using lists can help the _____ of your pages.

---

1. Because users may confuse it with linked text
2. Scannability

CRITICAL SKILL
14.3 Offer Printer-Friendly Pages

Even though many people use electronic documents to avoid having reams of paper on their desks, plenty of us still print lots of pages from the Web. The fact of the matter is, we are more likely to read long articles of text if they're printed. The problem with this is that most web pages were not created to be printed and, as such, don't print well.

PDFs

One solution to this problem is to enable users to download PostScript versions of the documents. A *PostScript* file, in contrast to an HTML file, was created with a printer in mind and contains specific instructions on how the file should be printed. Different types of PostScript files can be created from all kinds of software titles, regardless of the computer platform.

For example, Adobe's *Portable Document Format* (*PDF*) enables you to take any file from another program (such as Microsoft Publisher or Adobe InDesign) and save it in a universally recognizable file format, characterized by the .pdf file extension. Adobe PDF has become a standard in electronic document delivery because of its ease of use, reliability, and stability.

Unlike HTML pages, which look different depending on the browser and computer system, PDF files look the same across different platforms, even when printed. This makes it easy to distribute documents, such as your company's annual report or newsletter.

TIP

Some programs, such as Adobe Photoshop and Adobe InDesign, are automatically able to save their files as PDFs. Check with your page layout or publishing program's manual before purchasing Adobe Acrobat. Also, Mac users can save as PDF from most applications, by default.

To save text files in the PDF format, you typically must have the Adobe Acrobat software loaded on your system. Once you do, it's only a matter of selecting a few menu items before the file is converted to the PDF format.

To view PDF files, you typically must have the Adobe Acrobat Reader installed on your system. This free utility is available from Adobe's web site. Even if you've never downloaded the Reader, you may already have it because it's included with many other software titles and computer systems. If you do include a link to a PDF file on your web page, remember also to tell users what is needed to view the file and where to download the Reader.

NOTE

Visit **www.adobe.com/products/acrobat/readermain.html** to download the free Acrobat Reader.

Because users must have the reader to view a PDF, avoid using PDFs as the only means for electronically delivering important information. Whenever possible, it's good to have both an HTML version—for online viewing—and a PDF version—for printing—of important documents. (Visit **http://access.adobe.com** for tips on creating accessible PDFs, as well as tools for converting PDFs to HTML documents and vice versa.)

Printer-Specific Style Sheets

Ever visited a web page and seen a button labeled "click here for printer version" or something similar? While that link may have led to a PDF version of the page, it more likely led to another HTML version of the page—this one using a printer-specific style sheet.

As mentioned in Module 12, when using external style sheets it's possible to add the `media` attribute to your `link` tag to tell the browser when to use a particular style sheet. For example, the following shows some code that loads two different style sheets: one if the page is printed, and one if the page is displayed on the screen.

```
<link type="text/css" media="print" href="print.css" />
<link type="text/css" media="screen" href="screen.css" />
```

Once you've linked to your printer-specific style sheet, you just need to edit that style sheet to make the page display appropriately when printed. I recommend starting with a copy of your normal style sheet, and then editing as necessary. So what should you change? The following presents a few things to look out for.

Backgrounds

Always set your background color to white and remove any background images you might have already assigned to the page. This will ensure the user doesn't waste precious ink printing a black background with white text for no real reason. What may have looked attractive on screen might only be a big bleed of ink on the printed page.

```
body {background: white;}
```

Links

If you turned your link underlines off, be sure to turn them back on. Likewise, consider making them bold or otherwise emphasized so they'll stand out even when printed in black and white. CSS-2 even allows you to specify that links should display the linked URL after the link. This would be quite useful if someone prints your page and then wants to access its links at a later date, because the link addresses would be printed on the page. The following code specifies that the URL should be printed after both visited and unvisited links.

```
a:link:after, a:visited:after {
   content: " (" attr(href) ") ";
   }
```

If you have a lot of internal links on your pages, you may need to add your domain name
to this code. Without it, users might see only a portion of the URLs printed: index.html or
aboutus/address.html. The following shows how the code should look in order to make those
links display completely.

```
a:link:after, a:visited:after {
   content: " (http://www.mywebsite.com " attr(href) ") ";
   }
```

Finally, consider turning off any graphical navigation bars or buttons when styling a
printed version of the page. Not only do web navigation bars typically print poorly, but they
are frequently of no use to the reader of a printed page.

Fonts

The standard font measurement for printed pages is points. Therefore, if you used another
measurement for your screen pages, such as pixels, be sure to change that for your printer-
specific style sheet.

```
body { background: white;
       font-size: 12pt;
       }
```

Margins and Padding

If you've removed all margins and padding on your page to make things snug against the edges,
you should remove those style declarations in your printer version. I like to leave the margins
and padding at their default values so as not to have content cut off when printed. However,
many designers prefer to add a 5- or 10-percent margin to either side so the content has a good
amount of buffer space when printed.

Ultimately, the choice is yours. As with all web pages, it's important to test your printer-
specific pages (by printing them on at least two different printers) until you are happy with
the results.

NOTE
If you styled any aspects of your page to be absolutely positioned, consider removing
that declaration and allowing the content to flow freely on the printed page.

Final Tips for Printer-Friendly Pages

Whenever you create pages that will be printed, whether PDF files or printer-specific style sheets, remember the following things:

- **Page Size**   Whereas web pages are designed for screen format (landscape, 800×600 pixels, and so forth), printed pages should be designed for the paper on which they will be printed. Most users in the U.S. will probably print in portrait format on standard letter-size paper (8.5" by 11"). Be sure to leave at least a 1/2" margin on all sides.

- **Color**   Avoid dark background colors on printed pages. Many browsers don't print background colors anyway, so someone might end up with light-colored text on white paper and have trouble reading anything. Remember, many people have black and white printers as opposed to color, so printed documents should be readable in both formats.

- **Reference**   Always include the web page address (URL) on a printed page, so users can return to the page for more information as needed.

- **Image Resolution**   Images created for the Web are low in screen resolution (72 dpi) because that makes them quicker to download. It does not, however, make them pretty when printed. In fact, printed web graphics often look quite bad. Therefore, when creating alternate versions of web pages that will be printed, avoid graphics whenever possible.

Project 14-1 Optimize Text Content

Every web page can use an edit or two to verify the content is optimized for online reading (or scanning). This project asks you to perform such an edit on the home page created for Chop Point. The goal for this project is

- Edit a page of text content for online readability

NOTE

All the files needed to complete the projects in this book for Chop Point can be downloaded from **www.osborne.com** or **www.wendywillard.com**. In addition, you can view my version of the web site anytime by visiting **www.choppoint.org.** If you aren't using the Chop Point site, you can tailor the project to your particular needs.

Step by Step

1. Open your text or HTML editor and load the home page used in previous projects entitled index.html. (Most likely the last time you edited this file was in Module 7.)

2. Rework this page to focus solely on Chop Point Summer Camp by removing the introductory information listing the camp and school. The new title should be "Chop Point Summer Camp."

3. Using the guidelines from this module, edit the page for online readability. To begin, scan the page from a user's standpoint to determine the most important information and how it is portrayed.

4. Check to make sure any links are clear and concise.

5. Feel free to delete repetitive information or to move content to any of other pages you created as you see fit.

6. Save the file.

7. Open your web browser and choose File | Open Page (or Open File or Open, depending on the browser you are using). Locate the file index.html that you just saved. Quickly scan the page as a web surfer would do in order to make sure the file appears as you intended it.

8. If you need to make changes, return to your text editor to do so. After making any changes, save the file and switch back to the browser. Choose Refresh or Reload to preview the changes you just made.

9. Compare your pages with Figures 14-1 and 14-2 to see how a thorough edit for web-readability can make a big difference.

Project Summary

Given how little time most of us spend viewing many web sites, editing text content for online readability is an important skill for anyone maintaining a web site. This project gave you a chance to work on this skill using a page of unedited content from the Chop Point site.

TIP

For extra practice, add a style sheet to this page to focus on readability from a design standpoint. For example, which font styles are more readable? And which color combinations are more pleasing and encourage readability?

(continued)

14

Web Content

Project
14-1

Optimize Text Content

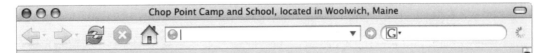

Chop Point

Chop Point is a non-profit organization operating a summer camp and PK-12 school in Woolwich, Maine.

Summer Camp

Chop Point received accreditation from the American Camping Association and opened as a camp in Maine in 1967. Before the founding of Chop Point, the property had been operated as Merrymeeting camp for over fifty years.

Chop Point Summer camp combines a strong residential camping program designed specifically for teenagers, with the excitement of an adventurous trip program. Each summer, 80 teenagers between the ages of twelve and eighteen come to Chop Point from all over the world to have one of the best summers of their lives. The camp is located two hours up the Maine coast in the town of Woolwich. The property includes 50 wooded acres of land at the end of a peninsula, and a mile of shoreline on picturesque and historic Merrymeeting Bay, on the Kennebec River.

Click this image to view a video clip of the inside of a girls' cabin. (2MB)

Buildings include a dining hall, a lodge, two homes, eight cabins, a new state-of-the-art gymnasium, and a boathouse. The boathouse was renovated into a Library and Learning Center, housing staff and computers in the summer. Chop Point also has a full size athletic field, tennis courts, basketball courts, a volleyball court and a well-equipped waterfront facility.

What's the greatest asset of Chop Point? Founder Peter Willard said it best: "We firmly believe our greatest asset is our top-notch staff. Sixteen counselors, having completed at least a year of college, come from throughout the world. They bring their skill, enthusiasm and love of teenagers to camp, and strive to be a genuine friend to each camper."

Chop Point is a recognized non-profit organization and strives to keep campers' and students' fees as affordable as possible. To do this, and still maintain the level of programs that we offer, we rely somewhat on outside donations. We have been provided with generous support from former campers, students, staff and friends. Many of the major improvements to the grounds, facilities and equipment are a direct result of their commitment to Chop Point.

Figure 14-1 This screen shows the index.html page before I edited it.

Chop Point Summer Camp, located in Woolwich, Maine

Chop Point Summer Camp

History

Chop Point received accreditation from the American Camping Association and opened as a camp in Maine in 1967. Before the founding of Chop Point, the property had been operated as Merrymeeting camp for over fifty years.

Program

Chop Point Summer camp combines a strong residential camping program designed specifically for teenagers, with the excitement of an <u>adventurous trip program</u>.

- **Capacity:** 80 campers
- **Ages:** 12-18
- **Camper/Counselor Ratio:** 4:1
- **Ethnicity:** Campers come from all over the world and all walks of life

Location

The camp is located two hours up the Maine coast in the town of Woolwich. The property includes 50 wooded acres of land at the end of a peninsula, and a mile of shoreline on picturesque and historic Merrymeeting Bay, on the Kennebec River.

Buildings include:

Click this image to view a video clip of the inside of a girls' cabin. (2MB)

- Dining hall
- Lodge
- 2 homes
- 8 cabins
- State-of-the-art gymnasium
- Boathouse (The boathouse was renovated into a Library and Learning Center, housing staff and computers in the summer.)
- Full size athletic field
- Tennis courts
- Bsketball courts
- Volleyball court
- Well-equipped waterfront facility

Staff

What's the greatest asset of Chop Point? Founder Peter Willard said it best: "**We firmly believe our greatest asset is our top-notch staff.** Sixteen counselors, having completed at least a year of college, come from throughout the world. They bring their skill, enthusiasm and love of teenagers to camp, and strive to be a genuine friend to each camper."

Donor Support

Chop Point is a recognized non-profit organization and strives to keep campers' and students' fees as affordable as possible. To do this, and still maintain the level of programs that we offer, we rely somewhat on outside donations. We have been provided with

Done

Figure 14-2 After an edit for web readability, the page can more easily be scanned by busy web surfers.

Module 14 Mastery Check

1. Fill in the blank: Most people don't *read* web pages, they _____ them.

2. Where should the most important information on a web page be?

3. What type of file is an example of one that contains specific instructions on how it should be printed?

4. Which file format has become a standard in electronic document delivery because of its ease of use, reliability, and stability?

5. True/False: You should avoid using all capital letters in text on a web page.

6. Why should you avoid underlining text on a web page?

7. Fill in the blank: Using lists can help the _____ of your web pages.

8. What is a reasonable range for column widths on web pages?

9. What are three key things to consider when designing a printable version of a web page?

10. What two words should be avoided as link labels on a web page?

Learn More

This module introduced you to the topic of writing for the Web, which has recently become a hot subject. Whole courses have sprung up at colleges and universities on this topic. If you've found this is something you're interested in, I encourage you to consider the following sources of additional information.

- **Jakob Nielsen**   Mr. Nielsen is an expert in web site usability, particularly in helping developers create web sites that work. His books on web usability are must-reads for anyone creating web sites. Mr. Nielsen's web site, **www.useit.com**, offers additional information about creating usable information technology.

- **usableweb.com**   This web site is a collection of links about human factors, user interface issues, and usable design specific to the Web. In particular, visit **usableweb.com/topics/001310-0-0.html** for links to articles about writing content for the Web.

Module 15
Dynamic Content

While HTML enables you to create static, or unchanging, web pages, JavaScript extends the capabilities of HTML, enabling you to create dynamic pages, which either change or react to users' input. The combination of JavaScript and Cascading Style Sheets (CSSs) gives us what's commonly called Dynamic HTML or DHTML. This section is not meant to teach you to be a web programmer, but rather to help you use it in simple formats in your pages.

To that end, this module gives a brief introduction into the how and why of JavaScript and DHTML, and then focuses on the presentation of a few typical examples of using dynamic content in a web page. If this whets your appetite for basic web scripting and you want to learn more, don't miss the great additional resources listed at the end of the module.

Understand the Concept and Uses of JavaScript and DHTML in Web Pages

Contrary to what its name implies, JavaScript is not the same as Java. Sun Microsystems created the Java programming language, while Netscape developed JavaScript. Unlike Java, which can run on its own as a mini-application, *JavaScript* is built into web browsers and cannot stand on its own. Essentially, it's just a set of statements, or scripts, that are instructions for the browser.

NOTE

JavaScript is not supported by all web browsers. In addition, users can turn off support for JavaScript from within their personal browser. This means you should use caution when relying on JavaScript to transfer important information to users.

When you write JavaScript, it's actually placed right within the HTML on your page. This means you can learn JavaScript from your favorite web sites, just like you can with HTML, by viewing the HTML source from within the browser.

But, before you can do that, you have to know what JavaScript *looks* like and where to look for it. The following is a basic example:

```
<html>
<head>
    <title>My Web Page</title>
```

```
<script language="JavaScript" type="text/javascript">
   document.write("I can write JavaScript!");
</script>
</head>
<body>
</body>
</html>
```

The opening and closing `script` tags are HTML, while everything in between them is written in JavaScript. This is an important distinction because JavaScript is quite different than HTML in several ways:

- JavaScript is case-sensitive; some forms of HTML are not.

- In JavaScript, quotes are required; in some forms of HTML, quotes are optional.

- JavaScript has a distinct format that must be adhered to; most forms of HTML are forgiving about spacing and formatting.

Given those restrictions, troubleshooting JavaScript can be a bit tricky. Whenever you copy a script from a web site or a book, be sure to copy it exactly as it is written, unless otherwise specified. For example, placing a line break in the middle of the previous example could produce an error when the page is viewed in a browser.

```
<script language="JavaScript" type="text/javascript">
   document.write("I can write JavaScript! ←──┐
");                            This misplaced line break can cause browsers
</script>                      to display an error when the page is viewed
```

Troubleshoot JavaScript

If you have a copy of a Mozilla-based browser, such as Firefox, you have a great way to troubleshoot your JavaScript. Type **javascript:** into the location box in the browser and

a console pops up with any error information. (If you've visited any web sites recently, chances are good you'll see plenty of errors, like I did when I took this screen capture!)

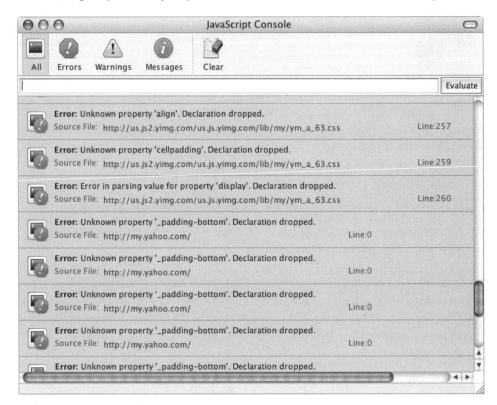

You can use this console to view errors on your pages or even to test strings of code, by typing them into the console and clicking the Evaluate button.

TIP

When a page displays with errors in Internet Explorer, you see a statement such as "Done, but with errors on page" near the bottom-left corner of the browser window. Click the icon to the left of the statement to reveal information about the error(s).

Hide Scripts

If you look at a few JavaScripts on the Web, you may notice many look like they are actually commented out—hidden—in the HTML.

This is the HTML code used to begin a comment

```
<script language="JavaScript" type="text/javascript">
<!-- This hides the script from older browsers
    document.write("I can write JavaScript!");
// This stops hiding the script from older browsers -->>
</script>
```

This is the HTML code used to end a comment

This is JavaScript's way of adding a comment. Without these double slashes before the closing HTML comment code (-->), the browser may become confused

This is done so that older browsers that aren't capable of understanding JavaScript will simply skip over the script and not produce any errors.

Terminology

You should learn several new terms before you use any JavaScript. The following examines the most common.

NOTE

Many web sites and other books contain the official JavaScript specifications. Refer to the "Learning More" section at the end of this module for details.

Objects and Methods

To understand these terms, let's first look back at the previous example and identify the pieces.

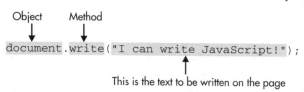

Object   Method

```
document.write("I can write JavaScript!");
```

This is the text to be written on the page

In this example, document is acting as a JavaScript object. Quite simply, an *object* is anything that can be manipulated or changed by the script. In this case, the object document tells the browser the code directly following it is referring to the HTML document itself.

Objects can have *methods*, which are actual things that happen to the objects (in this case, a document is written to). For example, the object "car" might have a method called "drive." Along those lines, what other methods might you imagine for the car object? (How about "clean" or "park"…) Methods are followed by a set of parentheses, containing any specific instructions on how to accomplish the method. In the previous example, the text inside the parentheses is written within the current document.

Properties

Just as an object, such as a car, has features (tires, brakes, and so forth) in the real world, JavaScript objects can have *properties*. This is useful if, for example, you want to manipulate a specific section of a document. Objects and properties are separated by periods. When you want to specify the *value* of a property, such as the color of the background, you add the value after the property, as in the following example.

```
document.bgColor="333333";
```
◄——————— Note the capital C in this property and remember JavaScript is case-sensitive

NOTE

An object can even have a property that is, in itself, another object. For example, `document.location.href` includes a `document` object, its `location` (an object itself and a property of `document`), and an `href` (a property of `location`).

Variables, Operators, and Functions

In JavaScript, a *variable* is something you specify for your own needs. You might think of variables as labels for changeable values used within a single script. To define a variable, type **var**, followed by the one-word name of the variable.

TIP

Remember, JavaScript is case-sensitive. If you capitalize a letter when you first define a variable, you must also capitalize that letter every time you refer to it.

```
var VotingAge;
```

An *operator* does something, such as a calculation or a comparison between two or more variables. The symbols used to do this (listed in Table 15-1) should look familiar because they are also used in simple mathematics. One place you can use operators is in defining values of variables, as in the following example:

Tells the browser we are defining a variable

Gives a name to our variable, so we can refer to it later

```
var VotingAge = 18;
```
◄—— Gives a value to associate with the variable

```
var DrivingAge = VotingAge - 2;
```
——————— Operator

Gives a name to this second variable

Refers to the variable associated with the variable named VotingAge (18)

Operator	Description	Operator	Description
+	Adds	-	Subtracts
*	Multiplies	/	Divides
++	Adds one	–	Subtracts one
=	Sets value	==	Is equal to
<	Less than	>	Greater than
<=	Less than or equal to	>=	Greater than or equal to
!=	Is not equal to	||	Or
&&	And		

Table 15-1 JavaScript Operators

Likewise, a *function* is a group of commands to which you give a name so that you can refer to the group later in the page. To create a function, type **function**, followed by the function name and a set of parentheses. Then, type the commands that are part of the function below the name and enclosed in curly brackets. This is shown in the following example.

```
function functionName()
     { commands go here
}
```

You can't use just any name for a variable or a function because there's a list of reserved words that have a special meaning in either JavaScript or Java. If you use one of these words (shown in Table 15-2) as a function or a variable, users may encounter errors when viewing your pages.

abstract	break	boolean	byte
case	char	comment	continue
default	delete	do	double
else	export	false	final
float	for	function	goto
if	implements	import	in

Table 15-2 Common Reserved JavaScript Words

instanceOf	int	interface	label
long	native	new	null
package	private	protected	public
return	switch	synchronized	this
throws	transient	true	typeof
var	while	with	void

Table 15-2 Common Reserved JavaScript Words *(Continued)*

Event Handlers

By contrast with other terms discussed here, *event handlers* needn't be placed within the opening and closing `script` tags. These pieces of JavaScript can actually be embedded within HTML to respond to a user's interaction and make a page dynamic. For example, placing the event handler `onClick` within an a tag (`<a>`) causes the event to occur when the user clicks the link. So, if I wanted to change the page's background color when a link was clicked, I could use the following code.

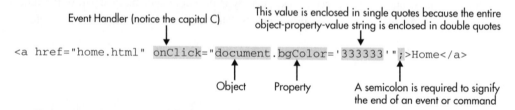

Table 15-3 lists popular event handlers, but more information can be found in the resources listed at the end of this module.

Event Handler	Specifies Action to Occur...
onAbort	...when the user stops loading the current page.
onBlur	...when the user moves away from an object (such as a browser window).
onChange	...when the user changes an object.
onClick	...when the user clicks an object.
onFocus	...when the user brings an object (such as a browser window) to the foreground.
onLoad	...when an object is fully loaded.

Table 15-3 Common Event Handlers in JavaScript

Event Handler	Specifies Action to Occur...
onMouseDown	...when the user presses the mouse button down over an object.
onMouseOver	...when the user moves the cursor over an object (such as an image or text).
onMouseOut	...when the user moves the mouse away from an object (such as an image or text).
onMouseUp	...when the user releases the mouse button after clicking an object.
onSelect	...when the user selects an object (such as a check box or another form field).
onSubmit	...when the user submits a form.

Table 15-3 Common Event Handlers in JavaScript *(Continued)*

JavaScript Logic

Given that scripts are essentially a set of instructions to the browser, you can often read them logically as a series of commands. For example, in the following script, I am telling the browser to write one thing if the user has Internet Explorer and something else if the user doesn't have IE.

This part of the script checks if the browser's name is Microsoft Internet Explorer. Notice the two equal signs (meaning "is equal to")

```
<script language="JavaScript" type="text/javascript">
<!-- Begin hiding script from older browsers
if (navigator.appName == "Microsoft Internet Explorer") {
    document.write("The Magic 8-ball says: Your browser is Internet Explorer.");
}
else {
    document.write("The Magic 8-ball says: Your browser is not Internet Explorer.");
}
// End hiding script from older browsers -->
</script>
```

This is what the browser is supposed to do if it is IE

This is what the browser is supposed to do if it is not IE

These types of *if...then* statements are called *conditionals* and tell the browser to do one thing if *x* is true, and to do something else if *x* is false. Notice the actual instructions on what to do are included within curly brackets, {}. The spacing here is important because the opening curly bracket should be on the same line as the `if` or `else`. The closing curly bracket is on a line by itself, after the instructions end. In addition, all statements (instructions) end with semicolons. The following is a simple example of the layout.

```
if (something) {
    do this;
}
else {
    do this;
}
```

It could also appear in the following form, which, although less common, easily splits the conditions from each other.

```
if (something)
{
    do this;
}
else
{
    do this;
}
```

Sample Scripts

The next few sections include sample scripts for you to try in your web pages. Remember, these are provided as examples only. They might not work in every situation. Because it's beyond the scope of this book to teach you JavaScript at the same level you've learned HTML, please refer to the additional resources at the end of this module for more help.

Add the Current Date and Time

The most basic way to add the current date and time to a web page is shown in the following script. Once you learn more about JavaScript, you can customize this script. For example, you might tell the browser to print only the month and day, or to print the month, day, and year in 00/00/00 format.

Place this script within the body of your web page wherever you want the date to appear.

```
<script language="JavaScript" type="text/javascript">
<!--
    document.write(Date());
// -->
</script>
```

Make Required Form Fields

To avoid receiving unusable form responses, you can use JavaScript to make certain form fields required. For example, if your page included a form for posting on a bulletin board, you might want to make the comments field required so that no one accidentally posts a blank message. Likewise, if you want to be able to respond to users via e-mail, you might want to make the field asking for their e-mail addresses required.

If you use this script and users don't enter any text in the required fields, the browser brings up an alert message telling them to do so before they can submit the form.

Instructions and Script

Place the JavaScript code enclosed by the `<script>` and `</script>` tags in the header of the HTML page (not in the body). Then, place the appropriate event handler in the `form` tag within the body of your HTML page.

Essentially, the script checks the input control (radio button, text field, and so on) to see if its value is blank (empty). If it is empty, it displays a pop-up window asking the user to complete that item. The final line of the conditional statement—return false—prevents the form from being submitted until all required input controls have been completed.

NOTE

The bolded text highlights pieces of the script you should customize.

```
<script language="JavaScript" type="text/javascript">
<!-- Start hiding script from older browsers
function checkInput(formName) {

    if (formName.fieldName.value == "") {
        alert("Please enter your name");
        formName.fieldName.focus();
        return false;
    }
}
// End hiding script -->
</script>
```

This names the function so we can refer to it later

This should be the name of your form, as specified in the name attribute of the opening `form` tag

This is the text the user will see if the required field is left empty

This should be the name of the field you want to require, as specified in the input control's name attribute

This `onSubmit` event handler needs to go in the opening `form` tag, and then the form needs to be named with the name attribute, like this:

```
<form onSubmit="return checkInput(this);" name="formName" action="processForm.cgi">
```

Need to make multiple form elements required? Simply repeat these steps by copying and pasting the conditional statement. The following is an example in which both the first and last names are required:

```
<script language="JavaScript" type="text/javascript">
<!-- Start hiding script from older browsers
function checkInput(contactForm) {
```

```
if (contactForm.firstName.value == "") {
      alert("Please enter your first name");
      contactForm.firstName.focus();
      return false;
   }
if (contactForm.lastName.value == "") {
      alert("Please enter your last name");
      contactForm.lastName.focus();
      return false;
   }
}
// End hiding script -->
</script>
```

Then continue with the rest of the form, making sure to name each form field appropriately:

```
First Name: <input type="text" size="20" name="firstName" /><br />
<input type="submit" value="submit" />
</form>
```

Replace an Image When the User Points to It

If you've done any amount of surfing on the Web, you've probably noticed that page elements sometimes change when you move the cursor over them. For example, have you ever moved your mouse over a graphical link and found it changed? This type of thing can be accomplished using event handlers in JavaScript.

You can use the onMouseOver event handler to replace an image when the mouse is moved over an image. This handler is placed within the a tag, so you can replace an image only when the user rolls over a link (either the image itself or a text link).

This script requires JavaScript in the header of the HTML page, as well as the body. Both the code at the top of the page and the code in the a tag must be present for the image swap to work.

You also need two versions of each image you want to change: one that's present when the page is first viewed and another for when the mouse is rolled over the image or link—and both of those versions should be the same size. Name your images so you can recognize which one should be used when. For example, the original link to a section called "camp" might be referred to as *campOff*, while the version appearing when the user rolls over it might be called *campOver*.

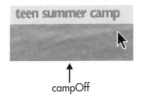
campOff

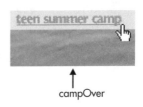
campOver

Instructions and Script

Place this script in the header of your page (in between the opening and closing head tags). The bolded text highlights pieces of the script you should customize.

This line gives the original image a name, so it can be referenced later

This line gives the location (URL) of the original image

```
<script language="JavaScript" type="text/javascript">
<!--
campOff = new Image;
campOff.src = "/images/link_campOff.gif";

campOver = new Image;
campOver.src = "/images/link_campOver.gif";

function replaceImg(oldImg,newImg) {
    document[oldImg].src=eval(newImg + ".src");
}

// -->
</script>
```

This line gives the replacement image a name, so it can be referenced later

This line gives the location (URL) of the replacement image

This part identifies the function we use to replace the image

Place the onMouseOver and onMouseOut event handlers in the a tag of the link for the image that should be changed. Place the name attribute in the img tag, to identify the image to be changed.

The following is an example of how the script looks when placed within an a tag for an image:

Here, we're telling the browser to look for the image named *campOff* . . .

. . . and replace it with the image named *campOver* when the mouse moves over the link

```
<a href="/camp/index.html"
    onMouseOver="replaceImg('campOff','campOver')"
    onMouseOut="replaceImg('campOff','campOff')">
    <img src="/images/lk_camp1.gif"
    alt="LINK: Chop Point Coed Summer Camp for Teens 12-18"
    name="campOff" width="122" height="18" border="0" />
</a>
```

. . . and change it back to its original state, named *campOff*

You must remember to identify the image using the name attribute inside of the img tag

Then, when the mouse moves away from the link, we tell the browser to look again for the location of the image named *campOff* . . .

Format a New Window

While you learned in previous modules that you could use the `target` attribute to load links into another browser window, you cannot control the size and style of that browser window with standard HTML. Instead, you can use JavaScript to specify settings such as how large or small that window should be and whether the scroll bars are present (see Figure 15-1).

Some of the characteristics you can specify include

- **toolbar=yes or no** Turns the browser tool bar—Back, Stop, Reload, and so on—on or off in the new window

- **location=yes or no** Turns the browser location bar on or off in the new window

- **status=yes or no** Turns the browser status bar on or off in the new window

- **menubar=yes or no** Turns the browser menus—File, Edit, View, and so on—on or off in the new window

- **resizeable=yes or no** Specifies whether users can resize the new window

- **scrolling=yes, no or auto** Allows or prevents scrolling, or leaves it up to the browser to decide as needed

- **width=#** Specifies the width of the new window in pixels

- **height=#** Specifies the height of the new window in pixels

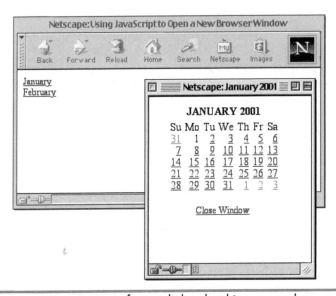

Figure 15-1 You can use JavaScript to force a link to load into a new browser window that is formatted to your specifications.

Instructions and Script

Place this script in the header of your page (in between the opening and closing head tags). The bolded text highlights pieces of the script you should customize.

In the beginning of the script, we see function NewWindow(link). This part identifies the function we use to open the new window, so we can reference it later. The end of the script—MonthWindow.focus()—brings the window named MonthWindow to the front of the screen.

```
<script language="JavaScript" type="text/javascript">
<!--
function NewWindow(link) {
    var MonthWindow = window.open(link, 'Month', 'toolbar=no,location=no,
status=yes,menubar=no,resizeable=yes,scrollbars=yes,width=200,height=200');
    MonthWindow.focus();
}
// -->
</script>
```

Even though it is misspelled, it is actually the proper way to write it! (The correct spelling is ignored by most browsers...)

This defines the characteristics of the new window. When typed in your text/HTML editor, these should be contained on a single line without any breaks.

Then, in the body of your page, reference the function created in the previous script from within the appropriate link. You can use the following code to load other links in the NewWindow, simply by changing the URL listed in the parentheses.

```
<a href="javascript:NewWindow('january.html');">January</a><br />
```

This tells the browser to perform the function called NewWindow

This gives the location of the page to load in the new window

```
<a href="javascript:NewWindow('february.html');">February</a><br />
```

If you want to give users the option of closing the window easily, you can add the following code to the bottom of the page that's loaded into the new window. So, in this case, the code was added to the january.html and february.html pages. Refer back to Figure 15-1 for an example.

```
<a href="javascript:window.close();">Close Window</a>
```

Create a Dynamic Navigation Bar

In Module 12, I discussed how you can actually have hidden layers of content within your web page. While the layers can be created and hidden with CSS, you use JavaScript to make them visible when a user interacts with the web page. The most common use of this in web pages is for dynamic navigations bars, where a submenu or drop-down menu appears after you click a link, providing additional link choices without refreshing the HTML page itself.

These dynamic navigation bars can become extremely complex, but the core concept is relatively simple, and that's what this section discusses—a bare bones method for invoking submenus. For more on how to make your navigation bar "bigger and better," refer to the resources section at the end of this module. Figures 15-2 and 15-3 show this basic DHTML in action, and the code used to accomplish this task is included in the following section.

Instructions and Script

Place this JavaScript in the header of your page (in between the opening and closing head tags). The bolded text highlights pieces of the script you should customize.

```
<script language="JavaScript" type="text/javascript">
<!--
function showLayer() {
    document.getElementById("aboutus-sub").style.visibility="visible";
}
function hideLayer() {
    document.getElementById("aboutus-sub").style.visibility="hidden";
        }
//-->
</script>
```

Replace this with the name of the layer whose visibility you're altering

Figure 15-2 This shows the navigation button before it's been clicked.

Figure 15-3 This shows how the hidden layer is made visible after I clicked the About Us button.

Next, adjust your style sheet to format the visible navigation button/link and the hidden submenu. Be sure to set the positioning so the submenu displays below the top menu. What follows is the style sheet I used to create the menus shown previously in Figures 15-2 and 15-3.

```
body {
    font-family: verdana;
    }
#aboutus {
    position: absolute;
    top: 20px;
    left: 20px;
    width: 100px;
    padding: 10px;
    text-align: center;
    background-color: #ccc;
    border:1px solid black;
    cursor: pointer;           ←——— This changes the cursor to a pointer, to
    }                                help indicate that the content is linked
#aboutus-sub {
    position: absolute;
    visibility: hidden;        ←——— I set the visibility to hidden so the
    top: 60px;                       submenu is not visible when the
                                     page first loads
```

```
        left: 20px;
        width: 100px;
        padding: 0px 10px;
        text-align: center;
        background-color: #333;
        color: #fff;
        border: 1px solid #999;
        cursor: pointer;
        }
ul {
        padding: 0px;
        margin: 0px;
        }
li {
        list-style: none;
        padding: 5px 0px;
        border-bottom: 1px dashed white;
        }
li a {
        color: #fff;
        text-decoration: none;
        }
.last {
        border: 0px;
        }
```

The final piece to this DHTML is the actual HTML code for the content, which is placed between the opening and closing body tags.

```
<div id="aboutus" onClick="showLayer('aboutus-sub');">ABOUT US</div>
<div id="aboutus-sub">
<ul><li><a href="history.html">History</a></li>
    <li><a href="location.html">Location</a></li>
    <li class="last"><a href="team.html">Team</a></li>
    </ul>
</div>
```

The onClick JavaScript event handler tells the browser to display the "aboutus-sub" layer when the user clicks anywhere within the "aboutus" content area

As mentioned previously, this really is just the tip of the iceberg regarding what is possible with DHTML. If it's inspired you to want to do more with JavaScript and CSS, don't miss the "Learn More" section at the end of this module.

15

Dynamic Content

Project 15-1 Use JavaScript to Launch a New Browser Window

JavaScript can add much to a web site, which wouldn't otherwise be possible with HTML. Many of the popular JavaScript techniques used on the Web make a site seem more dynamic. In this project, we use JavaScript to launch a new browser window from a link on the Chop Point Camp Adventure Trips page. The goal for this project is to use JavaScript to launch and control a new browser window.

NOTE

All the files needed to complete the projects in this book for the Chop Point site can be downloaded from **www.osborne.com** or **www.wendywillard.com**. In addition, you can view my version of the web site anytime by visiting **www.choppoint.org**. Those of you who aren't using the Chop Point site can tailor the project to your particular needs.

Step by Step

1. Open the file trips.html (saved from Module 9) in your text or HTML editor.

2. Add the necessary JavaScript to the header of the page to set up a function for launching a new browser window.

3. Name the window **MapWindow**.

4. Title it **'Map'**.

5. Turn the menu bar, the status bar, the tool bar, and the location off in the new window.

6. Set the scrolling to `auto`.

7. Format the new window to be 500 by 500 pixels in size.

8. Create a link from the phrase *Kennebec River* in the first canoeing trip description. Using JavaScript, specify that the text should link to a page called `canoetrip-map.html` and should open in the MapWindow.

NOTE

`canoetrip-map.html` was created for you and is located in the Module 15 folder for this book on the Osborne web site.

Project
15-1

Use JavaScript to Launch a New Browser Window

(continued)

9. Save the file.

10. Open your web browser and choose File | Open Page (or Open File or Open, depending on the browser you're using). Locate the file trips.html you just saved. Click the link labeled *Kennebec River* to verify that the linked page opens in a new browser window with the appropriate customizations.

11. If you need to make changes, return to your text editor to do so. After making any changes, save the file and switch back to the browser. Choose Refresh or Reload to preview the changes you just made.

TIP

Do you get an error or see nothing in the new browser window? Make sure the canoetrip-map.html page is located in the same folder as the trips.html page. If you receive other errors, verify your script against the following one or try using your browser's JavaScript console for troubleshooting.

```
<!DOCTYPE html PUBLIC "-//W3C//DTD XHTML 1.0 Transitional//EN"
"http://www.w3.org/TR/xhtml1/DTD/transitional.dtd">
<html>
<head>
<title> Optional Adventure Trips - 2006  </title>
<script language="JavaScript" type="text/javascript">
<!--
function NewWindow(link) {
    var MapWindow =
window.open(link,'Map','toolbar=no,location=no,status=no,menubar=no,resizeable=
yes,scrollbars=auto,width=500,height=500');
    MapWindow.focus();
    }
// -->
</script>
```

└── This entire section should be on one line, without any hard returns, or it will "break" the script

. . . The code in between these two sections remains unchanged.

```
<tr><td class="center">X</td>
    <td class="center"></td>
    <td>Canoeing</td>
    <td>2 days</td>
    <td><a href="javascript:NewWindow('canoetrip-map.html');">Kennebec River</a></td>
    </tr>
```

. . . The rest of the page remains unchanged.

Project Summary

Although JavaScript isn't the same as HTML, the two can be used together to make web pages more dynamic in nature. This project gave you a chance to practice one JavaScript technique—controlling browser windows.

✓

Module 15 Mastery Check

1. Fill in the blank: JavaScript is case-_____.

2. Name two ways JavaScript differs from standard HTML.

3. How do you hide JavaScript from older browsers that don't support it?

4. Fill in the blank: In the following code, _____ is the JavaScript object.

```
document.write("This is a text!");
```

5. True/False: A plus sign (+) is an example of a JavaScript variable.

6. When placed within the header of a web page, which opening and closing tags surround all JavaScripts?

7. Fill in the blank: Objects can have _____, which are actual things that happen to the objects, such as `write` in the following statement: `document.write("I can write JavaScript");`.

8. What term is given to an aspect of a JavaScript that you specify for your own needs, which is used as a label for a changeable value?

9. Fill in the blank: A _____ is a group of commands to which you give a name so you can refer to it later in the script.

10. Which aspect of JavaScript is embedded within the page's HTML and responds to a user's interaction?

11. How are conditionals used in JavaScript?

12. What does the following JavaScript do when added to an `a` tag on a web page?

```
onClick="document.bgColor='green'"
```

13. How do you specify that a new browser window should not have any scroll bars?

14. What punctuation ends all JavaScript statements?

15. What does `onFocus` do when used in a JavaScript?

Learn More

While I didn't expect this module would teach you everything you need to know about JavaScript or DHTML, I hope it gave you a basic understanding of what types of things these scripts can do. If you'd like to learn more, many sources of additional information are available on this topic. The following section lists some of the most popular.

Also, the sites listed here offer many free scripts that you may borrow and use on your own site. This is considered perfectly normal, so long as you give credit to the original author(s) in your code.

Online References and Scripts

- **SitePoint.com**   This site contains DHTML and JavaScript articles (**www.sitepoint.com/subcat/javascript**), as well as a whole blog about this stuff (**www.sitepoint.com/blogs/category/dhtml-css**)!

- **Web Reference JavaScript Articles**   This web site (**www.webreference.com/ programming/javascript**) includes tutorials, tips, and reviews of tools.

- **Mozilla Developer Center**   This section of the Mozilla Developer Center (**http://developer.mozilla.org/en/docs/DHTML**) is specifically geared toward anyone developing DHTML, and includes helpful documentation and support communities.

- **javascripts.com**   You can find thousands of free scripts and information about how to use them.

- **DHTML Center**   This site has thousands of free scripts you can download and customize, as well as tutorials and help forums (**www.dhtmlcentral.com**).

NOTE

Always look for the most recent references you can find when working with JavaScript and DHTML. The reason is this—older scripts were written for older browsers, and may or may not be valid today. Often, those older browsers required web developers to use special workarounds, called hacks, in their JavaScripts and DHTML. Many of those hacks are no longer necessary, and in some cases can even "break" in modern browsers.

Books

- *DHTML and CSS for the Web* (Visual Quickstart Guide) by Jason Cranford Teague is a good place for beginners to start.

- *JavaScript: The Definitive Guide* by David Flanagan offers more advanced information for users with a bit of previous programming experience.

- *JavaScript & DHTML Cookbook* by Danny Goodman is good for someone who's looking for easy-to-use recipe-style scripts.

- *The JavaScript Anthology: 101 Essential Tips, Tricks & Hacks* by Cameron Adams and James Edwards is another recipe-style book of scripts.

- *DHTML Utopia: Modern Web Design Using JavaScript & DOM* by Stuart Langridge is a book specifically geared toward the modern browsers, which means it avoids outdated hacks and inefficient code.

Module 16

Making Pages Available to Others

Throughout the course of this book, you've created and viewed web pages on your personal computer. At some point you'll undoubtedly want to show your web pages to other people. To do that, your site must be transferred or *uploaded* to a host computer with 24-hour access to the Internet, where it has a suitable domain name or URL. Then, to drive traffic to that site, you need to consider submitting your site to search engines and using other marketing techniques.

CRITICAL SKILL
16.1 Select Possible Domain Names for Your Site

Before diving into the actual meat of this module, I want to mention domain names briefly. Many people underestimate the power of a guessable and memorable domain name. Consider a company called Acme Landscaping Incorporated. While it may seem logical to its business owners to purchase the domain name *alinc.com*, this is probably not the first thing a potential customer would guess.

TIP

There are probably thousands of places online where you could research and register a domain. A couple of options include **www.networksolutions.com** and **www.godaddy.com**.

The name acmelandscaping.com would be my first guess, but if that were already taken, I might try acmelandscapers.com, acmelawns.com, or even something like beautifullawns.com. If more than one of those were available, you might even register both. Purchasing multiple domain names is an inexpensive way to bring in some additional customers and build your brand identity online. Whenever appropriate, you might also purchase the same domain name ending with different extensions, such as beautifullawns.com and beautifullawns.net.

CRITICAL SKILL
16.2 Determine the Most Appropriate Type of Hosting for Your Site

Many different options are available for those who want to publish a site on the Internet. For the purposes of this module, I group these options into two categories: personal site hosting and business site hosting.

Ask the Expert

Q: What are the valid characters for a domain name, and how long can a domain name be?

A: According to Network Solutions (**www.networksolutions.com**), you can use letters and numbers. You can also use hyphens, although they may not appear at the beginning or end of your web address. Spaces or other characters like question marks and exclamation marks are never allowed.

Your complete domain name (including the extension—such as .com, .edu, .net, .org, .biz, .tv, or .info) can be up to 26 characters long. Remember, "www" isn't included in the domain name you register, so you needn't count those characters. For example, *acmelandscaping.com* (19 characters) is acceptable, but *acmelandscapingincorporated.com* (31 characters) isn't.

Personal Site Hosting

When you want to publish a personal web site and you aren't concerned about having your own domain name (such as wendywillard.com), you have a wide range of free options available. For example, all the following sites offer free web space for personal sites to anyone who asks for it. If you currently have an e-mail account with any of these, you're already halfway there.

- **Yahoo! GeoCities (www.geocities.com)**

- **AOL Hometown (hometown.aol.com)**

- **Tripod (www.tripod.com)**

- **My Space (www.myspace.com)**

Because these sites are largely targeting beginners, they make uploading and maintaining your web pages a breeze. Most use web-based tools to do so, meaning you don't even need any additional software.

While these sites offer free hosting to anyone who requests it, remember to check first with your current *Internet service provider* (*ISP*). ISPs frequently throw in some free web space with dial-up Internet connections. If none of these free options suits your purposes or if you need to register your own domain, move on to the next section about business site hosting.

NOTE

Before you sign up with any ISP, be sure to check the terms of service to verify your site fits within the confines of the ISP's requirements. For example, the majority of ISPs prohibit sites distributing pornography or illegal copies of computer software. In addition, free ISPs usually limit the amount of space and/or bandwidth you can use. I mention these only to point out that restrictions do exist and you'd be wise to review all terms and details carefully to avoid incurring unexpected fees.

Business Site Hosting

On the business side, your options vary from onsite to colocated to offsite. In the case of *onsite hosting*, your business purchases a server, its software, and a dedicated Internet connection capable of serving your site to web users 24 hours a day, 365 days a year. For small businesses, this isn't a viable option because it requires expensive start-up costs and on-staff Information Technology (IT) talent.

For businesses that already own the appropriate equipment and have an experienced webmaster but don't want to spend the money for an expensive, dedicated Internet connection, *colocation* is an option. In this case, you use your own equipment and personnel but rent space and a high-speed Internet connection from a host company. Your equipment is housed in that space and can be reached any time of day by your personnel, thereby enabling you to maintain a higher level of control over your site as desired.

For the majority of small to mid-size businesses, *offsite hosting* is the most cost-effective and popular solution. This can be on either a *shared* or a *dedicated* server. While a shared server can be significantly less expensive than one dedicated to your needs, it may not be possible in all situations. For example, if your site runs custom web applications, requires a high level of security, or needs a large amount of space, a dedicated server is preferred.

Many service levels, and therefore, many price levels, exist within shared offsite hosting. For this reason, be wary of comparing apples to oranges. When you are considering two or more hosting providers, look closely at the fine print to be sure they offer similar services before making a final decision solely on price.

The following are some questions to ask when you look for business hosting.

- How much space on the server will I receive? How much extra do I have to pay if I go over that space?

- How much traffic can my site generate over a month? What are some average traffic rates for some similar sites you host? How much extra will I pay if the site generates more traffic than allowed?

- Is multimedia streaming supported? If so, how much traffic is supported for any given event and at what point will the system overload? What are procedures for dealing with excess traffic?

- How many e-mail accounts will I receive with this account?

- Can I use my own domain name(s) (as opposed to www.hostcompany.com/mybusiness)? Will you help me register my domain? (If you haven't already registered one.) Will you charge extra if I have multiple domain names for a web site? If so, how much more?

- What kind of access will I have to my web site? (For example, is FTP access available for uploading files?)

- What kind of support do you offer? (For example, if I need help adding password protection to my site, will you help me?) What hours is your support staff available?

- Can I load my own applications (database tools, e-commerce tools, and so forth) onto the server? What requirements or restrictions do you have regarding those? Are additional costs involved?

- What additional services do you offer? (For example, can you also host my online store and if so, how much would it cost me in addition to my current fees? Can I use the Microsoft FrontPage extensions if I want to?)

- How many Internet connections do you have? (The more connections a host has, the better chance your site has of staying "live" if one connection goes down.)

- How often do you perform backups? How easy is it for me to gain access to a backup if I need one?

- What are the start-up costs? What are the monthly costs? Are there any guarantees?

- Do you offer a service to measure statistics for my site, such as how many people have visited? If so, can I see an example?

- Can you also provide Internet access if I need it?

- Can you provide references?

Many services online let you compare different web site host companies. To get started, you might try

- **www.hostsearch.com**

- **www.cnet.com/internet/0-3799.html**

Or try searching in Yahoo! using the phrase *web site host* to see lists of hosting companies. In the end, you'll probably get the best ideas about which hosting provider to use by asking friends or business associates.

Search Engines and Search Directories

Many times in this book, I direct you to search for more information on the Internet. The majority of web surfers use a search engine or search directory at some point to locate information. If the Web were a large book, you might think of these as different types of indexes—some listing alphabetically, others by topic.

Search directories like Yahoo! (**www.yahoo.com**) organize huge lists of web sites by category and enable you to search these listings by keyword. Search directories usually include short descriptions next to each listing and sometimes even editorial comment. Other popular search directories are Open Directory (**www.dmoz.org**), LookSmart (**www.looksmart.com**), and Snap (**www.snap.com**).

In addition to these large search directories, thousands of smaller search directories exist for specific topics. So, if your site sells children's clothing, submitting the site to search directories of children's products or those specifically for parents might be wise. Search for these keywords to locate related search directories.

TIP

A great way to find out where you should list your site is to check your competition. If you enter **link:competitor.com** into AltaVista's search engine (where competitor.com is replaced with the URL of your competitor's web site), you can see all the sites that link to your competitor. Chances are good that if you want to acquire some of those customers from the competition, you could benefit by having links from those same sites.

Search engines maintain a large database of the content on the Web. You can search that database according to keyword to return pages of results. Some search engines are now adding directory features, trying to give users the best of both worlds. Popular engines are Google (**www.google.com**), AltaVista (**www.altavista.com**), MSN (**search.msn.com**), AOL (**search.aol.com**), and Go (**www.go.com**). A few of these engines now allow users to ask questions in sentence format, such as "How can I advertise my web site?" The most popular of these is Ask Jeeves (**www.ask.com**).

Search engines and search directories don't have to conform to any set of standards, so any details or special techniques you may read about them are subject to change. To help you keep current on these issues, visit **www.searchenginewatch.com**.

Prepare Your Site for Its Public Debut

Before you upload your site to a host computer and submit it to directories and engines, tidying it up a little is best. Consider the following dos and don'ts.

Do:

- *Make sure all your images have alternative text.* Directories and engines can't see the images—they only "look" at the alternative text for descriptions.

- *Give your pages descriptive 5- to 13-word titles, using keywords from the page.* Directories and engines look at the titles of your pages and often use them to list your site. So "Page 2" would definitely not entice as many visitors as, say, "Lawn Care Products for Sale."

- *Repeat keywords throughout the page.* On a page entitled "Lawn Care Products for Sale," you should include those same words in the headlines, body text, and alternative text for images on the page. This increases the relevancy of the page when someone searches for those words.

Don't:

- *Stray from the topic.* If a page is about lawn care products, don't include information about your favorite links or television shows on that same page. Extraneous information only weakens the relevancy of your pages because search engines typically show pages with the most relevant information at the top of the results list.

- *Repeat keywords too many times.* Search engines are known for dropping sites from their listings because of suspected spamming—a word repeated too many times on a page is a big red flag for spamming. Be realistic and honest. Use the words whenever they seem appropriate and you'll be fine.

- *Use irrelevant keywords just to draw in people.* Don't include keywords that aren't appropriate for your site. Users will get annoyed and complain, causing your site to be dropped from the search engine altogether.

Meta Tags

Finally, use `meta` tags to aid those engines or directories supporting them in identifying your content. `meta` tags are hidden instructions about your page, such as a description and keywords.

NOTE

Be aware that some engines and directories ignore meta tags altogether. For this reason, they shouldn't be relied on as the "be all and end all" of preparing your site.

These tags should be added to each page on your site in between the opening and closing head tags. The following is an example of how meta tags might be used on a page selling handmade children's clothing.

```
<head>
    <title>Wendy's Handmade Children's Clothing For Sale</title>
    <meta name="description" content="We sell handmade children's
clothing for boys and girls, sizes 6-12. Our children's clothing -
pants, shirts, dresses, and more - is made to last generations.">
    <meta name="keywords" content="kids children clothing clothes
handmade pant shirt suit dress skirt">
</head>
```

Customize the content of these tags to identify a description that properly explains the purpose of your site in a sentence or two (20–40 words is a good place to start) and keywords that parallel what users will probably search for. Because most users search for words in lowercase, you can avoid using capital letters in your keywords. The number of keywords you can use varies somewhat according to the search engine or directory; make sure your most important keywords are listed first because many limit the contents of your keywords to 900 characters.

You can also use the robots version of the meta tag to restrict a page from being indexed at all. This might be useful for a private page or a work in progress.

```
<meta name="robots" content="none">
```

Possible values for this tag include

- **all**   Index the page and follow its links (default)

- **none**   Don't index the page and don't follow any of its links

- **index**   Index the page

- **noindex**   Don't index the page

- **follow**   Follow all the links on the page

- **nofollow**   Don't follow all the links on the page

The last four values can be used together as needed, so content="index, nofollow" would tell the engine to index the page, but not to follow any of its links.

TIP

Visit Search Engine Watch (**http://searchenginewatch.com/webmasters/meta.html**) for more tips on using the latest `meta` tags.

Project 16-1 Add Meta Tags

As discussed, one way to help boost your rankings in some search engines is to add keywords and descriptions to all your web pages using `meta` tags. This project asks you to add these tags to some of the pages in the Chop Point web site. Goals for this project include using

● Research-related sites to determine appropriate keywords

● `meta` tags to add descriptions and keywords to web pages

Step by Step

1. Visit **www.google.com** with your web browser.

2. In the search box, enter keywords that might be appropriate for your organization. If you are using the Chop Point, these might be "maine summer camp", "teen summer camp", "adventure trip camp", and so on.

3. View the web sites listed on the first page of results to determine what keywords are included on their pages to make them rise to the top of the search results. If necessary, view the HTML source of the pages to view any `meta` tags.

4. Repeat this process in **www.yahoo.com** to see how different the results are.

5. Open the index.html file in your text or HTML editor.

6. Add `meta` tags to this page to identify the page's description and appropriate keywords.

7. Save the file.

Project Summary

Advertising your site is a necessary, but time-consuming, aspect of web development. This project gave you practice with two techniques used for improving search engine rankings. In the end, bringing your site to the top of the search listings (and keeping it there) involves dedication and patience—and a bit of luck.

TIP

For extra practice, try adding unique `meta` tags to all the pages you created.

CRITICAL SKILL

16.3 Upload Your Site to a Host Computer

After your site is finished and you're ready to make it "live" or accessible by visitors on the Web, it's time to transfer the pages to the host computer. You can use file transfer protocol (FTP) programs to do so.

The concept of using an FTP program is similar to moving things around on your own personal computer. The key difference is, instead of moving files from one folder to another on your computer, you're actually moving them from one folder on your computer to another folder on a different computer.

Just as you can change settings and information about who has access to view or edit a file on your own computer, you can also make these changes on a host computer. For information about how these settings might work, checking with your ISP or host company is best.

Depending on what type of computer you have and who's hosting your site, you may use one of many different types of FTP programs. Or you might use an FTP tool that comes with your HTML editor, if you have one. The next sections outline a few popular options.

Windows FTP Programs

One of the most popular FTP programs for the PC is WS-FTP. It comes in a free LE (lite) version or an inexpensive professional version, and is available for download from **www.ipswitch.com**. The following steps outline how to use one version of this free tool. However, there are hundreds of other FTP options available. This brief overview of WS-FTP is included just to show how most of these tools work.

To begin, you must choose which computer you want to access. If you want to upload your files to your web server, enter that computer's information in the Session Properties screen that comes up when you first start the program (Figure 16-1). (You may need to click the button labeled New first if a different computer's information is already filled into the blanks when you launch the program.)

NOTE

You should receive all the necessary information when you sign up for hosting service. If you're unsure, check your host company's web site or call its customer support line for assistance.

Give your setting a name

Unless your hosting provider specifies otherwise, leave this as "Automatic detect"

Enter the domain name or IP address of the computer you're trying to access

Enter your username, as specified by your hosting provider

Enter your password, as specified by your hosting provider

When finished, click this button

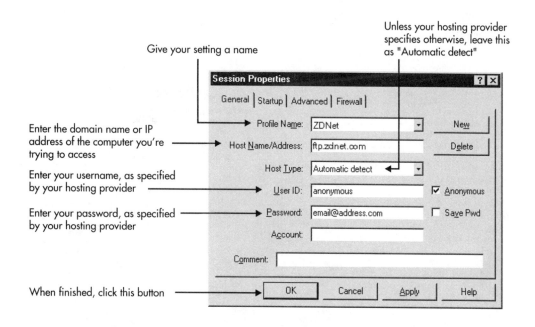

Figure 16-1 To begin, enter the information for the computer you want to access.

After entering all the appropriate information, click the button labeled OK to connect to that computer. If your connection is successful, WS-FTP displays the company you're accessing, referred to as the *remote system*, in the right window. Your local computer is visible in the left window (Figure 16-2).

You can transfer files between these two computers by first clicking the filename to highlight it, and then using one of the two arrows in the center of the screen to move the file.

You can also navigate through the directory structure of either computer by clicking the arrow at the top of the list of files to move back to the previous directory. Double-click the name of a folder to view the contents of that folder.

TIP

Notice near the bottom of the screen that you can transfer files in two different ways: ASCII or binary (the Auto option attempts to help you choose between these two). HTML and text files should be transferred in ASCII mode, while graphic, multimedia, and most other file types should be transferred in binary mode. This is true regardless of what FTP program you are using.

This is your computer

This shows which directory you're currently in on the local system

After highlighting a file on the remote system, click this arrow to download it to your personal system

This shows which directory you're currently viewing on the remote system

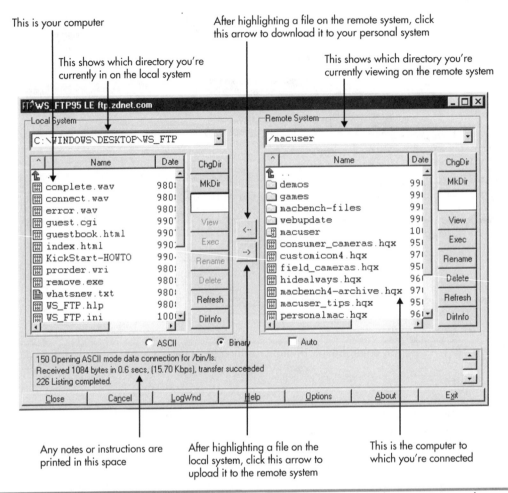

Any notes or instructions are printed in this space

After highlighting a file on the local system, click this arrow to upload it to the remote system

This is the computer to which you're connected

Figure 16-2 Once you're connected to another computer, it's displayed in WS-FTP's right menu and referred to as the *remote system*.

For more information about using WS-FTP, visit **www.ispwitch.com.** Or, if you prefer, try one of these other great Windows FTP programs.

- CoffeeCup Free FTP (**www.coffeecup.com**)

- CuteFTP (**www.globalscape.com**)

- FTP Voyager (**www.rhinosoft.com**)

Macintosh FTP Programs

When working on my Mac, I typically use Yummy FTP. This excellent FTP program is available in shareware and professional versions, which can be downloaded from **www.yummyftp.com**. Just as with the Windows FTP programs, these steps are included to give you an overview of the basic process. Feel free to use whichever program you like best.

To start the process, you have to enter all the information about the computer you intend to access. For example, you need the server's name (domain name or IP address) as well as your username and password. In Yummy FTP, this can be entered on the initial New Connection screen that appears when the program first starts. After setting up the new connection, click the Connect button.

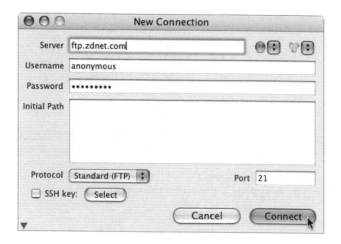

NOTE

You should receive all the necessary information when you sign up for a hosting service. If you're unsure, check your host company's web site or call its customer support line for assistance.

A window will display, showing your local hard drive on the left side and the computer you're accessing on the right (Figure 16-3). You can drag-and-drop files from one side to the other, as you would in other folders on your Mac. You can also right-click a file, or use the buttons across the top navigation bar, to perform functions like renaming, moving, or deleting files.

To upload or download a file, you must first highlight the file. Then, either drag it over to the other window or click the Transfer button in the top-left corner of the window. (When a

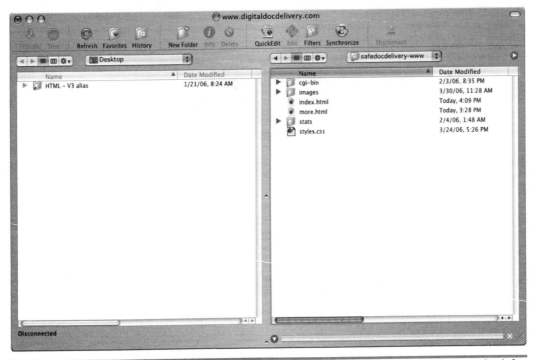

Figure 16-3 When connected to another computer, your local hard drive is shown on the left and the remote system is shown on the right.

file on the remote computer is highlighted, the button is labeled with a down arrow. Otherwise, it's labeled with an up arrow.)

For more information about using Yummy FTP, visit **www.yummyftp.com.** Or, if you prefer, try one of these other great Macintosh FTP programs.

- Fetch (**www.fetchsoftworks.com**)

- Interarchy (**www.stairways.com**)

- VicomsoftFTP (**www.vicomsoft.com**)

- Transmit (**www.panic.com**)

Web-Based FTP

If you are using a free service to host your web page, you probably have FTP capabilities through that company's web site. This is called *web-based FTP* because you don't need any additional software to transmit the files—in fact, you transmit the files right from within your web browser.

For example, Figure 16-4 shows the FTP capabilities for users of Yahoo! GeoCities. To use this web-based FTP, click the first button labeled Browse and locate the file on your hard drive that you'd like to upload. When you finish, click the button named Upload Files. Depending on the size of the files and the speed of your connection, you may experience a delay as the file is uploaded to Yahoo! GeoCities' servers.

When your files are uploaded, you can use Yahoo! GeoCities' File Manager to move, rename, or delete files, as well as to create and edit folders.

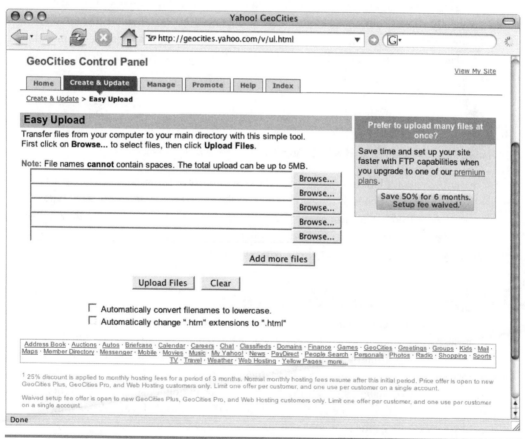

Figure 16-4 If available, web-based FTP can be an easy way to upload your files to a web server.

16.4 Test Your Site

After your site is uploaded to the server, you'll want to run through each page once more in order to verify everything transferred as expected. In addition, test to make sure all the links work and images appear.

Once you've made a cursory check, it's time to check for cross-browser and cross-platform consistency. Throughout the book, I have mentioned the importance of checking your pages in multiple browsers and on multiple computer systems to make sure they appear as you intended. However, if you weren't able to do so before because you didn't have another computer or browser handy, now's the time.

The .zip archive for this module (which can be downloaded from **www.osborne.com** or **www.wendywillard.com**) contains a testing checklist to help you complete this task. After your site is uploaded to the host computer, you should run through each page once more to verify that everything transferred as expected. In addition, test to make sure that all the links work and that each image appears.

TIP

Finding errors? Remember to check out Appendix C in regards to troubleshooting.

Even if you don't have more than one type of computer or browser, now that your pages are live, you can ask friends or family to test them for you. Have them record what type of browser they're using, what size monitor they have, what size screen resolution they're using, and what computer operating system they're running. That way, when they report bugs or errors on your pages, you'll have help in determining the problem.

16.5 Publicize Your Web Site

After your site is live, you can begin submitting its URL to search engines and search directories. When you submit your site to a search directory, you typically have to fill out a form detailing information about the site and its purpose. To begin the process, visit a directory and look for links where you can "Suggest a Site" (Yahoo!) or "Add URL" (Open Directory) to get your site listed. Be aware, though—changing a listing in a directory is difficult, so be sure to enter the correct information the first time. It can take as long as 8 to 12 weeks (Yahoo!) for your site to appear in a directory.

By contrast, submitting your site to an engine simply involves entering the URL of your web site and, perhaps, a contact e-mail address. Just like with directories, you should look for

16

a link labeled "Add URL" or "Add a Site." Your listing typically appears within a few days, but it may take as long as a week or so.

The different types of engines vary greatly according to how they index your site. Because most engines give results based on how relevant pages are to search terms, you might rank 10th on one day or $1,000^{th}$ on another. Another key aspect to keeping your site in the top of the search engines is to make it popular. Unfortunately, this may seem a bit like the chicken-and-egg syndrome.

Your site needs to be clicked (in the search results) to become "popular" (by search engine standards), but if your site is at the bottom of the search list because it's new, few people may ever find it to click it! This is why paid ads on search engines are such a big deal these days. Ever searched on Google and seen little ads appear on the right side that seem to be selling exactly what you searched for? These businesses are doing just that—they pay to "sponsor" certain search terms. So a summer camp might pay to appear each time a user searches for "summer camp" in Google. Theoretically, you'll only need to pay for these ads for a short time, provided they work and get people to click your web site link. Once your site becomes popular in Google, it will naturally rise to the top of the search results.

There are two schools of thought regarding how to submit your site to search engines and search directories. First, you can do this manually, by visiting each of the top eight to ten search engines or search directories (as well as any other smaller directories you choose) and submitting your URL.

TIP

You can use a site like **netmechanic.com** to help you organize the submission process when submitting your site to multiple search engines and search directories. This type of company is often referred to as a search engine optimization or SEO provider.

Second, you can pay someone else to do it for you. Unfortunately, finding a reputable service to do this is difficult and can be costly. Be wary of companies willing to boost your site to the "top ten" for a fee. These companies may bring you to the top ten of a popular engine for a single day or, even worse, to the top ten of some unknown search engine. If you do hire a company to help you with this, look for one willing to submit and resubmit your site over a period of six to nine months. For a checklist of what to consider regarding these services before signing up, visit Paul Bruemmer's article on the Workz Network entitled "Selecting a Reputable SEO Provider" (**www.clickz.com/search/opt/article.php/918341**).

Either way, this is a time-intensive process for whoever does it, and there's no magic solution.

NOTE

Because many search engines and search directories have their own set of rules and guidelines, reading through any tips or help files they provide before submitting your site is important. For example, on some sites, if you submit your site too often, they actually remove it from their listings altogether.

Marketing Tips

In addition to submitting your site to search engines and search directories, you can do many other things to promote your web site on- and offline.

- *Exchange links with related sites.* Consider asking sites with related content for links in exchange for a link to their site from yours. Don't forget about organizations you belong to like your local Chamber of Commerce or an industry association. These are great places to exchange links. Another place you can exchange links is with a group of related sites, called a *web ring.* Visit **www.webring.com** for some examples.

- *Create newsworthy content.* Everyone loves free publicity, and with the thousands of media outlets both on- and offline, you should be able to get a little publicity yourself. If you have an interesting product or a new twist on an old idea, tell someone! E-mail news agencies, send out a press release, write to your local paper, contribute to an association's newsletter . . . and don't forget to plug your web site.

- *Use your customers and tell everyone you know.* Give out free pins, bumper stickers, pens, or anything with your web site address to your existing customers. If your services and products are good, they'll have no problem telling others about them. In addition, spread the word through industry events where you can network and sell your business.

- *Don't forget traditional advertising!* If you have stationery, add your web site address. If you already run radio or print ads, include your web site address. Consider running a special ad promoting your new or revamped web site.

- *If you have the budget, consider paid online advertising.* Banner ads and paid listings in directories can be beneficial if targeted toward the right audience. Sometimes a less-expensive alternative might be to sponsor a related nonprofit web site. For example, if you sell school supplies, consider sponsoring a nonprofit homework help site. Another alternative is to sponsor free e-mail or Internet service providers. MySpace (**www.myspace.com**), whose web site service is free, generates revenue entirely through advertisements shown to all its users.

- *Most important, create useful content.* If your site is boring or otherwise useless, people won't come and they won't help you promote it. While the best marketer for *your* business is a satisfied customer, the best marketer for *your competition* is a dissatisfied one.

Make the Site Live!

As a final step in creating your web site, research possible hosting solutions. Refer to the beginning of the module for links and tips on finding personal and business hosting.

TIP

If you simply want to test the pages you created to learn HTML in this book, I suggest signing up for a free site with Yahoo! GeoCities (**geocities.yahoo.com**). You can then follow the onscreen instructions to use Yahoo!'s web-based FTP or use any of the popular FTP programs.

After selecting a hosting provider, use an FTP program to transfer your web site to the server. Test the pages in several browsers and on different computer systems to confirm you successfully created and uploaded your web site. For practice, try making a change to one of the pages after viewing it live. Then, re-upload the page and choose Refresh or Reload in your browser to review the change.

If appropriate, add your site to search engines and search directories, and continue with other marketing techniques. Remember, promoting your web site is an ongoing task and requires frequent maintenance.

Summary

Congratulations! If you've successfully uploaded your pages to a server and made them live, you certainly should be proud.

TIP

Ready to learn about more web technologies? Check out Obsorne's web site (**www.osborne.com**) for information regarding additional books in the Beginner's Guide series.

✓ Module 16 Mastery Check

1. Fill in the blank: ISP stands for _____.

2. Including the extension, what is the limit for characters in a domain name?

3. Which type of business hosting enables you to use your own equipment and personnel to maintain a server, but to lease space and use a high-speed Internet connection from a host company?

4. Name a key difference between search engines and search directories.

5. True/False: Some search engines ignore meta tags.

6. Add the appropriate code to the following to cause search engines to *not* index the page or follow its links.

   ```
   <meta name="              "  content="              ">
   ```

7. Where are meta tags placed within a web page?

8. True/False: All search engines use the same set of standards for indexing web pages.

9. Fill in the blanks: When testing a web site, you should test for cross-_____ and cross-_____ consistency.

10. What does FTP stand for?

Learn More

Many online tutorials can help you learn more about transferring files on the Internet. Check with your hosting provider because it probably will have additional help files on this subject. The following are some of the most popular:

- **Yahoo! GeoCities FTP Help (help.yahoo.com/help/us/geo/gftp)**

- **AOL's FTP Help (www.aol.com/nethelp/ftp/ftp.html)**

- **Web Know How (www.webknowhow.net)**   Contains online tutorials, as well as help with finding a web host.

- **WebMonkey (www.webmonkey.com)**   A great overall resource for web developers.

Search Engines and Search Directories

This module only scratched the surface of a complex issue for web developers—marketing a site on the Internet. I recommend you check out some of the following sources of additional information to help improve your site's standing in the market.

- Search Engine Watch (**www.searchenginewatch.com**) is considered one of the best places to look for information about improving your site's rankings online. It includes search engine tips and techniques, reviews, tests, resources, and the latest headlines.

- The Search Engine Guide (**www.searchengineguide.com**) offers search engine and directory news, marketing information, and general tips.

- **keywordcount.com** helps you analyze the most popular words on your web site, as well as compare them with that of your competition.

- Web Marketing Info Center (**www.wilsonweb.com/webmarket**) gives advice and links for articles about marketing on the Web.

- The Workz Network (**www.workz.com**) is a large network of information including a section about effective marketing of web sites both on and offline.

- Position Agent (**www.positionagent.com**) enables you to search by keyword for your site in ten of the top engines and directories at once.

In addition, the search engines and search directories themselves can be a great place to look for information about advertising your site. Most of them have sections of their site dedicated to answering users' questions about this very topic. The following is an alphabetical list of some key engines and directories.

- **Alta Vista (www.altavista.com)**
- **AOLNetfind (search.aol.com)**
- **AskJeeves (www.ask.com)**
- **Excite (www.excite.com)**
- **Go (www.go.com)**
- **GoTo (www.goto.com)**
- **Google (www.google.com)**
- **HotBot (www.hotbot.com)**
- **LookSmart (www.looksmart.com)**

- Lycos (www.lycos.com)

- Netscape (www.netscape.com)

- Open Directory (dmoz.org)

- SearchMSN (search.msn.com)

- Yahoo! (www.yahoo.com)

Part III

Appendixes

Appendix A

Answers to Mastery Checks

Module 1: Getting Started

1. **What is a web browser?**

A web browser is a software program that runs on your computer and enables you to view web pages.

2. **What does HTML stand for?**

HTML stands for hypertext markup language.

3. **Identify the various parts of the following URL:**
http://www.osborne.com/books/webdesign/favorites.html

_____://_____/_____/_____/_____

The various parts of the URL are as follows: protocol://domain/folder/folder/file

4. **What is WYSIWYG?**

WYSIWYG is the acronym for what-you-see-is-what-you-get. It refers to the idea that, for example, instead of typing code to cause a certain bit of text to be bold, you simply click a button that makes it bold.

5. **Fill in the blank: Every new version of HTML will be built on the foundation of _____.**

Every new version of HTML will be built on the foundation of XHTML 1.0.

6. **What is the program Macromedia Dreamweaver used for?**

Dreamweaver is a WYSIWYG web page development and editing tool.

7. **What is the most popular web browser?**

Microsoft Internet Explorer

8. **Fill in the blank: When you type a URL into your web browser, you send a request to the _____ that houses that information.**

When you type a URL into your web browser, you send a request to the web server that houses that information.

9. **What does the acronym "URL" stand for?**

URL stands for uniform resource locator.

10. **What organization maintains the standards for HTML?**

The World Wide Web Consortium (W3C) maintains the standards for HTML.

11. **How can you give your site's visitors visual clues as to where they are in your site's structure?**

The following list is not exhaustive; there are plenty of other good ideas the students may come up with.
A. Highlight the current section on the navigation bar.
B. Repeat the page name in the page title (at the top of the browser window).

C. Include the page name in the filename.

D. Include an appropriate headline on the page.

12. Fill in the blank: Good practice is to include a standard _____ on all pages for consistency and ease of use.

Good practice is to include a standard navigation bar on all pages for consistency and ease of use.

13. Fill in the blank: Selling products and recruiting potential employees are examples of web site _____.

Selling products and recruiting potential employees are examples of web site goals.

14. Fill in the blank: Before you can begin developing your web site, you must know a little about the site's target _____.

Before you can begin developing your web site, you must know a little about the site's target audience.

15. If your site represents a new company or one that doesn't already have information about its client demographics, where might you look for information?

Look to the competition. Chances are good that if your competition has a successful web site, you can learn from them about your target audience.

Module 2: Basic Page Structure

1. What file extensions do HTML files use?

HTML uses the .htm or .html file extension.

2. The following line of HTML code contains errors. What is the correct way to write this line:

```
<p    This is a paragraph of text    p>
```

```
<p>This is a paragraph of text</p>
```

3. At the very least, which tags should be included in a basic HTML page?

A basic HTML page should include the following tags: !DOCTYPE, html, head, title, and body.

4. Identify the tag name, attribute, and value in the following line of HTML code: <a href="page.html">

a is the tag name, href is the attribute, and page.html is the value.

5. Fill in the blank: XHTML requires all tags to be _____case.

XHTML requires all tags to be lowercase.

6. Which option is *not* acceptable for an HTML filename?
A. myfile.html
B. my_file.html

C. my file.html
D. my_file.html

C. my file.html is not an acceptable HTML filename.

7. **What is the named character entity used to add a copyright symbol to a web page?**

© is the named character entity used to add a copyright symbol to a web page.

8. **You just created a web page, and you're previewing it in a web browser when you notice an error. After fixing the error and saving the web page, which button should you click in the browser to view the changes made?**

Use the Refresh or Reload button to view the changes you have made.

9. **Which is the proper way to close the hr tag to make it XHTML-compliant?**
A. **<hr>**
B. **</hr>**
C. **<hr/>**
D. **<hr />**
E. **</ hr>**

D. <hr /> is the proper way to close the hr tag to make it XHTML-compliant.

10. **The tags in the following line of code aren't nested properly. Rewrite the code so the tags are nested properly: <p><strong><em>Hello World!</p></strong></em>**

<p><strong><em>Hello World!</em></strong></p>

11. **How can you rewrite the following text so it doesn't display when the page is viewed in a browser?**
Hide Me!

<!-- Hide Me! -->

12. **Which two options will the browser ignore when they are coded in a web page?**
A. **<p>**
B. **A tab**
C. **
**
D. **

**
E. **Single space with the SPACEBAR**
F. **Double space with the SPACEBAR**

Answers B and F are correct. The browser will ignore a tab and a double space made with the SPACEBAR, when they are coded in a web page.

13. **Fill in the blank: The p tag is an example of a _____ tag because it contains sections of text.**

The p tag is an example of a container tag because it contains sections of text.

14. The following line of HTML code contains errors. What is the correct way to write the code:

`< img src = "photo.jpg"  >?`

`<img src="photo.jpg />`

15. What symbols must surround all HTML tags?

Left and right angle brackets (<>) must surround all HTML tags.

Module 3: Color

1. What is the difference between decimal numbers and hexadecimal numbers?

Decimal number systems are based on the number 10, whereas hexadecimal systems are based on the number 16.

2. The second two numbers in a six-digit hexadecimal code refer to which color?

The second two numbers in a six-digit hexadecimal code refer to green.

3. How many colors are there in the web-safe palette?

There are 216 colors in the web-safe palette.

4. #036 is hexadecimal shorthand for which complete hex color code?

#003366

5. Fill in the blank: Instead of making up new characters to represent the remaining units after 9, the hexadecimal system uses the first six letters of the _____.

Instead of making up new characters to represent the remaining units after 9, the hexadecimal system uses the first six letters of the English alphabet.

6. Can you use RGB color values to specify color in traditional HTML code?

No, in traditional HTML code, you can only specify colors in HTML using hexadecimal codes and predefined color names.

7. In what additional way is CSS capable of specifying colors?

You can also specify colors in CSS using RGB values.

8. Fill in the blank: Each of the web-safe colors has decimal RGB values that are multiples of _____.

Each of the web-safe colors has decimal RGB values that are multiples of 51.

9. Which tag is used as a CSS selector when you want to change the color of a page's links?

The a tag is used as a CSS selector when you want to change the color of a page's links.

10. Which tag is used as a CSS selector when you want to change the background color of a page?

The `body` tag is used as a CSS selector when you want to change the color of a page background.

Module 4: Working with Text

1. What is the difference between physical and logical styles in HTML?

Logical styles name how text is to be used in a page, but not how it will look. Physical styles tell how the text should look when rendered in the browser, but not how they will be used on the page.

2. How do you close the `br` tag to make it XHTML-compliant?

Use the `<br />` tag.

3. What happens when you code three `p` tags in a row?

The browser uses only the first tag and ignores the others.

4. List two style sheet properties used for text alignment.

The CSS properties text-align and vertical-align are used for text alignment.

5. Name four possible values of the font-size CSS property.

Possible values of the font-size CSS property include point sizes (12pt, 14pt, and so on), pixel sizes (10px, 12px, and so on), em sizes (24em, 36em, and so on), and keywords (such as xx-small, x-small, small, medium, and so on).

6. What is a characteristic of text rendered in the style of the `tt` tag?

It is rendered in a typewriter font.

7. Fill in the blank: You use the _____ property when specifying the font name in which the text should be rendered.

You use the font-family property to specify the font name in which the text should be rendered.

8. Which tag is used to mark a reference to another source or a short quotation?

`<cite>` marks a reference to another source or a short quotation.

9. Name the four possible values of the `align` attribute or the text-align CSS property.

Four possible values of the `align` attribute and the text-align property are `left`, `right`, `center`, and `justify`.

10. Fill in the blank: The process of providing a backup font name in the font tag or the font-face property is also referred to as _____.

The process of providing a backup font name in the font tag or the font-face property is also referred to as cascading.

11. How is the `div` tag different from the `p` tag?

The p tag adds blank lines around paragraphs, whereas the div tag does not have any formatting properties of its own. Instead, the div tag carries the properties of any attributes used with it. This means placing a div tag in your page won't affect the look of it in the browsers, but placing `<div style="text-align:right;">` aligns the text elements after that tag to the right.

12. Fill in the blank: The `h` tag is an example of a _____ style.

The h tag is an example of a logical style.

13. True/False: The `blockquote` tag indents text on both the left and right sides.

True.

14. Which style sheet property is a better way to add horizontal lines to a page than the `hr` tag?

The border property is a better way to add horizontal lines to a page.

15. What does it mean when tags are deprecated by the W3C?

This means the W3C strongly discourages the use of these tags, usually in favor of style sheets.

Module 5: Working with Links

1. What does the `href` attribute do?

The href attribute gives the location of the content to which you are linking.

2. Which of these can be classified as a relative link?
A. <a href="../email.html">
B. <a href="http://www.yahoo.com/email.html">
C. <a href="/email.html">
D. <a href="http://email.yahoo.com">

Answers A and C are relative.

3. What must be installed and activated on a user's machine to take advantage of an e-mail link in a web site?

To take advantage of an e-mail link in a web site, the user must have an e-mail program, such as Microsoft Outlook or Mac Mail, installed and active.

4. How do you tell the browser to launch a link in a new window?

Add the name attribute to the a tag.

5. Which style sheet selector enables you to change the color of the links on your page after someone has clicked them?

a:vlink enables you to change the color of the links on your page after someone has clicked them.

6. **In Windows, what must users type to highlight the following link: <a href="contact.html" tabindex="2" accesskey="t">Contact Me</a>**

Windows users must type ALT-T to highlight the link shown.

7. **Fill in the blank: After successfully using the TAB key to highlight a link, you must press the _____ key to actually visit that link.**

After successfully using the TAB key to highlight a link, you must press the RETURN or ENTER key to actually visit that link.

8. **Fix the following code: < ahref="contact.html" >Contact Me</a>**

The correct code is <a href="contact.html">Contact Me</a>

9. **Add the appropriate code so that this link enables users to e-mail you at your personal e-mail address: <   > Email Me </ >**

The answer should be similar to this (with your e-mail address):
<a href="mailto:name@emailaddress.com"> Email Me </a>

10. **Which tag links to a section within the current page?**
```
A. <a href="page1">Page 1</a>
B. <a href="#page1">Page 1</a>
C. <a href="*page1 ">Page 1</a>
D. <a href="page1.html" >Page 1</a>
```

Answer B links to a section within the current page.

11. **Which common phrase should always be avoided when naming links?**

The phrase *Click here* should always be avoided when naming links.

12. **Fill in the blank: By default, all linked text is _____.**

By default, all linked text is underlined.

13. **True/False: A dot-dot-slash tells the browser to go up a level in the directory structure before looking for a file.**

True.

14. **Which links to a section named *Intro* within the web page named genealogy.html?**
```
A. <a href="genealogy.html">Intro</a>
B. <a href="genealogy.html#intro">Intro</a>
C. <a href="genealogy.html#Intro">Intro</a>
D. <a href="genealogy.html=Intro">Intro</a>
E. <a href="genealogy.html=intro">Intro</a>
```

Answer C links to a section named Intro within the web page named genealogy.html.

15. **What does _blank do when used as the value of the name attribute?**

It causes the browser to open the link in a new unnamed browser window.

Module 6: Working with Images

1. **What does the src attribute do?**

The src attribute gives the location of the image you're adding to the page with the img tag.

2. **Why is it important to specify the height and width of images in web pages?**

It is important to specify the height and width of images in web pages because this information enables the browser to continue displaying the rest of the page without having to wait and calculate the size of its images.

3. **Which style sheet properties enable you to add blank space around images?**

The CSS properties margin and padding enable you to add blank space around an image.

4. **Which attribute must be added to the img tag to designate the image as a client-side image map?**

usemap must be added to the img tag to designate the image as a client-side image map.

5. **Which two tags are used when defining a client-side image map's name and hot spots?**

map and area are used when defining a client-side image map's name and hot spots.

6. **You are creating the code for a client-side image map, and one of the rectangular hot spots has the following coordinates: 0,0 (upper left); 50,0 (upper right); 50,50 (lower right); and 0,50 (lower left). Which are used in the coords attribute: <area shape="rect" coords="_____" href="maryland.html">**

The correct code, using the upper-left and lower-right coordinates, is <area shape="rect" coords="0,0,50,50" href="maryland.html">.

7. **Fill in the blank: The value of the height and width attributes is measured in _____.**

The value of the height and width attributes is measured in pixels.

8. **Fix the following code: <img href="contact.jpg" /> **

The correct code is shown here: <img src="contact.jpg" />

9. **Add the appropriate style declaration to use wallpaper.gif as a background for the web page code shown next. Note that the graphic is in the same folder as the HTML file.**

```
body {                                      }
```

The correct code is

```
body {background-image: url("wallpaper.gif");}
```

10. **What are the four possible values of the clear property (used to clear floats)?**

Left, right, all, and none are the possible values of the clear property.

11. **Fill in the blank: The default value of the border property is ____ for linked images and _____ for nonlinked images.**

The default value of the border property is 1 for linked images and 0 for nonlinked images.

12. **True/False: You can achieve a layered look in your designs when an image in the foreground is placed on top of an image in the background.**

True.

13. **What value must be used with the display property before you can center an image using the method discussed in this module?**

```
img.centered {display:               ;
margin-left: auto;
margin-right: auto;}
```

The correct code is

```
img.centered {display:block; margin-left: auto; margin-right: auto;}
```

14. **Which attribute is used to add alternative text to an image?**

alt is used to add alternative text to an image.

15. **Which statement is not true about background images?**
A. All background images tile by default.
B. You can only include one image in the background.
C. Background images are added to web pages with the background tag.
D. Background images begin at the top of the page and run all the way to each of the four sides.

Answer C is correct, or in this case Answer C is the only statement that isn't true about backgrounds. Background images are added to a web page with the body tag and background attribute, not the background tag.

Module 7: Working with Multimedia

1. **What's the difference between a plug-in and a helper application?**

A plug-in helps the browser display a file, whereas the helper application does it for the browser.

2. **Which tag does the W3C recommend for embedding multimedia in a web page?**

The object tag is recommended by the W3C for embedding multimedia in a web page.

3. **How can users determine which plug-ins are installed on their computers, and/or download new plug-ins?**

Most users can look in the "plugins" directory within your browser's application or program folder. Internet Explorer users choose "Internet Options" from the Tools menu in the browser, then click the Programs tab and the "Manage Add-ons" button to view a list of all add-ons.

4. **What are two ways you can include multimedia files in a web site?**

You can include multimedia files in a web site by linking to them or embedding them.

5. **True/False: Clicking a link to a sound file automatically downloads the file and saves it for later listening.**

False.

6. **What are two ways to specify the height and width of multimedia files embedded with the `object` tag?**

You can specify the height and width either in the `object` tag itself, or in `param` tags nested between the opening and closing `object` tags.

7. **Fill in the blank: MIME stands for _____.**

MIME stands for Multipurpose Internet Mail Extensions.

8. **Fix the following code:**

```
embed href="sillyme.mov" height="100" width="50" />
```

The correct code is

```
<embed src="sillyme.mov" height="100" width="50" />
```

9. **Add the appropriate code here to link to wendy.mov. Note that the movie is in the same folder as the HTML file.**

```
<html>
<head>
    <title>Home Movie</title>
</head>
<body>
<                               >View my home movie!<        >
</body>
</html>
```

The correct code is

```
<html>
<head>
   <title>Home Movie</title>
</head>
```

```
<body>
<a href="wendy.mov">View my home movie!</a>
</body>
</html>
```

10. Which attribute can restrict a file from replaying after it has played through once?

`loop`

11. How might you provide an alternative way to view a file that requires a plug-in?

You can place the information (such as a link to the plug-in required) in between the opening and closing `object` tags.

12. True/False: A link to a multimedia file is the same as any other link because it also uses the a tag.

True.

13. What is the purpose of the `param` tag?

The `param` tag enables you to add any additional attributes for multimedia embedded with the `object` tag.

14. Which attribute of the `object` tag tells where the media file is located?

`data`

15. What are Java applets?

Java applets are miniapplications written in the Java programming language that can run within your browser window.

Module 8: Creating Lists

1. What's the difference between an unordered list and an ordered list?

An unordered list's items are not listed in a particular order, whereas an ordered list's items are. In addition, an unordered list's items are preceded by bullets, whereas an ordered list's items are preceded by numbers or letters.

2. Which tag is used to enclose list items in both ordered and unordered lists?

The `li` tag is used to enclose list items in both ordered and unordered lists.

3. You created an unordered list with four list items. All the content following the fourth list item that should be normal text is indented under the list. What is the most likely cause of this problem?

A missing closing tag, such as `</ul>`, is most likely the cause of the problem.

4. Which HTML attribute changes the numbering style of a list?

The `type` attribute changes the numbering style of a list.

5. **True/False: You can use more than one dd tag for each dt tag.**

True.

6. **Which HTML attribute changes the starting letter or number for a list?**

The start attribute changes the starting letter or number for a list.

7. **Fill in the blank: When displayed in a browser, each item in an unordered list is preceded by a _____, by default.**

When displayed in a browser, each item in an unordered list is preceded by a bullet, by default.

8. **Fix the following code.**

```
<dl>
 <dd>HTML</dd>
 <dt>Hypertext Markup Language is the authoring language used to
create documents for the World Wide Web.</dt>
</dl>
```

The correct code is

```
<dl>
   <dt>HTML</dt>
   <dd>Hypertext Markup Language is the authoring language used to
create documents for the World Wide Web.</dd>
</dl>
```

9. **Add the appropriate code to turn the following text into an ordered list.**

```
<html>
<head>
   <title>My favorite fruits</title>
</head>
<body>

        My favorite fruits, in order of preference, are:

        Raspberries

        Strawberries

        Apples

</body>
</html>
```

The correct code is

```
<html>
<head>
 <title>My favorite fruits</title>
```

```
</head>
<body>
<ol>My favorite fruits, in order of preference, are:
 <li>Raspberries</li>
 <li>Strawberries</li>
 <li>Apples</li>
</ol>
</body>
</html>
```

10. **Add the appropriate code to cause each item in the following list to be preceded by square bullets.**

```
<html>
<head>
    <title>My favorite colors</title>
</head>
<body>


        My favorite colors, in no particular order, are

        Red

        Blue

        Green


</body>
</html>
```

The correct code is

```
<html>
<head>
 <title>My favorite colors</title>
</head>
<body>
<ul type="square">My favorite colors, in no particular order, are:
   <li>Red</li>
   <li>Blue</li>
   <li>Green</li>
</ul>
</body>
</html>
```

11. **Fill in the blank: The dl tag stands for _____.**

The dl tag stands for definition list.

12. **True/False: When you nest unordered lists, the bullet style remains unchanged.**

False.

13. **What value is used with the `display` property to change a list from vertical to horizontal?**

Use `display: inline` to change a list from vertical to horizontal.

14. **How can you change a list from using Arabic numbers to lowercase letters?**

To change a list from using Arabic numbers to lowercase letters, you can use `type="a"`.

15. **Which CSS property is used to replace the standard bullet in a list with an image?**

The list-style-image property is used to replace the standard bullet in a list with an image.

Module 9: Using Tables

1. **What is the difference between the `td` and `th` tags?**

The `td` tag is used for standard table cells, whereas the `th` tag is used for cells containing header information. By default, the contents of `th` tags are made bold and centered.

2. **The `td` and `th` tags are contained within which other table tag (aside from the `table` tag itself)?**

The `td` and `th` tags are contained within the `tr` tag.

3. **How do you force a cell's contents to display along a single line?**

Use the white-space property in your style sheet, with a value of nowrap, to force a cell's contents to display along a single line.

4. **What is the most widely supported way to make all internal and external borders of a table invisible?**

Add `border="0"` to the opening `table` tag.

5. **True/False: You cannot use other HTML tags between opening and closing `td` tags.**

False.

6. **Which attribute affects the appearance of the internal table borders only, not external borders?**

The `rules` attribute affects the appearance of the internal table borders.

7. **Fill in the blank: The _____ attribute affects the space in between each of the individual table cells.**

The `cellspacing` attribute affects the space in between each of the individual table cells.

8. **Fix the following code:**

```
<table>
<td>HTML</td>
<td>Hypertext Markup Language is the authoring language used to
create documents for the World Wide Web.</td>
</table>
```

The correct code is

```
<table>
<tr>
<td>HTML</td>
<td>Hypertext Markup Language is the authoring language used to
create documents for the World Wide Web.</td>
</tr>
</table>
```

9. **What are two types of measurements you can use to identify a table's width?**

Pixels and percentages identify a table's width.

10. **Add the appropriate code to cause this table to fill the entire browser window, regardless of the user's screen size.**

```
<html>
<head>
   <title>A Big Table</title>
</head>
<body>
<table>
<tr>
  <td>X</td>
  <td>X</td>
  <td>O</td>
</tr>
</table>
</body>
</html>
```

The correct code is

```
<html>
<head>
   <title>A Big Table</title>
</head>
<body>
<table width="100%">
<tr>
  <td>X</td>
```

```
    <td>X</td>
    <td>O</td>
  </tr>
  </table>
  </body>
  </html>
```

11. Fill in the blank: You can add the _____ property to your style sheet to change the background color of the whole table.

You can add the background-color property to your style sheet to change the background color of the whole table.

12. True/False: To add a caption to a table, you use the `caption` attribute in the opening `table` tag.

False.

13. If you include a `thead` or a `tfoot` group in your table, you must also include which other group?

If you include a thead or tfoot group in your table, you must also include tbody.

14. Which CSS property (and value) is used to align all the text in a cell to the right?

Use text-align: right to align all text in a cell to the right.

15. True/False: If you had both `colgroups` and `theads` in a single table, the `colgroups` would be placed before the `theads` in your table structure.

True.

Module 10: Developing Frames

1. Fill in the blank: A group of frames is called a _____.

A group of frames is called a frameset.

2. Which basic structure tag of most HTML pages is not included in a frameset page?

The body tag is not included in a frameset page.

3. How do you tell the browser that a frame should fill whatever space is left over in the browser window after all other frames are placed?

Use an asterisk as a variable length value for the frame that should fill the screen.

4. To load a link in a particular frame, you must first do what in the `frame` tag?

To load a link in a particular frame, specify the frame's name with the name attribute of the a tag.

5. **True/False: To turn the frame borders completely off in the majority of browsers, add `frameborder="0"` to the opening `frameset` tag.**

   False.

6. **What is the default value of the `scrolling` attribute for frames?**

   `auto` is the default value of the `scrolling` attribute for frames.

7. **Fill in the blank: The _____ attribute adjusts the space between the content of a frame and the top and bottom edges of that frame.**

   The `marginheight` attribute adjusts the space between the content of a frame and the top and bottom edges of that frame.

8. **Fix the following code:**

   ```
   <frame cols="20%,80%">
   <frameset src="top.html">
   <frameset src="navigation.html">
   </frame>
   ```

   The correct code is

   ```
   <frameset cols="20%,80%">
     <frame src="top.html">
     <frame src="navigation.html">
   </frameset>
   ```

9. **Which two tags embed an inline frame within a web page?**

   `object` and `iframe` can be used to embed an inline frame within a web page.

10. **Add the appropriate code to create a frameset with two vertical frames—the first frame is 250 pixels wide, and the second takes up the rest of the browser window. Fill the first frame with `navigation.html` and the second frame with `content.html`.**

    ```
    <html>
    <head>
      <title>Frames</title>
    </head>


    </html>
    ```

    The correct code is

    ```
    <html>
    <head>
    <title>Frames</title>
    </head>
    <frameset cols="250,*">
    <frame src="navigation.html">
    ```

```
<frame src="content.html">
</frameset>
</html>
```

11. **Fill in the blank: Use the _____ tag and _____ attribute to force all the links on a page to load in a particular frame.**

    Use the `base` tag and `target` attribute to force all the links on a page to load in a particular frame.

12. **True/False: By default, relative-width frames are resizable.**

    True.

13. **Which tag displays content for non-frames-capable browsers?**

    The `noframes` tag displays content for non-frames-capable browsers.

14. **Which attribute should you add to the `frameset` tag to create two horizontal frames on the page?**

    Add `rows` to the `frameset` tag to create two horizontal frames.

15. **Fill in the blank: The _____ attribute of the `frame` tag tells the browser which HTML page to load into that frame.**

    The `src` attribute of the `frame` tag tells the browser which HTML page to load into that frame.

Module 11: Employing Forms

1. **Fill in the blank: _____ tags must surround all web forms.**

   `form` tags must surround all web forms.

2. **What are two types of text input in HTML web forms?**

   Single-line text boxes (text fields) and multiple-line text areas are two types of text input in HTML web forms.

3. **Which attribute identifies an input control so that it's correctly handled when the form is processed?**

   `name` identifies an input control so that it's correctly handled when the form is processed.

4. **Which input control is most useful for questions requiring a simple yes or no answer?**

   The radio button is most useful for questions requiring a simple yes or no answer.

5. **True/False: Radio buttons are small, round buttons that enable users to select a single option from a list of choices.**

   True.

6. **Which CSS property can prohibit text in a text area from being continued across long lines out of the visible window?**

   The overflow property can prohibit text in a text area from being continued across long lines out of the visible window when it is set to auto or scroll.

7. **Fill in the blank: The _____ attribute identifies the visible width of a text area based on an average character width.**

   The cols attribute identifies the visible width of a text area based on an average character width.

8. **Fix the following code so that users can enter multiple lines of data into the comment box, which should measure 30 characters wide by 5 lines tall.**
   Enter your comments here:

   ```
   <input size="30,5"></input>
   ```

   The correct code is

   ```
   Enter your comments here:
   <textarea cols="30" rows="5"></textarea>
   ```

9. **How do you cause three options in a select menu to be visible at once?**

   Use `<select size="3">`.

10. **Add the appropriate code to create a single-line text field in which, upon entry of data, all contents are displayed as bullets or asterisks in the browser. Name the field "secret" and make it XHTML-compliant.**
    Please enter your secret word:
    ```
    <                                  >
    ```

    The correct code is

    ```
    Please enter your secret word:
    <input type="password" name="secret" />
    ```

11. **Fill in the blank: _____ tags surround each item in a select menu.**

    option tags surround each item in a select menu.

12. **True/False: The `fieldset` tag is used to divide long select menus into categories of submenus.**

    False.

13. **Add the appropriate code to create a place where users can upload a graphic file from their personal computers to the web server. Name the field "upload" and make it XHTML-compliant.**

    Please select the file to upload:
    ```
    <                                  >
    ```

The correct code

```
Please select the file to upload:
<input type="file" name="upload" />
```

14. **Which attribute is added to the `form` tag to give the location where the form's information should be sent?**

The `action` tag gives the location where the form's information should be sent.

15. **Which attribute and value are added to the `form` tag to tell the browser to take all the data submitted with the form and send it to the server attached to the end of the file's URL?**

The `method="get"` attribute and value tell the browser to take all the data submitted with the form and send it to the server attached to the end of the file's URL.

Module 12: Positioning Page Elements

1. **Fill in the blank: _____ positioning takes an element out of the normal page flow and positions it in a particular place on the page.**

Absolute positioning takes an element out of the normal page flow and positions it in a particular place on the page.

2. **Which property determines whether a layer is hidden or visible?**

The visibility property determines whether a layer is hidden or visible.

3. **Which two properties are set in the `body` tag to ensure all browsers use the same "starting point" for page layout?**

The padding and margin properties should be set in the `body` tag to ensure all browsers use the same "starting point" for page layout.

4. **According to the W3C specifications, if you had a box that was 150 pixels wide, with 10 pixels of padding on all four sides and a 2-pixel border all the way around, what is the total horizontal space used by the box?**

174 pixels (150 pixels wide + 10 pixels left padding + 10 pixels right padding + 2 pixels left border + 2 pixels right border)

5. **Which version of Internet Explorer was the last one to not follow the W3C specifications for box and page layout?**

IE 5 was the last version of Internet Explorer to ignore the W3C box model specifications. IE 6 complies with W3C specifications for the box model and page layout.

6. **Which HTML tag is used to create sections of content to be formatted with style sheets?**

The `div` tag is used to separate content into formatting areas.

7. **Fill in the blank: The _____ attribute identifies the medium for which a particular external style sheet should be used.**

   The `media` attribute identifies the medium for which a particular external style sheet should be used.

8. **Add the appropriate code so the content area has a 20-pixel margin around the top, right, and left sides, but a 5-pixel margin around the bottom.**

   ```
   #content {

       }
   ```

   The correct code:

   ```
   #content {
           padding: 20px 20px 20px 5px;
   }
   ```

9. **Which HTML tag can be used to reference an external style sheet?**

   The `link` tag can be used to reference an external style sheet.

10. **Add the appropriate code to import a style sheet called design.css.**

    ```
    <style type="text/css">

    </style>
    ```

    The correct code is

    ```
    <style type="text/css">
        @import "styles.css";
    </style>
    ```

11. **Fill in the blank: _____ positioning is the default type of positioning.**

    Static positioning is the default type of positioning.

12. **True/False: Relative positioning adjusts an elements location on the page relative to itself.**

    True.

13. **Add the appropriate code to place the content area 50 pixels from the left edge of the browser and 150 pixels from the top edge.**

    ```
    #content {

        }
    ```

    The correct code:

    ```
    #content {
            left: 50px;
    ```

```
    top: 150px;
    }
```

14. **Which property is used to specify an element's stacking order on the page?**

The z-index property is used to specify an elements stacking order on the page.

15. **True/False: When adjusting an element's stacking order on the page, lower values take precedence over higher values.**

False. The element with the highest value is placed on "top."

Module 13: Creating Your Own Web Graphics

1. **Fill in the blank: _____ applications create graphics using tiny dots.**

Bitmap applications create graphics using tiny dots.

2. **Name three key issues that affect web design decisions.**

Key issues related to web design include platforms, target audience demographics, HTML, browsers, color, and bandwidth.

3. **If you are designing web graphics to fit without scrolling in a 640×480 monitor, what should be the largest width of any such graphics?**
   A. 640
   B. 600
   C. 540
   D. 500
   E. 480
   F. 400

Answer B is correct.

4. **What is a CLUT?**

Color lookup tables (CLUTs) are color swatches you can load into most graphics editors.

5. **True/False: Graphics generally look lighter on a PC than they do on a Mac.**

False.

6. **Name two ways to reduce a graphic's file size.**

To reduce a graphic's file size, do one of the following: reduce the actual height or width, reduce the number of colors, compress the image, or omit it completely.

7. **Fill in the blank: The standard file resolution for web graphics is _____.**

The standard file resolution for web graphics is 72 dpi.

8. **Which type of file compression requires data to be removed from the image to compress the file and make it smaller?**

   Lossy compression requires data to be removed from the image.

9. **What is the difference between binary and variable transparency?**

   Binary transparency requires each pixel to be either transparent or opaque, whereas variable transparency allows pixels to have partial transparency.

10. **What is the color mode of GIF files?**

    GIFs are restricted to no more than 256 exact colors.

11. **Fill in the blank: _____ is a process in which a graphic is displayed at multiple levels of clarity, from blurry to clear.**

    Interlacing is a process in which a graphic is displayed at multiple levels of clarity, from blurry to clear.

12. **True/False: The JPEG file format supports transparency.**

    False.

13. **In which file format should you save a photograph if it's going to be part of an animation?**

    Save a photograph as a GIF if it will be part of an animation.

14. **In what color modes can PNG files be stored?**

    PNGs can be stored in 8-bit, 24-bit, or 32-bit color modes.

15. **Fill in the blank: When saving a GIF, _____ can be used to give the appearance of gradations of subtle color shifts, but it adds to the file size.**

    When saving a GIF, dithering can be used to give the appearance of gradations of subtle color shifts, but it adds to the file size.

Module 14: Web Content

1. **Fill in the blank: Most people don't *read* web pages, they _____ them.**

   Most people don't *read* web pages, they *scan* them.

2. **Where should the most important information on a web page be?**

   The most important information on a web page should be at the top so that users can see it without scrolling.

3. **What type of file is an example of one that contains specific instructions on how it should be printed?**

   A PostScript file is an example of a file that contains specific instructions on how it should be printed.

4. **Which file format has become a standard in electronic document delivery because of its ease of use, reliability, and stability?**

PDF (Portable Document Format) has become a standard in electronic document delivery.

5. **True/False: You should avoid using all capital letters in text on a web page.**

True.

6. **Why should you avoid underlining text on a web page?**

Linked text is underlined by default, so it might be confusing to see linked and non-linked text both underlined on a page.

7. **Fill in the blank: Using lists can help the _____ of your web pages.**

Using lists can help the scannability of your web pages.

8. **What is a reasonable range for column widths on web pages?**

200–400 pixels is a reasonable range for web page column widths.

9. **What are three key things to consider when designing a printable version of a web page?**

When designing a printable version of a web page, consider size, color, and reference.

10. **What two words should be avoided as link labels on a web page?**

"Click here" should be avoided as link labels on a web page.

Module 15: Dynamic Content

1. **Fill in the blank: JavaScript is case-_____.**

JavaScript is case-sensitive.

2. **Name two ways JavaScript differs from standard HTML.**

JavaScript is case-sensitive; standard HTML is not. In JavaScript, quotes are required; in standard HTML, quotes are optional. JavaScript has a distinct format that must be adhered to; standard HTML is more forgiving about spacing and formatting.

3. **How do you hide JavaScript from older browsers that don't support it?**

By placing the actual script in between opening and closing HTML comments.

4. **Fill in the blank: In the following code, _____ is the JavaScript object.**
```
document.write("This is a text!");
```

In the following code, `document` is the JavaScript object.

5. **True/False: A plus sign (+) is an example of a JavaScript variable.**

False.

6. **When placed within the header of a web page, which opening and closing tags surround all JavaScripts?**

   `script` tags surround all JavaScripts when placed within the header of a web page.

7. **Fill in the blank: Objects can have _____, which are actual things that happen to the objects, such as `write` in the following statement: `document.write("I can write JavaScript");`.**

   Objects can have methods, which are actual things that happen to the objects.

8. **What term is given to an aspect of a JavaScript you specify for your own needs, as a label for a changeable value?**

   A variable is a term given to an aspect of a JavaScript you specify for your own needs, as a label for a changeable value.

9. **Fill in the blank: A _____ is a group of commands to which you give a name so you can refer to it later in the script.**

   A function is a group of commands to which you give a name so you can refer to it later in the script.

10. **Which aspect of JavaScript is embedded within the page's HTML and responds to a user's interaction?**

    Event handlers are embedded within the page's HTML and respond to a user's interaction.

11. **How are conditionals used in JavaScript?**

    JavaScript uses *if... then* statements called conditionals to tell the browser to do one thing if *x* is true and something else if *x* is false.

12. **What does the following JavaScript do when added to an a tag on a web page? `onClick="document.bgColor='green'"`**

    It changes the background color of the document when the user clicks the link.

13. **How do you specify that a new browser window should not have any scroll bars?**

    Add `scrolling=no` to the JavaScript.

14. **What punctuation ends all JavaScript statements?**

    A semicolon (;) ends all JavaScript statements.

15. **What does `onFocus` do when used in a JavaScript?**

    It specifies that an action should occur when the user brings an object (such as a browser window) to the foreground.

Module 16: Making Pages Available to Others

1. **Fill in the blank: ISP stands for** _____.

ISP stands for Internet service provider.

2. **Including the extension, what is the limit for characters in a domain name?**

The character limit in a domain name is 26, not including "www."

3. **Which type of business hosting enables you to use your own equipment and personnel to maintain a server, but lease space and a high-speed Internet connection from a host company?**

Colocation enables you to use your own equipment and personnel to maintain a server, but lease space and a high-speed Internet connection from a host company.

4. **Name a key difference between search engines and search directories.**

Search directories list pages by category.

5. **True/False: Some search engines ignore `meta` tags.**

True.

6. **Add the appropriate code to the following to cause search engines to *not* index the page or follow its links.**

```
<meta name="          "  content="          ">
```

The correct code is

```
<meta name="robots" content="none">
```

7. **Where are `meta` tags placed within a web page?**

`meta` tags are placed between the opening and closing `head` tags.

8. **True/False: All search engines use the same set of standards for indexing web pages.**

False.

9. **Fill in the blanks: When testing a web site, you should test for cross-_____ and cross-_____ consistency.**

When testing a web site, you should test for cross-browser and cross-platform consistency.

10. **What does FTP stand for?**

FTP stands for file transfer protocol.

Appendix B

HTML/CSS Reference Table

This resource serves as a reference table for the tags and properties learned in this book. It is organized alphabetically, with HTML tags and CSS properties included together for easy comparison. Because the scope of this book is at a beginner's level, I decided not to discuss a few tags and properties. If you come across something not listed here or in the index, try visiting an online reference library such as the following:

- **http://webdesign.about.com/od/htmltags/a/bl_index.htm**

- **www.w3schools.com/css/css_reference.asp**

NOTE

The latest version of the HTML specifications can be found on W3C's web site at **www.w3.org**.

Generic Attributes

The following groups of attributes can be used by a large number of tags in HTML. In the rest of the tables in this reference, a code is listed in the attribute column on a particular tag if it accepts any of the following groups of generic attributes.

- Core Attributes (*core) provide rendering and accessibility information to elements.

- Event Handlers (*events) provide a way of triggering an action when an event occurs on a page. Note: Not all event handlers are listed.

- International Attributes (*intl) provide a way of rendering documents using multiple language or character sets.

Group Type: Core

Attribute	Uses
accesskey	Assigns a keyboard shortcut to the element
class	Assigns a category label to an element
ID	Assigns a unique identifier to an element
style	Gives instructions on how to render an element
tabindex	Assigns the tab order of an element
title	Gives a brief description of an element

Group Type: Events

Attribute	Uses
onClick	Triggers an event when the element is clicked
onDblClick	Triggers an event when the element is double-clicked
onMouseDown	Triggers an event when the pointer is pressed down over an element
onMouseUp	Triggers an event when the pointer is released over an element
onMouseOver	Triggers an event when the pointer is passed over an element
onMouseOut	Triggers an event when the pointer moves away from an element
onKeyPress	Triggers an event when a key is pressed and released immediately
onKeyDown	Triggers an event when a key is pressed and held down
onKeyUp	Triggers an event when a key that was pressed is now released

Group Type: Intl

Attribute	Uses
dir	Indicates the direction of the content flow
lang	Indicates the language of the content

HTML Tags

The following table provides a reference for the HTML tags discussed in this book. Although I have removed most of the deprecated (outdated) tags from this table, there are some deprecated attributes that remain. Those are marked with a (D) to help make them easily recognizable. In most cases, these have been deprecated in favor of style sheets.

One additional note—some attributes are only deprecated in certain cases. For example, while it is not acceptable to use the `align` attribute with the p tag, it is OK to use it within a table (such as in the `colgroup` or `tr` tags).

HTML Tag	Attributes	Uses
<!--...-->	n/a	Inserts comments into the page that aren't seen when the page is viewed in the browser.
<!DOCTYPE>	n/a	Indicates the version of X/HTML used. Must be placed on the first line of the document.

HTML Tag	Attributes	Uses
<a></a>	*core, *events, *intl	Creates links and anchors.
	cords	*Defines the size of a hot spot in an image map.*
	href	*Specifies the location (URL) of the link.*
	name	*Identifies an anchor.*
	shape	*Defines the shape of a hot spot in an image map.*
	target	*Identifies the target window where the link will be displayed.*
<abbr></abbr>	*core, *intl	Indicates the content is an abbreviation.
<acronym></acronym>	*core, *events, *intl	Specifies an acronym.
<address></address>	*core, *events, *intl	Formats the contact information for a page.
<area />	n/a	Defines links and anchors within an image map.
	coords	*Specifies the size of the hot spot.*
	href	*Specifies the location (URL) of the link.*
	nohref	*Specifies that a hot spot isn't linked.*
	shape	*Defines the shape of a hot spot in an image map.*
	target	*Identifies the target window where the link will be displayed.*
<b></b>	*core, *events, *intl	Makes text bold.
<base />	n/a	Identifies the default path for links specified within the document.
	href	*Defines the location (URL) of the link.*
	target	*Specifies the window in which the URL should open.*
<big></big>	*core, *events, *intl	Formats the text as one size larger than the default size.
<blockquote></blockquote> (D)	*core, *events, *intl	Sets off a block of text, indenting it on both sides.
<body></body>	*core, *events, *intl	Encloses the content of the document.
	alink (D)	*Specifies the default color of an active link on the page. (Use the color CSS property instead.)*
	background (D)	*Defines a background image for the page. (Use the background-image CSS property instead.)*
	bgcolor	*Specifies the default background color of the page.*

HTML Tag	Attributes	Uses
	link (D)	*Specifies the default color of the links on the page. (Use the color CSS property instead.)*
	text (D)	*Specifies the default color of the visited links on the page. (Use the color CSS property instead.)*
	vlink (D)	*Specifies the default color of the visited links on the page. (Use the color CSS property instead.)*
	topmargin, leftmargin	*Specifies the size in pixels of the top and left margins. (Not in the official HTML specification; browser support varies.)*
	marginheight, marginwidth	

	*core, *events, *intl	Causes a line break.
	clear (D)	*Causes text to stop wrapping around an image and start again on the next line. (Use the clear CSS property instead.)*
<button> </button>	*core, *events, *intl	Creates a button.
	name	*Defines the name of the button.*
	value	*Specifies the value or type of button.*
<caption> </caption>	*core, *events, *intl	Defines a table caption.
<cite></cite>	*core, *events, *intl	Formats a short quote or reference.
<code></code>	*core, *events, *intl	Formats text as code (usually in a monospaced font).
<col />	*core, *events, *intl	Specifies subgroups of columns within a column group, to allow them to share attributes.
	align	*Aligns the subcolumn group horizontally.*
	span	*Specifies the number of columns the subcolumn group spans.*
	valign	*Aligns the subcolumn group vertically.*
	width	*Specifies the width of the columns using percentages or pixels.*
<colgroup> </colgroup>	*core, *events, *intl	Defines a group of columns.
	align	*Aligns the column group horizontally.*
	span	*Specifies the number of columns the group spans.*
	valign	*Aligns the column group vertically.*
	width	*Specifies the width of the columns using percentages or pixels.*

HTML Tag	Attributes	Uses
`<dd></dd>`	*core, *events, *intl	Defines the description of a term in a definition list.
`<del></del>`	*core, *events, *intl	Formats the text as deleted by marking a line through it.
	cite	References another document with a URL.
	datetime	Identifies the date and time of the deletion.
`<dfn></dfn>`	*core, *events, *intl	Specifies a definition.
`<div></div>`	*core, *events, *intl	Identifies a section (or division) of the page.
`<dl></dl>`	*core, *events, *intl	Creates a definition list.
`<dt></dt>`	*core, *events, *intl	Defines a term in a definition list.
`<em></em>`	*core, *events, *intl	Gives emphasis to text (usually by making it italic).
`<fieldset></fieldset>`	*core, *events, *intl	Creates a group of form controls.
`<form></form>`	*core, *events, *intl	Creates a form where users can enter information.
	action	Specifies the location (URL) of the script to process the form.
	enctype	Specifies the MIME type used to encode the content of the form.
	method	Defines how the form will be processed (get or post).
`<frame />`	id, class, title, style	Creates frames.
	frameborder	Specifies whether the border(s) between frames are visible.
	longdesc	Defines a location (URL) of the long description for the frame contents, for browsers that do not support frames.
	marginheight	Defines the size of the frame's top and bottom margins.
	marginwidth	Defines the size of the frame's left and right margins.
	name	Defines a name for the frame so it can be used as a target window.
	noresize	Specifies that the user cannot alter the frame's size.
	scrolling	Defines when the scroll bars appear in the frame (yes, no, or auto).
	src	Defines the initial document (URL) that should be loaded into the frame.
`<frameset></frameset>`	id, class, title, style	Creates a layout for a set of frames.
	cols	Defines the number and size of the columns in the frameset.
	rows	Defines the number and size of the rows in the frameset.

HTML Tag	Attributes	Uses
<h1></h1>	*core, *events, *intl	Creates six levels of headline (h1 being the largest and most important; h6 being the smallest and least important).
<head></head>	*intl	Contains the header information for the page (such as the title and information for search engines).
<hr />	*core, *events	Separates sections with a horizontal rule.
<html></html>	*intl	Contains and identifies the document.
<i></i> (D)	*core, *events, *intl	Formats text as italic.
<iframe> </iframe>	id, class, title, style	Creates an inline, floating frame.
	align (D)	*Aligns the frame in the page. (Use the text-align or float CSS properties, or other CSS positioning properties instead.)*
	frameborder	*Defines whether the frame's border is visible.*
	height	*Defines the height of the frame in pixels or percentages.*
	longdesc	*Contains the link (URL) to a long description of the frame contents.*
	marginheight	*Defines the top and bottom margins of the frame.*
	marginwidth	*Defines the left and right margins of the frame.*
	name	*Defines the name of the frame.*
	scrolling	*Defines when the scroll bars appear in the frame (yes, no, or auto).*
	src	*Defines the initial document (URL) that should be loaded into the frame.*
	width	*Defines the width of the frame in pixels or percentages.*
<img></img>	*core, *events, *intl	Embeds an image in a page.
	alt	*Specifies a text description of the image. (Required)*
	height	*Defines the height of the image in pixels.*
	longdesc	*Defines the location (URL) of a longer text description of the image.*
	src	*Defines the location of the image file.*
	usemap	*Defines the image as a client-side image map and specifies the location (URL) of the map properties.*
	width	*Defines the width of the image in pixels.*

HTML Tag	Attributes	Uses
<input />	*core, *events, *intl	Creates types of form input controls for users.
	accept	*Defines the file types allowed in a file upload control.*
	alt	*Defines an alternative text description.*
	checked	*Specifies that the input control should be checked by default when the page is loaded.*
	disabled	*Specifies that the input control cannot be used.*
	maxlength	*Defines the maximum number of characters a user can enter in a text field or password box.*
	name	*Defines the name of the input control, used when processing the form.*
	readonly	*Specifies that a user can read, but cannot edit, an input control.*
	size	*Defines the size of a text field or password box.*
	src	*Defines the location (URL) of an image used in an input control.*
	type	*Identifies the type of input control (text, checkbox, radio button, and so forth).*
	usemap	*Identifies the control as a client-side image map and specifies the location (URL) of the map properties.*
	value	*Defines the initial value of an input control.*
<ins></ins>	*core, *events, *intl	Formats text as inserted since the last change.
	cite	*References another document with a URL.*
	datetime	*Identifies the date and time of the insertion.*
<kbd></kbd>	*core, *events, *intl	Formats text as something the user should type on his or her keyboard.
<label></label>	*core, *events, *intl	Specifies a label for a form input control.
	for	*Identifies to which input control the label belongs.*
<li></li>	*core, *events, *intl	Defines an item in an ordered or unordered list.
	type (D)	*Specifies the style of the list. (Replaced by the list-style-type CSS property.)*
	value	*Specifies the initial value of the first item in the list.*

HTML Tag	Attributes	Uses
\<link>\</link>	*core, *events, *intl	Indicates a relationship between the current document and another resource (such as a style sheet).
	href	*Specifies the location of the resource.*
	rel	*Specifies the type of resource.*
	type	*Defines the MIME type.*
\<map>\</map>	*core	Defines the properties of a client-size image map.
	name	*Names the map so it can be referenced by other aspects of the page.*
\<meta />	*intl	Gives information about the document.
	content	Contains specified information.
	http-equiv	Assigns a header field, which then can be used to transfer the user to another page or otherwise process the document.
	name	Defines what type of information the content attribute specifies.
\<noframes>\</noframes>	*core	Provides alternative content for non-frames-capable browsers.
\<noscript>\</noscript>	*core	Defines the content displayed in browsers that don't support scripts.
\<object>\</object>	*core, *events, *intl	Embeds an object in the page.
	classid codebase	*Defines a URL indicating how the object should be implemented.*
	codetype type	*Specifies the MIME type of the code referenced by the classid attribute.*
	height	*Defines the height, in pixels, of the object.*
	name	*Defines the name of an object.*
	standby	*Defines the message to show while the object is loading.*
	usemap	*Identifies the object as a client-side image map and specifies the location (URL) of the map properties.*
	width	*Defines the width, in pixels, of the object.*
\<ol>\</ol>	*core, *events, *intl	Creates an ordered list.
	type (D)	*Specifies the style of the list. (Use the list-style-type CSS property instead.)*
	value	*Specifies the initial value of the first item in the list.*

HTML Tag	Attributes	Uses
<option></option>	*core, *events, *intl	Creates choices in a form select menu.
	disabled	*Specifies the specific option as viewable, but not selectable.*
	selected	*Defines the option as selected by default when the page is loaded.*
	value	*Defines the initial value of the option, used when processing the form.*
<p></p>	*core, *events, *intl	Specifies a paragraph of text (inserts a blank line by default above the paragraph).
<param />	id	Contains parameters for an object.
	name	*Defines the parameter's unique name.*
	value	*Defines the parameter's value.*
	valuetype	*Defines the MIME type of the value.*
<pre></pre>	*core, *events, *intl	Identifies text as preformatted (usually displayed in a monospaced font).
<q></q>	*core, *events, *intl	Formats a short quotation.
<samp></samp>	*core, *events, *intl	Formats text as a sample computer output, usually in a monospaced font.
<script></script>	None	Contains scripts, such as those written in JavaScript, executed in the page by the browser.
	defer	*Indicates the script is not going to generate any document content, and the browser can continue drawing the page.*
	src	*References an external script, by giving its location (URL).*
	type	*Specifies the MIME type of the script. (Required)*
<select></select>	*core, *events, *intl	Creates a form menu with choices (using the option tag) users can select.
	disabled	*Specifies the menu as viewable, but not useable.*
	multiple	*Enables users to select multiple choices.*
	name	*Identifies the name of the menu, used when processing the form.*
	size	*Defines the number of choices visible in the menu when the page loads.*
<small></small>	*core, *events, *intl	Formats the text as one size smaller than the default size.
<span></span>	*core, *events, *intl	Defines a section of content.

HTML Tag	Attributes	Uses
`<strong></strong>`	*core, *events, *intl	Gives stronger emphasis to text, usually by making it bold.
`<style></style>`	*intl	Adds an internal style sheet to a page.
	media	*Specifies the destination medium for the style information (such as print, screen, all, and so forth).*
	type	*Defines the MIME type of the content. (Required)*
`<sub></sub>`	*core, *events, *intl	Formats the text as subscript.
`<sup></sup>`	*core, *events, *intl	Formats the text as superscript.
`<table></table>`	*core, *events, *intl	Creates a table.
	align (D)	*Aligns the table on the page. (Use the text-align or float CSS properties, or other CSS positioning instead.)*
	bgcolor (D)	*Specifies the background color of the table. (Use the background-color CSS property instead.)*
	border	*Specifies the thickness, in pixels, of the border around the table.*
	cellpadding	*Specifies the amount of space around the content within the cells.*
	cellspacing	*Specifies the amount of space between the cells.*
	cols	*Identifies the number of columns.*
	frame	*Defines which of the table's edges are visible.*
	height	*Specifies the height of the table, in pixels or percentages.*
	rules	*Defines which of the table's interior seams are visible.*
	summary	*Specifies a summary of the table for speech-synthesizing or nonvisual browsers.*
	width	*Specifies the width of the table in pixels or percentages.*
`<textarea></textarea>`	*core, *events, *intl	Creates a form input control where users can enter multiple lines of text.
	cols	*Defines the height of the text area in the number of character columns visible.*
	disabled	*Prevents users from entering text in the area.*
	name	*Identifies the name of the text area, used when processing the form.*

B

HTML/CSS Reference Table

HTML Tag	Attributes	Uses
	readonly	*Specifies the text area as viewable, but not editable.*
	rows	*Defines the width of the text area in the number of character rows visible.*
`<tbody></tbody>`	*core, *events, *intl	Defines the table's body (must be used with tfoot and thead).
	align	*Aligns the cell contents horizontally.*
	valign	*Aligns the cell contents vertically.*
`<td></td>` `<th></th>`	*core, *events, *intl	Defines an individual cell (td) or header cell (th).
	align (D)	*Aligns the cell's contents horizontally. (Replaced with the text-align CSS property.)*
	bgcolor (D)	*Defines the cell's background color. (Replaced with the background-color CSS property.)*
	colspan	*Defines how many columns the cell spans.*
	height (D)	*Defines the height of the cell in pixels or percentages. (Replaced by the height CSS property.)*
	nowrap (D)	*Specifies that the content of the cell should stay on a single line. (Replaced by the white-space CSS property.)*
	rowspan	*Defines how many rows the cell spans.*
	valign (D)	*Aligns the cell's contents vertically. (Replaced with the vertical-align CSS property.)*
	width (D)	*Defines the width of the cell, in pixels or percentages. (Replaced by the width CSS property.)*
`<tfoot></tfoot>`	*core, *events, *intl	Defines the table's footer (must be used with thead and tbody).
	align	*Aligns the cell contents horizontally.*
	valign	*Aligns the cell contents vertically.*
`<thead></thead>`	*core, *events, *intl	Defines the table's header (must be used with tbody and tfoot).
	align	*Aligns the cell contents horizontally.*
	valign	*Aligns the cell contents vertically.*
`<title></title>`	*intl	Gives a name to your page that will be displayed in the title bar of the browser.

HTML Tag	Attributes	Uses
<tr></tr>	*core, *events, *intl	Defines a table row.
	align	*Aligns the contents of the row's cells horizontally.*
	bgcolor (D)	*Specifies a background color for the row. (Instead, use the background-color CSS property.)*
	valign	*Aligns the contents of the row's cells vertically.*
<u></u> (D)	*core, *events, *intl	Underlines text.
<ul></ul>	*core, *events, *intl	Creates an unordered list.
	type (D)	*Specifies the style of the list. (Can also be accomplished with the list-type-style CSS property.)*

CSS Properties

This table acts as a reference for the style sheet properties used throughout this book. Because this is a beginner's guide, this table does not include every possible CSS property.

When listing values, those within brackets, such as <length>, indicate value concepts as opposed to actual values. For example, when a value is listed as <length>, you might use a pixel dimension, as in 10px. By contrast, a value of "left" is an actual value term, an in float:left. Here are a few more tips regarding value concepts:

- Length units take two-letter abbreviations, with no space between number and unit, as in width: 100px or padding-top: 2cm.

- Percentage units are calculated with regard to their default size.

- Color units can be specified by hexadecimal code: color: #ffffff; RGB value: color: rgb(255, 255, 255); or name: color: white.

- URLs are relative to the style sheet, *not the HTML document*, and are defined like this: list-style-image: url(star.gif).

Property	Use	Values	Default Value
background	*Shorthand for any of the background properties.*		
background-attachment	Defines whether a background image scrolls when the page is scrolled, or remains fixed in its original location.	scroll | fixed	scroll

Property	Use	Values	Default Value
background-color	Defines the background color of an element.	\<color\> | transparent	transparent
background-image	Defines an image to be used as the background pattern.	\<URL\> | none	none
background-position	Defines the starting position of the background color or image.	\<percentage\> | | \<length\> | | top | center | bottom | | left | center | right	0% 0%
background-repeat	Specifies how a background image repeats.	repeat | no-repeat | repeat-x | repeat-y	repeat
border	*Shorthand for all the border properties.*		
border-collapse	Specifies whether the borders of each table cell are merged or separated from one another. Applies to table elements.	collapse | separate	collapse
border-color	Defines an element's border color. Can be specified for each side individually (as in border-top-color).	\<color\> | transparent	*Varies*
border-style	Defines an element's border style. Can be specified for each side individually (as in border-top-style).	none | hidden | dotted | dashed | solid | double | groove | ridge | inset | outset	none
border-width	Defines an element's border width. Can be specified for each side individually (as in border-top-width).	thin | medium | thick | \<length\>	medium
bottom	Specifies the location of the bottom of positioned elements.	\<length\> | \<percentage\> | auto	auto
caption-side	Specifies the location of a table caption.	top | bottom | left | right	top
clear	Specifies whether an element can have floating elements around it.	none | left | right | both	none
color	Specifies the color of the element, by hexadecimal code, RGB values, or keyword.	\<color\>	*Varies*

Property	Use	Values	Default Value
cursor	Changes the display of the cursor.	<URL> | auto | crosshair | default | pointer | move | e-resize | ne-resize | nw-resize | n-resize | se-resize | sw-resize | s-resize | w-resize | text | wait | help	auto
direction	Specifies in which direction the text flows.	ltr | rtl	ltr (left to right)
display	Specifies how the item should be displayed within the page flow.	inline | block | list-item | run-in | compact | marker | table | inline-table | table-row-group | table-header-group | table-footer-group | table-row | table-column-group | table-column | table-cell | table-caption | none	inline
empty-cells	Specifies whether to display empty table cells.	show | hide	show
float	Pushes an element to the left or right of other page elements. Can be applied to any element that is not absolutely or relatively positioned.	left | right | none	none
font	*Shorthand for all font properties.*		
font-family	Changes the font family in which text is displayed.	<family name> | <generic family>	*Varies*
font-size	Changes the font size in which the text is displayed. Absolute sizes include pixels, ems, points, and picas. Relative sizes are keywords such as small, medium, and large.	<absolute size> | <relative size> | <length> | <percentage>	medium

Property	Use	Values	Default Value
font-size-adjust	Adjusts the font size up or down, relative to the current font size.	\<number\> | none	none
font-stretch	Changes the horizontal width of the font.	normal | wider | narrower | ultra-condensed | extra-condensed | condensed | semi-condensed | semi-expanded | expanded | extra-expanded | ultra-expanded	normal
font-style	Adjusts whether text is italicized.	normal | italic | oblique	normal
font-variant	Adjusts whether text is displayed in small-caps.	normal | small-caps	normal
font-weight	Adjust the heaviness of the text.	normal | bold | bolder | lighter | 100 | 200 | 300 | 400 | 500 | 600 | 700 | 800 | 900	normal
height	Specifies the height of an element. (Does not apply to table columns or column groups.)	\<length\> | \<percentage\> | auto	auto
left	Specifies the location of the left edge of positioned elements.	\<length\> | \<percentage\> | auto	auto
letter-spacing	Adjusts the amount of space between letters.	normal | \<length\>	normal
line-height	Adjusts the amount of space between lines of text.	\<length\> | \<percentage\>	normal
list-style	Shorthand for all list-style properties.		
list-style-image	Uses an image before each item in a list.	\<URL\> | none	none
list-style-position	Specifies whether items in a list display inside or outside of the "bullet."	inside | outside	outside

Property	Use	Values	Default Value
list-style-type	Specifies the type of "bullet" that precedes items in a list.	disc | circle | square | decimal | decimal-leading-zero | lower-roman | upper-roman | lower-greek | lower-alpha | upper-alpha | upper-latin | lower-latin | hebrew | armenian | georgian | cjk-ideographic | kiragana | katakana | hiragana-iroha | katakana-iroha | none	disc
margin	Shorthand for all margin properties.		
margin-top margin-right margin-bottom margin-left	Defines the amount of blank space around the outside of an element's box.	<margin width>	0
max-height min-height	Defines the maximum and minimum allowable height of an element. (Does not apply to table elements.)	<length> | <percentage> | none	none
max-width min-width	Defines the maximum and minimum allowable width of an element. (Does not apply to table elements.)	<length> | <percentage> | none	0
overflow	Defines how to handle content that does not fit within a particular block-level box.	visible | hidden | scroll | auto	visible
padding	Shorthand for all padding properties.		
padding-top padding-right padding-bottom padding-left	Specifies the amount of blank space around the content, within a box.	<padding width>	0
position	Specifies how an element is positioned on the page.	static | relative | absolute | fixed	static

Property	Use	Values	Default Value
right	Defines the location of the right edge of a positioned element.	\<length\> | \<percentage\> | auto	auto
text-align	Defines the horizontal alignment of text and block-level elements.	left | right | center | justify | \<string\>	*Varies*
text-decoration	Adds lines above, below, or through text.	none | underline | overline | line-through | blink	none
text-indent	Specifies the amount text is indented.	\<length\> | \<percentage\>	0
text-transform	Changes the case of text.	capitalize | uppercase | lowercase | none	none
top	Defines the location of the top edge of a positioned element.	\<length\> | \<percentage\> | auto	auto
vertical-align	Specifies the vertical alignment of text and inline-level elements (including table cells).	baseline | sub | super | top | text-top | middle | bottom | text-bottom | \<percentage\> | \<length\>	baseline
visibility	Specifies whether/how an element is displayed on the page when it first loads.	visible | hidden | collapse	inherit (the default value is inherited from the parent element)
white-space	Defines how white space is handled within block-level elements.	normal | pre | nowrap	normal
width	Defines the width of an element. (Does not apply to table rows or row groups.)	\<length\> | \<percentage\> | auto	auto
word-spacing	Defines the amount of space displayed between words.	normal | \<length\>	normal
z-index	Specifies the stacking order of the element. (Applies only to absolutely or relatively positioned elements.)	auto | \<integer\>	auto

NOTE

All these properties can also have a value of *inherit*, which tells the browser to use whichever value has already been assigned to the element's parent/container object.

Appendix C

Troubleshooting (FAQs)

This resource lists some of the most common problems encountered when writing HTML. If none of these answers solves the trouble you're experiencing, try running your page through an online validator, such as the one offered by the W3C at **validator.w3.org**. A service like this tests your page against the HTML specifications and prints a list of errors that makes it easy to locate problems.

Or, you could use Dave Raggett's HTML Tidy program (also available from the W3C at **http://tidy.sourceforge.net**/). This handy program actually attempts to fix any problems on your page, if possible. It can also print a list of errors to alert you to things you can look for in the future.

Finally, you might consider posting a link to your site on one of the "Site Check" channels found in many popular web design forums, such as **www.were-here.com**. You're likely to get honest, real-world answers to your questions and advice on your site.

My Page Is Blank in the Browser!

Yikes! You lost everything? Don't worry—it's probably all there, but an unclosed tag or quote somewhere may be causing the browser to ignore everything else on the page. If you have Netscape, try viewing the HTML source of the page from within the browser. If an unclosed tag or quote is the problem, Netscape highlights the location of the error by changing its color or causing it to blink.

In my experience, the number one cause for a page displaying blank or empty in a browser is an unclosed `table` tag. So, if your page uses tables, go back through the code and identify each opening and closing `table` tag to make sure you didn't leave one off accidentally.

The number two cause of a missing section of a page is an unclosed quotation mark. For example, in the following code, the lack of closing quotes in the first a tag causes all the text after it to be considered part of the link URL. No text is displayed in the browser until another set of quotes is encountered that can be considered the closing quotes for the first link.

All I See Is Code in the Browser!

This occurs when the page doesn't have an HTML extension (such as `.htm` or `.html`) or when the page is saved in a format other than text-only. If you encounter this problem, return to your text editor and save the file again, making sure to choose "Text Only" or "ASCII Text" from any list of format types. When naming the file, be sure the text editor doesn't add a `.txt` extension because only .htm or .html extensions are recognized as HTML by a browser. Finally, make sure your page includes an opening and closing html tag.

My Images Don't Appear!

When images don't appear in a page, they are often replaced with a question mark graphic or a broken image symbol. Here's a quick checklist to run through if you encounter this problem.

- **Check filenames**   Perhaps you named a file image.jpg but, in the HTML, you referenced it as IMAGE.JPG. Any difference at all causes the image to appear "broken" in the browser. In addition, be sure your filename doesn't include spaces because those also cause problems.

- **Check file locations**   If you tell the browser your image is in the photos folder when you write your HTML, make sure to upload the image to that folder. If the image is in a different folder, the browser won't be able to find it.

- **Check file types**   Remember, most graphical editors can view only GIF and JPEG files (although newer ones can also view PNG files). Other file types, such as BMP or TIFF, may be displayed as a broken image if the browser doesn't understand them.

- **Check img tags**   It's common for beginners to write out image instead of img when referencing an image. The tag is img, however, not image and, therefore, you must write it as such.

I Tried to Change the Font, but Nothing Happened!

First, make sure the font name is spelled correctly. If it is spelled correctly, make sure you actually have that font running on your system. Try launching your word processor to see if the font is available in that program. If it isn't, chances are you don't have that font loaded on your system. You might try a different font or download the font in question. And, remember, your users may not have that font, either.

When I Use a Special Character, It Doesn't Appear!

This happens for one of two reasons:

- **Missing ampersand and/or semicolon**   Don't forget all entities—whether named or numbered—must begin with an ampersand and end with a semicolon.

- **Lack of browser support** Certain browsers don't support some entities. If you double-checked that you're typing the entity correctly and it still doesn't appear, it might not be supported by your browser.

In something like a trademark symbol, which is not supported by all the browsers, try using the superscript tag (<sup>) instead, as in the following example:

```
My Product<sup>TM</sup>
```

My Links Don't Work!

If your links don't work, check to make sure you typed them correctly. For example, a link to another web site should look something like this:

```
<a href="http://www.wendywillard.com">Wendy Willard</a>
```

while a link to another page in your site might look like this:

```
<a href="contactme.html">Contact Me</a>
```

Be sure to surround the link name with quotes and, if you are linking to another web site, don't forget the `http://`.

Unfortunately, if you are linking to another person's web site, it may be beyond your control to ensure the link works all the time. If a user clicks a link to another site from one of your pages and that site is unavailable, the link won't work. For this reason, it's important to check your links often, making sure they haven't become extinct. You might also contact the owner of the page you're linking to, as the owner might be able to provide a specific link address he or she can guarantee won't change.

My Page Looks Great in One Browser, but Terrible in Another!

Unfortunately, I must say this is a common problem. In most cases, though, the page's developer never takes the time to look at the site in another browser and, therefore, never knows how bad the page looks. Take heart—you're halfway to making your page look great in both browsers, just because you know there's a problem! The following are a few things to consider when you have this problem.

- *Did you use Microsoft Word or Microsoft FrontPage to create your page?* These programs sometimes create proprietary code that works great in Internet Explorer, but terrible in Netscape. You can use a validation service (such as **validator.w3.org**) to identify any code that isn't HTML 4.01–compliant. In addition, some HTML editors, like Dreamweaver, have a function to delete all the Microsoft HTML code from a Microsoft Word document. If that doesn't work, keep reading. . . .

- *Did you use cascading style sheets or other features of Dynamic HTML (DHTML)?* These newer technologies are supported differently by some older versions of the browsers. This means you may have to create multiple versions of your pages if the formatting is important to the page display, or just know your pages will look differently according to the browser used.

Finally, remember some HTML tags are rendered differently by some browsers. Even though you may have coded your page perfectly, there's a good chance it still might look different when viewed in certain browsers. The best advice I can offer you on this topic is to test, ask your friends to help you test, and test some more. Previewing your page in as many different browsers and computer systems as possible can help to ensure you know how it will look to the largest number of users.

When I Link My Images, They Have Little Colored Dashes Next to Them!

This happens when the browser finds a carriage return before it finds the closing a tag for a link, as in the following example:

```
<a href="home.html">
<img src="home.gif" alt="Return to the Home Page" width="25" height="25">
</a>
```

To eliminate those little dashes next to your images, run all the code on a single link, like this:

```
<a href="home.html"><img src="home.gif" alt="Return to the Home Page"
width="25" height="25"></a>
```

I Saved My Image as a JPEG, but the Browser Says It's Not a Valid File Format!

Open your image in a graphics program like Photoshop and check the color mode (in Photoshop, choose Image | Mode). JPEG files must be in the RGB color mode for the browser to be able to display them. It's not uncommon for JPEG images to mistakenly be saved in the CMYK color mode.

When this happens, the browser can't display the image, even though it's saved in the JPEG file format. To fix this, change the file format to RGB and resave the image as a JPEG.

Strange Characters Are at the Top of My Page!

If you used a word processor to write your HTML, you may end up with some characters you didn't type up at the top of your page when you view it in a browser. This occurs when the page contains hidden formatting instructions. To avoid this, return to your file in the editor and save it in Text Only or ASCII Text format, with an .html or .htm extension.

I Added Internal Links to Sections of a Web Page, but When I Click Them, the Browser Launches a Brand New Window!

This occurs when the internal links within the page aren't defined properly. For instance, suppose you were trying to create a link at the bottom of your web page that took users back to the top of the page. You might use the following code:

```
<a href="#top">Back to Top</a>
```

However, unless you actually add the code to tell the browser where the top of your page is, the browser won't know what to do and will just launch a new window. In this instance, you'd need to add the following code near the top of your page:

```
<a name="top"></a>
```

If you're saying, "Wait, I already had that code at the top of my page and it still doesn't work!" then make sure both the <a name> reference and the <a href> reference match exactly. So if you used "TOP" in the <a name> reference, make sure to use "TOP" and not "top" in the <a href> reference.

I Specified One Color but Got a Totally Different One!

This has happened to me several times, and it's caused by something that's easy to fix but hard to spot. Consider the following code:

```
<body bgcolor="#336699 text="#ffffff">
```

Did you spot the missing quotation mark after the background color value? That simple omission can cause the background color to be rendered as some odd concoction of the #336699 and #ffffff colors. So if your colors start behaving oddly, check your quotation marks.

I Need to Protect Some of My Pages from Unwanted Visitors!

Suppose you uploaded some photos of your children to a web site and now want to restrict the pages so only your friends and family can gain access. You can add simple password protection to your site to do just that, but keep in mind most simple password protection scripts won't keep the pros out. (If someone is really determined to get in, they'll be able to unless you add more secure features to the computer your site is hosted on.)

In any case, if you're interested in adding password protection to your site, check out some of the following sites for some scripts that'll help.

● **JavaScript** **http://javascript.internet.com/passwords/**

● **CGI** **http://cgi.resourceindex.com/Programs_and_Scripts/Perl/Password_Protection/**

I Need to Prevent People from Stealing My Images!

Along with the question about password protection, this is another one I am asked quite frequently: "How can I protect my photography from the casual Internet thief?" Quite honestly, you can't. And most likely, you don't need to. Consider what we're talking about here—in the vast majority of cases, any photos you put on your web site are only 72-dpi (screen resolution).

This means when someone goes to print your 72-dpi photo, they will see a pretty poor representation of the image because it's so low in file resolution. To really get a nice print of an image, you need at least 300-dpi in file resolution. My guess is that no one can get that high a resolution file from you without asking for it (or breaking into your house and stealing it off your hard drive), so there's little need to worry. Hey, if the Louvre Museum (**www.louvre.fr**) is okay with putting photos of *their* artwork on a web site, you can be okay with it too.

With that said, there are scripts available that can attempt to prevent users from right-clicking your images and saving them to your hard drives. One example can be found at **http:// javascript.internet.com/page-details/no-right-click.html**. However, users who know what they are doing can disable JavaScript in their browsers or otherwise find ways around this.

If you are a photographer or artist, I suggest you use Photoshop or another graphics program to add a copyright and watermark to your images.

I Tried to Send My Web Page in an E-mail, but the Page Looked Terrible!

Several things could be happening here. First, you need to make sure the person you're sending the e-mail to has an HTML-compatible e-mail program. Not all e-mail programs are capable of displaying HTML, and those that do sometimes support only certain aspects of HTML. For example, many e-mail programs don't support tables or frames, even though they do support images, links, and text formatting. Furthermore, those that are capable of doing so often give the user an option to turn OFF the display of HTML in e-mails.

I Updated My Web Page, but I Don't See the Changes in the Browser!

First, double-check that you saved the file. If you did, indeed, save your changes, and clicking the Refresh or Reload button doesn't help, try forcing a reload by choosing File | Open Page or File | Open Location and then selecting the file in question. This ensures the browser is looking at the latest version of the file.

In some cases, you may also need to clear the browser's cache on disk. The *cache* is a place where browsers store temporary copies of web page files, to avoid having to go back to the server to retrieve them multiple times. You can access your browser's cache by choosing Edit | Preferences | Advanced in Netscape and Tools | Internet Options in Internet Explorer.

My Whole Page Is _____!
(Fill in the Blank)

For example, your whole page could be bold or linked or orange, and so forth. Even though this may look like a terrible error, it's relatively easy to fix. Most likely you're just missing a closing tag somewhere. For example, if your whole page is a giant link, look in your code for the place you actually wanted to create a link to be sure you included the closing a tag. Or, if all the text on your page is bold, look to make sure you included a closing b tag. Typing something like the following is actually quite common

```
<b>Welcome to my Web site.<b>
```

where at first glance it looks great, but a second look shows the closing tag is actually missing a slash. It should look like the following instead:

```
<b>Welcome to my Web site.</b>
```

My Page Has a White Background in
Internet Explorer, but Not in Other Browsers!

The latest versions of Internet Explorer set the default background color of web pages to white, while some other browsers use a default color of gray. If you only test your pages in Internet Explorer and forget to specify a background color, other users may complain that your pages look drastically different. To avoid this problem, always specify a background color in your style sheet, even if you only want that color to be white.

```
body {background-color: white;}
```

TIP

When you do specify a background color, be sure to set the text color to something readable. This is a common reason for "blank" pages: the text and background are the same color!

I Shrank My Images, but They Still Take Forever to Download!

How did you shrink your images? Did you use HTML to do so, within the height and width attributes of the img tag? If so, then you didn't really shrink your images. You just specified that they should be displayed smaller within the browser. To really shrink your images and reduce their file sizes, you need to open them in a graphics editor and cut down the physical height and width of the images.

I Embedded a Flash File that Works Fine on My Computer, but Doesn't Work Properly on Other Computers!

I suspect the other computer doesn't have the latest version of Flash Player and you haven't included code to catch that incompatibility. If this is the case, you can notify and give manual instructions for an updated Flash Player on your web page. Or, if you're up for something a bit more advanced, try implementing the deployment kit, at **http://www.adobe.com/products/ flashplayer/download/detection_kit/**, which can detect cases in which users do not have the appropriate version of the Flash Player and automatically reroute them. (Most plug-ins automatically detect older players, but Flash Player does not in every case.)

My Tables Look Fine in One Browser, but Terrible in Another!

First, make sure you have closed your table tags, and all tr and td tags have opening and closing versions. Consider the following example:

```
<tr>
   <td>Cell 1
   <td>Cell 2
<tr>
   <td>Cell 3
   <td>Cell 4
```

While some browsers can be forgiving when they encounter sloppy HTML that doesn't include closing tags, others refuse to display the content at all. The key to making tables that look good across multiple platforms is to use proper HTML and to test it in several browsers ahead of time.

```
<tr>
  <td>Cell 1</td>
  <td>Cell 2</td>
</tr>
<tr>
  <td>Cell 3</td>
  <td>Cell 4</td>
</tr>
```

I Still Have Questions!

If the previous sections haven't answered your questions, the following are a few more things to try:

- *Take a break.* Looking at HTML code for hours on end can be quite straining, regardless of how experienced you are. If you're having trouble, take a break and don't come back to the problem page until you feel rested enough to look at the issue with fresh eyes.

- *Check for typos.* This may sound easy, but with HTML it's not. I can't tell you how many times I struggled with a certain page, only to find out three days later that it was all because I misspelled a tag or left out a quote. Printing the page and highlighting anything that seems like a potential problem area helps me. Also, reading the code on paper as opposed to on the screen can sometimes help you look at it differently. As much as 90 percent of HTML problems brought to my attention by students or co-workers involve typos!

- *Start fresh.* Begin a new HTML page and add to it from the problem page, piece by piece. For example, first add the `header` and `title` tags. Then save the page and try it in the browser. If that works, add something else. While this may take a while, it certainly can help you identify exactly where the problem lies if you didn't already know.

- *Reread the module.* If you're having trouble with tables, try returning to that module and, perhaps, even re-creating some of the examples. After all, practice makes perfect, right? Well, at least it helps. . . .

- *Ask someone else.* You could try posting your problem HTML on a troubleshooting bulletin board online to see if anyone else has had the same problem. I've set up a bulletin board on my web site for this very subject. If all else fails, feel free to post your question at an online web design community such as **http://www.were-here.com**.

Appendix D

Special Characters

n HTML, characters that use the SHIFT key should be rendered by entities instead of being typed out. Entities can be in the form of numbers or names, but all begin with an ampersand and end with a semicolon. Some entities aren't supported by all browsers, so be sure to test your pages in several browsers to ensure they appear as you intend. For more information, visit **www.htmlhelp.com/reference/charset**.

NOTE

The following table lists the most popular entities. Most nonstandard or minimally supported entities aren't included here.

Standard HTML Entities

Character	Numbered Entity	Named Entity	Description
	 	n/a	Space
!	!	n/a	Exclamation point
"	"	"	Double quote
#	#	n/a	Number symbol
$	$	n/a	Dollar symbol
%	%	n/a	Percent symbol
&	&	&	Ampersand
'	'	n/a	Single quote
(	(	n/a	Opening parenthesis
)	)	n/a	Closing parenthesis
*	*	n/a	Asterisk
+	+	n/a	Plus sign
,	,	n/a	Comma
−	-	n/a	Minus sign
.	.	n/a	Period
/	/	n/a	Forward slash (virgule)
:	:	n/a	Colon
;	;	n/a	Semicolon
<	<	<	Left angle bracket (less-than symbol)

Character	Numbered Entity	Named Entity	Description
=	=	n/a	Equals sign
>	>	>	Right angle bracket (greater-than symbol)
?	?	n/a	Question mark
@	@	n/a	"At" symbol
[	[	n/a	Opening bracket
\	\	n/a	Backslash
]	]	n/a	Closing bracket
^	^	n/a	Caret
_	_	n/a	Underscore
'	`	n/a	Grave accent, no letter
{	{	n/a	Opening brace (opening curly bracket)
|	|	n/a	Vertical bar
}	}	n/a	Closing brace (closing curly bracket)
~	~	n/a	Tilde (equivalency symbol)
™	™	™ (not widely supported)	Trademark symbol
			Nonbreaking space
¡	¡	¡	Inverted exclamation
¢	¢	¢	Cent sign
£	£	£	Pound sterling
¤	¤	¤	General currency sign
¥	¥	¥	Yen sign
¦	¦	¦	Broken vertical bar
§	§	§	Section sign
¨	¨	¨	Umlaut, no letter
©	©	©	Copyright symbol
ª	ª	ª	Feminine ordinal
<<	«	«	Left double angle quote (guillemotleft)
¬	¬	¬	"Not" symbol

Character	Numbered Entity	Named Entity	Description
	&#173;	&shy;	Soft hyphen
®	&#174;	&reg;	Registration mark
¯	&#175;	&macr;	Macron accent
°	&#176;	&deg;	Degree symbol
±	&#177;	&plusmn;	Plus or minus symbol
²	&#178;	&sup2;	Superscript two
³	&#179;	&sup3;	Superscript three
´	&#180;	&acute;	Acute accent, no letter
µ	&#181;	&micro;	Micro symbol
¶	&#182;	&para;	Paragraph symbol
·	&#183;	&middot;	Middle dot
¸	&#184;	&cedil;	Cedilla
¹	&#185;	&sup1;	Superscript one
º	&#186;	&ordm;	Masculine ordinal
>>	&#187;	&raquo;	Right double angle quote (guillemotright)
¼	&#188;	&frac14;	Fraction one-fourth
½	&#189;	&frac12;	Fraction one-half
¾	&#190;	&frac34;	Fraction three-fourths
¿	&#191;	&iquest;	Inverted question mark
À	&#192;	&Agrave;	Capital A, grave accent
Á	&#193;	&Aacute;	Capital A, acute accent
Â	&#194;	&Acirc;	Capital A, circumflex accent
Ã	&#195;	&Atilde;	Capital A, tilde
Ä	&#196;	&Auml;	Capital A, dieresis, or umlaut mark
Å	&#197;	&Aring;	Capital A, ring
Æ	&#198;	&AElig;	Capital AE dipthong (ligature)
Ç	&#199;	&Ccedil;	Capital C, cedilla
È	&#200;	&Egrave;	Capital E, grave accent
É	&#201;	&Eacute;	Capital E, acute accent

Character	Numbered Entity	Named Entity	Description
Ê	&#202;	&Ecirc;	Capital *E*, circumflex accent
Ë	&#203;	&Eulm;	Capital *E*, dieresis, or umlaut mark
Ì	&#204;	&Igrave;	Capital *I*, grave accent
Í	&#205;	&Iacute;	Capital *I*, acute accent
Î	&#206;	&Icirc;	Capital *I*, circumflex accent
Ï	&#207;	&Iuml;	Capital *I*, dieresis, or umlaut mark
Ð	&#208;	&ETH;	Capital Eth, Icelandic
Ñ	&#209;	&Ntilde;	Capital *N*, tilde
Ò	&#210;	&Ograve;	Capital *O*, grave accent
Ó	&#211;	&Oacute;	Capital *O*, acute accent
Ô	&#212;	&Ocirc;	Capital *O*, circumflex accent
Õ	&#213;	&Otilde;	Capital *O*, tilde
Ö	&#214;	&Ouml;	Capital *O*, dieresis, or umlaut mark
×	&#215;	&times;	Multiplication sign
Ø	&#216;	&Oslash;	Capital *O*, slash
Ù	&#217;	&Ugrave;	Capital *U*, grave accent
Ú	&#218;	&Uacute;	Capital *U*, acute accent
Û	&#219;	&Ucirc;	Capital *U*, circumflex accent
Ü	&#220;	&Uuml;	Capital *U*, dieresis, or umlaut mark
Ý	&#221;	&Yacute;	Capital *Y*, acute accent
Þ	&#222;	&THORN;	Capital THORN, Icelandic
ß	&#223;	&szlig;	Lowercase sharp *s*, German (sz ligature)
à	&#224;	&agrave;	Lowercase *a*, grave accent
á	&#225;	&aacute;	Lowercase *a*, acute accent
â	&#226;	&acirc;	Lowercase *a*, circumflex accent
ã	&#227;	&atilde;	Lowercase *a*, tilde
ä	&#228;	&auml;	Lowercase *a*, dieresis, or umlaut mark
å	&#229;	&aring;	Lowercase *a*, ring
æ	&#230;	&aelig;	Lowercase ae dipthong (ligature)

Character	Numbered Entity	Named Entity	Description
ç	&#231;	&ccedil;	Lowercase c, cedilla
è	&#232;	&egrave;	Lowercase e, grave accent
é	&#233;	&eacute;	Lowercase e, acute accent
ê	&#234;	&ecirc;	Lowercase e, circumflex accent
ë	&#235;	&euml;	Lowercase e, dieresis, or umlaut mark
ì	&#236;	&igrave;	Lowercase i, grave accent
í	&#237;	&iacute;	Lowercase i, acute accent
î	&#238;	&icirc;	Lowercase i, circumflex accent
ï	&#239;	&iuml;	Lowercase i, dieresis, or umlaut mark
ð	&#240;	&eth;	Lowercase eth, Icelandic
ñ	&#241;	&ntilde;	Lowercase n, tilde
ò	&#242;	&ograve;	Lowercase o, grave accent
ó	&#243;	&oacute;	Lowercase o, acute accent
ô	&#244;	&ocirc;	Lowercase o, circumflex accent
õ	&#245;	&otilde;	Lowercase o, tilde
ö	&#246;	&ouml;	Lowercase o, dieresis, or umlaut mark
÷	&#247;	&divide;	Division symbol
ø	&#248;	&oslash;	Lowercase o, slash
ù	&#249;	&ugrave;	Lowercase u, grave accent
ú	&#250;	&uacute;	Lowercase u, acute accent
û	&#251;	&ucirc;	Lowercase u, circumflex accent
ü	&#252;	&uuml;	Lowercase u, dieresis, or umlaut mark
ý	&#253;	&yacute;	Lowercase y, acute accent
þ	&#254;	&thorn;	Lowercase thorn, Icelandic
ÿ	&#255;	&yuml;	Lowercase y, dieresis, or umlaut mark

Appendix E

File Types

This table includes some of the popular file types you might encounter when creating web pages.

MIME Type	File Extension(s)	Name and Description
application/excel	.xl .xls	Microsoft Excel (spreadsheet)
application/futuresplash	.spl	Flash 1.0 file (animation)
application/mac-binhex40	.hqx	Macintosh Binhex format (file compression)
application/msword	.doc .word	Microsoft Word document (word processing)
application/octet-stream	.exe	Windows/DOS programs
application/pdf	.pdf	Adobe's Portable Document Format (PostScript/printer-friendly files)
application/postscript	.ai .eps .ps	PostScript document
application/rtf	.rtf	Rich Text Format (word processing)
application/vnd.m-realmedia	.rm	RealMedia file (audio and video)
application/x-director	.dcr .dir .dxr	Macromedia Director file (presentation/animation/multimedia)
application/x-javascript	.js	JavaScript file
application/x-macbinary	.bin	Macintosh binary file (file compression)
application/x-shockwave-flash	.swf	Macromedia Flash 2.0+ file (presentation/animation/multimedia)
application/x-stuffit	.sit	Stuffit Archive (file compression)
application/zip	.zip	ZIP archive (file compression)
audio/basic	.au .snd	AU/mlaw (basic audio)
audio/vnd.m-realaudio	.ra .ram	RealAudio file
audio/x-aiff	.aif .aiff .aife	Audio Interchange File Format

MIME Type	File Extension(s)	Name and Description
audio/x-mpeg	.mp3	MP3 audio file
audio/x-mpegurl	.m3u .mp3url	MP3 text file (links to sound file)
audio/x-wav	.wav	Windows Waveform audio format
audio/x-midi	.mid	Musical Instruments Digital Interface (MIDI) sound files
audio/x-pn-realaudio	.ra .ram	RealAudio file
audio/x-pn-realaudio-plugin	.rpm	RealAudio plug-in page
image/gif	.gif	Graphic Interchange Format (GIF)
image/jpeg	.jpeg .jpg	Joint Photographic Expert Group (JPEG)
image/pict	.pic .pict	Macintosh picture
image/tiff	.tif .tiff	TIFF image
image/x-bitmap	.xbm .bmp	Windows Bitmap Format (BMP)
text/html	.html .htm .shtm .shtml	Hypertext Markup Language document (HTML)
text/plain	.txt	Plain text document (no formatting)
text/xml	.xml	Extensible Markup Language document (XML)
video/vnd.m-realvideo	.rv	RealVideo file
video/quicktime	.qt .mov	QuickTime refers both to the file format and the helper application or plug-in used to play it
video/x-msvideo	.avi	Audio/Video Interleave Format is the standard nonstreaming Microsoft Windows Video format
video/mpeg	.mpg .mpeg .mpe	MPEG Video file

Index